Benjamin Woolley

THE KING'S ASSASSIN

The Fatal Affair of George Villiers and James I

PAN BOOKS

First published 2017 by Macmillan

This paperback edition first published 2018 by Pan Books
an imprint of Pan Macmillan
20 New Wharf Road, London N1 9RR
Associated companies throughout the world
www.panmacmillan.com

ISBN 978-1-5098-3708-3

A CIP catalogue record for this book is available from the British Library.

Typeset by Palimpsest Book Production Ltd, Falkirk, Stirlingshire
Printed and bound by CPI Group (UK) Ltd, Croydon, CR0 4YY

Visit **www.panmacmillan.com** to read more about all our books
and to buy them. You will also find features, author interviews and
news of any author events, and you can sign up for e-newsletters
so that you're always first to hear about our new releases.

In memory of Anthony Sheil, 1932–2017,

and Professor John Henry, 1939–2007

*

With special thanks to Nicholas Martin and Matthew

Contents

Act II
Two Venturous Knights

Act III
The Greatest Villain in the World

Act IV

We the Commons

List of Illustrations

Dramatis Personae

Anne of Austria	Queen of France, wife of Louis XIII, daughter of Philip III of Spain, sister of the Infanta Maria
Anne of Denmark	Wife of King James, mother of Charles
Aston, Sir Walter	James's permanent ambassador in Madrid
Atkins, Dr Henry	President of the College of Physicians, Mayerne's deputy as royal physician
Bacon, Francis	Lord Chancellor, George's mentor
Beaumont, Anthony	Mary's father
Beaumont, Henry	Provided a home for Mary in her early teens, Leicestershire MP who had served alongside Sir George Villiers
Beton, Dr David	French physician, one of James's doctors during his final illness
Brett, Arthur	Groom of the royal bedchamber who became contender for royal favourite in 1624
Carr, Robert, Earl of Somerset	James's favourite from 1607 until his downfall in 1616, following the discovery of the Overbury plot
Chamberlain, John	Letter-writer and commentator
Chambers, Dr James	One of James's Scottish physicians

Chevreuse, Duc de	Protestant French duke, Charles's proxy at his marriage, George's host during his visit to collect Henrietta Maria
Chevreuse, Duchesse de	Marie de Rohan, wife of the Duc de Chevreuse, mistress of Henry Rich, lady-in-waiting to Anne of Austria
Coke, Edward	Lawyer, MP and Francis Bacon's rival
Coloma, Carlos	Spanish ambassador 'extraordinary', 1622–24
Compton, Sir Thomas	Mary's third husband, George's stepfather
Conway, Sir Edward	Royal secretary
Cottington, Sir Francis	Charles and George's companion during the Madrid escapade
Craig, Dr John	One of James's Scottish physicians
Cranfield, Lionel	Disgraced Lord Treasurer, and member of the pro-Spanish clique
D'Ewes, Simonds	Lawyer and diarist
D'Effiat, Marquis	Antoine Coëffier de Ruzé d'Effiat, French ambassador
Digby, John, Earl of Bristol	James's special ambassador in Madrid, responsible for the Spanish match negotiations
Eglisham, George	James's Scottish physician, friend of James Hamilton, and author of *The Forerunner of Revenge* alleging George's poisoning of Hamilton and King James
Eliot, Sir John	Cornish MP, Vice Admiral of Devon, and latterly George's fiercest critic

Elisabeth of France	Queen of Spain, wife of Philip IV, daughter of Marie de' Medici
Elizabeth	James's daughter, wife of Frederick, Count Palatine; known as the 'Winter Queen' following her short reign as Queen of Bohemia
Elizabeth I	Final Tudor monarch of England and James's predecessor; died in 1603
Erskine, Thomas	Lord Fenton (or Fentoun), Earl of Kellie, James's loyal Scottish servant, received the Order of the Garter in 1615, with George's support
Ferdinand II	Holy Roman Emperor, member of the Habsburg dynasty
Frances	Daughter of Lady Hatton and Edward Coke, wife of John, George's brother
Francesco, Don	François de Carondelet, Spanish envoy recruited in 1624 to deal with George
Frederick, Count Palatine	Husband of Elizabeth, James's daughter; Protestant ruler of German provinces around the Rhine and bordering the modern Czech Republic collectively known as the Palatinate, briefly King of Bohemia
George	George Villiers, first Duke of Buckingham
Gondomar, Conde de	Diego Sarmiento de Acuña, Spanish ambassador in London 1613–18, 1620–22, 1624; known, thanks to his closeness to James, as one of the 'Two Diegos'

Goring, Sir George — One of the 'Master Fools' who helped introduce George to court in 1615, later an MP and proxy for George in the House of Commons

Graham, Sir John — George's first champion, introduced him to James

Graham, Sir Richard — George's Master of the Horse and bodyguard during Madrid escapade

Gresley, Walsingham — Steward to John Digby, James's ambassador in Madrid

Hamilton, James — George Eglisham's childhood friend, Marquis of Hamilton, allegedly poisoned by George

Harvey, Dr William — One of James's English physicians, later Charles's personal doctor and medical pioneer

Hatton, Lady — Elizabeth, wife of Edward Coke, mother of Frances, wife of John, George's brother

Henrietta Maria — Sister of Louis XIII of France and wife of Charles

Henry, Prince of Wales — James's son and heir, who died in 1612

Herbert, Philip — Earl of Montgomery, brother of William, James's hunting companion and Baynard's Castle conspirator

Herbert, William — Earl of Pembroke, Baynard's Castle conspirator, introduced George to court in 1615

Hinojosa, Marquis de — Juan de Mendoza, Spanish ambassador 1623–24

James	James VI of Scotland and I of England, member of Stuart dynasty; son of Mary, Queen of Scots
Kate	Kate Villiers, née Manners, George's wife, daughter of the Earl of Rutland
Lister, Dr Matthew	Royal physician and 'censor' of the College of Physicians
Louis XIII	King of France
Maestro, Father	Friar Diego Lafuente, Spanish 'agent' in London, 1623–24
Mansfeld, Count	German mercenary hired to retake the Palatinate
Maria, Infanta of Spain	Charles's proposed bride, daughter of Philip III of Spain, sister of Philip IV of Spain and of Anne of Austria
Mary	George's mother, daughter of Anthony Beaumont, second wife of Sir George Villiers, became Countess of Buckingham in 1618
Mayerne, Sir Theodore	James's chief physician
Medici, Marie de'	Mother of Louis XIII, King of France
Moore, Dr John	Physician, said to be a Catholic, who attended James's final illness
Olivares, Conde de	Philip IV of Spain's *valido* or chief minister and favourite
Paddy, Sir William	Former president of College of Physicians and one of James's most senior doctors

Philip III	King of Spain, father of Philip IV, Anne of Austria and the Infanta Maria, member of the Habsburg dynasty
Philip IV	Son and heir of Philip III, King of Spain after his father's death in 1621; brother of the Infanta Maria and Anne of Austria
Porter, Endymion	George's Spanish secretary and companion in Madrid
Ramséy, Dr Alexander	One of James's Scottish physicians
Remington, John	Mary's doctor, from Dunmow in Essex
Reynor, Sir William	Mary's wealthy second husband, George's stepfather
Rich, Henry	Earl of Holland, England's ambassador in Paris
Rich, Robert	Earl of Warwick, friend of George
Rutland, Earl of	Francis Manners, father of Kate, George's wife
Stuart, Esmé	French cousin of James and the king's first favourite
Stuart, Ludovick	Duke of Lennox and Richmond, loyal Scottish servant of James, son of Esmé Stuart
Villiers, Sir Edward	George's half-brother, son of Sir George by his first wife
Villiers, Sir George	George's father
Villiers, John	George's eldest brother
Villiers, Kit, or Christopher	George's younger brother

Villiers, Susan — George's sister

Villiers, Sir William — George's half-brother, eldest son of Sir George, inheritor of the Villiers estate

Williams, John — Lord Keeper of the Privy Seal, Bishop of Lincoln and member of the pro-Spanish clique

Winwood, Sir Ralph — Royal secretary, supporter but then enemy of Carr, responsible for his downfall by discovering the Overbury plot

Wriothesley, Henry — Earl of Southampton, and one of George's occasional rivals and enemies

Prologue

The group portrait hangs in a 'private area' of Highgrove House, the country residence of Charles, the current Prince of Wales. A valuable and rather puzzling historical artefact, it is only available for direct inspection by members of the royal household, as it is in 'a very high security location . . . impossible to access', according to a representative of the Surveyor of the Queen's Pictures.

It shows a family: two children dressed in white, three women in scarlet, three men and an older woman in black. It was probably commissioned by Prince Charles's namesake and ancestor, Charles I, some time between January 1628, when its youngest subject was born, and 23 August of that year, the day its central figure was assassinated.

It is a dreadful painting, awkwardly arranged and cluttered with ostentatious detail. The statue of a lion to one side is almost comical, squatting on an improbably large plinth, the menacing growl that the artist presumably intended looking like an awkward grimace, and his tousled mane like a dandy's wig.

On the opposite side of the scene, an open glass doorway provides a glimpse of a terrace or balcony with a marble balustrade, beyond which lies a formal garden and the rolling pastures of the family estate.

On the floor is a scarlet Turkish rug, overhead a dark blue awning or canopy. To either side there are what appear to be statues of Greek gods or satyrs, bare-chested, their right hands clutching what might be sconces or candle holders. In the muddy dark background, two strange images are just visible, probably lion heads, perched, like the other classical characters, on fluted columns.

The clumsy composition extends to the figures spread out across the centre of the canvas, the crudeness of the painting's execution highlighting the gaudiness of the subjects.

They are members of the most powerful clan of the age: the Villiers family, who came to prominence during the reign of James VI of Scotland and I of England. To the left is Susan – Countess of Denbigh at the time the portrait was painted. Little is known about her, which perhaps reflects her even-tempered character and relatively uneventful life. She sits next to her sister-in-law, Kate, the Duchess of Buckingham, an anxious, needy but resourceful woman who lost her mother when she was an infant, and had to fight to escape the influence of a controlling, irascible father.

The two men standing to the right are John, the mad, philandering Viscount Purbeck, and Christopher or 'Kit', the Earl of Anglesey, a feckless and unemployable drunkard. Adopting a casual pose in the picture, John was prone to outbursts of violent mania, followed by periods of catatonic stupor. Kit, known to be vicious as well as lazy, looks more apprehensive, grabbing on to a chair arm with one hand while resting the knuckles of the other on the lion's plinth.

In the foreground are two children. The older is Mary, known as 'Mal' to King James, who treated her as a grandchild and delighted in watching her play in his privy chambers when her parents were away. Next to her is her infant brother George, presented like a trophy on a black velvet cushion brocaded in gold. He would grow up to become an incorrigible political schemer and celebrated wit. The young woman propping him up and staring blankly to one side is probably Susan's teenage daughter, another Mary, the child bride of James, Duke of Hamilton.

Looming behind the group is a framed portrait, the only known image of Sir George Villiers – of Brooksby, Leicestershire – the patriarch. The large woman sitting beneath his picture, the roundness of her face, the spread of her arms and her shapeless dress suggesting a middle-aged woman running to fat, is his widow, another Mary, the Countess of Buckingham. Sitting to the right of the countess is her second and favourite son, George, responsible for the family's rise from rural obscurity to become the most powerful aristocratic dynasty in the country. He is the reason the portrait was painted and now hangs in royal splendour.

The sexual charisma for which he was famous, the 'magic thraldom' he held over those who came under his spell, the arresting looks that made him 'a man to draw an angel by' – none of it is detectable in this depiction of him. Neither is there much evidence of the dashing bravado that enchanted his friends, or the appealing humility that beguiled his enemies.

His mother, the countess, has a hint of guardedness, emphasized by her huge ruff, and the slight parting of her lips makes her appear startled. George's sideways glance out of the picture, on the other hand, makes him look shifty. It adds an unsettling mood to the entire scene, as though something dreadful is about to happen, if it has not already occurred.

ACT I

Christ Had His John and
I Have My George

The King's Way

In the early seventeenth century, the writer and cleric John Earle spelled out the plight of the younger brother. Under the principle of primogeniture that meant the eldest male child inherited his father's entire estate, the younger brother's prospects were miserable. He was at the 'mercy of the world', Earle wrote, either 'condemned' to join the Church (Earle was writing from personal experience – he would go on to become a bishop), or, worse, headed for the 'king's road', 'a more crooked path yet' which led through a life of aimless dissolution and debauched resentment to Tyburn's tree, the infamous setting of London's gallows.

Languishing in the condemned cell at Newgate or the King's Bench, under the shadow of Tyburn's twisted limbs, the younger brother's only hope of a reprieve would be desperate appeals to the older brother, who, out of family pride rather than fraternal love, must be prevailed on to use his inheritance and influence to secure a royal pardon. But even if a pardon was granted, relief was short-lived. The restless search for some kind of purpose as well as living would continue, perhaps taking him across the Channel to the war-torn Low Countries, 'where rags and lice are no scandal, where he lives a poor gentleman of a company, and dies without a shirt'.

These were the prospects facing George Villiers. If anything, they were even more hopeless. He was a younger brother in a second family. His father, Sir George, a Leicestershire MP and landowner, had died suddenly in 1606, when the younger George was thirteen years old. He left behind crippling debts, six children by a first marriage, and a further four by Mary, George the younger's mother. Sir George had not left a will, so the entire estate had gone to his eldest son by his first marriage, William. Any provision for Mary or her children was now dependent on the generosity of a stepson who was openly hostile.*

Mary had no land or wealth of her own to fall back on. She had pedigree: her ancestors, the Beaumonts, had been earls of Leicester in the thirteenth century, and her gravestone would insist she was 'descended from Five Kings of the most powerful kingdoms of All Europe'. But the line had since dwindled into obscurity. By Mary's generation, the most notable members of her clan were no longer mighty kings and noble earls, but petty lawyers and struggling dramatists.

Her father was Anthony Beaumont, a Leicestershire squire. In her early teens, Mary had been sent to live with her father's richer kinsman, Henry Beaumont of Coleorton, who had served as an MP for Leicestershire during the reign of Queen Elizabeth. There she had served as a 'waiting woman' to Henry's wife Elizabeth, a socially ambiguous position that embraced many roles – maid, dresser, drudge, adornment, a companion for social outings, a conspirator in domestic disputes.†

It was at Coleorton she met her future husband, George Villiers senior. He was a distant relative of the Beaumonts and had come to stay with the family soon after the death of his first wife. His arrival might have brought a whiff of masculine rivalry to the household, as George had just acquired one of the sleepier Beaumont estates, Goadby Marwood, in 1575, and had set about 'enclosing' it. This was a practice his family had already successfully and ruthlessly applied to the main Villiers seat at Brooksby, about twenty miles from Coleorton, the other side of Leicester. It involved evicting tenant farmers who had for centuries been cultivating small

---

* In 1599 William had taken his stepmother Mary, along with his father, to court to establish his entitlement to the family estates, after it emerged that Sir George senior had used the property as security against his mountainous debts.

† There is some debate about the social position of a 'waiting woman' and how it impacted on Mary. In Shakespeare's *Othello*, Emilia is the waiting woman and confidante to Desdemona, Othello's unfortunate wife. In *The Scornful Lady* by Mary's distant cousin Francis Beaumont, Abigail is a waiting woman trapped by her servitude into becoming an ageing spinster and predatory nymphomaniac.

plots of land on the estate and enclosing the fields with fencing so they could be grazed by sheep. The enterprising, opportunistic George had begun a similar process at Goadby, with the result that he now boasted possession of the impressively refurbished 'ancient mansion house', standing amid rolling pastures, deserted cottages and rusting ploughshares.

The Villiers clan was known to be a colourful, sometimes thuggish local presence. George's roguish uncle, Sir John, had sired a bastard son and famously confronted a local magnate by riding into town at the head of a posse of 'eight or nine horses' with a 'sword and buckler by his side', which he threatened to use if anyone dared to arrest him.

Mary was evidently impressed with the glamorous visitor. Barely in her mid-teens, she made her 'handsome presence' known to the forty-year-old widower, and he 'became very sweet on her'. He reportedly offered her £20 to buy a dress that would flatter her 'beautiful and excellent frame', and she obliged. As a result, his 'affections became so fired' that to 'allay them' he proposed marriage.*

They had their first child, a boy called Samuel, in June 1590, suggesting they were married before October 1589 (assuming George's affections were not 'fired' prematurely). Samuel survived only a month. Four more children followed in quick succession: John (perhaps named in honour of the roguish uncle), Susan, George (named after the father), and Christopher or 'Kit'. All except Susan seemed to suffer from ill health. John had what was politely termed 'giddiness of the head', which manifested as fits of violent rage, while Kit, the youngest, suffered from a 'weak brain', a kind of moral lassitude that 'could not buoy him up from sinking into that distemper that drowns the best wits'.

Then there was George. He nearly died of a childhood illness, and he would continue to suffer lapses of health throughout his life. Like his older brother, he could be volatile, later admitting that

---

* Mary's age is a matter of conjecture. Nativity and horary charts drawn up by Richard Napier (Bodleian MS Ashmole 329, f66v) suggest she was born on 23 December and was thirty-six years old in April 1610, giving a birthdate of 23 December 1574. This makes her rather younger than is generally accepted. For example, the *DNB* gives her birthdate as *c.*1570.

as a child he would 'nothing else but unreasonably and frowardly wrangle'. But these weaknesses only served to show off his strengths. For in George, Mary had her paragon: a charismatic, handsome young man, with an athletic if delicate frame, and a precociously confident manner tempered by a disarming humility and sometimes desperate vulnerability. Even his 'froward wrangling' added to his charm, acting as a register of emotional honesty, a candour that snuffed out feelings of hatred or disgust before they could take hold.

Though she remained fiercely protective of all her brood, Mary put everything into the raising of George, her 'domestic favourite', as one family friend later put it. He became the embodiment of her hopes and instrument of her ambitions. For his part, he reciprocated by later expressing his feelings of a 'more than ordinary natural love of a mother which you have ever borne me'.

By the 1590s, the family as a whole was beginning to thrive, and no expense was to be spared in increasing its status. This inevitably meant stretching the finances to such an extent that, in 1592, perhaps in response to a looming crisis, a list of creditors was drawn up. This showed that George senior owed over £2,500 – more than ten times the annual income generated by the family estates. Nevertheless, it was money well spent: £20 9s on entertainment, £30 – a decent annual income for a craftsman – on a hat and coat. After all, reckless extravagance, rather than thrift, was the signifier of social ambition in an age of swaggering ostentation.

In January 1594, the extravagance was rewarded with a knighthood. It came for no obvious reason from the Lord Deputy of Ireland rather than the king, making it somewhat dubious, but that would have been of little concern to the former waiting woman who, now in her early twenties, could call herself Lady Mary. In 1603, the ascent continued with Sir George being selected as one of Leicestershire's two Members of Parliament alongside Mary's former benefactor, Henry Beaumont (also now a knight, though receiving the honour nearly a decade later than her husband).

Commensurate with this rising status, Mary cultivated an atmosphere of metropolitan sophistication at the Villiers residence that must have amused her more down-to-earth neighbours. For example, she decided to hire a personal musician, who lived with the Villiers some time in the mid-1590s, while George the younger was still in his cradle. Thomas Vautor would go on to write exquisite madrigals dedicated to his patroness and her son, songs celebrating the courtly arts of seduction and deceit.

To prepare George the younger for a place on the family's upward trajectory, Mary arranged for him to be tutored by Anthony Cade, the Cambridge-educated vicar of nearby Billesdon, who advertised himself as teaching 'some nobles and many other young gentlemen of the best sort'.

All of this progress came to a shocking halt with Sir George's sudden death in 1606. He had probably been in London at the time, attending King James I's first Parliament. He may have been a victim of the plague, struck down in the latter stages of a dreadful epidemic that had already killed tens of thousands.

The death transformed Mary from lady of the manor into a 'relict', the genteel term for a widow that cruelly captured her ruined status. Her children too were suddenly at risk. Her teenage daughter Susan was unmarried, and it would now be all the harder to find a suitable husband. None of her boys, not even George, had the education or intellect for a life in the Church, university or law; they apparently faced the alternative John Earle had so vividly described: the king's road to Tyburn's tree.

The Malcontent

'At last, with easy roads, he came to Leicester,' Shakespeare wrote in *Henry VIII*. And so, in 1606, came Shakespeare's acting company, the King's Men. Thanks to the wealth generated by the wool its increasingly enclosed pastures produced, the city of Leicester had become a centre of culture as well as trade in the English midlands, and a regular stopping-off place for London's acting troupes as they toured the country.

The King's Men were booked to appear at Leicester's Guildhall, and among their repertoire of productions was a play especially commissioned for that year's season called *The Malcontent* by John Marston, which had been revised in collaboration with John Webster. Drama was now firmly established as a semi-official medium for airing public anxieties too sensitive to discuss directly, and the King's

Men's version of *The Malcontent* touched upon the most sensitive and current matter of all: the xenophobic fear that England was being taken over by a Scottish elite of corrupt deviants.

In March 1603, Queen Elizabeth had died without heir, ending the Tudor era and throwing England into a state of anxious uncertainty about the future. Under a secret deal hatched by the government's chief minister Robert Cecil, James VI of Scotland, Elizabeth's cousin and a member of the Stuart dynasty, was proclaimed her successor.

Within weeks of Elizabeth's death, the new king had arrived in London with a large retinue of Scottish courtiers, becoming James VI of Scotland and I of England (being the first monarch south of the border to bear that name). The change of regime produced a deep cultural as well as political shock at the very highest levels. James's entourage appeared to behave in a manner at odds with the more reserved English courtiers, particularly in their taste for flamboyant displays of public emotion and raucous feasts and entertainments – a habit apparently learned from the royal courts of France, making it all the more distasteful. The vulgar masculinity of their behaviour was hard to reconcile with the more restrained practices and habits that had evolved over the four decades of Elizabeth's reign.

A major concern was the new king's weakness for 'favourites' – male acolytes chosen for their good looks and charming manners rather than noble birth or financial wealth. To the horror of James's English nobles, advisors and ministers, he relied on them not only for emotional and, it was suspected, sexual succour, but political and diplomatic advice.

James made little effort to disguise his feelings for these men. In 1584 a narrative poem called 'A Metaphorical Invention of a Tragedy called Phoenix' was published in Edinburgh as part of an anonymous poetry collection. It told the story of an exotic bird that landed in Scotland, attracting a great deal of admiration. Other birds became envious of the attention the phoenix was getting, and attacked it, forcing it to find refuge between the narrator's legs. Eventually, it took flight, and was consumed by the flames from which it had emerged.

James, who was seventeen when he wrote the poem, was widely known to be the author of this strange 'Metaphorical Invention', and he did not make it difficult to identify the subject. An acrostic in one of the poem's verses spelled out the name of Esmé Stuart, a cousin of James's murdered father, Lord Darnley, who had come from France to join the thirteen-year-old king's Scottish court in 1579. James's infatuation for the much older Esmé (he was thirty-seven when they first met) left little doubt as to whose thighs had provided the phoenix with shelter. The king had exuberantly celebrated Stuart's 'eminent ornaments of body and mind', his 'comely proportions' and 'civil behaviour', and had been seen at public events to embrace him in a 'most amorous manner'. Esmé, suspected by James's predominantly Protestant court of being an agent of the Catholic cause, had been forced into exile in 1582, and had died in May the following year. James had received soon after a 'kist' (small coffer) containing Esmé's embalmed heart, a gesture that provoked the feelings poured into the 'Metaphorical Invention'.

James's attitude towards Esmé had been well known in England, it being noted with disapproval that the Scottish king had become 'altogether . . . persuaded and led' by him, 'for he can hardly suffer him out of his presence, and is in such love with him, as in the open sight of the people, oftentimes he will clasp him about the neck with his arms and kiss him'. Christopher Marlowe made a sly allusion to Esmé in the opening lines of his 1594 history play *Edward II*, which mentioned King Edward's notorious favourite, Piers Gaveston, having 'swum from France' to 'smile' and take the king in his arms. The play also referred to the king's weakness for 'minions' and 'ganymedes', words that carried strong associations with homoeroticism and pederasty.

Since James's arrival in England, it was noted how such minions and ganymedes had been congregating in the royal bedchamber, sleeping with him, pandering to him, and, to the even greater shock of government ministers forced to wait at the door, deciding who should have access to him.

The new version of *The Malcontent* commissioned by the King's Men in 1604 had played on these anxieties, and as such would have found a receptive audience among the burghers and gentry of Leicester, worried about the gossip reaching them from London.

The play began with a warning against taking offence at what was to follow, as the 'old freedom of the pen' must be allowed to 'write of fools, while it writes of men'. And offence duly followed.

Like the best satires, what was most deplorable the play brought most luridly and vividly to life – in this case, London's courtly corruption thinly disguised by being relocated to Genoa in Italy. The first stage directions for the first act literally set the tone, by calling for the sound of 'the vilest out-of-tune music'. The music, it turned out, was coming from the chamber of the malcontent of the title, Malvole, the deposed and exiled Duke of Genoa who has returned to his court in disguise to try to settle scores and recover his title. As the dreadful din sent winces through the auditorium, Pietro, who had usurped the dukedom, entered with his entourage, including Ferrardo, described as Pietro's 'minion'. Ferrardo called to Malvole, provoking a tirade: 'Yaugh! God-a'-man, what dost thou there? Duke's Ganymede, Juno's jealous of thy long stockings. Shadow of a woman, what woulds't, weasel? Thou lamb o'court, what dost thou bleat for? Ah, you smooth-chinned catamite.'

Plenty there to shock a provincial audience: the reference to Ganymede; to Juno, the Roman name for Zeus's wife, supposedly jealous of her husband's lustful infatuation with his cupbearer; to effeminacy ('shadow of a woman'), and to prepubescent boys used by older men for sexual entertainment ('smooth-chinned catamite'). Also, the littering of references to 'bawbees', Scottish pennies, 'Scotch barnacles' and a 'Scotch boot' made contemporary parallels all the more obvious.

For an ambitious gentlewoman, though, a recent widow facing obscurity and penury, it was perhaps not these scandalous pronouncements that would stick in the mind, nor Malvole's relentless diatribes against a duplicitous and deviant elite that had usurped his position. It would have been a soliloquy given by Malvole's antagonist Mendoza, a powerful speech delivered direct to the audience describing what it was like to be a royal favourite:

> What a delicious heaven it is for a man to be in a prince's favour! . . . O sweet god! O Pleasure! O Fortune! O all thou best of life! . . . To be a favourite! A minion! To have a general timorous respect observe a man, a stateful silence in his presence, solitariness in his absence, a confused hum and busy murmur of obsequious suitors training him; the vassals licking

the pavement with their slavish knees . . . O blessed state! What
a ravishing prospect doth the Olympus of favour yield!

All We Here Sit in Darkness

Following the death of her husband, Mary Villiers no longer had
any property of her own. She had been allowed to stay at Goadby
Marwood, but as tenant rather than mistress, with an antagonistic
stepson for a landlord. This was a very weak position if she was to
realize her impossibly ambitious plans to get George into the royal
court. She also had to think of her daughter. Susan's sweet nature
and good looks had attracted the interest of an eligible husband:
William Feilding, the son of a Warwickshire gentleman. Though a
man of 'modest abilities', he was heir to estates that yielded an
annual income of £200, enough to keep Mary's daughter relatively
comfortable and independent. However, William's father was
demanding a dowry of £2,500 – a vast sum for an impecunious
widow. If she was ever to pay it, her only hope was to find a rich
husband of her own.

Sir William Reynor was in his eighties, a former Sheriff of
Nottingham with several lucrative estates to his name and no male
heirs. He had also known Mary's late husband – indeed he was one
of his largest creditors, being owed £330 by Sir George in 1592.

Though some suspected that Mary had 'compassed by . . .
enticement and persuasions' the aged widower, others claimed that
he had been 'an earnest suitor for marriage'. And why not? She
was 'beautiful and provident', and in her early thirties, the same
age as Sir William's daughter by his first marriage.

However, within a few weeks of the wedding, it became clear
that Sir William was not prepared to provide the support for her
family that Mary expected. So, on 23 September 1606, his new
bride decided to take matters into her own hands.

Suffering from 'some extremity of sickness', Sir William had
moved from his house at Stanton-upon-the-Wolds, Nottinghamshire
to his family's main property at Orton Longueville in Cambridgeshire.
Hearing the news, Mary, together with a band of her most loyal
servants, set off on the fifteen-mile journey to Stanton. There they

'entered into the dwelling house . . . and with false keys, picklocks, and other instruments and engines, broke open the doors and locks of the parlours, chambers, studies and closets, and did rifle and ransack the said chambers, parlours, studies, closets, chests, trunks, and cupboards and did convey away £2,000 in money'.

Stanton had a large sheep farm, and a secure 'wool house' stood next to the main house to store the fleeces. Mary had a key to one of the doors, but there was a second blocking the way, so she ordered her men to break it down. Bales or 'staples' of wool amounting to £300 in value were revealed, which were loaded onto a cart. Mary set off back to Goadby with the portable loot, sending the cart on to Leicester, where the wool was to be sold.

Unfortunately for her, Sir Robert Pierpoint, a friend of Sir William's, seems to have been alerted to the break-in and, with 'diverse others', managed to intercept the cart, which they returned along with its load to Stanton.

Sir William was in no condition to recover his property, but the following month, 'while sick in body but of good and perfect remembrance (thanks be to God)', he drew up a will excluding his new wife and her children from his inheritance. Instead, everything was to go to Elizabeth, his daughter by his first marriage. He died a month later, and Mary promptly attempted to have a legal 'caveat' or stay put on the execution of her dead husband's will, which seems to have been unsuccessful.

Around the same time, Elizabeth, Sir William's daughter and sole beneficiary, took action. She had powerful connections. Her first husband, and the father of her daughter Anne, was Henry Talbot, son of the sixth Earl of Shrewsbury. Her second was the irascible MP Sir Thomas Holcroft, who not only boasted close links to Robert Cecil, the king's chief minister, but had a history of violence involving at least two ferocious altercations, one resulting in a fatality.

Drawing on these links, Elizabeth was able to bring a case against Mary which culminated in February 1607 with a hearing before the Star Chamber. There Mary was accused, 'at the relation of Sir Thomas Holcroft', of 'conspiracy, fraud, unlawful assembly and embezzlement'. These were serious charges, brought by the Attorney General, the government's chief lawyer, and heard in

England's highest court, presided over by members of the Privy Council and the country's most senior judges. A widow less formidable than Mary might have been overwhelmed by the onslaught. But she would not be intimidated, arguing that she had been forced to take the goods 'under distress for a fifteenth' – to pay overdue taxes due on her husband's property.

The outcome of the case is unrecorded, but it hardened Mary's resolve to rebuild her family's fortunes. Drawing on her contested gains, she managed a swift conclusion of Susan's marriage negotiations, and within weeks had found a more suitable candidate for a third husband.

Sir Thomas Compton was quite unlike Sir George Villiers or Sir William Reynor, boasting neither a flamboyant lineage nor prospects of an imminent inheritance. He was a log merchant variously described as 'low-spirited' and 'backward'. History bothers to record only one incident from his youth, concerning a quarrel with a 'roaring captain' called Bird. Bird had taken to taunting young Compton for his slow-wittedness, eventually goading him into a duel. The challenge was accepted but, in a further provocation, the captain insisted that, in order to stop his opponent running away, the confrontation should take place in one of Sir Thomas's 'saw pits', a deep, narrow trench in the ground used for the manufacture of planks. They duly met, and the blustering captain, brandishing his sword, shouted 'Come, Compton, see what you can do now', whereupon Sir Thomas ran him through with his weapon, 'which,' as a chronicler of the incident noted, 'should teach us that strong presumption is the greatest weakness'.

Mary, a shrewd judge of men and opportunity, made no such presumption about the slow log merchant. She had met him via his mother, Frances Hastings, daughter of the Earl of Huntingdon, who had links with the Beaumonts. Sir Thomas's fortunes were on the rise. His father Henry was a Warwickshire landowner with extensive estates, and his brother William, Lord Compton, was a glamorous star of the Accession Day Tilts, the annual jousts that celebrated the date of the monarch's accession to the throne. Through his marriage to the daughter of the alderman Sir John Spencer, London's lord mayor, William was also heir to a fortune said to be the biggest in the country.

It was probably William's celebrity that led to 'Master Thomas Compton, brother to the Lord Compton' being selected as one of the members of a lavish embassy appointed by King James in 1604 to go to Spain. The aim was to finalize a new peace treaty that would end decades of war. This was a controversial policy that to many English politicians revealed the Scottish king's suspected Catholic sympathies. For James, however, it was a natural development. Scotland had no history of enmity with Spain, and his new English administration was so cash-strapped, he could not afford any further costly confrontations with Europe's maritime and economic superpower.

Thomas had received his knighthood from the king on his return from Madrid, enhancing further his financial position and connections to the royal court – exactly the qualities Mary needed in a husband. They were married some time after October 1607.

Meanwhile, Mary's efforts to improve George's prospects through his education were proving unproductive, his tutor Anthony Cade finding that he was 'by nature little studious and contemplative'. So, 'not without aim (though far off) at a courtier's life', she decided to focus on developing his more social or 'conversative' qualities, 'as dancing, fencing and the like'. He quickly flourished, his teachers deciding that he was of such 'dextrous proclivity' that he should be taught on his own rather than with his brothers, for fear he would be held back.

While his conversative qualities began to flourish, when he turned sixteen, in May 1609, it was decided that George needed to 'gain experience'. Mary's new husband Sir Thomas drew on his courtly connections to procure a pass from the king's Privy Council allowing George, chaperoned by his elder brother John, to 'repair unto the parts beyond the seas'. They left for France later that year, accompanied by four servants.

Little is known about the adventures of the two Villiers boys. Letters home appear to have been sparse, forcing a desperate Mary to resort to astrology to find out what was happening to them. She had been consulting the famous astrologer-physician Richard Napier since 1609, mostly on matters concerning her health and that of her fragile youngest son, Kit. However, in the autumn and winter of 1610, she asked Napier to draw up several 'horary' astrological charts, perhaps hoping, like many mothers and wives in her position at the time, that the stars would cast at least a dim light on the welfare and whereabouts of her absent boys.

It was not until 1612 that she opened the door at Goadby Marwood to see them safely returned, three years after they had set out. A mother's unbounded delight must have been multiplied by the transformation of her beloved George. While his 'natural' demeanour was unchanged, and though he had managed to avoid the 'affected' manners that were the 'ordinary disease of travellers', it was obvious he had acquired a dazzling polish. Sojourns in places like Blois, the country seat of the French monarchy, and Angers, famous as a centre for learning the noble arts such as horse riding, had lent him the Gallic air of sophistication and 'nobility' that, thanks to French influence over the Scottish court, was now becoming highly prized in England.

George would remain at Goadby for a year under the 'wing and counsels' of his mother, so that she could add finishing touches. Then, some time in late 1613 or early 1614, she decided he was ready.

'Where the court is,' wrote John Holles, an MP and desperate seeker of royal office, 'there shines the sun only; all we here sit in darkness.'

Mary had spent a lifetime in the darkness, in the penumbra of the provincial gentry where prominence and wealth shaded into obscurity and penury. The time had come for the Villiers family to head into the light, and George would lead them there.

Debateable Lands

The easy road from Leicester to London was seventy-eight country miles, according to a travel guide from the time of George's journey to the capital. It followed a well-trodden route. The traveller would set out along Fosse Way to High Cross, a journey of some sixteen miles, where the old Roman road to Winchester intersected with Watling Street, leading to London.

Once the journey taken by thousands of pilgrims heading for the shrine of St Alban, the road was now thick with young men like George, second sons and younger brothers jostling to make a name for themselves through courtly celebrity rather than religious devotion.

Though George had experience of travelling, to any twenty-year-old looking forward to a life in the capital, the approaches to London must have been daunting. The first landmark on the final leg of the long journey was 'Mount Calvary', a hill made up of bones excavated from London's overflowing cemeteries, topped by a windmill. A little further on, the main road began to drop down as it entered the gentle slopes of the Thames valley. From here, the exhausted traveller had his first view of the capital.

Mass migration from the countryside, the arrival of so many hopefuls like George, had turned London and its surrounding towns and villages into a sprawling conurbation, threaded together by the broad ribbon of the Thames and the rivers feeding into it. The City itself, separated off from its surroundings by its imposing but disintegrating Roman wall, was dominated by the Gothic bulk of St Paul's Cathedral, rising out of a thicket of church spires. To the west, upriver from the City, hugging the banks, lay a cluster of aristocratic mansions and cramped lawyers' inns, leading on to the palace complexes of Whitehall and Westminster, the London bases of the Crown and Parliament respectively.

Continuing down towards Aldersgate, the traveller now found himself sinking into the melee of a great slum that had formed around the fringes of the City wall, passing the stinking ditch at its foot, filled with rotting food, sewage, carcasses and other debris of city life. Using a handkerchief to cover his nose, he carried on, following the line of the wall towards Smithfield meat market, where the stench of decay was replaced by the tang of slaughter. Cow Lane curved round towards the river, revealing a large painted sign of an Arab warrior, famous for its ferocity, which marked the location of the Saracen's Head Inn, the terminus for journeys from Leicester.

The new arrival had a chance to wash off the dust in Holborn's 'conduit', a spout fed by the Fleet River which filled a trough opposite the inn's entrance, before following the slope of Snow Hill down to Ludgate. Here was the fulcrum of the city. On the far bank of the Thames, the Globe Theatre was just visible, recently reconstructed after cannon fired in a production of Shakespeare's *Henry VIII* set its thatched roof ablaze. To his left, through the archway of the city gate, the precincts of St Paul's could be seen, where booksellers and pamphleteers had their stalls, selling useful books such as a *Guide for Cuntrey men In the famous Cittey of London.*

George would turn his back on the City, heading up Fleet Street and the Strand, passing Charing Cross as he made his way to the Palace of Whitehall, the king's London seat. Here was a disappointingly empty thoroughfare, lined with low-rise buildings. Those on one side catered for royal entertainments – tennis, cockfighting, bearbaiting, bowls. Behind a long wall was the tiltyard where George's step-uncle, William, Lord Compton, had performed daring feats, and beyond lay gardens, orchards and stables leading into St James's Park, the king's private hunting ground. On the opposite side of the thoroughfare, next to the river, were the royal apartments.

For a young man who had travelled so far, from provincial obscurity, via some of the Continent's most sophisticated centres of aristocratic culture, who had heard about if he had not seen the great royal palaces of the Louvre in Paris and the Escorial in Castile, Whitehall would have seemed underwhelming, even a crushing disappointment. Originally built by Cardinal Wolsey when he was Archbishop of York, and surrendered to Henry VIII following Wolsey's plunge from grace, it was little more than a ramshackle complex of squat buildings.

The main point of architectural or navigational significance was a structure that joined together the two sides of the palace complex – east and west, court and cockpit, work and play. The Holbein Gate (named after Henry VIII's favourite painter, who is thought to have lived there) was a graceful three-storey structure of chequered stone and flint with two octagonal turrets. But passing through the gate seemed to lead nowhere, or rather into a courtyard and another gate, beyond which lay Westminster, a separate palace that acted as the seat of Parliament.

The result was a royal residence that daunted its visitors not through the architecture of grandeur, or intimidation, but confusion. With some two thousand rooms, the Palace of Whitehall, like the royal court in general, was designed literally to amaze anyone who attempted to navigate its corridors and conventions. It was a labyrinth, with the king as the minotaur, and his bedchamber his lair.

To the yeoman at the guard chamber, George would have been just another provincial turning up in his country weeds, the connection to Lord Compton sufficient to get him into the presence chamber, one of the outer reception rooms that served as a meeting place for petitioners and other visitors, and a very occasional venue for royal appearances. Young hopefuls would mill around there, hoping for a chance to make themselves known to one of the privy councillors or, even better, a gentleman of the bedchamber, as they emerged briefly from the passageways that led deeper into the palace.

Mild interest was aroused by the new arrival. The Villiers name rang distant rural bells, and the Compton connection added a dash of glamour. But there was condescension too. George had decided to dress himself in 'French garb' to cut a dash, but it failed to impress. This was still another country bumpkin 'in no greater a condition than fifty pounds a year is able to maintain'.

He artfully turned the snobbery to his advantage. Seen as harmless, he was able to slip past rivals and by mid-1614 had managed to make his way into the household of one of the most important families in the king's entourage.

Sir Roger Aston was one of the king's closest friends. The illegitimate son of a powerful Cheshire landowner, he had spent most of his life in Scotland, where a combination of sporting prowess, toughness and charm had led to him becoming barber, hunting companion and confidant to James, as well as the husband of Marjory Stuart, one of the king's cousins and a lady-in-waiting to the queen consort, Anne of Denmark.

Sir Roger had died unexpectedly in 1612, and his wife soon after, leaving behind considerable wealth and four daughters. The youngest, Ann, was unmarried and a relationship quickly flourished between her and George, and, to the horror of friends of the Aston family and delight of court gossips, they became betrothed.

If George had hopes that the journey from Leicestershire to London meant leaving the past behind, they were to be dashed. Ann's guardian and her father's executor was Sir William Heyricke, an enterprising goldsmith and moneylender. He knew the Villiers family well, having lent considerable sums to George's spendthrift father, some of it to buy pearls for Mary. So he was in a good position to assess the son's financial prospects.

Ann's older sister, Elizabeth, had recently married one John Grymesdyche, and Heyricke had negotiated the marriage settlement. It allowed for a £2,000 dowry to be paid to the groom's family, and in return Elizabeth was granted a life interest in Mr Grymesdyche's extensive Northamptonshire estates. As Heyricke well knew, George, with no inheritance or estates of his own, was in no position to offer a similar deal for an equally eligible bride. Indeed, to Sir William, George's charm and 'French garb' only added to the impression that he was a fortune hunter. So, Sir William set about wrecking the romance by setting terms that George could only interpret as insulting: there was to be no dowry from Ann, and George would have to deposit a hundred marks (£66 6s 8d) – a sum well beyond his personal resources – as a 'jointure' or security, which would become Ann's in the event of his death or their separation.

Whatever the obstacles, Ann and George seemed set on one another. She insisted that she would proceed with the marriage 'in despite of all her friends', while he declared it 'the height of his ambition' to be her husband, and that she was the only reason he remained 'a hanger on upon the court'.

However, George's sincerity was about to face a test sterner than any Sir William Heyricke could devise. The argument over the match had brought George's presence to the attention of Sir John Graham, a senior courtier who had served alongside Ann's late father as a gentleman of the royal bedchamber. He saw in the young man what the teachers of his courtly manners had seen: a refreshing English charm and attractiveness that James might appreciate – and for which there was a sudden and desperate demand.

Hailing from the gloriously named 'debateable lands', marking the fragile frontier between Scotland and England, the Graham clan had a noble tradition going back to Roman times of patrolling the borders to fight off English incursions. This gave Sir John an appreciation of the ancient rivalry between the two kingdoms, which seemed to have intensified rather than diminished since James had taken over both thrones. 'The Scottish monopolize his princely person,' John Holles complained, 'standing like mountains betwixt the beams of his grace and us'. The result was 'jealousy, distrust or unworthiness' among his English subjects. 'We most humbly beseech his Majesty his Bedchamber may be shared as well to those of our nation as to them,' Holles had pleaded, and in this curious, charismatic twenty-one-year-old Englishman, Sir John wondered if he might have discovered a candidate capable of redressing the balance.

So he set about giving George 'encouragement to woo fortune in court' rather than with Ann. It was a fortune that, while fraught with danger, would take him into realms of influence and extravagance he could barely imagine, redeeming his family's ancient line, and setting his beloved mother at the pinnacle of society, where she most manifestly belonged, and from which the failures of so many hapless or useless men had left her excluded.

'O sweet god! O Pleasure! O Fortune! O all thou best of life!' Malvole's antagonist, Mendoza, promises in *The Malcontent*. 'To be a favourite! A minion!' This is what George had been groomed for, what his mother, through so many travails, had strived for, and what now seemed to be within grasp, if only he would surrender love for ambition.

Apethorpe

King James was a restless spirit. The 'cradle king', as he styled himself, had been crowned King of Scotland when he was barely a year old, in the midst of a murderous power struggle between his barons. 'Nourished in fear', as he later described it, he had been forced into exile in his own kingdom, kidnapped by his own subjects and throughout his childhood was under constant threat of assassination. As a result, he did not feel safe anywhere, and so would spend the year in ceaseless motion, moving from one location to the next, his court – ministers, nobles, bishops, gentlemen, grooms, clerics, clerks, purveyors, cooks, couriers and pages – forced to follow.

This restlessness took on a more ritual and formal purpose every summer, when James would embark upon his annual progress, his official tour of the country. Hundreds of carts – as many as 600 in one particularly extravagant year – would form a train that snaked across the kingdom, stopping off at the houses of local nobles along the way, each competing to bankrupt themselves with displays of ostentatious hospitality.

These progresses came like a plague of locusts to the local economy. An ancient royal prerogative known as 'purveyance' allowed the monarch's officials to requisition provisions for the journey at a price of their choosing. This inevitably resulted in rampant corruption and produced an outpouring of complaints. But the progresses also acted as a way for James's subjects to behold their king's grandeur and acknowledge his supremacy. During a trip through Huntingdonshire, for example, the king found himself surrounded by a throng of people calling to him for his help. Sir John Spencer, the fabulously rich alderman whose daughter had married George's step-uncle Lord Compton, had 'very uncharitably molested' local common land, they complained. They pleaded with the king to intercede against a powerful figure, 'beseeching his Majesty that the commons might be laid open again, for the comfort of the poor inhabiters thereabout; which his Highness most graciously promised should be performed according to their heart's desire'. Whether or not they would ultimately receive satisfaction, his assurances seemed to relieve the locals' distress, and, 'with many benedictions of the comforted people', the king's carriage passed on.

One of James's favourite places to stay during these progresses was Apethorpe, in neighbouring Northamptonshire, home of the retired diplomat Sir Anthony Mildmay. Mildmay was a man equal to his name, a reluctant ambassador during Elizabeth's reign, an unassuming MP for his county, who had made little political impact and an 'honourable fast friend' who liked to stay at home and read his books or tend to his estate.

Apethorpe was one of those distinctively English stately homes that managed to combine domestic intimacy with stately grandeur. James had first visited in 1603, as he made his way from Edinburgh to London to take the English throne. Mildmay had greeted the king with a dinner 'most sumptuously furnished', the tables resplendent with 'costly banquets, wherein every thing that was most delicious for taste, proved more delicate, by the art that made it seem beauteous'. To round off proceedings, Mildmay had presented James with 'a gallant Barbary horse, and a very rich saddle', gifts well calculated to win the king's approval.

Sir Anthony may well have come to regret his hospitality, as James would become a regular and very costly visitor at Apethorpe. The king even insisted that he build an extension, to make it more suitable for his 'princely recreation' and 'commodious entertainment', as well as a convenient base for his favourite pursuit: hunting in the nearby royal forest of Rockingham.

In July 1614, James was at Hawnes Hall in Bedfordshire, en route to Apethorpe, when news reached him that his brother-in-law, Christian IV, King of Denmark, had turned up unexpectedly at Somerset House, Queen Anne's London residence. James immediately rode back to London, managing the journey in less than a day.

The Danish king was infamous for his carousing, even among the rowdier elements of the British court. During a previous visit, one witness of a particularly drunken evening's revel remarked that 'the Danes have again conquered the Britons, for I see no man, or woman either, that can now command himself or herself'.

Christian did not disappoint on this occasion either. The entertainments included a private drinking competition between the two kings, 'where some dozen or fifteen healths passed to and fro', followed by a riotous feast in Whitehall's Banqueting House. A few days later, James escorted Christian back to his ship at Great Yarmouth, and saw him off before hastening back to his progress, 'overtaking his hounds' in his eagerness to reach Apethorpe.

The court, marooned in the Midlands and wondering what to do, erupted with speculation on the reason for the Danish king's surprise visit. Some suggested Christian was trying to draw James into the military hostilities on the Continent, others insisted it concerned James's controversial plans to marry off his son Prince Charles to the daughter of the Spanish king. Whatever the purpose, the diversion had left James in an exhausted and crapulent mood, which resulted in a spat with his secretary, Sir Thomas Lake, whose efforts to find out what was going on were interpreted as interference. Sir Thomas was put on half-rations for his pains.

But once the king was settled at Apethorpe, the mood relaxed.

It was 4 August, a Thursday evening. In Mildmay's commodious hall, the tables were once again prepared for costly banquets, including the famously delicious candies prepared by Lady Mildmay, who was considered to be 'one of the most excellent confectioners in England'. A gallery at one end of the hall provided a place for musicians to play, and for those with suitable permissions to gawp.

James took his seat at the high table, with his hosts and closest courtiers. As the serving of the evening's meal commenced, he might have recited some poetry, or terrified a local cleric by inviting him to sit by his side and discourse on theology, or forced a guest to listen to his strong and idiosyncratic opinions on the dangers of witches and tobacco.

Behind the door of the garderobe, the service room connecting the kitchen to the hall, stood a nervous George Villiers, dressed in new livery chosen by Sir John Graham to flatter the young man's athletic physique. George had been given the role of 'extraordinary' (probationary) cupbearer, an attendant whose job was to serve at the 'upper end of the board at dinner' where the king sat, replacing one of James's usual attendants, who, despite protests, had been demoted to serve at the lower tables.

What was about to happen was a highly unusual and dangerously presumptuous exploit for all concerned. Graham would have had to call in considerable favours to achieve it. James's reign had been marked by several attempts on his life, and if he was startled by an unfamiliar face was liable to react with terror or fury. Furthermore, the demands on cupbearers were daunting. These young ganymedes were expected not just to serve wine, but to entertain and delight. Success required an almost impossible alchemy of opposing elements: frailty combined with confidence, innocence with knowingness, masculinity with effeminacy. They had to be coy yet seductive, spontaneous yet calculating, lithe and quick, yet careful and watchful. So, when a gentle push from his patron propelled George into the banqueting hall for the first time, clutching a gilded flagon and an embroidered napkin, it would have been with a sense of trepidation for all concerned.

First impressions of the royal presence would have been confusing. There was nothing regal about James. The forty-eight-year-old was an unprepossessing, to some even slightly repulsive figure, of 'middling stature'. He had a snub nose with pronounced bags beneath large eyes, like the awnings of a sail in a slack wind, giving him a doleful look. His red moustache and beard were 'very thin' and framed bulging, misshapen lips. As a cupbearer would be only too aware, his tongue was too large for his mouth, causing him to slobber and spill drink and food over his front. His complexion was 'as soft as taffeta sarsnet', the most delicate of fabrics, and he was rumoured never to wash his hands, only rubbing his finger ends slightly with the wet end of a napkin. He had a distracted air about him, his gaze roving around continuously, and was constantly fiddling about his codpiece. But he was also good company: erudite, sensitive and clever, eager to be entertained and generous and sincere with his emotions and affections.

All eyes would have been on George as he approached the king, assessing with minute care the royal reaction. The initial response was promising – a flicker of interest over the rim of the goblet.

Then, disaster. While carrying a tray of meat to the royal table, George was given a knock by the cupbearer whose position he had taken, causing food to spill over his new clothes. Withdrawing to clean himself up, he returned to the hall soon after and confronted his adversary, giving him a 'box on the ear'.

The impetuous act caught the attention of Robert Carr, the irascible and jealous Earl of Somerset, the king's current favourite and the most powerful of his courtiers. Sitting at the top table, near to James, he had spotted the king's interest in the newcomer, and, sensing the presence of a potential rival, decided to take action. He demanded that George should face the customary punishment for starting a fight in the royal presence of having his hand cut off. But, to Carr's consternation, the king intervened, pardoning George, 'without any satisfaction to the other party'. It was a sensational outcome, reinforcing Carr's conviction that the upstart must be destroyed.

George now became the focus of fierce curiosity as the royal progress continued on to Nottingham and Oxford. It was noted that the young man was as 'inwardly beautiful as he was outwardly', that he had the sort of elegant frame and 'sweet' disposition the king liked; his 'delicacy and handsome features' were praised, along with his 'especially effeminate and curious' hands and face. One admirer stared at him 'about half an hour's space at least' to try and comprehend his magnetism. Another was simply overwhelmed: 'From the nails of his fingers, nay, from the sole of his foot to the crown of his head, there was no blemish in him. And yet his carriage and every stoop of his deportment more than his excellent form were the beauty of his beauty.'

Thomas Erskine, Lord Fenton, who had known James since he was a boy, noticed the blossoming of a new infatuation. A few weeks after the first encounter, he was reporting to a cousin of this unknown 'youth' who 'begins to be in the favour of his majesty'. It was a measure of George's obscurity that Erskine assumed he was just a local boy from Northamptonshire.

In November, after the court had returned to London, a vacancy came up in the royal household for a groom of the bedchamber. It was a junior but nevertheless key position. A staff of twenty or so were responsible for the king's daily care, the grooms ranking between the pages and the gentlemen. They came into regular and intimate contact with the royal person, attending to him in shifts around the clock, quite often sleeping on a pallet at the bottom of the royal bed. They would wash him, dress him, pamper him, fetch for him, but were also expected to entertain and amuse him. They might even be put in charge of the 'privy purse', the king's own money, as necessity required.

Sir John Graham, as a gentleman of the bedchamber, seized the opportunity to put George forward as a candidate. The king had evidently enjoyed the young man's company, and would surely appreciate his presence in the bedchamber. But James turned Sir John down flat, leaving him puzzled and hurt, and George out on a limb.

The reason for the rebuff emerged in an extraordinary letter the king wrote to his current favourite Robert Carr, complaining of his jealous behaviour during the summer progress. It ran to several pages, and, while brimming with emotion, was clearly the product of hours of careful drafting. Prompted by the debacle over the young groom's appointment, it expressed the 'infinite grief of a deeply wounded heart' rather than the anger of a disobeyed master.

James was bewildered by the 'strange frenzy' that had overtaken Carr since George's appearance, 'so powdered with and mixed with strange streams of unquietness, passion, fury and insolent pride, and (which is worst of all) with a settled kind of induced obstinacy as it chokes and obscures all these excellent and good parts that God hath bestowed on you'. That choking obstinacy had led Carr to appoint, without James's knowledge or permission, his illegitimate kinsman William Carr to the role Sir John Graham had sought for George. This had forced James into the embarrassing position of having to turn his 'countenance' from his faithful old friend Sir John, 'the like whereof I never did to any man without a known offence'.

It was all part of a pattern in the favourite's behaviour, the king complained. He noted Carr's 'long creeping back and withdrawing . . . from lying in my chamber, notwithstanding my many hundred times earnest soliciting you to the contrary'.

Revealing his weakness and dependence, James also sought to reassure Carr. He would never, he promised, 'suffer any to rise in any degree of my favour except they may acknowledge and thank you as a furtherer of it, and that I may be persuaded that they love and honour you for my sake'.

Carr's response to the letter was to become even more difficult and demanding. He even claimed that he no longer felt 'inward affection' for the king, but would instead act only as a dutiful servant.

In the midst of these histrionic battles, George was all but forgotten. An adventure that had begun just a few months before, that had given him a tantalising glimpse of the glamour of court and brought him within touching distance of the king, had come to an end. Fortune had passed him by, and his efforts to run after it became desperate.

George was spotted at a horse race at Newmarket. The royal entourage was passing through in January 1615, and he was hoping to rejoin the carnival. But abandoned by his sponsors, he had become indistinguishable from all the other wretched petitioners reaching for the king's hem as he swept by. Dressed only in 'an old black suit, broken out in divers places', he could not even afford a room in a local inn, but had to rely on the charity of a local gentleman 'of a mean quality', who offered him a place to sleep on a 'trundle bed'.

Baynard's Castle

The humour in London in the winter of 1614/15 was sour. After a decade on the English throne, King James had yet to settle into it. He continued his restless touring of the country, from palace to hunting lodge to rural retreat, hawking or hunting or watching masques or feasting with his friends. He made little effort to address public concerns, was reluctant to summon Parliament – which served at his pleasure – and ran up enormous expenses which threatened to bankrupt the treasury. He was easily distracted, his interest in the affairs of state diverging wildly between schemes of enormous constitutional significance undertaken with casual presumption, such as a union of England with Scotland, and pet projects in which he became obsessively engaged, such as producing a definitive English edition of the Bible.

The public mood had started to deteriorate seriously following the death in 1612 of James's eighteen-year-old son and heir Henry, Prince of Wales. Henry had been a focus of adoration and hope in England, a paragon of princely virtues: 'Tall . . . strong . . . well proportioned', with 'eyes quick and pleasant . . . his whole face and visage comely and beautiful . . . with a sweet, smiling, and amiable countenance . . . full of gravity'. But in October of that year he had fallen ill with a mysterious wasting disease, to which he succumbed on 6 November. It was noted that the king did not even bother to attend the funeral, the enormous procession being led by the forlorn figure of Henry's twelve-year-old brother Charles.

Robert Carr appeared to be filling the vacuum Henry had left behind, arousing growing resentment in court and beyond. His rise was seen as the reason for the royal bedchamber in London becoming so thick with Scottish accents. When it was discovered that James was teaching Carr Latin, a courtier quipped that he should first teach him some English.

Like George, Carr was a younger brother without prospects of an inheritance, though from a more aristocratic background. His father had been the Laird of Ferniehirst, a closet Catholic whose clan, like Sir John Graham's, patrolled the Scottish–English borders. In 1585 an encounter between Ferniehirst's men and their English counterparts had resulted in a brawl that left one prominent English aristocrat dead. The laird's death a year later had helped prevent a serious escalation, but the Carrs were not popular in English circles – less so soon after James came to England, when Robert was appointed a groom of the royal bedchamber, one of those who blocked the 'beams' of royal benefaction from the English.

At a 1607 jousting competition staged to celebrate James's accession to the English throne, the young Carr, barely twenty years old, was given the task of riding into the tiltyard with a ceremonial shield to present to the king. As he dismounted, his horse had reared and he fell, breaking a leg. James immediately lost all interest in the tilt and called for Carr to be carried to a nearby house to be attended by royal physicians. Over the following days it was noticed how the king spent hours at the groom's bedside, fussing over his treatment and diet, deep in conversation with a young man not known for any 'great depth of literature or experience'. James seemed to flourish in the role of self-styled physician, as it provided him a chance both to show a fatherly concern for his patient as well as to admire Carr's smooth-skinned, pale complexion and well-formed frame, later said to share 'the beauty of both sexes'. For jealous English courtiers, looking for an excuse to challenge the king's choice of courtiers, this suggested an infatuation that had gone beyond the bounds of decency.

'Wondrously in a little time', James's passion for Carr had become public. It was noted how James 'leaneth on his arm, pinches his cheek, smoothes his ruffled garment', and would gaze adoringly at him even as he spoke to others. Carr responded by carefully honing his appearance and manner in ways that would maintain his master's fascination. He learned 'rather than to be, outwardly to seem', as the Tudor poet Sir Thomas Wyatt bitterly characterized the courtier's art. He would regularly change his tailors and 'tiremen' (dressers) so that he was always attired in the latest fashions. He became exquisitely sensitive to the king's particular likes: for a flowing garment, for clothes that were 'not all of one sort, but diversely coloured', for collars that fell 'somewhat down', for ruffs 'well stiffened and bushy', managing to combine any resulting flamboyance with 'some sort of cunning and show of modesty' in a way that utterly beguiled his rivals. He learned not to 'dwell too long on any one subject', to 'touch but lightly' on the controversial issue of religion, and always to heap praise upon the king's 'roan jennet', his favourite horse. It was an exhausting list, and vigilance as well as dedication were required to see that it was observed in every detail.

'We are almost worn out in our endeavours to keep pace with this fellow in his duty and labour to gain favour,' wrote one courtier to a country friend, 'but all in vain; where it endeth I cannot guess, but honours are talked of speedily for him.'

Honours duly followed. In 1608 Carr was given the manor of Sherborne in Dorset, worth about £1,000 a year (which had been confiscated from Queen Elizabeth's favourite Sir Walter Ralegh, who now languished in the Tower), followed by the barony of Winwick in Northamptonshire and the custody of the castle of Rochester, as well as lands in Westmorland and Durham. Every man now clutched his property closer for fear it would be snatched by the king as a gift for the favourite.

Carr also began to meddle directly in English politics. In 1610, he was suspected of spreading rumours to discredit Sir Robert Cecil, the man who had negotiated James's succession and was now his chief minister. Soon after, he became Viscount Rochester, with the right to sit in the House of Lords, the first Scottish peer to do so, and in April 1612 was appointed to the English Privy Council, the body that ran the government.

In 1613, Carr was created Earl of Somerset, and, in December of that year, in a lavish court wedding financed by the king, he had married Frances Howard, linking him to one of England's most ancient and powerful noble families. By the following summer, he had secured his political ascendancy by acquiring the roles of Lord Privy Seal and Lord Chamberlain.

As his wealth and status had risen, so had his sense of importance and control over the king. Even the Howards bemoaned the flatteries that had to be lavished on Carr to get his cooperation. 'Will you say the moon shineth all the summer?' Thomas Howard, the Earl of Arundel, complained to a friend. 'That the stars are bright jewels fit for Carr's ears? That the roan jennet surpasseth Bucephalus, and is worthy to be bestridden by Alexander? That his eyes are fire, his tail is Berenice's locks, and a few more such fancies worthy your noticing?'

By the time the king had returned from his summer progress of 1614, a group of grandees had decided something had to be done to halt Carr's rise, and loosen the Scottish grip on James's inner circle. The story of how and precisely when this group came together is fragmentary, but it begins with a meeting called in or around December at Baynard's Castle, the imposing fortress on the bank of the Thames that was home to the powerful Herbert family.

The ringleaders were William Herbert, Earl of Pembroke, and his younger brother Philip, Earl of Montgomery. Both had positioned themselves advantageously in the early days of James's English court, happy to engage in its sometimes boisterous antics, and skilful at cultivating the king's affections. The Venetian ambassador described William as 'a handsome youth' who once 'actually kissed His Majesty's face, whereupon the king laughed and gave him a little cuff'. Knowing how much he hated frogs, James put one down William's neck, causing much hilarity, and William got his revenge by putting a pig in the royal lavatory. Philip Herbert, meanwhile, had an 'indefatigable industry in hunting' that made him a favoured royal riding companion. Both, however, had found their ambitions thwarted by Carr's growing dominance at court. Their resentment culminated with his appointment as Lord Chamberlain, an office Pembroke had expected for himself.

There were plenty of other disgruntled courtiers ready to join the Herberts in bringing Carr down, including Edward Seymour, the Earl of Hertford, and Edward Russell, the Earl of Bedford. Passing along Fleet Street en route to Baynard's Castle, one of the group noticed a portrait of Carr hanging in a painter's stall, and instructed his footman to throw dirt at it.

The strategy this secret cabal chose to deal with the problem was simple: to 'drive out one nail with another'. And a new nail was at hand: the currently unemployed sensation of the previous summer's progress, George Villiers.

With the king distracted by so many demands, 'many arts' would be needed to spark 'the beginnings of new affection', and, this being the age of Shakespeare, the one chosen by the Baynard's Castle plotters was drama.

While in London, the king, whose mood had been low, had started to 'come forth' more regularly 'to see pastimes and fooleries'. It was decided that this provided the best opportunity for bringing George back to royal attention.

Three 'Master Fools' – Sir George Goring, Sir Edward Zouch and Sir John Finit – were recruited to perform an introductory entertainment that would get James into a receptive mood. Goring was the most accomplished of these 'fools'. He had a 'jocularity of humour' that was known to amuse the king.

Together, Goring and his fellow master fools staged a bawdy show that culminated with two of James's dwarves, David Droman and Archie Armstrong, performing a mock tilt, in which they rode piggyback on 'other fools' until, to gales of laughter, 'they fell together by the ears'.

The 'jollity' having cheered up the melancholy king, George was 'ushered in'. Magnificently dressed by the Herberts' tailor and seamstress in clothes made of the 'curious' materials that James appreciated, George stood before the royal throne and the royal eyes glistened promisingly.

A few weeks later, George was invited onto an even bigger stage. For Twelfth Night, when by tradition the Christmas revels reached their peak, the playwright Ben Jonson – Shakespeare's protégé – had been commissioned to write a masque (a short drama with highly elaborate sets and costumes) entitled *Mercury Vindicated from the Alchemists*. 'The principal motive' for staging it, according to one source, was 'the gracing of young Villiers and to bring him on the stage'. It was to be an extravagant affair, with the king, whose finances were already stretched, agreeing to contribute £1,500 towards the production costs.

'Ben's plays are works, where other works are plays', went the jibe, and, for those not distracted by the gorgeous costumes, staging and sets, *Mercury Vindicated* was particularly hard work. The language was highly allusive and allegorical, and difficult for many to interpret. But it had to be. It was a gentle but nevertheless arousing caress of the most sensitive issue preoccupying the court: the king's power to 'create' men like Carr.

The masque opened in an alchemical workshop illuminated by a great furnace – perhaps a welcome source of real as well as theatrical heat for a show being performed in the depths of a hard winter in a draughty Whitehall chamber. In their efforts to discover the Philosopher's Stone, the alchemists have trapped Mercury, in this context not the messenger of the gods but the personification of the vital spirit that brings dead matter to life. They need him to perform their experiments. Mercury tells the audience he is their 'crude and their sublimate; their precipitate and their unctuous; their male and their female; sometimes their hermaphrodite; what they list to style me'.

The ensuing drama was filled with references to the ingredients needed to 'make men' – 'not common ordinary creatures, but of rarity and excellence, such as the times wanted, and the age had a special deal of need of; such as there was a necessity they should be artificial; for Nature could never have thought or dreamt of their composition'. There were interludes with hideously deformed 'anti-masquers', half human, half chemical flask (their upper bodies dressed as 'lambics' or alembic distillation vessels), who performed a wild dance to screeching music until the audience rolled in laughter. There were mentions of a phoenix and of a *monsieur* – clear allusions to James's first 'made man', his French cousin and favourite Esmé Stuart – and of the dangers of creating with 'fire and art' a hideous distortion of what was achieved by the 'Sun and Nature'.

At which point, in a coup de théâtre, the alchemists disappeared and the scene was magically transformed from a fiery forge into a 'glorious bower', a canopy of fresh plants, flowers and branches, in which sat Nature and Prometheus, surrounded by twelve 'masquers'.

'How young and fresh am I tonight,' sang Nature, gesturing to the masquers, as 'Twelve my sons stand in their Maker's sight.' And there was George, one of these twelve, the others various gentlemen of the court, standing 'in their maker's sight', who as part of the finale ran off the stage and into the audience to choose a lady to dance with.

And George, everyone could agree, was an exceptional dancer. 'No one dances better, no man runs or jumps better', it was remarked. To see him move was to behold 'the best made man in the world, with the finest looks'. None could match his 'exquisite manner'. The elegant movement of his elegant limbs 'rendered himself the admiration and delight of everybody'.

Dance demonstrated George's charms to be a product of his natural 'plight', created 'without affected forms', as his friend Sir Henry Wotton put it. To this extent, he seemed to transcend the troubling question the production raised, about whether the qualities and powers of James's 'made men', his other courtly creatures, were genuine or fake. In an environment as mannered and constructed as the court, how could the real be distinguished from the counterfeit? James, whose fragile vanity was balanced by a keen intelligence, would have enjoyed pondering such questions. But the dazzling appearance of this young man from – where was it? Northamptonshire? Leicestershire? Somewhere – his qualities were so manifest, so captivating, so spontaneously invoked, they must surely be real.

James was smitten. 'Strucken' was the word used by the chronicler Arthur Wilson, a contemporary. But the king, whose turbulent upbringing had left him wary of confrontation, did not want to provoke Carr. Nor did he want others to think him 'changeable' or prone to 'a sudden affection'. So he instructed his 'confidents' to reintroduce George to his circle 'by degrees', 'at too great a distance' to arouse suspicions of favour – out of Carr's way, in other words, but within the king's sight.

St George's Day

In the early months of 1615, George somehow managed to keep far enough away from the king to avoid another clash with Carr. According to the French ambassador, James had persuaded the favourite that George had only been allowed back into court to act as a token Englishman, to quieten the complaints about Scots monopolizing the royal household.

With Carr placated, the focus of the Baynard's Castle plotters now turned to Anne of Denmark, James's sociable, formidable wife. The queen's relationship with her husband was complex. Being the sister of a Danish king and Holy Roman Emperor, she saw no reason why she should defer to him. Her principle was that 'honour goes before life', and certainly before marriage, which made her quick to take offence, and slow to offer forgiveness. She openly resisted any efforts by James to control her. In 1593, for example, she had gone riding in bad weather while in the early stages of pregnancy, against his instructions. Further efforts to confine her were frustrated until she agreed to be more compliant, but only if he gave her 'the greatest part of his jewels'. The birth of Henry, a male heir, in 1594 had improved her standing in the Scottish court, but she was distraught and furious when James, fearing his son would be used as a pawn in the ongoing feuds with his barons, insisted that the child be brought up by foster parents. The king was also occasionally embarrassed by her Catholic sympathies, which had become increasingly obvious. At their joint English coronation, she refused to take the Anglican communion, causing consternation among the bishops.

Since her arrival in London with James in the summer of 1603, an 'open diffidence' had been observed between them. Ending any pretence at cohabitation, she had set up her own household at Somerset House, one of London's most magnificent mansions, renovating it to her Scandinavian tastes. In a gesture of patriotic defiance and regal independence, she had also renamed it Denmark House.

Despite their estrangement, however, James trusted her. He continued to rely on his wife to vet royal appointments, because he knew it was not in her interests to allow anyone into his household who might plot to overthrow him. So, in order to ease George deeper into the royal ménage, the Baynard's Castle plotters knew they had to win over the queen.

Fortunately, Anne did not care for Robert Carr. His high-handed manner rankled with her sense of dignity. Nevertheless, she had been 'bitten with favourites' before, and 'was very shy' to promote another. In an effort to win her over, George and his sponsors approached George Abbot, the Archbishop of Canterbury, a close friend of the queen. Abbot's influence over James was at a low ebb, in part due to Carr, and he was eager to find a way of recovering his standing. In backing the charming and apparently pliable twenty-two-year-old George, he saw how this could be achieved.

Heavy snow fell across London in January and February of 1615, and the freeze continued well into March. Despite the weather, the king decided to resume his restless touring of the country, George now a discreet presence among the serving staff. The great, creaking machinery of royal conveyance dragged itself across the snow-covered countryside, visiting Newmarket and Theobalds, James's country mansion in Hertfordshire. In Cambridge he heard a sermon by the poet and clergyman John Donne and watched a play entitled *Ignoramus: a Common Lawyer* starring the versatile dwarf Dominic Drummond, which succeeded in provoking howls of outrage from the legal fraternity, and so impressed the king that he decided he would return to Cambridge later in the year to see it again.

While James was away, Archbishop Abbot managed to persuade the queen to sponsor George's promotion to the post of gentleman of the king's bedchamber. Her agreement came with a warning. 'My lord,' she wrote to him, 'you and the rest of your friends know not what you do. I know your master better than you all, for if this young man be once brought in, the first persons that he will plague must be you that labour for him. Yea, I shall have my part also' – meaning that she too would suffer; 'the King will teach him to despise and hardly entreat us all, that he may seem to be beholden to none but himself.'

'Notwithstanding this,' Abbot wrote years later, and with a nod to hindsight, 'we were still insistent, telling her Majesty, that the Change would be for the better: For George was of a good nature, which the other [Carr] was not; and if he should degenerate, yet it would be a long time before he were able to attain to that height of evil, which the other had.' In other words, all these grandees were confident that, once their objective had been achieved, they could rely on George, at least in the medium term, to be obedient to their bidding, and thereby help strengthen their influence over James.

And so the plan was 'stricken while the iron was hot'. An auspicious date was set: 23 April, St George's Day. However, no sooner were arrangements in place than they started to unravel. James had returned to the capital for the anniversary of his English coronation, but, following rather lacklustre celebrations, he decided to remove himself to his suburban palaces at Hampton Court and 'Oking' (Woking). At the same time, Anne fell ill with a condition 'not without danger'.

Then the queen rallied a little, and managed to entice James back to London. She also decided to involve her younger son in the plan, perhaps in the hope of helping Prince Charles, the current heir, to overcome his shyness and his awkward, even marginal presence in his father's court. She had become 'passionately attached' to her fourteen-year-old boy, calling him her 'little servant' and taking a keen interest in the crucial matter of his marriage prospects. Like his older brother Henry, he had been taken away from her during his early years, but since he had turned eleven he had been 'admitted to the Queen's service', becoming a regular presence at Denmark House.

On the appointed day, Anne sent instructions to George to dress in the clothes and 'curious linens' his sponsors had bought for him and repair to Denmark House, where he was to wait close by the queen's private chambers. She then arranged for her husband and her son to come to her bedchamber.

The king arrived to find Archbishop Abbot already there, along with the Herbert brothers, William and Philip, the earls of Pembroke and Montgomery, and other leading Baynard's Castle plotters. James must have been puzzled, if not a little alarmed, to discover the primate and such senior nobles attending his sick queen.

Anne then rose from her bed and, with husband and son standing before her – two fidgety figures with symptoms variously attributed to rickets and cerebral palsy – she asked Charles to hand her his rapier. The king flinched – memories of the bloody confrontations that had marked the early years of his Scottish reign had made him nervous of naked blades, even when they were wielded by his own son. But Anne was shrewd enough to have anticipated such a reaction, and turned shock into delight by producing from behind an arras – metaphorically if not actually – the twenty-two-year-old George.

Drawing on the conversative qualities he had worked so hard to cultivate and that so potently amplified his natural appeal, George played his part impeccably, entrancing the jaded monarch and overcoming his instinctive wariness. Without the need for any further prompting, the king instructed him to kneel and used Charles's sword to knight the glamorous young man on the spot.

And so the dreams of George's sponsors seemed to become

reality, with the immediate swearing-in of the former cupbearer to the king's bedchamber, the position closest physically as well as politically to the centre of royal power.

Word of the apparently impromptu proceedings soon reached Carr, who instantly recognized the threat. It was too late to reverse the knighthood, so he sent a message 'importuning' James to promote Villiers to the lower rank of groom rather than gentleman. But the Herberts, with the queen's and the archbishop's continuing support, prevailed on the king to keep to their course, and Sir George arose as a fully fledged gentleman of the bedchamber.

After the ceremony was over, Archbishop Abbot watched George go off with the king, the young man's first experience of direct and private contact with the monarch. He emerged soon after alive with excitement, and came looking for the archbishop. He found him in the queen's privy gallery, where he embraced him. 'He professed that he was so infinitely bound unto me, that all his life long he must honour me as his father,' Abbot recalled later, emphasizing his own central role in George's dizzying ascendancy. 'And now he did beseech me, that I would give him some lessons how he should carry himself.'

The lessons the archbishop gave were predictably pious, but tinged with pragmatism: George should pray every day 'upon his knees' for the king and for the 'grace studiously to serve and please him', he should 'do all good offices' in support of the king's relations with his wife and his son Prince Charles and he should 'fill his Master's ears with nothing but truth'. He made George repeat his promises three times.

The archbishop ruefully noted several years later that George was grateful for the advice 'for a few days, but not for long'. Abbot quoted the Roman historian Tacitus, who 'hath somewhere a note' to the effect that acts of kindness, 'while they may be requited, seem courtesies; but when they are so high that they cannot be repaid, they prove matters of hatred'. He had conveniently forgotten that his own involvement had been as much out of self-interest as charity, and that it was a mistake on the part of all the Baynard's Castle plotters to take their apparently pliant protégé for granted and assume he would remain subservient to their interests and wishes.

The Matter of the Garter

John Holles, an experienced observer of courtly affairs, was amazed at the 'daring' of George's insurgency. He told his brother that the upstart's supporters – known as the 'braccoes' for their strutting confidence – showed a ferocity and determination with which 'this tame generation of ours is not acquainted'. Yet when it came to the flow of royal favour he could not believe they had the capacity to 'turn the stream down another channel'. George had numbers, certainly, but Carr . . . he had the weight of office and tenure. Perhaps a shift in James's affection might 'bring something forth', but not enough, surely, to 'raze' an incumbent 'rooted by long service, and many offices of great latitude in our state'.

A significant test came a month after George's promotion to the bedchamber, at the ceremony to install two new Knights of the Garter, England's most ancient chivalric order. The candidates were William Knollys, a veteran English soldier and courtier, and Thomas Erskine, James's Scottish Groom of the Stool. Knollys was close to Carr's in-laws, the Howard family, so had the backing of the favourite. George responded by declaring that he would join Erskine's entourage, an apparently innocent gesture of Anglo-Scottish cordiality which was quickly recognized as a chance to test the strength of Carr's support.

As the day of the investiture approached, John Chamberlain, a well-informed and perceptive gossip, was quick to realize the significance. In a letter to a friend in Holland, he speculated on which of the two knights would attract the more impressive following. He had taken it for granted that Knollys would prevail 'by reason of his alliance' to Carr's supporters, which included the Howard clan and 'many other great families that will bring him their friends'. 'Yet,' he pointed out, 'most are persuaded, that the other will bear away the bell' – that the underdog Erskine would win. This was because he had not only the support of 'the best part of the Court' and an escort of 'an hundred of the Guard, that have new rich coats made on purpose', but was backed by 'Sir George Villiers, the new favourite'.

On the day, George was forced to watch the investiture from

the sidelines. James had forbidden him from taking part, fearing it would trigger another outburst from Carr. To that extent, the king's efforts were successful, as the event went off without a hitch. However, it turned out that the real action was taking place not in the pageantry of the ancient ceremony, but in the royal box. Sir Ralph Winwood, the king's secretary and thought to be a Carr loyalist, was seen to be watching the event alongside George. Chamberlain noted that Winwood's 'presence had been better forborne, in my judgement, for many respects', not least to prevent an escalation of courtly infighting, 'but that every man abounds in his own sense'.

Winwood had become increasingly concerned about Carr's domination of government affairs. A veteran of Queen Elizabeth's diplomatic service, Sir Ralph had been a key figure in the early stages of James's English reign, helping to implement the king's pacifist foreign policy towards Europe. In 1612, the post of Secretary of State, responsible for foreign affairs, had fallen vacant, and Winwood was clearly the best qualified candidate. He had lobbied hard to get the job, focusing his efforts on Carr, who had been delegated by James to deal with government appointments.

No one could have indulged in more humiliating and, at times, expensive, sycophancy than Sir Ralph in his efforts to win his prize. He had helped arrange the wedding of Carr to Lady Frances Howard in 1613, and had attended the nuptials in showy style, wearing an enormously expensive black suit made for the occasion. He had showered the couple with presents and when the bride needed horses to draw her new coach through the streets of London, offered her the pick of the thoroughbreds he had imported from Flanders.

For more than a year he had endured the 'misery and beggary' and 'vexation of spirit' of this intensive courting until, finally, in March 1614, he was given the job. But it turned out he was Secretary of State only in name. Carr continued to keep a tight grip on the seals of office and the diplomatic bags, and ensured that all foreign correspondence was routed through his office. He treated Winwood, more than twenty years his senior, with breathtaking condescension. When Sir Ralph, for example, had suggested Carr should write to the English agent in Brussels on an important matter of state, he was told dismissively that he 'should not trouble himself' with such matters, as Carr 'would do whatsoever was requisite'.

In July 1615, two months after the Garter investiture of Erskine and Knollys, Sir Ralph's defiant gesture of loyalty to George produced the result he had craved: he was told he would finally be receiving the seals of office. For a moment, it looked as though Carr was accepting the inevitable. But by this time, the favourite's jealous petulance was out of control and, at the last minute, he changed his mind and snatched the seals back, leaving Sir Ralph once again humiliated and empty-handed. It was the last straw. Carr had done this 'in so scornful a manner' that Winwood gave up all further efforts at flattering him and pledged to 'endeavour' his ruin.

Around this time, Carr embarked with the king on the annual royal progress, with George snapping at his heels. It was a long and dry summer, producing 'the best and fairest melons and grapes' ever seen in England, and as the royal party wound its way along the narrow country lanes from one market town to the next, past dense hedgerows frothing with blossom and butterflies and fields abundant with crops, the factionalism seemed to ease.

Winwood, meanwhile, had been told to stay behind in London to deal with the menial business left by Carr. With the court away, he took the opportunity to visit Mary Talbot, Countess of Shrewsbury, then a prisoner in the Tower of London. What prompted the meeting with Sir Ralph is unknown, and what transpired was too convenient to suggest an accident.

The countess told him of a rumour she had heard concerning a flamboyant and fierce-tempered friend of Carr's, Sir Thomas Overbury. Overbury had been sent to the Tower two years previously, ostensibly for refusing a foreign post offered to him by James, but really because he had become bothersome to Carr's and the king's efforts to boost the favourite's position at court. Locked away, it was convenient to all parties that Overbury be left to rot, and he had apparently obliged. He started to suffer severe vomiting, stopped eating, complained of being permanently thirsty, and, when physicians were called to treat him, produced urine samples that smelled unusually foul. He died on 15 September 1613, his body buried that evening, ostensibly because of the dreadful odour.

There was nothing particularly suspicious about his death – fevers of various sorts were common and often fatal in prisons at the time. However, the countess was convinced he had been poisoned. She had heard it, she told Sir Ralph, from no less an authority than the Keeper of the Tower, Sir Gervase Elwes, suggesting that he must have been involved in the plot, as he controlled access to the prisoner.

It was surely not chance that had delivered this useful information to Sir Ralph just when he needed it, suggesting a tip-off by one of George's supporters. Whatever the circumstances, Winwood decided to investigate further. At a meal organized by the countess's husband, perhaps with promises of his wife's release, Winwood met the keeper, who confessed he had been forced to poison the prisoner by Carr and his wife Frances.

As Winwood was making these sinister discoveries, the mood of the ongoing summer progress was beginning to change. While George had maintained a demeanour of serene self-possession, Carr had become tormented by self-doubts, making him increasingly needy and demanding. In an effort to resolve the issue, the king ordered Sir Humphrey May, an accomplished courtier and politician known for his warm manner and persuasive eloquence, to act as an intermediary. Though close to Carr, May had also been among the first to offer himself as a 'wise servant' to George.

May suggested to George that he should go to Carr and offer to become his 'creature'. May then approached Carr and advised him not to spurn his rival, but to 'embrace him'. If he did so, he would 'still stand a great man, though not the sole Favourite'. When Carr resisted, Sir Humphrey told him 'in plain terms' that it was the king's will, and that George would be coming to him 'to cast himself into his protection, to take his rise under the shadow of his wings'. Sir Humphrey then took his leave, and within half an hour George appeared in Carr's chamber and dutifully said to him: 'My Lord, I desire to be your servant, and your creature, and shall desire to take my Court-preferment under your favour and your Lordship shall find me as faithful a servant unto you as ever did serve you.'

Carr's reply was terse and decisive. He told George that he

would have 'none of your service, and you shall none of my favour. I will, if I can, break your neck, and of that be confident.'

Carr then went to the king. With hostile forces closing in on him, and perhaps warned of Winwood's investigations in London, he asked for a general pardon, an ancient royal prerogative that would give him immunity from punishment for all past crimes. General pardons were rarely granted and usually highly controversial. News of Carr's efforts began to leak, prompting speculation about the offences he might have committed; some suggesting that it was because he had 'appropriated a considerable quantity of the Crown jewels'.

Hoping to calm his volatile favourite, James agreed to the pardon. But in a sign of growing concerns about the king's lenience towards Carr, the Lord Chancellor Thomas Egerton, risking his own career, refused to put the royal seal to it. At a meeting of the Privy Council on 20 August 1615, as the progress was passing through the West Country, matters reached a head. Carr complained of 'the malice of his enemies' that had 'forced' him to ask for a pardon, and confronted the Lord Chancellor, demanding 'if he knew anything against him, to say it there'. James spoke up in Carr's favour. He summoned Prince Charles into the room and, in a move that must have perplexed his councillors as much as it humiliated his son, he placed a hand on the fourteen-year-old heir and proclaimed that the purpose of the pardon was so that his son 'may not be able to undo that which I have done'.

The strange performance did not have its intended effect. Egerton fell on his knees before the king, pointing out that there was no precedent for such a warrant and that awarding it would amount to giving Carr 'the jewels, the hangings, and the tapestry, and everything' the king owned. James 'grew very angry, saying that he ordered him to pass it, and that he was to pass it', and stormed out of the council chamber. But Egerton stood firm, continuing to withhold the seal. Frantic efforts by Carr to find a legal precedent that might force the issue drew a blank, and the queen, still acting as George's champion and Carr's enemy, persuaded James to let the matter drop.

Some time in August, the royal progress reached Gotly, a West Country property belonging to one of George's stepfathers. There the king was 'magnificently entertained', and perhaps met for the first time the formidable Mary Villiers, who held the property as part of a marriage settlement. James's relationship with his mother, Mary, Queen of Scots, had been a distant and troubled one, ending in him being effectively complicit in her execution by the English in 1587, after she spurned his efforts to help her. In contrast, Mary Villiers showed a fierce maternal devotion and determination that evidently impressed and moved the king, and explained the confident and self-assured manner of her son.

The next stop on their journey was Farnham Castle, the palace of the Bishop of Winchester, romantically set on the side of a wooded hill, overlooking the prosperous market town of Farnham and the gentle billow of the Surrey downlands. Here, in a mood relaxed by the Villiers hospitality, in a bedchamber commanding glorious views of the soft, luscious English countryside pullulating with summer ripeness, James's love affair with George was consummated.

Many years later, when the relationship was in crisis, George would recollect the encounter to remind his 'dear dad' James of the emotional as well as physical intimacy they had exchanged, 'the time which I shall never forget at Farnham, where the bed's head could not be found between the master and his dog'.

George had long referred to himself as James's 'dog', and there is little question from the way the two addressed one another that the use of the term was more than an expression of social subservience. James needed the comfort and consolation of a companion who showed unfaltering devotion and loyalty. He had been brought up in an atmosphere thick with fear, in which physical contact was usually violent and often deadly, in which love was sparse and sex strategic. But he was also a man of deep emotions, who craved tenderness, wanted to be generous with his feelings, displayed affection through contact, measured loyalty through closeness. He was starved of the warmth of another's body next to his. He had not shared a bed with his wife for years. Esmé Stuart, the phoenix who had sheltered between his legs, was frozen in memory. Carr was now estranged, having been 'long creeping back and withdrawing' from lying in his chamber. It was no surprise, then that 'in his passion of love to his new favourite . . . the King was more impatient than any woman to enjoy her love' and George – with his charm and wit, his confidence and humility, his youthful strength and yielding spirit – provided it. Reflecting some time later on their relationship, George expressed his amazement that one so high as the king should 'descend so low' with his 'good fellowship'. None showed expressions of more care than James did for him – not any master for his slave, not any physician for his patient, nor any father for his child, or any friend for his equal; not 'between lovers in the best kind', nor between a man and his wife. James was George's purveyor, his 'good fellow, my physician, my maker, my friend, my father, my all'.

Later in the month, as the summer progress was about to pass into a dream, they were at Theobalds together and, at this still early and highly impressionable moment in their relationship, James took George on a hunt.

Few, not even the sons of country gentlemen, had experience of the elaborate rituals of the royal hunt. For James, it was the most manly and noble of pastimes, 'specially with running hounds, which is the most honourable and noblest sort thereof'. It was an initiation into a world of sensual masculinity, of which James wanted to make George a part.

Theobalds had originally been the country seat of James's chief minister, the late Robert Cecil. Knowing of James's enthusiasm, Cecil had turned it into a hunting paradise, filling its woodlands with game and diverting a river to beautify the park. He did such a good job that James took it over, making it his main retreat and hunting ground. He enlarged the park by absorbing nearby Enfield Chase, and the commons of Northaw and Cheshunt, and enclosed it within a brick wall ten miles in circumference to keep the wildlife in and the poachers out.

This autumn hunt of 1615 was late in the season, and more dangerous for it, as the stags were in rut, and liable to attack rather than run. Nevertheless, if James was in residence, it was the huntsman's job to find suitable quarry, whatever the conditions.

The hunt took place on 25 September, just over a year after George had first served James at Apethorpe. It began with the 'assembly' at the edge to the park, the royal party and guests sitting in a pavilion erected for the occasion, or on blankets draped across the grass. James, George and the huntsmen were joined by various female companions – the 'cunts', as James called them on such occasions – who were to act as spectators. The hunting party itself was small, a group of the rougher sort that James preferred to accompany him. A huntsman arrived as breakfast was being eaten, and he spread across the ground the 'fumes' or dung of potential quarry, freshly gathered that morning. The king inspected the pellets, looking at their shape, considering their smell, and selected the most promising sample. The huntsman was then dispatched to lay a trail of markers leading to the chosen quarry's harbour, from where the hunt would begin.

At the appointed time, the men mounted their horses and trotted off into the woodland, watched by the women. They quietly followed a trail of snapped branches and broken twigs left by the huntsman. As they approached the quarry, the pace slowed. Once the huntsman was spotted, they came to a halt.

The stag broke cover, crashing through the undergrowth, prompting the huntsman to blow his horn, releasing the hounds, and the hunting party spurred their horses.

At a gallop they hurtled through the woods, horns blaring, hounds baying, men yelling, the buck glimpsed through the trees, threatening to confound the pursuit as it doubled back and darted off, or found a stream or river to break the trail. In the heat of pursuit, George could show off his horsemanship, the physical risk adding to the thrilling sense of vitality, as they thundered through the trees, leapt hedgerows and broke into the park. Some could not keep up, some fell; Nicholas Brett, one of George's servants, suffered a terrible accident and died. But the chase continued, until the speed, strength and guile of the quarry became exhausted, and the beast slowed and turned its crown of antlers towards its pursuers. As it confronted the hounds, now held at bay by their handlers, the huntsman leapt at it from behind, and slashed its hamstrings with a knife, so it dropped to the ground. The king and his party dismounted, drew their swords and hacked at the creature's neck to deliver the final blows.

An exultant blast of the hunting horns announced the kill, and the party gathered round the corpse for the unmaking – the ritual cutting up of the carcass – which it was the privilege of the king to perform. James slit open the creature's belly, and pulled out the steaming entrails to feed the howling pack of dogs. Then he anointed George with a smear of the creature's hot blood on his face, and morsels of the tender meat, still warm with life, were fed to the triumphant, ravenous hunters.

As these ancient bonding rituals were being performed in the country, in London, Sir Ralph Winwood was also on the hunt, and closing in on his prey, contacts in Holland revealing that a young apothecary had admitted to supplying poison to Carr.

As soon as the court was back in London, Winwood presented his findings to James. The king's reaction went unrecorded, but he clearly took the accusations seriously, as he referred them to his lawyers before withdrawing from London to await their decision at his retreat at Royston.

A trial was eventually held in May 1616, which led to the conviction of both Carr and his wife Frances. But what should have been a sweet moment for Ralph Winwood quickly turned sour. Because of his earlier association with Carr, he came under suspicion of involvement in the poisoning plot he had helped to expose. The strain led to him falling ill and he died the following year. As for Carr, before being committed to the Tower, where his victim had met his fate, he went to see the king. Two contemporary accounts of their final parting were circulated. According to one, presumably preferred by Carr's enemies, he approached James with characteristic petulance, announcing the verdicts 'to be a great presumption'. But the king told him he must accept that the evidence was decisive – indeed, he suggested (improbably) that even he would have accepted the verdict if he found himself in similar circumstances. According to the other, more dramatically satisfying version, Carr came to take his leave of the king, 'embraced and kissed him often', 'shewed an extreme passion to be without him' but as soon as his back was turned remarked ruefully as well as prophetically 'with a smile' that he would never see the king's face again.

Within a few weeks of Carr's fall, and perhaps as an acknowledgement of his enthusiasm for the hunt, George was made Master of the Horse. The title was one of the court's most coveted, replete with romance, glamour and chivalric honour. Even Carr had failed to secure it for himself, despite repeated efforts. George's success demonstrated not only the king's enthusiasm for his new minion, but that the young man was no amateur when it came to gaining power and position.

Then suddenly George's rise faltered. Everyone held their breath. It was rumoured that he had caught smallpox – the 'gift of a friend' was one sardonic observation. Smallpox would have left that beautiful face scarred, and his ambitions destroyed. It had been noted how since his rise George had 'lost much affection of his particular friends and generally of all men', and a certain grim satisfaction seemed to spread through the court. 'The favours of princes are looked on with many envious eyes,' warned Lionel Cranfield, a merchant who had become an advisor to George, and those eyes were now eager to catch the king's.

Then George recovered and rallied. There were scandalized reports that he was going to receive the Order of the Garter – '*non credo*', unbelievable! one commentator complained. But the rumours were true. The twenty-three-year-old shared his investiture with the Earl of Rutland, a delicious moment for George and his mother Mary, no doubt, as the earl was a member of the Manners family, one of those Midlands dynasties that had flourished while the Villiers and Beaumont lines had languished.

Around the same time, George's faithful promoter and mentor Sir John Graham died. The old Scot was buried 'in the night at Westminster with better than 200 torches', and a not inconsiderable number of lords, including Thomas Erskine, whose own Garter ceremony had been such a focus of Carr's fall and George's rise. To some the solemnity and extravagance was 'pompous': in Tothill Fields, near Westminster, several 'rude knaves' performed an 'apish imitation' of the ceremony with a dead dog.

Neither a God nor an Angel

A delicious heaven, Marston had described it in *The Malcontent*, and with a smooth ease, George seemed to have entered it. Using his natural charms and instinctive guile, he had become a royal favourite. Vassals licked the pavement with their slavish knees. He was received with a general timorous respect, and surrounded by the confused hum and busy murmur of obsequious suitors. But he was also dangerously exposed, the focus of powerful rivalries and personal jealousies. The death of Sir John Graham had deprived him of perhaps his only dependable friend at court. The former friends and allies of Robert Carr, the man he had displaced, were already plotting his downfall, while the self-appointed 'braccoes' who had pushed so relentlessly for his promotion now presumed him to be their creature, and expected him to do their bidding.

On 2 May 1616, George received a letter from Francis Bacon, the king's Attorney General. The fifty-four-year-old veteran of court politics had been appointed to oversee Robert Carr's prosecution. Bacon was a controversial presence in royal circles, arousing strong reactions. Many saw him as extravagant and pompous, a clever man flawed by greed and perversity. Rumours of his 'most horrible and secret sin of sodomy' dogged him throughout his career. He was later described by the antiquarian and biographer John Aubrey as a pederast, and a canon of St Paul's Cathedral with a grudge against him claimed in 1619 that he had engaged in sodomy with one of his 'catamites' during a sermon.

Others saw such flaws as minor blemishes in a man rightly hailed to be not only a brilliant jurist and politician, but 'the greatest philosopher since the fall of Greece', possessing 'the very nerve of genius' – claims that were not exaggerated for a scholar who in influential works such as *Novum Organum* was to shape the emergence of modern scientific thinking.

George did not care about either his depravity or accomplishments. He recognized him to be a figure whose vulnerabilities provided access to his strengths, a brilliant operator who might be prepared to give up some of the secrets of the deadly arts of courtly politics in return for the new favourite's flattering attentions.

Bacon's initial contact with George was innocuously bureaucratic, copying George into the confidential correspondence he had been having with the king about the conduct of the case against Carr. The king wished to ensure that the former favourite be found guilty without having to face the death penalty – a tricky outcome when the charge was murder. Bacon informed George that he was to be the 'third person' whom the king had 'admitted to this secret' desire.

George intuitively grasped the significance of Bacon's gesture, and responded enthusiastically, even flirtatiously. Bacon later mentions burning an 'inward' – surely meaning intimate – letter he had received around this time from the new favourite. 'But', the excited lawyer could not resist adding, 'the flame it hath kindled in me will never be extinguished.' Subsequent missives echoed this confidential tone, culminating with a long letter in which Bacon shared what he called his 'country fruits', opinions developed after much thought in his rural retreat about how George could consolidate his position as Carr's replacement.

He began with a carefully worded warning against greed. Thanks to the king's generosity, George's 'private fortunes' might seem 'established', but he must not appear too grasping in his pursuit of them; 'for assure yourself', Bacon counselled, 'that fortune is of a woman's nature, that will sooner follow you by slighting than by too much wooing'. Instead, he urged George to focus on the exercise of influence, to draw on a still shallow reservoir of royal love and trust to shape James's regime.

When he was at the height of his powers, Carr had effectively acted as James's prime minister, deciding on the appointment of ministers and officials. But, Bacon informed George, his fragile self-confidence and paranoia had led to men of calibre, such as Sir Ralph Winwood, being 'by design and of purpose suppressed', turning the Privy Council into a 'wilderness' of talent. George was now in a similar position to shape James's regime, so must reach beyond his brotherhood of braccoes to 'countenance, and encourage, and advance able men and virtuous men and meriting in all kinds, degrees, and professions'. 'Money, and turn-serving, and cunning canvasses, and importunity', Bacon complained, had been allowed to 'prevail too much'. Their influence must be suppressed – but not completely. For, as Bacon admitted, it was sometimes necessary to use 'cunning and corrupt men', but George must 'keep them at a distance; and let it appear that you make use of them, rather than that they lead you'.

It was the advice of a Machiavellian. Bacon was an early English scholar of the works of Niccolò Machiavelli, an admirer of the

Italian political theorist's role in making the Medici family the dominant dynasty in Renaissance Florence. By exercising the same combination of guile, ruthlessness and pragmatism, Bacon was suggesting, George could achieve similar, epoch-making results. He could ensure that he 'shall not be a meteor, or a blazing star, but *stella fixa*', a fixed star in the firmament, 'happy here, and more happy hereafter'.

In August 1616, James decided to raise George to the nobility. But first an estate was needed worthy of the dignity of an aristocratic title. The lush countryside surrounding Whaddon, Buckinghamshire, said to be worth £1,500 a year, had been forfeited to the Crown from Thomas, Lord Grey of Wilton, a convicted traitor who had died in the Tower in 1614. James decided to give it to George.

Bacon, whose snobbery gave him a sensitive appreciation of the importance of titles and names, fretted over what an ennobled George should be called. Baron Whaddon was suggested, but the king decided George should be a viscount, a higher aristocratic rank, and Bacon thought 'Viscount Villiers' to be best, as it was 'a well-sounding and noble name, both here and abroad; and being your proper name, I will take it for a good sign that you shall give honour to your dignity, and not your dignity to you'.

The title was conferred at Woodstock, the beautiful royal hunting lodge outside Oxford, in the late summer of 1616. The ceremony was enacted with the sort of courtly playacting that made the young man so attractive to the king. George was initially brought into the royal presence as Baron Whaddon. He then withdrew, changed his garments, and returned as Viscount Villiers, clad in a 'surcoat of crimson velvet, girt with his sword'. With the queen and Prince Charles as spectators, James 'performed the ceremonies of that action with the greatest alacrity and princely cheerfulness'. The new viscount and his supporters then retired to supper, but later 'came all joyfully up in their robes with glasses of wine in their hands, kneeled all round about the King before he was risen from supper, and drank to His Majesty's health; which he very graciously and cheerfully pledged'.

James's generosity began to run wild. He offered George Carr's manor of Sherborne. But George, reflecting Bacon's careful advice, tactfully refused 'in a most noble fashion, praying the King that the building of his fortunes may not be founded upon the ruins of another'. The king then decided George must receive lands of equivalent value to make up the deficit. This entailed various legal complications, but Bacon cleverly worked round them, and soon suitable properties were being added to George's flourishing portfolio.

At the end of 1616, court gossip held that George 'doth much decline in the King's favour', and John Chamberlain reported a '*sourd bruit*' – a faint rumour – that the favourite's fortunes were in decline, 'as if the blazing star at Court were toward an eclipse'. But it proved to be wishful thinking. As a gift to celebrate the new year of 1617, the king sent George a miniature of himself with his heart in his hand – a declaration of love as romantic as any by an ardent suitor. A few days later, during a 'day of oblation and sacrifice', Viscount Villiers became Earl of Buckingham at Whitehall.

The following month, the relentless promotion continued when George, Earl of Buckingham, Lord Lieutenant of Buckinghamshire and Master of the King's Horse was introduced to the Privy Council as its latest member, at twenty-four years of age the youngest ever to serve. George's charisma, and Bacon's relentless support in the background, had been translated into political power. When James's ministers objected to someone so callow having such seniority, the king delivered a speech choked with emotion: 'I, James, am neither a god nor an angel, but a man like any other. Therefore I act like a man, and confess to loving those dear to me more than other men. You may be sure that I love the Earl of Buckingham more than anyone else, and more than you who are here assembled. I wish to speak in my own behalf, and not to have it thought to be a defect, for Jesus Christ did the same, and therefore I cannot be blamed. Christ had His John and I have my George.'

The king did not confine his startling, embarrassingly candid expressions of devotion to closed meetings of his council. A scandalized Venetian ambassador reported how, during a royal banquet, the king 'as a recreation' decided to get to his feet and read out verses he had written expressing his adoration of the favourite, the guests forced to stifle any amusement or consternation as they listened to the mawkish tribute.

Keeper of the Seal

In an address to his people, King James once remarked that he had no family – 'no father, mother, brother nor sister'. But when George came into his life, he seemed to find a substitute. The favourite's noisome, curious, vigorous kin gave him the kind of family life he had been denied, complete with its surface tiffs and tensions as well as a deeper love and loyalty.

He became particularly attached to George's mother, Mary. She has been variously described as 'busy, intriguing, masculine, and dangerous', a 'Jezebel' and 'from first to last ambitious and unscrupulous'. Her activism on behalf of her relatives was relentless; she spared no effort to advance what were sniffily referred to as her 'poor' relatives, particularly her other, less eligible and more difficult sons, John and Christopher, for whom 'young maids' were being busily sought as marriage partners. It was jealously noted that within months of her son's promotion to the royal bedchamber, she was 'always so much at court' – at one point even George found her interference too insistent, pleading with her 'not to intermeddle with business'.

But James enjoyed her company. He encouraged Queen Anne to include her in her household and receive her kinsmen. By June 1616, Mary was enjoying private dinners with the Countess of Salisbury, and a queue of senior courtiers made themselves 'great followers and observers', having 'feasted and entertained her by turn'. 'All the entertainment was chiefly intended and directed to her and her children,' it was noted. Reflecting her growing eminence, the senior diplomat Sir John Digby asked her to be godmother to his son. Soon, it emerged she was to be made 'a countess, or marchioness', even though her husband Sir Thomas Compton, now a rather dejected figure, was 'not to rise, but to continue where he is'. 'I should not write these unlikely things,' John Chamberlain noted, 'but that nowadays what seems most improbable mostly comes soonest to pass.'

Thanks to Mary and George's efforts, in June 1616, John, the troubled eldest son, received a knighthood. He also became his younger brother's heir. As favourite, George could not envisage having the time or opportunity to find a wife and produce an heir himself, so decided to 'entail' his titles and estates to John. This meant finding a wife as quickly as possible for him, so that he and his children would be able to secure the family's new aristocratic status in the event of George's death, an objective towards which Mary now turned her formidable energies.

Meanwhile, hectic arrangements were underway for James to make his first – and belated – visit to his Scottish kingdom since first coming to London in May 1603. George was to be his companion, and Bacon would be left with the royal seals of government, giving him overall responsibility for managing royal business during the king's absence. Brimming with gratitude and pride, Bacon credited George with the promotion. In a letter of thanks, he apologized for his failure to express adequate gratitude by word of mouth, but claimed that it was in the nature of 'cares and kindness, that small ones float up to the tongue, and great ones sink down into the heart with silence'. 'You are the truest and perfectest mirror and example of firm and generous friendship that ever was in court,' he added. 'And I shall count every day lost, wherein I shall not either study your well doing in thought, or do your name honour in speech, or perform you service in deed.' He proudly signed the letter 'C. S.', *Custos Sigilli* – Keeper of the Seal.

James and George left London on 15 March 1617. They slowly headed north, covering between ten and twenty miles a day, stopping off en route at various country estates. They crossed the Tweed on 13 May, and James entered his motherland for the first time in over fourteen years. Three days later, they reached Edinburgh.

James's Scottish Privy Council – the appointed body that had been left to run the country with only minimal royal interference during the king's absence – had gone to great lengths to get the city ready for his arrival and ensure it was 'seemly in the eyes of the many English nobles and gentlemen who will be in his train'. It was noted that 'strangers' coming with him 'will be so much the more careful narrowly to remark and espy the carriage and conversation' of the citizens, so it was important that a good impression was made. To that end owners of guest houses were ordered to spruce up their bed linen and furnishings, cattle were removed from the royal parks, stables were filled with fodder, streets were cleaned, middens cleared, 'idle beggars and vagabonds' harried back to wherever they had come from, and supplies of food and drink ordered, including large quantities of French wine. Holyrood House, the king's empty palace at the foot of the city's Royal Mile, was refurbished and a total prohibition on all hunting declared in order to ensure sufficient game for the king's 'recreation, exercise, and pastime in the fields'.

The 'salmon-like instinct' that James claimed pulled him back to his homeland also made him nervous. Memories of the kidnapping and assassination plots that had surrounded his time in Scotland came flooding back. In a candid letter sent to the Scottish Privy Council before his departure from London, he wondered if he might be met by an 'unwelcome coldness', and during a tour of undersea coal works at Culross he had panicked, becoming convinced of 'some plot against his liberty or life' and shouting 'Treason!'

Keeping George close seemed to steady his nerves, so James made sure his favourite was at his side as he processed into Edinburgh for the formal welcome. Apart from the king himself, George was the only member of the royal entourage to be mounted, riding 'upon the king's stirrup', dressed in his chivalric insignia and flattering riding breeches, while the other English lords followed on foot in their long, heavy robes. The king also made him the first Englishman to be appointed to the Scottish Privy Council.

At the opening of the Scottish Parliament, George stood by the king, an epitome of the sort of English nobility James decided tactlessly to eulogize. At the Tollbooth, Edinburgh's imposing medieval parliament building, the king told the assembled members that he intended to 'reduce the barbarity' of Scotland to 'the sweet civility' of England. The Scots, he said, should learn to be as 'docible' to the best aspects of English culture as they were prone 'to limp after' the worst: 'to drink healths, to wear coaches and gay clothes, to take tobacco, and to speak neither Scottish nor English'.

From London came Bacon's regular reports. He was clearly wallowing in his new status. 'This matter of pomp, which is heaven to some men, is hell to me, or purgatory at least,' he complained unconvincingly to George, but was gratified to see the 'king's choice' of regent – in other words, himself – was so 'generally approved' by the public, not because it flattered his vanity, but because it made him a 'fitter instrument' to do James and George service.

Some were not so approving. 'Within ten days after the king goes to Scotland, Bacon instantly begins to believe himself king,' a courtier in James's Scottish entourage reported. He 'lies in the king's lodgings, gives audience in the great Banqueting House, makes all other councillors attend his motions' and 'with the same state the king used' would allow 'audience to ambassadors'.

Bacon's luxurious purgatory was soon disturbed. Rumours reached London that George had died in Scotland. Bacon later reported the panic he had felt: 'I thought I had lived too long,' he lamented. 'That was (to tell your Lordship truly) the state of my mind upon that report. Since, I hear it as an idle mistaking of my Lord Evers for my Lord Villiers. God's name be blessed, that you are alive to do infinite good, and not so much as sick or ill disposed for any thing I now hear.'

It was a false alarm, but it served as a reminder of the ephemerality of George's titles, and prompted Mary to redouble her efforts to find a bride for John and secure the line of inheritance. Despite her son's apparent eligibility, finding a willing mate was not easy, since John was now manifesting the early signs of serious mental illness. However, persistence paid off and Mary eventually found an apparently suitable candidate: Frances, the fourteen-year-old daughter of Sir Edward Coke.

A bitter personal as well as professional rivalry existed between Coke and Francis Bacon. Sir Edward had been the government's most senior lawyer, handling vital legal matters in the early years of James's English reign. He had also been due to lead the trial of Robert Carr, until the rise of George and manoeuvrings by Bacon had led to his plunge from grace. An alliance between his daughter and the Villiers family provided hope of redemption, so he leapt at it.

He began negotiations with Mary, but kept them secret from his wife Elizabeth, knowing she would disapprove of their daughter being married off to a provincial upstart like George. A fiery, impetuous woman, Elizabeth Coke was known at court as Lady Hatton, after her more famous first husband, the late Sir Christopher Hatton. This was a humiliation that Coke had been forced to endure as most of the family wealth was in her name, having been inherited from Sir Christopher.

When Lady Hatton heard of Coke's secret plan for their daughter she was furious. Concerned about her own estates falling into the hands of the Villiers clan, and perhaps mindful of John's unstable temperament, she set about trying to block the match. 'Uncivil words' were exchanged with George's mother Mary, some involving the queen, with the upshot that Elizabeth found herself excluded from court.

However, the redoubtable Elizabeth was not going to let the matter rest there. She took Frances from the family home, and hid her away, hampering her husband's efforts to recover his daughter by moving her between a series of safe houses.

All this left Bacon uncomfortably compromised. On the one hand, he had to maintain his loyalty to George. On the other, he wanted to frustrate Coke's efforts to recover his position at court. With George absent in Scotland, Bacon's hatred of Coke prevailed, to the extent that he had even offered to use his office as Lord Keeper to help Lady Hatton in her efforts to obstruct the marriage.

Sir Francis wrote to George, advising him against the match on the grounds that George's brother would be marrying into 'a troubled house of man and wife' – Coke and Lady Hatton were known to be at loggerheads – and that George would lose 'all such your friends as are adverse to Sir Edward Coke' (excepting, of course, Bacon, 'who out of a pure love and thankfulness shall ever be firm to you').

George received this letter as he and the king were in the midst of a tour of Scotland's towns, castles and universities. At first he ignored Bacon's advice, but then news began to arrive from London of a situation running rapidly and farcically out of control. Mary, it transpired, had tried to get Bacon to issue a warrant to allow Coke to repossess his daughter, but Bacon had refused. Coke then discovered where his wife was hiding their daughter and broke down 'divers doors' to reach her. He snatched Frances back and set off by coach to his house in London. Lady Hatton had immediately given chase, managing to remain 'at his heels, and if her coach had not tired in the pursuit after him, there was like to be strange tragedies'. Thwarted in her efforts, she went to Bacon's house while the Lord Keeper was resting and, told to wait outside his bedchamber, she instead 'bounced against' his bedroom door 'and waked him and affrighted him'. Apologizing for the interruption, she explained the urgency of the matter, and Bacon, recovering his composure, issued a warrant ordering Coke to surrender his daughter to the Privy Council.

Coke, however, refused, handing his daughter to Mary, who took Frances and some horsemen from Coke's house and set off to another secret location, with Lady Hatton once more in pursuit accompanied by what were described as sixty 'tall fellows' armed with pistols. Mary managed to escape her pursuer, preventing what would have been a bloody confrontation with Clem Coke, Sir Edward's 'fighting son'.

By now this had become a Privy Council matter, with Sir Edward being summoned to answer charges of 'riot and force' before his enemy Bacon. Mary was also ordered to appear, apparently as a witness.

As he sat as the council's chairman, resplendent in his robes and chains of office, with Coke seemingly defenceless before him, little did Bacon realize that Coke's associates had been hard at work in Scotland, agitating for the match and reporting to George the poor treatment of Mary and John. A few days later, a letter arrived from the king in Scotland commanding Lady Hatton to return Frances to her father 'and not again entice her away'.

Bacon responded by writing to George reminding him of the earlier letter 'wherein I gave you my opinion touching your brother's match'. He followed it up with a letter addressed directly to James, reiterating his concerns, and claiming that as a 'true friend' to George he would 'rather go against his mind than against his good'.

The road from Scotland fell quiet. For days, no messages arrived for the Lord Keeper. Bacon began to fret. He wrote again to George, noting: 'Your Lordship writeth seldomer than you were wont.' Still nothing.

Then, almost a month later, a letter arrived. It was from George, explaining that he had felt 'excused' from responding more promptly because Bacon had 'found another way of address' – a tart reference to him writing about the matter of John's marriage directly to the king. George suggested that such a move was a sign of Bacon having become 'weary of employing' him. And he mentioned almost in passing that with respect to 'this business of my brother's that you overtrouble yourself with', he had heard from friends in London 'that you have carried yourself with much scorn and neglect both toward myself and my friends; which if it prove true I blame not you but myself, who was ever, Your Lordship's assured friend, G. Buckingham.'

This devastatingly calm, almost casual dismissal was a powerful demonstration to Bacon that his once naive protégé had become a political creature. 'There is rarely any rising but by a commixture of good and evil arts,' Bacon once noted, and here was evidence that George had the strength of purpose and character to use both.

Bacon moved quickly to redeem himself. Within days, a letter was winding its way north in which he promised to show his 'acquiescence to the match' of John and Frances. Once more, his pleas were met with silence, so Bacon wrote to the king, begging him to intercede with George, confessing that he had been 'a little parent-like', but only for the favourite's benefit, as he would 'spend' his life 'and that which is to me more, the cares of my life' for George.

Meanwhile, Mary and John were treating Bacon 'with some bitterness and neglect', and he wrote again to George, asking that he not be made 'vassal to their passions'. George maintained his silence, leaving it to the king to answer by castigating Bacon's presumption in describing his actions as 'parent-like'.

By this point, James and George were on their way back to London, and Sir Edward Coke, taking advantage of his change of fortunes, was rushing north to meet them. They met at Coventry, and Coke immediately set about courting George, becoming, it was tartly observed, 'as close' to the favourite 'as his shirt'. An associate of Bacon's described George's mood as 'very fervent', having been 'misled by misinformation'. Combining reassurances with threats, George had told the associate that he 'would not secretly bite' those who had 'any interest or tasted of the opposition to his brother's marriage'; instead, he would 'openly oppose them to their faces, and they should discern what favour he had by the power he would use'.

Two days later, George wrote directly to Bacon complaining of the number of letters he had received from him. As for Bacon's 'unkind dealing with me in this matter of my brother's, time will try all'. With that chilling expectation, the by now distraught Bacon was left to stew for a month as the royal entourage slowly made its way south.

The court eventually trundled into London in mid-September, and George returned to Cecil House, his new residence on the Strand, to recover from the journey. Repeated messages arrived from his servants to notify him that Bacon was apparently waiting in the corridor outside his bedchamber, having been there since his homecoming. George decided to ignore him, ordering that he be removed to a room 'where trencher-scrapers and lackeys attended'. There he was made to linger for two days, sitting on an old wooden chest. Anthony Weldon, one of the courtiers who had returned with George from Scotland, noted what a dejected figure the Lord Keeper made, the 'Purse and Seal' resting on his lap now 'of so little value, or esteem'. Without them, Bacon 'merited nothing but scorn, being worst among the basest'.

Eventually, George admitted the poor Lord Keeper. 'At first entrance' Bacon 'fell down flat on his face' and kissed George's feet, 'vowing never to rise till he had his pardon'. George reached down and raised the grovelling minister from the floor.

A few days later, George wrote to Bacon, pointing out that his fervent 'offer of submission' had 'battered so the unkindness that I had conceived in my heart for your behaviour towards me in my absence' that he would let bygones be bygones. And, in a gesture of reconciliation, 'out of the old sparks of my affection towards you' he had decided to 'sound his Majesty's intention how he means to behave himself towards you'. The king, George admitted, was still in a mood of 'deep-conceived indignation' about Sir Francis's 'confused and childish' behaviour, and indeed was nurturing a 'rigorous resolution' to 'put some public exemplary mark upon you'. So George had fallen upon his knees on his old friend's behalf, 'to beg of his Majesty that he would put no public act of disgrace upon you'. As a result, James had agreed reluctantly – at least according to George's account, aimed at demonstrating the lengths to which he had gone to help his mentor – to give a 'kingly' but general reprimand to all those privy councillors involved in the affair of Frances Coke's daughter, without naming anyone in particular.

Weldon noted with admiration the effect of George's handling of Bacon, observing how his former mentor became 'so very a slave' that he 'durst not deny the command of the meanest' of George's kindred, 'nor oppose any thing'.

Frances was eventually won over to marrying John, if only for the sake of her father. In what was hardly a declaration of love, but a mature and pragmatic acceptance of her position, she also accepted that John was 'not to be misliked'. The wedding took place at Hampton Court on 29 September 1617, Michaelmas Day, and James gave the bride away.

Sir Edward Coke was given back his place in the Privy Council, and George staged a public reconciliation between his mother and Frances's at Cecil House. Lady Hatton responded by hosting the Villiers family at Hatton House, her home in Holborn. It was a 'very magnifical' occasion, according to John Chamberlain. 'The King graced her every way, and made four of her creatures knights.' But, he noted, 'the principal graces and favours lighted on the Lady Compton', George's mother, along with the rest of the family – the 'country kindred' so derided when George had first come to court. The king 'praised and kissed' them, 'and blessed all those that wished them well'. This was now his family, and he would do everything in his power to protect them.

Made or Marred

By the late 1610s, the mental condition of George's eldest brother John had become so alarming their mother had been forced to seek medical help. She took him to see the astrologer-physician Richard Napier, but efforts to find a cure were proving futile. This presented George with an urgent need to find a more suitable heir for his growing portfolio of titles and estates. Courtly expectation was that marriage would be 'very dangerous' for the favourite, as the competition for his affection was likely to arouse the king's jealousy. Nevertheless, with the deterioration of his elder brother's condition, it became clear that, to secure his legacy, George was in need of a wife to provide him with a son.

Many of the court's most eligible and beautiful debutantes were eager candidates, but he chose Katherine, daughter of Francis Manners, the sixth Earl of Rutland. Despite her pedigree, she seemed an unlikely choice for such a glamorous and desirable suitor. As even portraits commissioned by George show, Katherine's lively, intelligent face did not conform with conventional notions of female beauty. There were also financial and religious obstacles. The dowry demanded by George's mother was considered too high. Katherine was also known to come from a Catholic family, which was bound to arouse controversy among Protestant activists at court and in Parliament.

The greatest obstacle, however, was her father. As one of the great magnates of the English midlands, the thirty-eight-year-old earl had received the Order of the Garter from the king in 1616 at the same time as the twenty-three-year-old George, and he had evidently resented being upstaged by a man he would not in any other circumstances have dignified with his dog, let alone his daughter. So he had obstructed George's efforts to woo Kate, preventing them from meeting, and attempting to pre-empt George's efforts by casting around for an alternative partner.

Nevertheless, George had persisted. The Manners family were from the county of his birth. He had spent his childhood in the shadow of their ancestral home, the imposing Belvoir Castle. During their long exile in provincial obscurity, the Villiers family had been forced to pay homage to the earl. Now was a chance to turn the tables.

As with her elder son John, it was George's mother Mary who, with characteristic decisiveness, broke the deadlock. She paid a visit to Kate at the earl's London residence, and invited her to supper at her newly acquired mansion in Chelsea. Kate accepted, but the apparently innocent offer of hospitality took on a different complexion when they were joined by George. Kate spent the night at Mary's house, where, as one gossip scurrilously put it, she was either 'made or marred'. When Mary returned Kate the following day to her father, he refused to take her in, forcing her to stay with an uncle. Soon after, George received a furious letter from the earl in which he complained that it had never occurred to him that he should 'advise my daughter to avoid the occasion of ill' – that is, the sort of predatory abduction that Mary and George had apparently perpetrated. The crime had been compounded by his daughter's own collusion in surrendering the family honour, in respect of which, the earl wrote pessimistically, 'I hope I shall arm myself with patience, and not with rage'. George replied in a tone of surprised indignation, explaining to him that he took 'unkindly' to the 'harsh usage of me and your own daughter', claiming that 'she had never received any blemish in her honour but that which came by your own tongue'. George therefore decided he would 'leave off the pursuit' of Kate, 'putting it in your free choice to bestow her elsewhere to your best comfort'.

The earl's bluff was called, and he duly surrendered. They were married in a private ceremony in London, the earl in attendance, having agreed to hand over a dowry of £10,000 in cash and estates worth some £4,000 to £5,000 a year.

Kate proved to be an astute choice of partner. If anything, she succeeded in bringing George closer to the king, who treated her as a daughter rather than a rival. The two developed an affectionate and playful relationship, corresponding frequently and freely, fussing over each other's and George's health.

The reason for the king's enthusiasm is suggested in a portrait of the couple by the Dutch master Van Dyck, probably commissioned by James to celebrate the marriage. Known as 'Venus and Adonis', the figures are recognizably George and Kate. But the picture subverts conventional portrayals of its classical subject, making the man the focus of attention and object of desire. He is a magnificent specimen of male potency, with a strong chest and muscular thighs emphasized by a lithe greyhound curled around his leg, eager to lure him to the chase. She, in contrast, is hunched and flat-chested, hooked-nosed and weak-chinned. While he stares adoringly at her, she gazes out of the picture with a shrewd, almost complacent expression, challenging the viewer to make his or her own judgement on the nature of human beauty and desire. It advertised the reason for James's infatuation for George, and why

Kate could be a loyal companion, but never the exclusive object of his desire.

George used the windfall of Kate's dowry to buy Burley-on-the-Hill, a property neighbouring the earl's Rutland estates. Burley had romantic associations for George and James, as they had stayed there after the king had first caught sight of the handsome cupbearer at Apethorpe in 1614. James was invited to the housewarming, a lavish event at which, bareheaded (to demonstrate the informality of the occasion), the king toasted the health of his host and openly, perhaps tactlessly, speculated on who loved George the most, his wife, his family or his sovereign. He even wrote some verses, as the king was wont to do for occasions that touched his heart, in which he noted how nature had blessed the occasion with a smile, giving hope of 'a smiling boy within a while'.

Following the nuptials, James wrote a letter to his 'only sweet and dear child, blessing this morning and also his daughter', trusting that 'the lord of heaven send you a sweet and bright wakening, all kind of comfort in your sanctified bed, and bless the fruits thereof that I may have sweet bedchamber boys to play me with, and this is my daily prayer, sweet heart'.

For James, the title of 'dear dad' now began to shift from one of affection to something more meaningful and, in his mind, literal. When, in 1622, Kate produced their first child, named Mary after George's mother, James nicknamed her Mal, and referred to her as his grandchild. More children would follow and, as a French diplomat noted, while James 'never much cared for women', he was happy to have his court 'swarming' with George's offspring, 'so that little ones would dance up and down the privy lodgings like fairies'.

And so the rise of the Villiers family continued. Following Bacon's advice, George cultivated an ever-widening but carefully chosen circle of clients and dependents, magnanimous with those who were loyal and helpful, and, as he had been with Bacon, harsh on those who obstructed him. As a physician who got on the wrong side of George later remarked, 'his temper was exceeding good, & he could manage his affections . . . with much serenity & moderation' but once crossed 'could not think of anything but a revenge'.

Wickedest Things

In the late 1610s, some copies of a Latin work entitled *Corona Regia* or 'Royal Crown' began furtively circulating through London. It looked like an official publication. According to its frontispiece it was the work of Isaac Casaubon, a respected scholar and historian who had died in 1614, and it carried the London imprint of the royal printer John Bill. It could easily have been mistaken for one of the many 'panegyrics' published at the time, lavishing praise on the king. But following its apparently conventional opening, it became clear this was no ordinary work of royal flattery.

For example, a few pages in, it praised James for managing to conceal his 'natural tendencies under a veil of righteousness and integrity'. 'If you cannot be good, you should at least be thought so by your subjects,' wrote the author, who was very obviously not the loyal and deferential Casaubon. 'To pretend and invite is kingly', even though the mind 'takes pleasure in the wickedest things'. As it proceeded, it became increasingly explicit about these wickedest things. In a passage full of phallic imagery, it compared James to the whale, which 'raises itself like a pillar and violently discharges a deluge'. It noted how the king had enjoyed 'clandestine nights so full of pleasure' with partners of both sexes. 'The words of Christ were "suffer little children to come unto me". You summon boys – the very fair ones in particular – and appreciate the benefactions and miracles of nature in them.' It noted the king's 'unequalled generosity', conferring gifts not upon 'people of any age, but at the attractive prime of life', not for service to the kingdom, 'but upon those who serve you well'. As evidence, it produced an impressively well-informed list of James's favourites since coming to the English throne: John Ramsay, Philip Herbert (who became George's promoter) and Robert Carr, 'followed by the incomparably youthful beauty' of George Villiers, 'introduced by the queen herself into your chamber'. The writer concluded by seeing this as evidence of the British being 'acorn eaters', a euphemism for those who engage in fellatio.

The work was first brought to the government's attention by an English agent in Brussels, who had found a copy and discovered its 'highly offensive' nature. It was already in wide circulation on the Continent, according to the agent, who had seen two Jesuits reading it on a boat, 'fulsomely praising its style, language and subject matter'. This triggered a command direct from the king for an investigation into who had written and published it. 'His Majesty expects justice in this matter,' the king's secretary wrote to the Brussels agent, and if the authorities there did not provide it, 'he will retaliate to save his honour from being besmirched in this heinous manner.' But in the thriving print markets of London and Brussels, efforts to suppress it proved futile.

Simonds D'Ewes recorded his shock at seeing the work, describing it as 'terrible and wholly against the king himself, accusing him of atheism, sodomy etc. . . .' But, as for many, the shock did not necessarily indicate disbelief. A devout Protestant law student freshly down from Cambridge, D'Ewes complained how the 'wicked city' of London was rife with corruption at all levels and of all sorts. He wrote to a friend about the 'true story' of a French usher who had 'buggered a knight's son' and, despite being arrested and arraigned on what was a capital charge, been freed – at the king's instigation, ''twas thought'.

The gossipy John Chamberlain had noted a similar trend. He observed how some were beginning to 'tax' the king – that is, take him to task – for his liberal distribution of largesse among favourite courtiers, particularly George and his family. Scurrilous poems were doing the rounds, one of which Chamberlain quoted:

> Above in the skies shall Gemini rise,
> And Twins the court shall pester,
> George shall call up his brother Jack,
> And Jack his brother Kester.

Other, lewder poems began to turn up in the streets. One began as an apparently jolly celebration of the king, but quickly degenerated into a bawdy assault on George and his mother, 'old Bedlam Buckingame':

> Heaven bless King James our joy,
> And Charles his baby
> Great George our brave viceroy

> And his fair Lady.
> Old Bedlam Buckingame,
> With her Lord Keeper.
> She loves the fucking game
> He's her cunt creeper.

The same poem goes on to list in exhaustive detail the members of the Villiers family who had apparently benefited from George and his mother's distribution of carnal as well as political favours, including George's siblings, his stepfather, his sister-in-law, his half-sister by his father's first marriage, several cousins, a groom of the bedchamber who eloped with a woman betrothed to his brother Kit, and so on, ending with a satirical swipe at the rampant favouritism that had produced their promotion:

> These be they, go so gay
> In [the] court & city
> Would you have an office pray
> You must be this witty.

'You are a new-risen star, and the eyes of all men are upon you,' Bacon had told George. 'Let not your own negligence let you fall like a meteor.' But as the books and poems showed, he was ignoring the advice, and the results were coming to notice. The fall of Carr had revealed deep corruption at the heart of court, and a widespread opinion was forming that it was being perpetuated by and through George.

For example, he had arranged for a distant relation, a grasping 'projector' called Sir Giles Mompesson, to receive a royal patent for the licensing of inns. This gave Sir Giles an exclusive right to force any alehouse owner or innkeeper who took guests to buy a licence for £5 or £10. George also backed the appointment of one Sir Robert Naunton to become Secretary of State on condition that Naunton made his brother Kit his heir. He arranged for Kit, who unlike their older brother John had yet to secure a lucrative marriage partner, to be given the monopoly over the trade in gold and silver thread, used extensively (and expensively) in the clothing so crucial to courtly ostentation.

The bounty extended to his feckless half-brother Edward Villiers, who was given a knighthood and quickly set about using his enhanced status to promote a series of dubious deals and enterprises. Sir Edward invested in Kit's gold and silver thread monopoly and in a patent for licensing Irish alehouses, which he sold on to a friend. When the patent caused unrest and had to be revoked, he negotiated an annuity of £250 in compensation.

Bacon was essential to organizing such deals, and, revelling in the recovery of his influence, forgot his own warnings. He did everything he could to help George, and by the same token took all that was available – the perks of office, the debts of gratitude, the credit for others' achievements – to support the lavish lifestyle he thought he deserved and certainly craved.

To celebrate his sixtieth birthday, Bacon hosted a banquet in January 1621 at York House, his great medieval mansion on the Strand. His present from the king was the promise of becoming Viscount of St Albans. Ben Jonson, the court's most popular playwright, wrote a poem to celebrate:

> Hail, happy genius of this ancient pile!
> How comes it all things so about thee smile?
> The fire, the wine, the men! And in the midst,
> Thou stand'st as if some mystery thou didst!

Poor George Villiers

That winter, while Bacon and his guests were warmed by the fire, the wine and the men, outside a 'great frost' was gripping London and the country. Winds and high tides drove the snow and ice into 'heaps' which lay 'like rocks and mountains' around the capital, with 'a strange and hideous aspect'. The Thames froze over for the second time in a year, leaving the watermen who kept the capital supplied and its population moving 'quite undone'. Food prices soared as shortages spread. Developments on the Continent added to the economic pain. Religious and political tensions had triggered the first skirmishes in what would develop into Europe's disastrous Thirty Years' War, creating an economic crisis that was already eroding Britain's vital trade in cloth, its main export.

A clamour began to grow in the raw winter air for the king to do something, at the very least reduce tariffs and enforce trade agreements. But his options were limited – he had no money.

Since James's English succession in 1603, the royal exchequer had been in chaos. Being a foreign monarch whose claim to the throne was genealogically distant, and whose Scottish origins were treated with ill-disguised disdain, James had a lot to prove in England, and he saw courtly extravagance as the best way of proving it. He had spent lavishly and relentlessly to bolster his status, on masques, hunts, luxurious clothes, glittering jewels, grand ceremonials and sumptuous progresses.

With the help of officials such as Bacon, he had managed to exploit a number of often obsolete or obscure royal prerogatives to finance this profligacy. He had raised rents on Crown lands, and put offices, titles and privileges up for sale, reinventing the baronetcy to give provincial gentry a taste of aristocratic status for £1,000 a go, and offering monopolies over basic commodities and services to the highest bidder. He had extended tariffs on goods, such as tobacco newly imported from the Americas, and exploited wardships, a medieval 'incident' going back to feudal times which entitled him to a share of an estate left to an underage heir. But these often inventive initiatives, combined with ever-rising debts and dubious accounting practices, had failed to fill the deficit, and a chronic state of insolvency had set in.

The only way of relieving the problem was taxation, but under constitutional conventions going back to Magna Carta, only a 'common counsel of our kingdom', which had come to mean Parliament's House of Commons, could levy taxes. This required MPs to pass a so-called 'supply' bill, which would trigger an inefficient process whereby tax collectors scour the country, levying a 'subsidy' or special tax on trade and extracting one or more 'fifteenths' (or 6.66 per cent) of the wealth of property owners – a highly unpopular measure which MPs were not unnaturally reluctant to inflict on their electors.

A combination of factors had made the English House of Commons one of only a few representative assemblies to have survived in Europe. The spread of absolutist regimes across the Continent, notably in Spain and France, had reduced many of its

Continental equivalents to little more than instruments of royal power.

The Commons was not democratic in the modern sense. The king chose when it met, and could dismiss it at will, and the processes for selecting candidates and conducting elections were vulnerable to corruption and routinely flouted. A rule going back to the fifteenth century, however, meant that anyone with property worth more than 40 shillings was eligible to vote, and, thanks to inflation, by the early seventeenth century that had come to include as much as a quarter of the adult male population. This had made the Commons, as one royal official complained, so 'big and audacious' that the king's very authority would be under threat 'if way be given into it'.

If any institution comprising around four hundred members can be said to have a collective character, that of the Commons was a fragile and sometimes prickly sense of pride. This had been stimulated by James's dismissive attitude towards it. Having apparently succeeded in sidelining its Scottish counterpart, he had initially tried to treat it in a similar manner, regarding it as 'nothing else but the King's great council', with no powers over his government's policy. Since 1614, he had tried to rule without it altogether, in the hope that an efficiency and austerity drive would make him financially self-sufficient. But the spending had continued, and, to avoid bankruptcy, he had been forced to issue writs for fresh elections in November of 1620, the first in seven years.

Bacon was James's representative in negotiating the new parliamentary programme, and there were early signs of a cooperative mood among MPs. The Lord Chancellor was able to secure a guarantee of a supply bill of two subsidies, which promised to yield between £150,000 and £200,000. There was, however, a price: the king had to accept the setting up of a parliamentary committee to enquire into public grievances. As James ruefully observed, he was never so well informed 'of all the grievances of his people as in time of Parliament'. But, managed properly, Bacon calculated that such an investigation would be tolerable.

Sir Francis's lavish banquet at York House had barely had a chance to be digested before the new Parliament gathered at Westminster on 30 January 1621. The MPs were sworn in, and over the following days a series of votes were held to decide on the membership of various parliamentary committees. To Bacon's horror, the man selected to head the enquiry into grievances was his irrepressible rival Sir Edward Coke, now an MP for Liskeard in Cornwall. Sensing danger, Bacon advised George to revoke some of the monopolies given to him by the king and being enjoyed by his 'special friends'. This would 'put off the envy of these things (which I think in themselves bear no great fruit), and rather take the thanks for ceasing them, than the note for maintaining them'. This idea was discussed by the Privy Council, but it was decided that no action should be taken, as it might be seen as a 'humouring of the Parliament'.

Coke's committee responded by focusing its efforts on George's relatives, in particular Sir Giles Mompesson and his dubious monopoly over the licensing of inns. Mompesson's grasping efforts to force every innkeeper in the land to buy a licence to operate, a power previously and more discriminately exercised by local magistrates, had provoked outrage. It was eventually decided to refer the matter for debate by the entire House of Commons, which resolved to put Mompesson into the custody of the sergeant-at-arms while requesting the House of Lords to punish him for his abuses.

Complaining bitterly of being 'traduced', Mompesson wrote to George, pleading for help, but was held in limbo for more than a week as the wrangling over how to deal with him continued. Eventually, it was decided he should be escorted back to his home by guards in order to gather together materials he would need for his defence. Feigning an attack of illness, he asked to be allowed a private moment in his wife's bedroom, from which he escaped, showing a 'fair pair of heels' as he fled to the Continent. When news reached the Commons of Mompesson's flight, there was uproar. His house was searched and his papers seized, which revealed the full extent of the extortion. George quickly moved to distance himself from Mompesson, complaining he had been 'wronged and abused by this offender' who had so recently written to him 'protesting his innocency'.

For the sake of keeping his hopes of a tax bill alive, James, ultimately responsible for granting Mompesson's patent – indeed, who had in a fit of enthusiasm, personally put the seal upon it himself – was forced to revoke it and disassociate himself from the whole business, describing it as 'hateful and offensive' that his people 'should be so injured, molested, vexed or oppressed'.

Matters reached a head in March 1621, as Coke's committee was preparing to report on its conclusions. George's half-brother Sir Edward decided, with exquisite ill-timing, to demand the enforcement of the gold and silver thread monopoly, which he had found 'now lay a-bleeding'. This resulted in several thread-makers, lowly craftsmen who worked in the City, being rounded up and thrown into prison. Powerful merchants, including the goldsmiths who sold the thread-makers' wares, began to protest, forcing one of the MPs who acted as George's proxy in the Commons' chamber to intervene by declaring that the favourite had given Sir Edward 'no encouragement or comfort' in the matter.

George's initial reaction was to try to persuade James to dismiss Parliament, which the king was entitled to do. But James, still desperate for the tax revenues, resisted. Instead, a charm offensive was staged, which culminated in a strange piece of political theatre conducted in the House of Lords. It began with James arriving in the chamber to speak in George's defence, explaining that the favourite had been more 'troubled' by petitioners and suitors 'than ever any that served me'. It had been 'purgatory for him', the king said. He recognized that 'rascals' had been complaining about George 'in inns and alehouses', but their lordships should judge him not as a favourite but as a man. 'I desire you not to look of him as adorned with these honours as Marquess of Buckingham, Admiral of England, Master of my Horse, Gentleman of my Bed Chamber, a Privy Counsellor and Knight of the Garter, but as he was when he came to me as poor George Villiers, and if he prove not himself a white crow he shall be called a black crow.'

Whereupon George, who by virtue of the titles given to him by James sat in the Lords, went up to the king, and answered upon his knees: 'Sir, if I cannot clear myself of any aspersion or imputation cast upon me, I am contented to abide your Majesty's censure and be called the Black Crow.'

The performance might be thought to have been rehearsed. But, according to at least one contemporary, George was genuinely worried about his position. The 'jealousies hatched in hell' and unleashed by the parliamentary investigations had robbed him of 'all peace of mind'. The king had made it plain that, stripped of all the titles, he was just 'poor George Villiers', and with the 'arrow of vengeance' having 'grazed near to himself' which is shot at his brother' Sir Edward Villiers, he was extremely vulnerable.

Foreign observers beheld these developments with excited anticipation. The Florentine agent was confident that George would now face a full parliamentary investigation. The French ambassador thought he was doomed to go the same way as Robert Carr, and that the prospects of this had reduced the favourite and his followers to '*une grande melancholie*'. The fact that James had not sent any 'meat from his table' to George's for the Easter celebrations that year was taken to be 'the strangest news of all', as it was a sure sign of his fall from favour.

'Swim with the tide,' a friend advised George, 'and you cannot be drowned.' So he sent a conciliatory message to both Houses, declaring that he would not defend his brothers, but 'leave them to the censure of the parliament'. As for his own conduct, he humbly accepted that he needed to understand better the 'wisdom of Parliaments' and he would 'submit himself, as a Scholar, to it'.

Charges of corruption and bribery duly followed – but they were not aimed at George; they were brought against Bacon. Their origin is unclear, but from George's point of view, they could not have been more timely. Suddenly, parliamentary scrutiny switched away from the favourite to the Lord Chancellor – MPs voting to break off 'all other business' as they set about investigating him.

Bacon wrote to George, pleading for protection. 'Your Lordship spake of purgatory. I am now in it,' he complained. 'I know I have clean hands and a clean heart; and I hope a clean house for friends or servants. But Job himself, or whosoever was the justest judge, by such hunting for matters against him as hath been used against me, may for a time seem foul, specially in a time when greatness is the mark and accusation is the game.'

Having just a few months earlier been celebrated by Ben Jonson as a 'happy genius', Bacon's plunge from power was astonishingly fast. Within days of the charges being brought, he faced impeachment by his own peers in the House of Lords, an ancient procedure that had not been used since 1449. A few days later, James appeared before the House to declare that 'no private person whatsoever' was more precious to him than the public good, effectively signalling that he was prepared to surrender the Lord Chancellor if it settled the corruption matter. By the end of March 1621 Bacon's loss of office seemed inevitable; on 10 April he wrote his will.

Some were convinced that Bacon would be saved by George. They were both 'enslaved by wickedness and held captive by the devil', their enemies claimed, having engaged in the 'most abominable and darling sin' of sodomy. The writers of doggerel were once again busy, and a sheet of paper was found nailed to the door of Bacon's home:

> Within this sty a hog doth lie
> That must be hanged for sodomy.
> A pig, a hog, a boar, a bacon
> Whom God hath left, and the devil taken.

But according to a member of Bacon's staff, George was to be Bacon's destroyer rather than saviour. During an audience with James, the king had made it clear to the Lord Chancellor that he should 'submit himself to his House of peers' so that George would escape a similar fate. The satirists seemed to see it that way, one of them wondering how 'Bacon should neglected be when it is most in season', speculating that 'perhaps the game of Buck hath vilified the boar?'

The hunting image was a telling one, and would be used repeatedly in popular ballads as well as courtly gossip throughout George's career. It captured his status as an object of desire, pursued just as enthusiastically by those who wanted to glory in his magnificence as by those who wanted to bathe in his blood. It also captured the perilousness of his position, that this was a race to the death, his only chance of survival being to keep ahead of the pack.

As the pressure on Bacon increased, he fell ill. George visited his sickbed on several occasions, and presented mitigation on his behalf when he failed to attend the parliamentary hearings against him. And when it finally came to a vote on Bacon's guilt, George was the only member of the Lords to dissent, even though there was no possibility that the gesture would save him. Soon after, the man who had once ruled England like a king was exiled to

Gorhambury, his country retreat in Hertfordshire. Among Bacon's rivals, a ferocious competition now began to take possession of York House, the disgraced Lord Chancellor's coveted London residence on the banks of the Thames. Thanks to his increasing ability to exploit the political arts he had learned from his mentor, George comfortably won the contest, the court's 'new risen star' now seemingly secure as a fixture in the firmament.

ACT II

Two Venturous Knights

The Favourite and the Fountain

In 1611, a factory in Florence was frantically producing a series of small, bronze sculptures based on the works of the Flemish master sculptor, Giambologna, famous for his marble statue known as *The Rape of a Sabine*, a centrepiece in Florence's main piazza. They were being made for Prince Henry, King James's heir, on the orders of Cosimo II, the Grand Duke of Tuscany, whose daughter he hoped might be a match for the British prince.

The bronzes were presented to Henry in May 1612: a kneeling woman, a horse and bull, a bathing Venus, Hercules with his club, a birdwatcher, two shepherds – one blowing on bagpipes, the other drinking from a bottle – and a miniature horse. They were laid out in a private gallery set aside for their display in St James's Palace, accessed via a secret garden and a spiral staircase. In terms of the history of art, these objects were of great significance. As far as is known, they were the first Renaissance bronzes ever to reach England, where sculpture was still the preserve of tombmakers.

Perhaps in a demonstration of aesthetic appreciation, or childish possessiveness, when Henry first saw his collection laid out in his gallery, he picked one of the sculptures up and kissed it. He fondled the others, admiring the details and craftsmanship. An older courtier who was with him at the time admired the miniature horse and said that Henry's younger brother Charles might like it. 'No, no, I want everything for myself,' Henry replied.

Later, Henry protectively took the sculptures to a cabinet in one of his rooms, and arranged them carefully. He managed to get hold of three more, until his collection amounted to eighteen in total, including the miniature horse.

Henry's eleven-year-old brother Charles heard about his older brother's petulant refusal to share the horse, and it was to have a poignant role in their relationship.

Charles could not have been more different from Henry. Henry was athletic and tall; Charles was short, fragile and suffered from weak ankles. Henry had an attractive manner and commanding presence; Charles was aloof, reserved and stammered badly. Yet Charles adored Henry. When they were separated, as they usually were, he would send letters pathetically imploring his brother to visit, and would try to impress him with reports of his latest achievements in the schoolroom or the riding stables.

According to Francis Bacon, Henry was 'indulgent' with Charles. But he could be cruel, too. A possibly apocryphal story tells of the two of them waiting in the presence chamber with the Archbishop of Canterbury for an audience with their father. Henry snatched the primate's mitre off his head and put it on Charles's, saying that when he became king, he would make him archbishop, because he was such a bookworm and his vestments would hide his crippled legs.

Then Prince Henry had fallen ill. It was during celebrations for the wedding of Henry and Charles's adored sister, Elizabeth, to Frederick, ruler of a patchwork of provinces in central Germany known as the Palatinate. Despite the symptoms, Henry continued with his duties until he finally succumbed to a 'great pain in his head', forcing him into his sickbed. The doctors gave him a 'lenitive glister' and 'cordial julep' with ingredients that included 'bezoar' (a stone found in the digestive systems of various animals) and 'unicorn horn' (usually the powdered tusk of the narwhal). After expelling a 'great store of putrefied choler', he rallied, and played a game of cards with Charles. But soon after he relapsed, and within days, weakened by continual 'ravings' and 'convulsions', he was close to death. Frantic efforts were made to treat him, which included pigeons and cockerels being cut in half and placed on his head.

Fearing the worst, the royal family came to Henry's sickbed. As the prince lay exhausted, his head shaved, his shoulders covered in scarifications used to draw blood, his face 'pale and parched', his eyes 'hollow and of a wan colour', little Charles pressed the miniature bronze horse, which he had fetched from St James's Palace, into his brother's hand.

Within a week, Henry was dead, throwing the nation into convulsions of grief.

When Charles led the funeral cortege a month later, the dejected, delicate figure seemed barely to be noticed. 'Our Rising Sun is set', the Earl of Dorset declared, 'ere scarcely did he shine', overwhelming Charles's pallid glow as he passed along the streets of London. The man who interrupted the solemnity of the funeral procession by running naked through the crowd crying out that he was Henry's ghost seemed to get more notice than the new heir to the throne. When Charles was installed as Prince of Wales in 1616, the Bishop of Ely, leading the prayers, called him Henry by mistake.

Fatherly feelings did not come naturally to James. He doubted his own paternity – there was always a suspicion he was the son of David Rizzio, his mother's Italian lover, rather than of her husband and Rizzio's murderer, Henry Stuart. The wags of court eagerly played on these anxieties by whispering the joke that the self-styled British Solomon was in fact the son of David. While no one ever suggested that any of the king's children were illegitimate – James showed no interest in having mistresses – he seemed to have difficulty reconciling his relationship with them. He saw Henry more as a rival than a son – a feeling that had once surfaced during a hunting party, when the king rowed violently with the prince, but found himself humiliatingly abandoned when Henry stormed off, and most of the royal entourage followed.

James might have had a more fatherly attitude to Charles. The younger son was less assertive, less competitive than the older, and had more in common with the king. He shared James's interest in books and theological issues, and the self-consciousness and insecurity that came from suffering similar physical disabilities. But where James had harboured jealousies of Henry, he felt only disappointment in Charles. When the two made a royal visit to Cambridge University in 1615, an overeager don hailed Charles 'Jacobale' and 'Jacobissime Carole' – little James, so very James-like, prompting the king to tell him to curb the comparisons.

Then came St George's Day of 1615, the day George Villiers was introduced to the royal bedchamber. The appearance of this fascinating, glamorous figure of his older brother's age and build seemed like a miraculous resurrection of princely charisma in a royal household left drab and traumatized by Henry's death. And Charles had been given a central role in the miracle of transubstantiation, providing the very blade the king used to turn a provincial commoner into a chivalrous cavalier. For a while, Charles must have wondered whether James had given him back the brother he so badly missed.

But George, it turned out, was a rival, not a substitute sibling. The favourite seemed blithely unaware of Charles's efforts to get his attention, and the prince could only watch on helplessly as James lavished upon the favourite an intensity of feeling that the son never received. It was as if he had been tricked by his mother into providing the instrument of his own exclusion.

Once again, Charles found himself eclipsed. An 'uncessant swarm of suitors importunely' hung upon George, James once pointed out, 'without discretion or distinction of times'. But few paid much attention to Charles. In 1616, his efforts to get a learned and well-qualified divine called Dr George Carleton appointed Bishop of Carlisle were humiliatingly spurned, James instead choosing to give the job to one Robert Snowden, 'an obscure fellow', who had 'come in at the window' (in other words from nowhere) and shut Carleton out.

Two incidents show Charles's miserable position. In March 1616, he admired a ring that George was wearing, and asked to borrow it. The following day, George asked for it back, but Charles claimed to have 'forgot it and lost it'. George mentioned the matter to the king, 'who chided the Prince so severely as to bring him to tears'. James 'forbade' the humiliated Charles from being in his father's presence 'till the ring was restored'. It was soon discovered by one of Charles's servants in his bedchamber, and the prince fooled nobody when he explained to the favourite that it had been found in the back pocket of 'yesterday's breeches'.

The second incident happened two months later. James and George, flanked by the royal flunkies, were enjoying a stroll through Greenwich Park, when Charles 'in jest' decided to turn the jet of a fountain on the favourite, soaking George's no doubt exquisite and expensive clothes. The king was so incensed by the prank that, in front of George and all the royal staff, he boxed the prince's ears.

A Masque on Twelfth Night

In 1616, Francis Bacon, George's mentor, gave his pupil a warning about Charles. 'The prince groweth up fast to be a man,' he noted. 'It would be an irreparable stain and dishonour, having that access unto him, if you should misread him, or suffer him to be misused by any loose or flattering parasites: The whole kingdom hath a deep interest in his virtuous education; and if you, keeping that distance which is fit, do humbly interpose yourself, in such a case, he will one day give you thanks for it.'

Initially, George, preoccupied with the king's inexhaustible needs and his own personal ambitions, ignored the advice. But gradually he became aware that, if he was to secure his position in the complicated and emotionally fraught royal household, he needed a relationship with the hapless Charles.

A turning point came early in 1618. James had just made George a marquis, and, 'beyond all expectation', causing consternation among the earls and other lords whose precedence had been over-turned by the young upstart, had decided to make the title hereditary, to be passed on to the 'male heirs of his body'. Charles, in a last-ditch effort to gain his father's attention and approval, decided to organize a Twelfth Night masque to celebrate the promo-tion, expending 'extraordinary pains' on arranging what promised to be a spectacular event.

The festivities were a highly significant and keenly anticipated affair, marking the moment when Christmas at court shifted from a mood of ceremonial reverence to carnivalesque revelry. That year they were to be given added significance by the king's decision to invite the Conde de Gondomar, who after five years as Spain's ambassador in London, was returning to Madrid.

Since the ambassador's arrival in England in 1613, James had quite fallen for him. They seemed so inseparable, they became known as the 'Two Diegos' (Diego, Gondomar's first name, being Spanish for James). The king warmed to the Spaniard's combination of stiff, Castilian formality and wry, understated humour. And complaining to his masters in Madrid of James's 'vanity', Gondomar expertly played on the king's feelings of isolation and inadequacy. They were both foreigners surrounded by a condescending English establishment, sharing a dislike of London, a seedy, rotting city swelled by waves of impoverished immigrants. James even confided to Gondomar how unpopular he felt, how his English subjects would say unspeakable things about him. And the king revelled in the Spanish ambassador's expert flattery. Gondomar once told him that, while he spoke Latin badly, like a king, James spoke Latin well, like a scholar – just the sort of thing James, who yearned more than anything to be considered an intellectual, wanted to hear.

The Two Diegos were also close on the matter of Charles's future. In 1618, they had come up with a daring, if potentially delusional, plan to marry the prince to the Infanta Maria, the twelve-year-old daughter of Philip III of Spain. The earlier, disastrous unions of Henry VIII with Katherine of Aragon, and 'Bloody' Mary, Henry VIII's daughter, with Philip II of Spain, and the Spanish Armada's attempted invasion of England in 1588 were all still vivid in the English collective memory, making the idea of a so-called 'Spanish match' unpopular. But Scotland had never been at war with Spain, and by uniting his own family, the Stuarts, rulers of Protestant Great Britain, with the Spanish Habsburgs, the Continent's most powerful Catholic royal family, James not only flattered his dynastic ambitions but would cement his self-appointed position as the reunifier of a divided Christendom.*

In response to the king's growing affection towards Gondomar, George started to cultivate his own relationship with the Spanish ambassador. Gondomar was at first wary, assuming the favourite to be anti-Catholic. But he warmed to him as George became increasingly involved in the negotiations over Charles's bride. He even offered the favourite an annual pension of 6,000 ducats which, unlike a long list of other senior figures in James's government,

---

* Thanks to James's first Parliament frustrating his plans for a union of his kingdoms, Great Britain had yet to be formally created. However, it was recognized as a *de facto* entity by many foreign rulers, and treated as such by James himself.

George, initially at least, refused – not in a mood of patriotic indignation, but tactfully on the basis that he had yet to do anything to deserve it. But he did give the Spanish ambassador access to crucial correspondence, and when the king asked Gondomar if he trusted George, he replied that he did. 'You do well to do so,' said James, 'for he is as Spanish as you are!'

Now that Gondomar's embassy was drawing to a close, James was becoming increasingly emotional at the prospect of losing his close friend, and Charles hoped his Twelfth Night masque might lift his father's spirits as well as provide a suitable send-off.

The great hall at Whitehall had been fitted out 'like a theatre, with well secured boxes all round'. A stage had been erected at one end, with the king's throne placed before it, 'under an ample canopy'. This was the setting for the masque by the ever-popular Ben Jonson. It was entitled *Pleasure Reconciled to Virtue*, and promised a series of tableaux, dances and drinking songs to celebrate Comus, 'the God of Cheer, or the Belly'. Anticipation had been building over the holiday season, and the Venetian diplomat Horatio Busino sent a detailed and excited account of the event back to his masters.

It began a little inauspiciously, Busino and his fellow citizens, 'all perfumed' for the event, finding themselves 'so crowded and ill at ease' in their assigned box 'that had it not been for our curiosity we must certainly have given in or expired'. They had to endure the 'additional infliction' of a member of Gondomar's staff, 'who came into our box by favour of the master of the ceremonies' Charles. He asked for 'two fingers breadth of room, although we ourselves had not space to run about in, and I swear to God that he placed himself more comfortably than any of us'.

Nevertheless, Busino and his compatriots managed to distract themselves by 'admiring the decorations and beauty of the house' with its 'festoons and angels'. Six hundred of the 'most noble and richly arrayed ladies' were there, wearing 'delicate plumes over their heads, springing from their foreheads or in their hands serving as fans; strings of jewels on their necks and bosoms and in their girdles and apparel in such quantity that they looked like so many queens'. He also noted a 'mixture of husk and straw' among the 'grain': some of the 'plump and buxom' women displaying their 'bosoms very liberally', while those who were 'lean' went 'muffled up to the throat'. Farthingales were much in evidence, emphasizing the hips and rear, but he was unimpressed to discover that the women were all wearing 'men's shoes or at least very low slippers'. 'They consider the mask as indispensable for their face as bread at table,' he noted, 'but they lay it aside willingly at these public entertainments.'

After a two-hour wait in the stifling atmosphere, cornets and trumpets 'to the number of fifteen or twenty' blasted a fanfare to announce the arrival of the king with his honoured guest, followed by the male members of court. James processed into the hall, and seated himself on his throne. Gondomar was placed on a stool next to him, while 'the great officers of the crown and courts of law' sat upon benches behind him. Then, possibly on Charles's signal, a large curtain dropped, revealing a scene of a tent made of gold cloth, standing in a field against a background painted blue, powdered all over with golden stars. The figure of Atlas then appeared, whose 'enormous head was alone visible up aloft under the very roof of the theatre', his eyes and head moving 'very cleverly'.

What followed was an array of scenes and effects that clearly impressed the Venetian: twelve masked boys dressed as frogs, a guitar player in a gown 'who sang some trills', high priests wearing gilt mitres, culminating with a dozen 'cavaliers' all attired in crimson hose, with plaited doublets of white satin trimmed with gold and silver lace, who descended from the heavens in pyramid formation, 'of which the prince formed the apex'. Once they had landed, they began to dance, 'preserving for a while the same pyramidical figure, and with a variety of steps'.

Up until this stage, Busino seemed to be enthralled by the spectacle; but then things began to go wrong. Charles, in his role as the leading member of the dance troupe, was evidently struggling. He managed to 'cut few capers', but soon ran out of breath – 'owing to his youth' Busino charitably explained, but more likely due to his physical infirmities. English members of the audience began to get bored. 'Nothing in it extraordinary,' the jaded letter-writer John Chamberlain later pronounced. 'The invention proved dull.'

Suddenly James ('who is naturally choleric', the Venetian noted) lost his patience. He shot to his feet and shouted at the revellers: 'Why don't they dance? What did they make me come here for?

Devil take you all, dance!' Catastrophe. All Charles's hard work seemed to be undone. But then George, the new Marquis of Buckingham, 'sprang forward, cutting a score of lofty and very minute capers, with so much grace and agility that he not only appeased the ire of his angry lord, but rendered himself the admiration and delight of everybody'. The mood lifted and the hall was alive with capering cavaliers, one managing thirty-four dances, but none coming up 'to the exquisite manner of the marquis'.

George may have eclipsed the prince, but he had also saved him, and over the following months, Charles seemed eager to embrace the favourite as a friend rather than a rival to his father's attentions. The new alignment was cemented when a family argument broke out over Anne of Denmark's will. The queen had fallen dangerously ill around the time of the Twelfth Night masque and had summoned her son to her bedside. Charles had suggested to his mother that she leave her jewels to him, which she apparently agreed to do. Since they were rumoured to be worth an astronomical (though probably exaggerated) £400,000, it was perhaps not surprising that the cash-strapped James was furious at the news, and soon after George sent Charles a letter warning him of the king's reaction.

Charles wrote in desperation back to George, appealing for help. He addressed him using James's pet name, 'Steenie'.* 'There is none that knows me so well as yourself what dutiful respect and love I have ever, and shall ever, carry to the king.' George would therefore know the 'grief' Charles felt at his father's displeasure. He claimed to have acted on a 'command' James had given him 'a while ago that I should use all the means I could to make the queen make a will, whereby she should make over to me her jewels'. He had therefore assumed he would receive the king's 'approbation' for doing 'that which I thought he had desired'. He explained he was not claiming any right to the jewels, and begged George to tell his father 'that I am very sorry that I have done anything that may offend him and that I will be content to have any penance inflicted upon me, so he may forgive me'. He had never meant to displease

---

* A Scottish diminutive of Stephen, referring to St Stephen, who, according to tradition, had the face of an angel.

him, yet he accepted that he deserved 'to be punished for my ill-fortune'.

The pathetic plea was George's cue to recall the advice of his mentor Bacon, and 'humbly interpose' himself in the prince's miserable position.

George did so by staging a great feast for the king and Charles in London, 'the end whereunto it was designed, of reconciling' the prince with his father and the favourite. Charles grabbed at the opportunity with all-too-evident relief, declaring the event a 'Friends' feast'. James responded by deciding that it was also the 'Prince's feast', and drank a toast to his son. With the cup in his hand, he could not restrain himself from also raising it to George, as well as other members of the family, including Mary, along with Lady Hatton – now a firm friend as well as a sister-in-law – and several other members of the Villiers 'race', drinking a 'common health to all the noble family', which the king 'professed he desired to advance above all others'.

The Spanish Match

As the Christmas revels were underway, Queen Anne lay alone in her sickbed pondering her boy's future as well as her own mortality. Since the death of her eldest son Henry in 1612, she had been central to plans concerning Charles's marriage prospects, princes and kings from various foreign courts, including Tuscany and Savoy as well as Spain and France, courting her support for their daughters. Reflecting her religious sympathies, she had initially supported the idea of a Spanish match. In this she had been heavily influenced by her politically shrewd and witty lady-in-waiting Jane Drummond. Drummond had been Charles's wet nurse in Scotland and had close links to the Spanish ambassador, Gondomar, who paid her a generous pension to spy on Anne's court and influence the queen's deliberations.

With the queen's support, negotiations over the match had begun to gain traction. A treaty for the marriage was circulating as early as March 1615, and discussions had continued since, with new drafts going back and forth between London and Madrid. Religious issues had remained a sticking point, but Anne's backing had at least offered hope of overcoming them. It was even suggested that the queen and Drummond could provide a suitably Catholic establishment to accommodate the infanta when she came to live in England. And a plan had been discussed that would allow the infanta to raise her children, even the heir to the British throne, in the Catholic faith for the first few years of life – a major and highly controversial concession that was bound to provoke public hostility.

Then, in 1617, Anne had aroused shock and consternation by renouncing the match in favour of either Christine or Henrietta Maria, the two young sisters of the French king, Louis XIII. It turned out the queen had been vacillating for some time, confiding to the Venetian ambassador that she would 'sooner see' Charles 'married in France than in Spain' as early as 1615. A falling out with Sir John Digby, James's ambassador in Madrid, seemed to harden her view. She had then dismissed Drummond, on the pretext of her interfering in the appointment of a member of Charles's staff.

One explanation for the volte-face was the arrival of the Frenchman Piero Hugon as her page. She was known to have a penchant for male favourites in her inner circle. Hugon's predecessor Robert Lloyd (or Floyd), a 'sewer' in her privy chamber, had been knighted and raised to the curious rank of 'Admiral to the Queen', before suffering a mysterious fall from grace around the time of Hugon's arrival. Having swiftly displaced both Lloyd and Jane Drummond in the queen's 'affairs of trust and expense', Hugon had become heavily involved in her religious devotions, giving him the opportunity to shift her sympathies away from Spain and towards a daughter of France.

The queen's opposition to the Spanish match had become a major obstacle to it proceeding, and contributed to the complex treaty negotiations going adrift. However, in December 1618, as her illness had become dangerous, Anne had switched her position again, suddenly becoming 'very anxious' for Charles to marry the infanta, wanting in her final days to do her 'utmost to that end'. 'She hates a French marriage,' the Venetian ambassador reported, 'and opposes it openly.'

Whatever prompted the second change of mind is as unclear

as the first, but it was in the painful, final days of his mother's life that Charles was among the first to become aware of it.

On 1 March 1619, by now attended only by her faithful Danish maid Anna Roos, the forty-four-year-old queen's condition worsened dramatically and she lost her sight. Roos rushed to tell Charles that she was about to succumb, and the two of them were at her bedside when she died in the early hours of the following day.

Soon after it was discovered her jewels, the subject of the controversy over her will, had been stolen by Hugon. Some trunks that he had sent to France were subsequently tracked down, and found to contain not only the loot, but Catholic paraphernalia, revealing the extent of Anne's commitment to the old religion.

The queen was buried in May, James upstaging the funeral by suffering a dramatic deterioration in his own health, complaining of 'pain in his joints', probably gout, and 'nephritis'. Other complications soon began to develop, including 'fainting, sighing, dread, incredible sadness, intermittent pulse'.

Convinced that he too was about to follow his wife into the grave, he summoned Charles, George and leading members of his Privy Council to hear his deathbed speech, which the obsequious Bishop of Lincoln, John Williams, found of such profound importance he wrote that it deserved to be 'written in letters of gold'. James charged his lords and bishops with 'the care of religion and justice', and to look after 'that disciple of his whom he so loved in particular', George. And he ended 'with that heavenly advice, to his son, concerning that great act of his future marriage'. Charles should make his own choice of bride, he gasped, reaching for a final few breaths, but urged him to pursue the Spanish match.

These theatrics coincided with a period of fast-moving and dramatic international events. Barely a week after Anne's death, news arrived that the Archduke of Austria, Ferdinand II, had become Holy Roman Emperor.

The Holy Roman Empire, famous for not being either of its adjectives, nor hardly its noun, was made up of a collection of states and kingdoms spanning central Europe, roughly covering the territory of modern Germany, Austria and the Czech Republic, as well as parts of northern Italy, Poland and Slovenia. Though it was separate from the kingdom of Spain, the emperor and the Spanish king were both Catholic and members of the same Habsburg family, their confession and kinship ensuring that the two powers usually worked in unison.

The predecessors of the new emperor had tolerated a mixture of religious views among the dukes and princes of the empire's dominions, but Ferdinand, a devout Catholic, wanted to establish religious uniformity across his domains. This policy was tested almost as soon as he took the imperial throne, when the Kingdom of Bohemia rose in a state of rebellion against Ferdinand's rule. A group of protestors broke into the royal palace at Prague and threw two imperial representatives out of a high window, re-enacting a revolt that had taken place in the early fifteenth century, the so-called 'Defenestration of Prague'. The rebels then offered the Bohemian crown to Frederick, ruler of the Palatinate and husband of Elizabeth, the daughter of King James and Queen Anne. This was, if anything, an even more provocative act, as Frederick was, after his British father-in-law, the most powerful Protestant prince in Europe.

Going against James's advice, Frederick accepted the Bohemian throne, and on 4 November 1619 received the crown of St Wenceslas at St Vitus Cathedral, a heavily pregnant Elizabeth at his side.

By this stage, James had recovered from his illness to find his entire foreign policy thrown into turmoil by these events. His son-in-law's precipitate behaviour had upset 'all Christendom by the ears', unleashing convulsive forces that threatened to push the entire Continent into religious and dynastic war. Thanks to the family connections, Frederick had managed to draw Britain into the fray, putting James, who styled himself *Rex Pacificus*, the king of peace, into an extremely awkward position.

At the beginning of the year, James had made George 'Lord Admiral of the Fleet', succeeding the eighty-year-old Charles Howard, the heroic leader of the fleet that had defeated the Spanish Armada in 1588. George had revelled in his new role, attending formal events dressed in a suit of armour engraved with crossed anchors. But, to James's alarm, the favourite had also begun to adopt an appropriately warlike stance towards the developments on the Continent, arguing in the Privy Council that the king should give his son-in-law and his allies full military backing. He had won the support of several of his fellow councillors, including William Herbert, the powerful Earl of Pembroke, who seemed convinced that for 'the cause of religion, his son's preservation, and his own honour', the king should surely 'perform whatsoever belongs to the Defender of the Faith, a kind father-in-law, and one careful of that honour which I must confess by a kind of misfortune hath long lain in suspense'.

Even the usually shy and cautious Charles, who was now 'very friendly' with George, had joined in with the military tattoo, impressed that Frederick had shown himself to be 'of so ripe a judgement and of so forward an inclination to the good of Christendom'. It demonstrated the kind of princely daring and political idealism that had characterized his late brother Henry. 'I will be glad to not only assist him with my countenance,' Charles announced, 'but also with my person, if the King my father will give me leave.' But James would not give him leave. In fact, he would not allow anything to be done to support his impulsive son-in-law.

The result was political gridlock and incoherence. The French ambassador wondered if James had become deranged: 'It seems to me that the intelligence of this King has diminished. His timidity increases day by day as old age carries him into apprehension and vices diminish his intelligence.' The king told a foreign envoy about a letter he had received from his five-year-old grandson Frederick Henry, pleading for him to come to the aid of his exiled father and mother. He admitted that the child's entreaties had put him in a 'great strait', and lamented that he was being drawn 'to one side by his children and grand-children, his own flesh and blood, and to the other side by the truth and by his friendship' towards the Holy Roman Emperor.

James's only consolation was news that his old friend, Diego Gondomar, was on his way back to London. Philip III of Spain had decided to dispatch his emissary soon after Frederick's coronation in Prague. Gondomar had been reluctant to leave, claiming that he had not yet recovered from an illness that had forced his departure from London two years before. 'The matter of England requires someone who is healthy and robust,' he told his masters. He was also, despite appearances during his previous embassy, ambivalent about the idea of continuing peace with Britain, concerned it was allowing the country to build up commercial wealth and naval power at Spain's expense.

His objections were ignored, and in January 1620, Gondomar set off. He arrived in London in early March, and headed straight for Theobalds, where the king was staying. He was greeted by George and other courtiers and shown into an upstairs meeting room. As they were waiting for the king, the floor gave way, plunging several dignitaries, including the Earl of Arundel, into the room beneath. Gondomar was saved by standing in a doorway, and quipped in a letter home that 'the puritans have tried and are trying to have me killed'.

Despite the inauspicious reception, the reunion of the Two Diegos was warm, James gently chiding him for his absence by proclaiming that the man before him looked just like an old friend of his, the Conde de Gondomar!

Their private talks began with James trying to explain, in over-wrought and self-pitying tones, his predicament. 'I hear,' he said, 'from Buckingham, that when you shook his hand you squeezed his sore finger hard enough to hurt him.' The ambassador, he warned, must not squeeze so hard, as James, too, was tender. He had suffered terribly from the imbroglio in Bohemia, fearing that it had destroyed all their hard work to bring Britain and Spain closer together. 'I give you my word,' he said, taking Gondomar's hand, 'as a king, as a gentleman, as a Christian, and as an honest man, that I have no wish to marry my son to anyone except your master's daughter,' adding for good measure 'that I desire no alliance but that of Spain'. Having said his piece, he took off his hat, as if exhausted by the effort, and wiped his sweating forehead with a handkerchief.

Others did not find the ambassador's reappearance so welcome. During his first night in London, the battle drums were being beaten up and down the streets to summon a volunteer force to be sent to Bohemia to help Frederick and Elizabeth, and the following morning Gondomar found a placard nailed to the door of his lodgings inviting men to enlist to fight Spanish tyranny. The Venetian ambassador noted that 'the Protestants and the generality' viewed Gondomar 'with jaundiced eyes'. 'One already hears bitter speeches and very improper remarks, vigorously expressed, about the peace of these kingdoms if the marriage takes place.'

Elizabeth now began to write to George, adding to the pressure. She mentioned the 'many testimonies of your affection' she and her husband had received, and implored him to use his 'best means' to persuade her father 'to show himself now, in his helping of the prince here, a true loving father to us both'. In June 1620, an open letter addressed to George began to circulate the streets of London, pointing out the failure of previous unions between England and Spain, and urging the favourite to use his 'many talents' for 'God's glory and your honour' by 'dissuading privately by humble entreaties, and opposing publicly by your solid reasons, this Spanish Match'.

Then, in November, news reached London that Frederick and Elizabeth had been deposed. Imperial troops had routed Frederick's poorly organized and supplied forces just outside Prague, a clash that became known as the Battle of the White Mountain. In an apparently coordinated move, his Catholic rival, the Duke of Bavaria, had occupied parts of the Palatinate, his ancestral lands in Germany. As a result, Frederick and Elizabeth had been forced to flee to the Hague, the capital of the Protestant Dutch Republic, with little more than the clothes on their backs and a bag containing the Bohemian Crown Jewels.

The reaction in London was intense. 'Tears, sighs and loud expressions of wrath are seen and heard in every direction,' a diplomat reported. 'They have even found letters scattered in the streets, against the King, threatening that if his Majesty does not do what is expected of him, the people will assuredly display unmistakably their feelings and their wrath.' James, who was in Newmarket at the time, pronounced himself 'very sad and grieved', and 'remained constantly shut up in his room', forbidding his courtiers from indulging in 'any kind of game or recreation'.

In the turmoil of the unfolding events abroad, and the growing sense of Protestant fury at home, all hopes for the Spanish match seemed to disintegrate. The forces used to support the Holy Roman Emperor's attack on Prague and to seize Frederick's ancestral lands had included troops raised in the Spanish Netherlands, the region of the Low Countries under Spanish rule, and were led by an Italian general in Spain's service. This made a matrimonial alliance with Spain, the Holy Roman Empire's main ally, seem like a betrayal of the Protestant religion as well as James's daughter and grandchildren.

Matters reached their lowest point in October 1621, when Sir John Digby, James's veteran ambassador in Madrid, returned from a mission to Vienna to negotiate with the Holy Roman Emperor over the fate of the Palatinate.

Digby, regarded by many at court as being too close to the Spanish, gave a furious report of his humiliation at the hands of the emperor and his ally, the Duke of Bavaria, who refused all efforts at achieving a peaceful settlement. Digby told the king in the presence of the entire Privy Council that James must go to war, to restore honour and the Palatinate to the Stuart line. The council called for immediate retaliation, proposing a diversionary attack on the Spanish Netherlands. But James played for time. He agreed to send £40,000 to his son-in-law to help him maintain a court in exile. He also decided to recall Parliament, which had been adjourned since the previous June, in the hope of raising more money.

The king's reaction plunged the court into a state of confusion and frustration. 'The idea is now being put about with various and ill grounded reports, that it is not possible to do anything to help,' the Venetian ambassador wrote. James had 'several times remarked that he never wished to meddle in the affairs of Bohemia, and he clearly foresaw these disasters'. On this occasion, however, the impression of royal weakness was misleading. Digby's declaration had prompted James into an uncharacteristic burst of decisive activism, but in a direction quite opposite to that clamoured for by his councillors and Parliament. *Beati pacifici* – blessed are the peacemakers – was his motto, and he was not about to abandon it.

A reconciliation with George and Charles seems to have given added vigour to the king's plans. Having felt increasingly isolated from them, he managed to draw them into a secret strategy which he was sure would satisfy all parties and re-establish some kind of order. The deathbed declaration of support for the Spanish match by Charles's mother had left the prince open to the idea of maintaining relations with Spain, but only if it could be reconciled with saving his sister Elizabeth. This was what James now argued could be achieved.

As Digby's declaration had made clear, though the attack on Bohemia and the Palatinate had involved Spanish troops, it had been done in the name of the Holy Roman Emperor, not the King of Spain. If Charles were to marry into the Spanish royal family, then that would surely make it possible for the prince to prevail on his father-in-law, Philip, to put pressure on his kinsman the emperor to reach a peaceful settlement on the restoration of the Palatinate.

Parliament was recalled in late November 1621. On 24 November, Digby was allowed to repeat before a joint session of both Houses his angry denunciation of the Holy Roman Emperor. He did not hold back. In the interests of preserving peace, James had reached a point from which could 'descend no lower', Digby said, so the king 'must resolve either to abandon his Children or prepare for a war'. He urged MPs to raise £900,000 immediately to finance a relief force that would retake the Palatinate.

This was music to the members' ears, having adjourned the previous session pledging to offer the king financial assistance 'to the utmost' if the Palatinate were not restored.

Meanwhile, James had a private meeting with Gondomar to explain that Digby was being allowed to make these allegations to shift the focus of parliamentary anger away from Spain to the Duke of Bavaria, the emperor's ally, who had led the attack on the Palatinate. He also revealed that he had a plan to dissolve Parliament in the event of it threatening to declare war with Spain. He and George were going to disappear to Newmarket, leaving Charles 'with a secret commission' to prevent Parliament from meddling 'in any matter other than in conceding him a supply of money for the succour of the Palatinate'. If it was to veer from that course, then James would call for its immediate dissolution.

A few days later, secret letters between the Holy Roman Emperor and the King of Spain, intercepted by Dutch spies, were handed to the king. These showed that the young Philip IV, who had inherited the Spanish throne following the death of his father Philip III in March of that year, was increasingly nervous about the emperor's uncompromising stance, suggesting a gap was opening up between Spain and the Holy Roman Empire.

James acted promptly. George sent a message to his parliamentary proxy, Sir George Goring, telling him to deliver a speech to the Commons. He instructed his old friend to introduce a motion that the House should draw up a 'protestation' to the king, declaring that, if Philip IV did not 'give over' his military support of the Holy Roman Emperor's occupation of the Palatinate 'either direct or indirectly, then we may have a thorough war with him'.

Goring had been one of the 'Master Fools' recruited by the Baynard's Castle plotters to introduce George Villiers to court in 1615. He was popular at Westminster. According to the Venetian ambassador, 'people of all constitutions' were drawn 'wonderfully to him'. However, he was no heavyweight, 'a man more given to joking than to affairs', according to one hostile colleague. He was also known to be one of George's placemen. This made his bellicose intervention all the more startling. The Commons was prohibited from dealing in foreign policy matters. When it had strayed into such areas in the past, trouble would usually result and dissolution very likely follow. But here was this joker, best known for being a lackey of the favourite, inviting, perhaps luring them to do just that.

Confused by and suspicious of what they had witnessed, the MPs duly referred the matter to a committee.

After lodging the motion, the equally mystified Goring wrote back to George, reporting that, though his speech had been taken 'wonderfully well', 'the House was much distracted therewith'. Nervous that 'I have undone myself at Court' by publicly expressing such views, he reassured George that he had spoken 'the very words' he had been instructed to use, delivered with 'as much circumspection in every kind for his Majesty's service as my poor judgment could afford'. Tellingly, he added in the margin that 'His Majesty's end is not known to any flesh' (crossing out the word 'flesh') – an indication that the plot, though instigated by George, had originated with James.

Whatever qualms parliamentarians may have had about the dangers, Goring's intervention unleashed an explosion of anti-Spanish and anti-papist sentiment. James had presumably hoped to provoke a simple motion for war against the Holy Roman

Emperor to recover the Palatinate that would be voted through unamended, since it accurately reflected the views of MPs during the previous Parliament. There were even hopes a much-needed subsidy bill might result. But the MPs could not stop themselves from loading Goring's proposal with clauses against Catholics and the Spanish match until it threatened to become a wholesale protestation at the general state of affairs. Charles became particularly incensed at a demand that he should only marry someone 'of our own religion', writing to George that he would 'wish that the king would send down a commission' so that 'such seditious fellows' who had dared question the prince's matrimonial plans 'might be made an example to others'. In the end, James obliged, dismissing Parliament and personally tearing out from the official Commons Journal the page carrying the final version of the protestation.

This outcome has been taken as a sign of a catastrophic misjudgement on James's part. But Goring's original message had been aimed at Gondomar and the young King of Spain, rather than the MPs. Just before Goring had stood up to make his speech, one of his colleagues, the intemperate but glamorous Sir Edward Sackville, had suggested hypothetically to the Commons that, if James were to threaten direct military action over the Palatinate, 'it will not be long before we discover plainly whether the king of Spain be our enemy or no. Which if he be, then will the king without question, understanding our affections and inclinations, proclaim a general war against him and then shall we have our desires.' Goring's statement had effectively been a high-stakes challenge designed to put this proposition to the test. The hawkish MPs had assumed that the Spanish king would be shown to be their enemy. But they had not known about the secret letters James had seen between King Philip and the Holy Roman Emperor Ferdinand, which suggested the perplexed teenage Spanish king might show himself to be a friend, willing to push for the peaceful restoration of the Palatinate as part of a marriage settlement, if only to counterbalance the rampant and destabilizing ambitions of his older, more assertive, German cousin Emperor Ferdinand.

The initial signs were that James's gamble had failed. In the immediate aftermath of the vote on the Commons protestation, Gondomar had suggested to his masters that he might threaten to break off relations with James and return straight to Madrid. He had also alerted a colleague in Brussels to the possibility of an attack by the English on Spanish Netherlands.

However, within a few months of Parliament's dismissal, there were clear signs of a shift. In early 1622, reflecting a warming of relations with Spain, James sent Digby back to Madrid to resume the marriage negotiations. Soon after, news reached London that the Spanish king wanted Gondomar back in Madrid to take part in the discussions, and James, eager to encourage the growing mood of cooperation, gave his blessing to the recall.

Just before he was due to depart, Gondomar was invited to dine at Greenwich with the king, Charles and George. All three had over the past two years spent considerable time with the urbane ambassador, and were going to miss him. James was visibly moved by the prospect of losing his old friend again, and took a diamond ring from his finger to give to Gondomar, making him promise to return. Charles did the same.

As he was about to leave, the prince also took the ambassador aside to tell him 'in great trust and secrecy' that he was prepared to go to Madrid 'incognito with two servants' to woo the infanta. It was an astonishing offer, honouring with appealing gallantry his mother's dying request. Gondomar took it as a sign of the prince's sincerity, and even that he might convert to Catholicism.

Since the Continental crisis had brought his marital prospects to the fore, Charles had certainly undergone something of a transformation – the timid, hesitant, twenty-one-year-old prince emerging as a passionate and assertive champion of the Spanish match. Having been for so long neglected and dismissed, he had literally become the embodiment of his father's foreign policy and country's destiny, its only hope of success.

The prince had been sending letters to Digby in Madrid, pestering him for a portrait of the bride. What he eventually received depicted a young woman in her late teens with fair hair and a round face with blue eyes, a pale pink complexion, full mouth and the distinctive protruding Habsburg lip – not beautiful, perhaps, but attractive enough for an infatuated young man. The ambassador accompanied the picture with tantalizing descriptions of her at a masque, dancing 'as well as any that ever I saw'. 'And I dare boldly say unto Your Highness,' the ambassador added, perhaps to test the prince's recently acquired linguistic skills, 'that it was not so seldom as an hundred times repeated that night "*Plugiera a Dios que el Principe de Inglatierra la viese. O que linda, que hermosa, que angel*"' – if only, please God, the Prince of England could see her, how exquisite, how beautiful, how like an angel she is.

Endymion Porter, George's secretary and Spanish envoy, filled out the picture: 'She has fine hair and complexion, of a middling stature, being of late well grown, she hath the fairest hands I ever saw, she is very straight and well bodied and a likely lady to make you happy.' Not to mention, another diplomat added, a dowry that would be 'the greatest portion that was ever given in Christendom', capable of solving his father's chronic financial problems at a stroke without having to pander to another Parliament.

Charles began to wonder when he should start writing love letters to his angel. Having received a note from her modestly expressing her devotion, he contacted Gondomar in Madrid, asking him to pass on to her his best wishes, and thanking the ageing diplomat for acting 'in that honourable office, of my principal *Alcahuete*' – his procurer or pimp.* Charles, in short, had become besotted with the idea of the Spanish match, to such an extent that his father teasingly referred to it as his son's 'codpiece point'.

Behind the transformation of the once timorous, retiring adolescent into this assertive, rapacious prince stood the figure of George, his sexual magnetism adding a propulsive dynamism to Charles and James's dynastic hopes. He worked tirelessly to promote the match, reassuring Gondomar when Spanish enthusiasm seemed to droop that the prince was 'full ripe' for the nuptials, and that there was a longing to see 'an issue proceed' from the prince's 'loins'.

Through these interventions, a passionate, volatile royal ménage

---

* According to Glyn Redworth, who first brought this letter to the attention of British historians, 'though this word might be used to describe a patron or go-between, by the seventeenth century it was indelibly associated with the eponymous protagonist of Fernando de Rojas's immortal drama of sexual intrigue and licence, the brothel-keeper Celestina. It had come to mean "pimp" – or, in the case of the crone, "procuress". Being the sole Spanish word that Charles employed in this suspiciously brief note, it was of some consequence.'

was born. A heady combination of erotic desire and political ambition had brought together the two troubled figures of James and Charles, luring them into a daring mission that promised to transform Britain's place in Europe and save the Continent from a catastrophic war.

Periwigs

On 11 March 1623, a small group of men, unshaven and scruffy, but curiously well dressed, were chasing a kid goat on the road leading to the French city of Bayonne. With Lent prohibiting the serving of meat in local inns, a gruelling cross-country trek from Paris to this southwestern corner of the Basque country had left them famished and exhausted, and they were desperate for a decent meal.

Two of the men were known as Tom and John Smith, poor disguises for Prince Charles and George Villiers. The others were their servants and bodyguards. They had been on the road for nearly a fortnight, and doubts must have begun to set in as to what on earth they were doing there.

They had spotted the goat on the road as they approached the town. George's Master of the Horse, Sir Richard Graham, a man from the Scottish borders, had suggested catching the creature. Overhearing this, 'Tom' (Charles) chided him from resorting to his wild borderland ways and insisted that they should pay the owner for whatever they took. Having found the goatherd, they gave him 'good contentment', and George, together with one of his servants, began chasing the kid around a haystack. Losing patience, Charles shot the creature from his horse 'with a Scottish pistol'.

After Charles had first broached to Gondomar his plan to travel 'incognito' to Madrid, developments had proved frustratingly slow. Sexual, political and diplomatic frustrations became entwined. Encouraging letters had been received from Spain, but as late as Christmas 1622, there were still no signs of concrete progress. 'Talk of the Spanish Match lay somewhat dead,' reported the lawyer and diarist Simonds D'Ewes. Carlos Coloma, Gondomar's replacement as Spanish ambassador in London, described a meeting with James and Charles during which the prince kept muttering of Spain making him wait for a 'remedy'. In reply to Charles's letters about the delays and begging for news about the infanta, John Digby noted that 'the little god' – Cupid – 'hath been somewhat busy with you'.

Then, on 2 January 1623, George's secretary, Endymion Porter, had returned from a mission to Madrid with new proposals. Porter had connections to the Spanish court going back to his childhood, and there were hopes he could draw on them to get an insider's perspective on Spanish intentions. The expedition had been an exhausting and dangerous one, during which Porter had lost one of his servants in the sea, suffered a broken shoulder, been imprisoned at Calais, and lost most of his papers. But he had good news – or what was taken to be good news, when good news was all the recipients could bear to hear: reassurance from the Spanish king and his ministers that they were prepared to intercede at least diplomatically in the Palatinate crisis, and that they were serious about Charles marrying the infanta.

Breaking diplomatic protocol, Gondomar had also written a personal note to George in Spanish (rather than French, the usual language of diplomatic correspondence). He described the envy he felt for the carrier of the message, 'since he will get to kiss the hands of the marquis of Buckingham personally'. He also sent kisses for the hands of George's mother Mary and his wife Kate. Then, echoing George's carnal language, he revealed that as far as the Spanish were concerned, 'the decision has already been made, and with very great enthusiasm that the Prince of Wales should mount Spain'.

Encouraged by these diplomatic signals, Charles and George set about persuading James to allow the secret expedition to go ahead, skilfully exploiting the king's weakness of romance. 'How gallant and how brave a thing it would be,' they told him. James was reminded of his own marriage to Anne, how that too had been delayed, at first by the endless negotiations that had made him look like an 'irresolute ass', then by a tempest in the North Sea which had carried his bride's ship off to Norway. He had acted the chivalrous suitor, declaring when he heard the news of her detour that he would sail to Norway and fetch her himself, 'ay, upon the instant'.

The memory of that great venture cast a nostalgic glamour across his sweet boys' scheme. Nevertheless, when George and Charles spelled out some of the details, he fell into a 'great passion with tears'. He had gone to fetch Anne with a military escort of 300 men. These two were proposing to go with just two servants, on a journey of more than a thousand miles across land during the depths of winter. He feared for their safety, worried about losing the son he was supposed to protect and the man he loved.

To reassure the king, George and Charles offered to take Endymion Porter along with the prince's secretary, Sir Francis Cottington, who had led the most recent negotiations in Madrid and had extensive experience of the Castilian court. This eased James's concerns a little, as both had made the journey from London to Madrid many times, and would be prepared for eventualities that George and Charles 'would never think of'. He balked at their insistence that neither escort should be told the true nature of the expedition until the point of departure, so it was agreed that George and Charles would inform them beforehand in secret.

In the event, it was James who told Cottington. Sir John's reaction was 'such a trembling that he could hardly speak'. When they later all met, he voiced his opposition. His objections were concerned with the diplomacy as much as safety. He pointed out that for such a tiny, vulnerable party to turn up in Madrid uninvited would expose the prince to terrible risks and make it impossible to challenge Spanish demands in any subsequent negotiations.

George was furious with Cottington's bid to undermine the scheme, pointing out he was only being consulted so he could advise them on the best route.

Cottington's intervention added to James's anxieties. 'I am now so miserable a coward, as I do nothing but weep and mourn,' he wrote to George. 'I rode this afternoon a great way in the park without speaking to anybody, and the tears trickling down my cheeks, as now they do that I can scarcely see to write.' He pledged to 'pry into the defects' to harden his heart against the whole idea, 'and of every mote to make a mountain'. But it was no good, for as his efforts 'proceed from love' so they could not 'but end in love'.

And so it proved – love prevailed, or at least a pragmatic realization that, without some sort of bold intervention, James was not going to be able to keep alive his hopes of recovering the Palatinate for his son-in-law by peaceful means.

A carefully coordinated plan swung into action at seven in the morning on Monday, 17 February 1623. A sullen Cottington, having just written his will and said goodbye to his wife of four days, set off from Holborn for Dover with the objective of hiring the ship that would take the party across the Channel. He was accompanied by a puzzled Porter, who had been kept in the dark. Charles and George left Theobalds, and headed for New Hall, George's Essex home. That evening the two feigned casual bonhomie at a lavish dinner held for the prince and local dignitaries. The following morning, they slipped away, disguised in false beards, accompanied by Sir Richard Graham.

The journey that followed was described by Sir Henry Wotton, a contemporary of George's and a seasoned traveller himself, who did not spare posterity from the farcical as well as notable details.

The quickest route to Dover was via Gravesend, where a ferry crossed the Thames estuary. Here the plan faced its first obstacle, as neither George nor Charles had thought to bring any change. Paying the ferryman with a gold piece worth 22 shillings, suspicions were aroused that these were two wealthy men setting off to duel on the Continent, an activity the king had recently banned. The ferryman dutifully reported them to a local official, who immediately alerted the authorities in the nearby city of Rochester.

The party had by that stage managed to hire some post-hackneys (small horses used by couriers) and passed through the city unnoticed. But on the road to Canterbury – barely forty miles into a journey of around a thousand – they spotted the French ambassador, escorted by the 'king's coach', coming towards them on the way from Dover to London. Fearing they would be recognized, they 'baulked at the beaten road', forcing their horses 'to leap hedges' as they continued on a less conspicuous but much slower cross-country route.

Eventually reaching Canterbury, they went to the nearest stable to hire fresh horses, but found themselves confronted by the mayor, who had been tipped off by the authorities in Rochester about the suspicions of the ferryman at Gravesend. Perhaps overawed, possibly terrified by having to confront the aristocratic belligerents, the mayor claimed to have a warrant for their arrest from the Privy Council, the Royal Master of Ceremonies and the Lieutenant of Dover Castle, 'all of which confused fiction' prompted George to unmask himself and explain that, in his capacity of Lord Admiral, he was taking some 'slight company' on a confidential mission to review the royal fleet at Dover. 'This, with much ado, did somewhat handsomely heal the disguisement', and the party was allowed to continue.

Their 'disguisement' did not have long to recover, however, before a baggage post-boy, commissioned to deliver their luggage, somehow got a 'glimmering of who they were', forcing George to silence him with bribes and intimidation.

No doubt exhausted by these continuous emergencies, they finally reached Dover at six in the evening, where they were met by Porter and Cottington, who were waiting with one Kirk, a Scotsman, and James Leviston, a groom of the prince's bedchamber. It was too late to sail that evening, so they lodged at an inn and left early the following morning, by which time the weather had turned 'tempestuous'. Enduring a rough crossing during which George, the Lord Admiral, suffered acute seasickness, they arrived in Boulogne at two in the afternoon.

Having finally reached foreign soil, they abandoned their disguises and set off on the main road for Paris. However, two days later, as they approached the outskirts of the city, they met two German tourists who happened to be returning from a trip to Newmarket, where they had seen Charles and George riding with the king in the royal coach. Recognizing the illustrious travellers, the intimidating Sir Richard Graham was forced to 'persuade them they were mistaken'. This, as Wotton pointed out, was easily done, 'the very strangeness of the thing itself' convincing them of the impossibility that 'so great a prince and favourite' could be 'so suddenly metamorphosed into travellers, with no greater train'. It was enough 'to make any man living unbelieve his senses', if not conclude the prince and favourite had taken leave of theirs.

The next hazard was getting through Paris without being recognized. For such high-ranking foreigners to enter the capital uninvited had the potential to cause a serious diplomatic incident, and could even lead to their arrest. James had raised this very point before their departure, and they had strenuously argued that they would be able to get through the city before news of their adventure got out. So they were annoyed to find a messenger from England waiting for them with instructions from James that they should inform the French king of their arrival.

Bridling at the interference, they wrote back, insisting that everything was fine and they could manage on their own. But a reply arrived post-haste that humiliatingly contradicted their reassurances: 'My sweet boys and dear venturous knights, worthy to be put in a new romance,' James wrote soothingly, 'I thank you for your comfortable letters. But, alas, think it not possible that ye can be many hours undiscovered.' He explained that, despite the hedge-leaping and balking at the beaten Dover road, they had been spotted by the French ambassador, who had already made attempts to get news of their clandestine adventure to Paris. James had closed all the ports to prevent him, but there are 'so many blind creeks to pass at' that he could not guarantee that the ambassador's efforts had been thwarted. As a result, he felt he had no option but to send a letter 'of my own hand' directly to Louis XIII 'to show him that respect that I may acquaint him with my son's passing unknown through his country'. As a final, irritatingly meddlesome piece of advice, he reminded his 'Baby Charles' that he should probably write a thank-you letter to the French king once he had reached Spain.

Despite James's intervention, George and Charles decided not to make themselves known to their hosts but instead invest in periwigs to 'overshadow their foreheads'. Maintaining a curious overconfidence in their skills at the arts of disguise, and eager to experience the city as tourists rather than dignitaries, they decided to break their journey and spend the day sightseeing.

Roughly the same size as London in terms of population, Paris far outclassed the English capital in grandeur and style. The formidable queen mother, Marie de' Medici, a daughter of the powerful Florentine banking family, had introduced the Renaissance to medieval Paris, commissioning magnificent piazzi and palazzi modelled on the landmarks of her homeland. This would have provided Charles and George with their first experience of a post-medieval urban landscape: Baroque mansions instead of looming citadels, elegant rows of matching townhouses instead of jumbled alleyways of hovels, straight avenues of slender trees instead of winding paths and rutted roads, light instead of dark. They could cross the recently completed Pont Neuf onto the Île de la Cité and admire from the river the Louvre and the spires of Notre Dame, the Place Dauphine – enough to overwhelm a visiting prince and favourite with awe and envy.

That evening, they passed through the formal gardens of the Tuileries and smuggled their way into a viewing gallery in the palace, from where they could watch the French king 'solacing himself with familiar pleasures' – Wotton's prudish allusion to Louis's supposedly dissolute character – and the queen mother feasting 'at her own table'. 'Tom' and 'John' congratulated themselves on the effectiveness of their new periwigs. One Monsieur Cabinet, 'lately ambassador on England', had seen them both, yet failed to recognize them. Later that evening, emboldened by their anonymity, they overheard that rehearsals for a royal masque were underway, and approached Marie de' Medici's Lord Chamberlain, seeking permission to watch it. Accepting their pose as minor members of the English gentry (or perhaps indulging them, having been forewarned by the king's officials of their true identity), he allowed them entry 'out of humanity to strangers', where they had 'full sight' of the French queen, Anne of Austria, the elder sister of Charles's bride-to-be Infanta Maria, and Henrietta Maria, Louis's thirteen-year-old sister.

The sight of Anne, a vivacious twenty-one-year-old, had a powerful effect on both men. Her vivacious spirit had 'wrought in me a greater desire to see her sister', Charles reported in a letter home, penned later than night. George commented that of all the women he saw that evening, the queen was the 'handsomest'. She had married the youthful Bourbon king when they were both fourteen – a match cementing an alliance between two great dynasties in exactly the manner intended by the escapade of James's venturous knights. The marriage had flourished in the early years, but a series of miscarriages and Louis's dalliances at court, together with the dominating presence of Louis's mother, had soured the relationship. As a result, Anne had spent the last year in a state of dejection, restricted in her movements, her friends and finances meticulously managed by Marie de' Medici.

As she pirouetted entrancingly across the dance floor, enjoying a rare moment of freedom, Anne's eye caught that of George in the throng of spectators, and, despite the absurdity of his periwigged disguise, was as struck by his looks as he was by hers. Later that evening, after Charles had returned to their lodgings, he approached her. It is hard to imagine a more reckless act. If he was caught, it would not only ruin his reputation and seriously embarrass James, but bring the entire Madrid mission to an end, setting back the Spanish match by months if not permanently. In the event, affirming once again his sublime self-assurance and the delirious, life-affirming potency of risk, he found himself let into her apartment. What transpired is unknown, but the repercussions were severe for Anne. Her indiscretion with this apparently unidentified visitor was reported back to her husband, whose outrage led to a ban on all males entering her quarters except when he was present, which was rarely.

Oblivious to the scandal he had caused, George, together with Charles and their companions, set off in the early hours of the following morning for the next leg of their trip through the Loire and Gascony. The going was difficult. Possibly caught out by the Continental calendar, which was ten days ahead of the English one, they found they were travelling during the fast for Lent, and, in the depths of winter, food had become scarce. They stopped off for a night at Bordeaux, where they bought clothes to help weather the cold. Unable to resist choosing five fetching riding coats 'all in one colour and fashion, of a kind of noble simplicity', their aristocratic couture and carriage attracted local interest and came to the attention of the Duc d'Epernon, who invited the visitors to call at his chateau in nearby Cadillac. Cottington had to put the duke off, explaining they were 'gentlemen of mean degree, and formed yet little in courtship' – commoners, in other words, whose fine French clothes disguised a lack of breeding and courtly manners.

This brought them, famished and exhausted, to Bayonne, where Charles sat on his horse with a smoking pistol in his hand, George and his servant stood next to a haystack trying to recover from their exertions and the rest of the party looked on with amusement and empty stomachs at a dead goat lying on the road with a bullet in its side. They took the carcass back to their lodgings, where they feasted on it. It was their first proper meal for six days.

Their coats once more attracted the unwelcome attentions of a local noble, this time the Comte de Gramont, the town's governor. Being a strategic port on the Atlantic coast, the arrival of the unlikely posse had aroused suspicions and they were threatened with being detained. But somehow they once again eluded arrest, and 'he let them courteously pass'.

And so began the final leg of their French journey. Setting off on the road along the coast heading south, they ran into Walsingham Gresley, steward to Sir John Digby, carrying dispatches from Madrid to London. Breaking protocol, Charles and George opened the letters to see if there was any news concerning the Spanish match, but found only cypher and, in the parts they could read, evidence of Spanish prevarication – particularly on the vital matter of getting dispensation from the pope for the Catholic infanta to marry a Protestant prince. Concerned about the effect of this news on the king, and anxious to get to their destination as quickly as possible, they kept the letters and prevailed upon Gresley to accompany them out of France and into Spain.

Guided by their experienced escort, the party rode through the wild fringes of the Basque country, passing the Pyrenees where the mountains fall towards the sea, and crossed into Spain. In the ancient border town of Irun, Charles and George penned a letter to their 'dear dad and gossip', reporting that they had arrived 'free from harm of falls', and in 'as perfect health as when we parted'. They could also not resist bragging that they had made it across France 'undiscovered by any Monsieur'. Having 'saucily' opened Gresley's letters, they claimed to be reassured from the parts they could read that their journey was worthwhile, as it would defeat Spanish efforts to stall the negotiations 'upon pretext of making preparations'. Signing off as 'your majesty's humble and obedient son and servant Charles and your humble slave and dog Steenie', they sealed the letter and sent Gresley on his way.

They felt more at ease on Spanish roads, Charles a Don Quixote, George his rather grand Sancho Panza, 'venturous knights' heading south through the hills of Navarre. Only one event stuck out of an otherwise uneventful final leg of their journey: they met a Spanish diplomat who had visited England, and Charles struck up a conversation with him, mentioning his memories of Spanish embassies in London. He recalled a son of one of the ambassadors, mentioning that he was far too ugly for a beautiful wife, not realizing he was addressing that son. The diplomat immediately challenged Charles to a duel, and was only prevented from going ahead with it by being told his adversary's true identity.

The House of the Seven Chimneys

At 5 p.m., on 7 March 1623, Sir John Digby was sitting in his privy chamber in the House of the Seven Chimneys, the ambassador's elegant sixteenth-century residence on the Calle de las Infantas in Madrid, when a servant came up to his room to report that a mysterious English messenger had arrived. He brought news that the ambassadorial courier, Gresley, had 'fallen into thieves' hands and all his letters taken away'. He also said the visitor had injured his leg so would not be able to get up the stairs to the ambassador's chamber.

Digby sent down his son, who returned a little later in a flustered state to announce that the messenger was none other than the Marquis of Buckingham, George Villiers. 'In a kind of astonishment', Digby then came down himself, to discover George in the hall, and Charles waiting outside 'in the dark'.

The ambassador managed to disguise his reaction better than George his identity, but the bewilderment and dismay must have been profound at what he later described as this 'sudden & unthought arrival'. A solid, round-faced forty-three-year-old man from the English midlands, Digby was no novice to the shocks and banalities that characterized the world of diplomacy, but he had never encountered anything as impetuous, confounding and potentially disastrous as this.

Nevertheless, here they were, with George flourishing letters from James making him 'extraordinary ambassador and principal commissioner in all the treaty'. Speed was now of the essence, with George demanding that they immediately 'discover the wooer' – reveal Charles – to the Spanish king, because the swift reopening of ports following their departure from England meant that news of their secret mission was likely to reach Madrid 'within twelve hours' of their arrival.

Despite the clear indication that he was being demoted and sidelined, Digby stifled his indignation and humiliation, 'called for pen and ink', and dispatched a post that night to England reporting the pair's safe arrival. He also set about engineering the delicate business of breaking the news of Charles's arrival to the Spanish court, in violation of all the usual rules of royal and diplomatic protocol.

He sent a message to Gondomar, mentioning only that George had appeared at the embassy, seeking an audience with King Philip. The former ambassador to London turned up at the House of the Seven Chimneys early the following morning, bragging that he had known of Charles's presence within hours of the prince's arrival. The reunion with George was a warm one, the disgruntled Digby watching as they embraced and exchanged fond memories of Gondomar's visits to George's riverside house in London.

Gondomar went off immediately to break the news to Gaspar de Guzmán – Conde de Olivares and Duque de San Lúcar la Mayor – Philip IV's *valido* – chief minister and favourite, a man whose influence over the Spanish king was not dissimilar to George's over James. On seeing Gondomar in such an agitated state, Olivares was said to have asked him jokingly if he had come to announce the arrival of the King of Great Britain, to which Gondomar's sardonic reply was that it was only his son.

At four in the afternoon, a coach arrived for George and Digby. They were joined by Gondomar and Sir Walter Aston, a permanent member of the embassy staff. The coach took them to a discreet location in the grounds of the Alcázar, the imposing palace built by Charles I and Philip II on the site of the Islamic citadel that gave it its name. As they passed by the fortress's massive bastions, George could not be but impressed by the scale of a structure that dominated the surrounding landscape, sitting on the edge of a ravine that plunged down to the Manzanares river and overlooked the vast Casa de Campo royal hunting park.

The coach came to a halt and rocked violently as the huge figure of Olivares climbed in and squeezed onto the seat facing

George. The necessary courtesies concluded, Digby and Gondomar were asked to leave so the two royal favourites could be alone, with Aston acting as interpreter.

The count-duke's imposing physique, sombre dress and startling looks were quite at odds with George's delicate frame, flamboyant tastes and handsome features. Dressed in black velvets and silks, his jowly head, tiny in proportion to his massive body, protruded from a ruff of the finest white gauze, suggesting a small body hiding in a giant's costume. Dark hair cut with a high fringe emphasized the imposing dome of his forehead, which sloped down to deep-set eyes. Thick red lips protruded through the whiskers of a beard trimmed into a long brush, and a wide moustache reached almost to his sideburns, acting as an ornate plinth for a prominent, knobbly nose. A great key was stuck in his belt, to demonstrate his capacity to open and lock the doors of power.

He had the settled composure of an aristocrat with an impeccable pedigree – Olivares's family traced its roots to Spain's eleventh-century nobility. He was also bred in the arts of diplomacy, his father being Spanish ambassador to Italy, so any hint of condescension towards this upstart envoy of an upstart prince would have been well hidden.

Though there might be something intriguing, even quixotic about this ludicrous English adventure, it was an irritating interruption to the *valido*'s busy schedule. Olivares had to deal with foreign as well as domestic affairs on a scale unimaginable even to England's Lord Admiral. He had to manage colonies that girdled the globe, from Peru to the Philippines, and Spain's unruly northern European possessions in Flanders, while supporting the Austrian branch of the Habsburg family, whose grip of the Holy Roman Empire was, in large part thanks to Charles's impulsive brother-in-law Frederick of the Palatine, threatened with disintegration. In this great map of responsibilities, Britain was a small island floating in a sea of inconsequence whose king was a relatively minor and not particularly prepossessing character on the global stage, and whose military power, as he would later complain to Gondomar, was exaggerated.

Nevertheless, the sheer audacity of the escapade had piqued royal interest, so Olivares escorted the little party by a 'back way' to the king's privy chambers.

If George was daunted by meeting the most powerful monarch in Europe, he did not show it. The Habsburgs were famous for their aloofness and solemnity, and courtly manners in Spain demanded a certain decorum lacking in James's more turbulent household. So when George launched with 'alacrity and freeness' into the royal audience with Philip, a terrified Digby, already irritated at being upstaged, expected a diplomatic incident. Yet, to his amazement and perhaps with a touch of jealousy, he noticed that even the famous Habsburg reserve could not resist the Villiers charm, and for the first time in the old ambassador's decades of experience he witnessed all the 'Spanish gravity' being 'laid aside'.

The same day, Gondomar announced to Charles that an 'Englishman' had been made a member of the Council of State, the Spanish equivalent of the Privy Council. It turned out he meant himself, as the count claimed to have become 'an Englishman at heart'. Thus planting himself at the centre of the negotiations, he arranged for the prince to have his first sight of the princess.

Despite the informality and warmth that seemed to have developed between the two sides, there was no prospect of the 'wooer' prince having an impetuous tryst with his lover. If Charles was to be given even a glimpse of the infanta, it would have to be under the conditions of the strictest Spanish propriety. The next day, a Sunday, Gondomar and George accompanied Charles in an 'invisible coach' (meaning with curtains drawn) to the Paseo del Prado, a boulevard on the outskirts of the city that ran through an ancient monastery meadow. There they waited for the king, his queen and the infanta, who were to parade through later in the morning and stop at a strategic location for a rest.

Crowds gathered, and the carriages duly arrived. Charles could identify the infanta by a blue ribbon tied around her arm. According to Endymion Porter, when the prince looked at her through the gap in the curtains, he developed 'such a liking to his mistress that now he loves her as much for her beauty as he can for being sister to so great a king'. 'She deserves it,' Porter added, in a letter to his wife, 'for there was never seen a fairer creature.'

Though supposed to be incognito, 'the searching vulgar' somehow managed to spot Charles, and 'did so press about the coach to see him, that we could not pass through the streets, insomuch that the

King's guard was forced to beat them from it and make way through the multitude'. According to Porter, they knew who Charles was, 'and cried "God bless him", and showed as much affection generally as ever was seen among people, only they took it ill he showed not himself to them in a more public manner'.

Later that evening, Olivares told George in the typically exaggerated language of courtly diplomacy that 'the king longed and died for want of a nearer sight of our wooer', initially suggesting that he would come to meet Charles at the embassy. There was horror at the suggestion. The receiving of a monarch in such a relatively humble setting would put Charles in considerable debt to his host. Instead, it was decided that more neutral territory should be found for the rendezvous, agreement settling on a return to the Prado.

Thus began an extraordinary piece of courtly theatre described by George and Charles in an excited joint letter sent to James the following day. Olivares came to the embassy in his coach to collect George, and the two set off. According to George, they then encountered Philip, King of Spain, Portugal, Naples, Sicily and Sardinia, Duke of Milan, ruler of the Netherlands and Count of Burgundy, Emperor of the Americas and the Philippines, 'walking in the streets, with his cloak thrown over his face, and a sword and buckler by his side'. The coach door was opened, and 'he leaped in, and away he came to find the wooer,' Charles, who was waiting for him at an appointed place along the Prado promenade.

The seventeen-year-old Spanish king, five years Charles's junior, was tall, with a rather pale, doughy face, protruding lips shaded by a downy moustache, his eyes heavily hooded, the outer edges of the lids brushed by soft lashes. His hair was curled in a Castilian manner that would have seemed curious to English eyes, with a wide and very prominent quiff furled above the forehead and long locks that dangled around the ears.

According to George, 'there passed much kindness and compliment' between the king and the prince, Endymion Porter acting as Charles's interpreter. Philip was particularly curious to hear about their journey across France to Madrid, evidently impressed, if perhaps a little puzzled by it. The king then escorted Charles and

George back towards the House of the Seven Chimneys, their coaches hitting a pothole and nearly overturning along the way.

Back at the embassy, Charles and George had an opportunity to recover from and assess the meeting. Despite the occasional mishap, they could congratulate themselves on an impressive achievement. James had boasted of his mission to collect his bride Anne, stranded in Norway, but he had been accompanied by an armed escort, and been travelling to a neutral country. Charles and George had come uninvited and more or less defenceless into a potentially hostile kingdom, relying on no more than charm, guile and Sir Richard Graham's intimidating presence to keep them safe.

Judged at least by 'outward shows' and 'general speeches', this high-risk strategy was starting to pay off. A combination of youthful recklessness, romantic imagination and even carnal impatience had succeeded in reinvigorating negotiations stalled by diplomatic inertia. The ambassadors were to be 'condemned', George told James, 'for rather writing too sparingly than too much' about the possibilities of progress. Philip, George reported, had a 'sensible' understanding of Charles's position, and in Olivares he felt that, with careful cultivation, they might have an ally.

Exhausted, isolated, exhilarated, they suddenly beheld a prospect of success. If realized it would lead to a complete realignment of European politics. The son of an indebted landowner from the English midlands would have transformed a timid, lame, stammering boy into one of the great princes of the Continent, uniting the Scottish Stuarts with the mighty Habsburgs. They would have challenged the pope's insistence on treating all Protestants as heretics. They could put pressure on the Spanish to restore the ancestral lands of Charles's brother-in-law Frederick, thus helping to relieve the growing tensions in the Holy Roman Empire. And to top all this, they would have secured a £600,000 dowry that would at last pay off the royal debts.

Within days of their first introduction to the court, a public welcome was staged for Charles. Spain's financial health was precarious, and one of Olivares's earliest reforms as Philip's first minister had been to impose austerity measures at court, which included a ban on extravagant clothing and lavish entertainment. To disguise this from the visitors, these restrictions had to be temporarily lifted, to reinforce the British impression of Spanish opulence and wealth.

By tradition, a great royal celebration such as a wedding or succession was marked with the granting of a pardon. So, on Friday 14 March, hundreds of prisoners were released, including several Englishmen who had been caught committing acts of piracy and sentenced to serve as galley slaves.

The following evening, a royal emissary arrived with two horses from Philip IV, who told Charles to select whichever he wanted to use for the procession into the city the next day. Charles went to admire them in the embassy garden and 'took pains and pleasure to try them both, to the end that if there were a difference, he might take the less excellent to himself, and return the other to the king'.

On Sunday, barely a week after the arrival of the two 'venturous knights', the main ceremonies began. James had decided to bestow on Charles the rank of 'sworn king of Scotland', a title the Spanish seemed prepared to acknowledge. The now familiar seven chimneys of the British embassy provided the backdrop for the arrival of royal emissaries to welcome the Scottish 'king'. A receiving chamber had been set up, with pictures of great knights and statesmen, as well as of the English Parliament – a curious, perhaps pointed gesture, since Spain had no equivalent representative assembly.

The emissaries conducted Charles and George to the Monastery of San Jeronimo, where they joined Philip for a meal. Afterwards, with solemn, reverential and exhausting formality, Charles spent several hours being presented to a parade of the Spanish councils, each representing the various realms, military orders and offices of state.

The royal party then went down to the gate of the monastery, where they all mounted horses, and set off for the city. They were met at the gate by twenty-four *regidores*, or city officials, who unfurled a 'large canopy of rich tissue' lined with crimson cloth of gold under which the kings of Spain and Scotland were to parade through the streets, with George and Olivares following behind. 'All the streets were adorned, in some places with rich hangings, in others with curious pictures', while at various stages along the way 'representations were made of the best comedians, dancers and men of music, to give contentment to that royal pair'.

They were received at the Alcázar by Philip's exquisite, if rather forbidding, twenty-year-old wife, Queen Elisabeth of France, who conducted them to three 'equal chairs' set up beneath a 'cloth of state'. The queen sat in the centre, with Charles and her husband on either side. 'The room,' an English diplomat observed, 'was as richly furnished as may well be imagined, but the chief riches thereof consisted in the living tapestry of ladies, noblemen and children called "*menines*", which stood and garnished all the room round about close by the walls.'

Once the formalities were completed, Charles was conducted to the opulent apartments of the palace which were provided for him for the duration of his stay. As he was settling himself in, the queen brought 'sumptuous and curious' welcoming presents including 'a fair great basin of massy gold' carried by two men, 'a curious embroidered nightgown', two great trunks bound with golden locks and keys, lined with tan leather and filled with 'several delicacies of linen and perfumes', and a desk 'every drawer whereof was full of rarities'. 'Fireworks were made, and torches set in all the windows of Madrid' as the celebrations and formalities continued 'for three nights together'.

Charles installed George in a room next to his, and ordered that his companion was to be 'served with a full and plentiful diet, and to be also nobly attended'. The grandees who continued to turn up every day were expected to pay their respects to George as well as Charles, in an effort to shore up his position as the prince's chief negotiator and representative.

A few days later, a rushed and muddled letter arrived from James in which he reported that he had broken off diplomatic relations with the Holy Roman Emperor over the Palatinate. If that business was to be 'brought to a good end, it must now be done by the king of Spain's mediation', he declared. Feeling exposed and edgy at this critical turning point in their plan, he also urged Charles to speed up the 'long delay' in reaching a settlement, and was concerned that Philip might 'if not lessen, at least protract the terms for payment of the dowry'. But he remained optimistic. If the Spanish 'love themselves', they would see the marriage through.

'Here am I, now in a chamber alone,' George wrote back to James. Charles was out hunting with Philip, as the celebrations of his arrival continued. George commiserated with James over his current health problems, in particular his lameness, and hoped that by the next letter from England, news would arrive that 'you are marching upon your well-shaped legs again'. There was a hint of nervousness about his continued absence from James's side, a fear that others might be trying to fill the gap he had left behind. He strained to express the debt of gratitude he owed the king – most recently for the favour shown to his 'little deserving' dipsomaniac brother Kit, just made Earl of Anglesey. 'I may ease my heart in saying something,' he wrote, 'but never satisfy the debt or debtors in saying enough.'

George also enclosed 'consolatory' letters to be forwarded to his wife Kate and to his beloved but 'fearful sister' Susan, who continued to worry about his safety. Kate had maintained a regular and affectionate correspondence with her husband, sympathizing with him of the 'grievous time of this our grievous absence'.

'You could never had a one that could love you better than your poor, true, loving Kate doth,' she wrote, 'poor now in your absence, but else the happiest and richest woman in the world.' She consoled herself that she was 'that happy woman to enjoy you from all other women', perhaps a warning not to yield to the temptations she could only imagine surrounding him in the Spanish court. Her father, the Earl of Rutland, was more forthright, warning George that if he 'court ladies of honour you will be in danger of poisoning or killing' and that if he had 'whores, you will be in danger of burning' – catching venereal disease. George's secretary Endymion Porter, ever present as his interpreter, felt obliged to tell his own wife, Olive, to 'remember my humble service' to George's wife, and pass on 'that my lord and I wish you were both here very often', adding a suspiciously superfluous reassurance that 'we live very honest and think of nothing but our wives'.

In the midst of all this, the infanta seemed to have become lost – literally so, as far as Charles and George were concerned. Kate had even sent her husband 'spy glasses' to help him find this distant and elusive creature.

On the rare occasions Charles was allowed sight of his bride-to-be,

Olivares noted that the prince gazed upon her 'as a cat doth a mouse'. A cat-and-mouse game duly ensued in the days and weeks following the prince's installation in the Alcázar. The aim seems to have been to use Charles's carnal desires to tempt him into becoming a Catholic, linking consummation to conversion.

The infanta played her part in the game impeccably, maintaining an air of inscrutable formality and Catholic piety. She was rarely to be seen in public, and never put in a position where she might exchange so much as a glance with Charles. For his part, Charles made regular and ever more fervent appeals to see her, but was ignored.

Reinforcing the link between the union and religion, he was finally given another chance to see the infanta at Easter. Being, from a Catholic point of view, a heretic, Charles could take no part in the festival, though an English Catholic, a Jesuit who had become a religious refugee in Madrid, was allowed to distribute alms amounting to £2,000 on Charles's behalf – a remarkably ecumenical concession on both sides.

Charles's chance for another glimpse of the infanta came on Palm Sunday, at the beginning of the week's festivities, when the royal family processed through the corridors of the Alcázar palace. Charles was positioned behind a screen, and as the royal party passed, it slowed down, tantalizing him with 'a very good view of the lady infanta', possibly even a hint of her perfume.

Then, on Easter Sunday, at the height of the celebrations, the teasing reached a climax. The frustrated 'wooer' was finally to be allowed a meeting with the wooed. Charles had to borrow somewhat oversized clothes from Olivares for the occasion, those he had ordered from England having yet to arrive, though he did manage to decorate them with diamonds and the insignia and garter of the Order of St George, England's patron saint. In this ill-fitting but highly decorated garb, Charles was told to wait outside the royal chapel while King Philip finished his Easter prayers. The two then set off for the apartments of the queen, who was waiting for them with the infanta.

A meeting of excruciating formality ensued, the couple sitting silently on chairs either side of an unsmiling queen. The chamber began to fill with the whispers of watching courtiers. Charles rose.

The queen stood to hear him. The whispers subsided. The prince, whose stammer could be worse at times of heightened tension, spoke a few words, presumably thanking the queen for the opportunity to introduce himself. There was a pause for the interpreter. He then stepped past her to address the infanta directly. He kissed her hands, and told her via his interpreter that he had come to Spain to make a 'personal acknowledgment' of the friendship between her brother and his father and 'to continue and increase' it. She stared blankly at him as she listened to the translation. She replied that she greatly valued what he had said. He then enquired after her health, having heard that she had recently been unwell. She thanked him for asking. Offered no further encouragement, a tongue-tied Charles returned to his seat, and a half hour later left the room with King Philip.

The awkwardness and lack of encouragement on the part of the infanta had the expected effect, stoking Charles's desires. Sir Francis Cottington, their travelling companion since Dover, guessed that she 'will be with child before she gets to England'.

A month later, however, Charles was still awaiting a second encounter. The negotiations had once again become bogged down in disputes over religious issues, and the Spanish seemed to be dragging things out. Meanwhile, expenses were escalating, only partially relieved by the arrival in April of ships from England, bringing the much-needed clothes, more jewels (said to be worth as much as £200,000), and a party of nobles and knights to act as Charles's entourage, including Lord Compton, the glamorous brother of George's stepfather, and Archie Armstrong, James's court jester.

As the scorching summer temperatures set in, arguments with the Spanish became increasingly heated. On 24 April, King Philip arranged for a panel of Catholic theologians to interview Charles. The venue was one of the king's private chambers, and Philip greeted Charles when he arrived. But before proceedings began in earnest, the king left, saying he could never allow himself 'to listen to a word against the Catholic religion'. It was an ominous start to what proved to be another awkward confrontation.

George had already attended two secret discussions, to explore the difficult issues of heresy, Catholic toleration and papal supremacy

George Villiers, Duke of Buckingham, in his pearl jacket,
by Michiel J. van Miereveld, 1625.

Villiers family portrait, *British School*, c.1628. [*left to right*]
Susan, George's sister; Kate, George's wife; Mary or 'Mal', George
and Kate's eldest child; George Villiers, Duke of Buckingham,
in the same pearl-studded jacket he wore posing for Miereveld;
his son and heir George, propped up on a cushion probably by
Mary, Susan's daughter; John, George's mad older brother;
Mary, Countess of Buckingham, George's mother;
Christopher or 'Kit', George's feckless younger brother.

Robert Carr,
Earl of Somerset.
James's favourite and
George's rival.

Esmé Stuart,
James's cousin and
first favourite.

James VI of Scotland, I of England, by Paul van Somer, *c.*1620, soon after his relationship with George had begun to flourish.

Anne of Denmark, dressed in hunting gear. James's formidable and independent wife and George's early patroness, by Paul van Somer, 1616.

Francis Bacon, George's brilliant, extravagant, pompous mentor.

Sir Edward Coke, judge, MP and Bacon's rival.

George and Kate as models for *Venus and Adonis* by Anthony Van Dyck, *c*.1620.

Left. George's wife Kate by Van Dyck, *c.*1633.

Below. George, Kate and their children Mary and George, painted in 1628 by Gerrit van Honthorst soon before George's assassination.

– whether the pope's religious authority as church pontiff exceeded James's as Supreme Head of the Church of England. This was the first opportunity for Charles himself to be interviewed on these matters. The prince claimed there was nothing to talk about. He did not 'scruple' about his faith.

The mood darkened when one of the Spanish monks quoted Luke's gospel, when Jesus says to Simon Peter, the 'rock' of the church and the apostle considered to be the first pope: 'Simon, Simon, behold, Satan hath desired to have you that he may sift you as wheat, but I have prayed for thee that thy faith fail not; and thou, when thou are converted, strengthen thy brethren.' Charles asked twice for the verses to be repeated in French. Realizing the implication that Charles needed to convert to Catholicism to be accepted by Christ, George flew into a rage, throwing his hat to the ground and stamping on it before storming out of the room.

A stand-off ensued, with George refusing Olivares's efforts to arrange further conferences, and Olivares denying Charles further opportunities to meet the infanta.

Finally, Charles decided to revive the tactic that had brought him to Spain in the first place: an impetuous, romantic gesture to cut through the diplomatic deadlock. He discovered that, during May, the infanta was in the habit of visiting the summerhouse in the Casa de Campo. She went to gather 'maydew', the dew that gathered on freshly sprouting plants, which was believed to have medicinal qualities.

On Saturday 17 May, accompanied by Endymion Porter to act as his interpreter, Charles called at the summerhouse. He was let into the house and the garden, but informed that she was in the orchard, which was protected by a high wall and a gate with a double lock. Fetching a ladder, Charles scaled the wall and jumped down the other side. Seeing him, the infanta 'gave a shriek and ran back'. An elderly marquis who was acting as her guardian then approached the prince and, on bended knee, begged him to leave, as he 'hazarded his head if he admitted any to her company'. The humiliated Charles complied, and the orchard gate was opened to let him out.

Spring melted into summer, and the heat became so intense Charles had to send one of his older courtiers back to London to recover. The negotiations fell into a state of lethargic paralysis. It was now clear that Charles's conversion to Catholicism had become a Spanish objective, if not an explicit condition, of the marriage. It even transpired that Ambassador Digby had encouraged Olivares to believe that conversion was a possibility, which it had never been, nor could be.*

There was also the position of Charles's sister Elizabeth to consider. The hope remained that Philip would intercede in favour of her and her husband Frederick if Charles married the infanta. But Archie Armstrong, the king's clown, had learned from the Infanta Maria herself of the lack of sympathy in the Spanish court for Frederick's predicament. She pointedly remarked how 'strange' it was that Frederick's Protestant forces had lost to a Catholic army about half its size, suggesting that it must be the result of divine intercession.

A despondent mood set in at the English camp. George wrote to James of the latest version of the papal dispensation for the marriage becoming 'clogged' with yet more conditions. Relations with Olivares, the man he had once hailed as 'so full of real courtesy', had broken down, and the two were now only communicating in writing.

Before George and Charles had set off from England, James had proposed making his beloved 'Steenie' a duke. George had resisted the offer, fearing it would provoke the jealousy of his rivals. Dukedoms were by convention reserved for members of the royal family. To honour a commoner with such a title signalled that James might have ambitions to give George royal status, perhaps so his children could marry those of Charles's sister, Elizabeth. By this time, James already saw George as a member of his family. His letters, including the one that mentioned the dukedom, were filled with news about George's wife Kate and James's beloved 'grandchild', Mal.

The patent formally conferring the title arrived in Madrid in late May, with a message from James's Lord Keeper informing George

---

* The reasons for the breakdown of negotiations is highly controversial, with Glyn Redworth blaming a culture clash but others, such as Robert Cross, seeing Charles's concern for his sister and brother-in-law as a decisive factor.

that 'his majesty is most constant, and in some degrees more
enflamed in his affections to your grace than formerly' and that the
title had been conferred so 'your honour might be no less than
the Conde-Duke Olivares the Great Privado of King Philip'. A thank-
you letter overwrought with gratitude and humility made its way to
England by return of post. 'You have filled a consuming purse, given
me fair houses, more land than I am worthy of, to maintain both
me and them, filled my coffers so full with patents of honour, that
my shoulders cannot bear more,' George told James. 'You have
furnished and enriched my cabinet with so precious a witness of
your valuation of me, as in future times it cannot be said, that I rise
as most courtiers do, through importunity' – in other words, as a
result of annoying persistence. 'For which character of me, and
incomparable favour from you, I will sign, with as contented, nay
as proud a heart, Your poor Steenie, as Duke of Buckingham.'

The promotion made no difference to the negotiations, however.
They ground on without any sign of resolution, apparently propelled
by a momentum of their own. An optimistic outlook had to be
maintained. As late as July, Endymion Porter would write to his
wife that a deal had been done and that he and George 'shall be
at home suddenly'. But behind the scenes, the millstones of the
'*junta grande*' appointed by King Philip to discuss the diplomatic
details and a Vatican council, assembled to agree on the religious
aspects, slowly and remorselessly ground down any hopes of success.

A previous English envoy in Madrid had described the Spanish
court as 'the hospital of hope and the grave of the living'. George
called it a 'labyrinth, wherein we have been entangled these many
years'. A cartoon circulating in Rome, and noticed by an English
envoy there, showed Charles and George trapped in a cage, James
standing to one side in a 'fool's coat', Philip on the other side holding
a key.

If they were stuck in a cage, it was a gilded one. Escaping the
inferno of the summer heat, they were left free to wander the
Alcázar's cool, marble corridors and galleries, admire the pictures
and furnishings, run a finger along the bookcases in its libraries
and across the inlay decorating its cabinets. And as the weeks wafted
by, interesting lessons began to be learned about the power dynamics
of Habsburg courtly culture – that it preferred to demonstrate its

power through impression rather than expression, that it used grace to produce obedience, elegance to yield subservience, splendour to impose authority. Art was one of the chief instruments for achieving these effects, and it was everywhere.

Back home, Charles owned only twenty-four paintings, most by second-rate Flemish and British artists who had failed to make a more lucrative living in Continental courts. Philip had 2,000 by some of the great Renaissance masters – Titian, Tintoretto, Leonardo da Vinci. There were paintings from across Europe – Venice, Germany, Holland, Bohemia, France; paintings by exciting new artists such as Velázquez, who had arrived in Madrid the year before Charles; and paintings on subjects unknown to British eyes – still lives, subtle meditations on nature and death, and dream-like visions, such as Hieronymus Bosch's triptych *The Garden of Earthly Delights*. There were cabinets of curiosities stuffed with strange objects brought from Spain's New World colonies and the East Indies. There were volumes on the fabled worlds of Orinoco and El Dorado, and novels relating picaresque adventures: *Don Quixote*, *El Pícaro* and *Celestina*, the latter a romance that included an episode uncannily like Charles's scaling of the orchard wall to reach the infanta. There were vast tapestries that made English ones look threadbare, huge marble statues that dwarfed those in London. Charles was taken on a tour of the royal 'garden', where, according to a Spanish connoisseur, he was 'much delighted with the pictures of Raphael de Urbino, and Michelangelo, and with the alabaster fountain which the illustrious great Duke of Tuscany gave my lord cardinal, the Duke of Lerma: he was served with it; it is the portraiture of Cain and Abel'.

It was flabbergasting – opulence on a scale they could barely conceive, the magnificence of an imperial court. Britain had an empire now, of sorts: the privately funded colony of Virginia had begun to flourish after a precarious start, sustained by tobacco plantations (grown using seed stolen from the Spanish). Britain had a fledgling artistic culture too, though one more or less confined to the vulgarities of the playhouse. But it had no fruits or riches to compare with these.

Both George and Charles went on a spending spree, buying up paintings and objets d'art worth over 10,000 *reales* each month. They commissioned Velázquez, still finding his feet as a court artist, to sketch a likeness of Charles (since lost). They carefully studied an equestrian portrait of the Duke of Lerma, Olivares's predecessor as royal *valido*, by Peter Paul Rubens, an image that captured with such vivid intensity its subject's majestic confidence and power neither would forget it. Charles bought two Titians, *Woman in a Fur Wrap* and *Allegory of the Marquis of Vasto*, two very different subjects, but both featuring bare-breasted women delivering a powerful erotic charge rarely seen in art available in Protestant England.

When they ventured out, they saw bullfights and fiestas and toured the great palaces built by King Philip's Habsburg forebears. They spent time at the Escorial, the enormous, forbidding royal palace-cum-monastery-cum-necropolis dedicated to St Lawrence, set in the barren foothills of the snow-capped Guadarrama mountains. Its austere, rectangular layout was said to be inspired by the gridiron used in St Lawrence's martyrdom.

They arranged for five camels and an elephant to be sent home to add to James's menagerie. They attended banquets and concerts, saw a descendant of Montezuma, the Aztec emperor, presented at court, and listened to singers whose voices had 'more power to give life to all creatures sensitive and vegetative than ever Orpheus's silver-stringed lyre had'.

Here was a model of monarchy quite different to the dingy and insular sort projected by James. This showed what they could have had and, now that the negotiations teetered on the edge of collapse, what they were about to lose.

Secret Intelligencers

Wallingford House stood next to Whitehall's Tilt Yard, opposite the king's London residence, and a short walk from the Houses of Parliament. In Tudor times, it had been a small plot of wasteland used as a carpenter's yard. In the 1570s, the plot was leased by the prominent Elizabethan courtier Sir Francis Knollys, who used it to build a 'convenient house'. The building was inherited by Sir Francis's son, William, who later became Lord Wallingford, hence the name.

In 1618, family ties had implicated Lord Wallingford in efforts to undermine George's position, and Wallingford lost his job as Master of the Wards, one of the most lucrative offices of state. Exiled from court and desperate to regain favour, Wallingford had agreed to sell his home to George for a very reasonable £3,000.

George had set about making it a residence fit for a favourite, with fifty-four rooms, a long gallery, a great drawing room, a dining room, a chapel with a gallery (for a choir or musicians) and a 'White Parlour'. And, as the residence of King James's newly appointed Lord Admiral, it would eventually become known as the Admiralty.

Before leaving for Madrid, George had hired some 'secret intelligencers' – spies and reporters – to keep him informed of affairs back home and 'maintain the grandeur of his lordship', in other words, head off attempts to undermine his position. The group met 'frequently' at Wallingford House with the task of sending him 'notice of common talk or secret whispers that might concern him'.

In early May 1623 the intelligencers were busy, as the city was abuzz with news that, after the interminable negotiations, a papal 'dispensation' had been issued that would allow the infanta to marry a Protestant prince. In England, it was recognized by supporters and enemies of the Spanish match to be the document that would determine whether or not the match could go ahead – 'the furnace to make or to mar the wedding-ring'.

The dispensation had been delivered to James in a sealed box. It was accompanied by a letter from George and Charles asking him to be 'secret in the conditions' the dispensation contained, otherwise 'it will beget dispute, censures, and conclusions' which would be 'to our prejudice'. John Williams, Lord Keeper of the Privy Seal, was among those kept in the dark, and wrote to George directly, concerned that the secrecy was breeding suspicion. 'We all wonder at his majesty's reservedness,' he complained, as a result of which 'we all think, and the town speak and talk of the worst, and of very difficult conditions'. Williams was in favour of the match, but was aware of the growing controversy at home over papal interference, and was beginning to wonder if George was having second thoughts.

Speculation erupted, and was picked up by the diarist Simonds

D'Ewes. He guessed that whatever was contained in the mysterious box sent by George to James must be bad news for the Spanish negotiations, as it had 'joyed the hearts a little of drooping Protestants' while 'controlling the late insolent boastings of the popish crew'. Two days later, he was confidently providing a spurious list of the conditions the pope had apparently laid down: that James 'should renounce his style of defender of the faith; that he should declare himself an enemy of the Hollanders' – of the Dutch Protestants who were currently providing refuge for Charles's sister Elizabeth – 'that he should grant a general and full toleration of the popish religion . . .' and so on and so on: a scintillating catalogue of every Protestant's worst nightmares.

James Hay – the Earl of Carlisle and James's envoy to France – arrived in London a few days after the dispensation. He had made a brief visit to Madrid, and, according to the letter-writer John Chamberlain, was being 'very silent' about whatever he had discovered there. However, both Chamberlain and D'Ewes did learn that he had met the infanta, who had given him 'leave to kneel' before her 'above an hour', news that reversed the rumours of the match being off, and promoted, as Chamberlain put it, a frenzy of preparation among 'our great ladies' to think of how they could most graciously 'demean themselves' to their new princess.

However, with the rumours came counter-rumours of a rift opening up between George and Sir John Digby. The duke and the ambassador had become 'strangers in the business', with Digby being excluded from the negotiations. Other reports suggested that, while Digby remained close to the Spanish, George and Charles were becoming increasingly alienated. As a result, to get access to the infanta, James Hay had apparently been forced to present himself 'through the commendatory letters of the King and Queen of France' rather than as an emissary of James.

Meanwhile, there was wider unease about signs of growing Catholic toleration. At the opening of the short-lived Parliament of 1621, James had promised the strongly Protestant MPs that the Spanish match would not lead to the spread of Catholicism. The 'recusancy' laws, which penalized those who did not regularly engage in Protestant worship, would, he assured them, remain in place. However, under a secret accord with the Spanish, James was allowing

Catholics freedom to worship privately in their own homes. Somehow, news of this had leaked out, and a mood of political as well as religious unrest, even betrayal began to build.

Vigilant 'Puritans' (a derogatory term for Protestant radicals) complained of the 'Romish foxes' coming 'out of their holes'. Debate between Catholics and Protestants seemed to be officially tolerated, even encouraged. Jesuits, previously regarded as the foot soldiers of a Catholic insurgency, were preaching openly. D'Ewes recorded a 'disputation' at the home of a London lawyer between two Protestant theologians and two Jesuits, with 'our side' having to demonstrate the existence of Protestant doctrines 'before Luther', while 'their side' pointed out that their Church had been in continuous existence for 'the first 600 years after Christ'. In the Midlands, a priest who had served in Spain during Elizabethan times was seen parading around in episcopal vestments, posing as a Catholic bishop. Londoners walking across St James's Park on their way to Whitehall or the City could not fail to notice the building of a new Catholic chapel prominently positioned near St James's Palace, apparently in preparation for Charles's bride the infanta.

George's own family contributed directly to fears of a Catholic revival. His irrepressible mother Mary had openly proclaimed her conversion, and there were suspicions about George's wife Kate and her father the Earl of Rutland.

Fears swept through the country of a return to religious turmoil and sectarian violence – that the uneasy Protestant settlement established by Elizabeth and supposedly upheld by James, was eroding, and that the match would sweep it away. These fears sharpened when news broke in May that a deal on the match might have been done, and that Charles was about to return with his Spanish bride. A fleet was being readied at enormous cost to collect them. The 1,500-ton *Prince Royal* was to act as the flagship, a vessel of 'wonderful lines, strength and beauty', 'one of the fairest in the world'. A bridal cabin had been prepared for the infanta, decorated with a 'rich cloth of gold' and furnished with a bed of 'crimson velvet with a rich gold fringe and lace'. Three vice admirals – 'all three, rank papists', according to D'Ewes – had been appointed, lords Morley and Windsor together with George's father-in-law, the Earl of Rutland, who was given command of the ship. According to John

Chamberlain, everything was being 'so carried as if were to receive some goddess'.

Around the same time, two senior members of the Privy Council were dispatched to Southampton to organize the official reception for the prince and his bride (D'Ewes noting sourly that 'men of meaner rank might have served to have done this'), and James ordered that 'special honour' be shown to the Marquis of Hinojosa, sent from Madrid to join the current ambassador, Carlos Coloma. A startling figure, Hinojosa had a severely disfigured face and a 'careless' rather than stately carriage 'as if he should persuade men to imagine that all that he had was within'. On his way to London, he stopped off in Canterbury, where 'many persons' reportedly 'declared themselves papists', raising worries that he could become a figurehead for Catholic agitation. A man called Broome welcomed him by toasting the 'confusion' that was soon to be unleashed among 'all Protestants'.

William Whiteway, a Dorchester merchant, noted in his diary the busy traffic of magnates and emissaries between London and the western ports, and also heard a rumour that the fleet sent to collect Charles had mutinied, the Protestant crew having 'ducked' from the main yard Lord Morley, one of the 'rank papists' put in command.

The Wallingford House circle became alarmed at the cacophonous 'tympani' of gossip and speculation generated by all this activity, and became concerned about the impact on George's position. They wrote him a stark letter, urging him to 'set the match' between Charles and the infanta 'back by degrees'. They also warned him that he 'must look to stand by the love of the people as well as the king'. Popular opinion was becoming increasingly nervous and hostile towards the match. 'Unless the treaty for the great marriage was quashed', they concluded, it could prove fatal to his standing in the government and the country. A 'storm will fall upon your lordship', he was warned. 'Suffer no longer delays in Spain', as his continuing absence had allowed a great 'insolency' to breed among his enemies. John Williams, the Lord Keeper and a supposed ally, was identified as a particular threat, as he was close to the estranged ambassador in Madrid, Sir John Digby, and was said to be building a 'great and more powerful party in Court than you imagine', powerful enough to secure George's overthrow.

Then, on 14 June, Francis Cottington, Charles's secretary and companion since the prince's departure for Madrid, arrived in Greenwich with a letter from Charles and George which James was to burn as soon as he had read it. As he seems to have followed that instruction, its contents are unknown, but in reply, James told his 'sweet boys' that whatever they had written 'hath strucken me dead'.

A Farewell Pillar

George and Charles had been in Madrid for three months. Frustration soured into reckless bravado. Olivares, George's opposite number, was beginning to find Charles's companion boorish and untrustworthy. He was disgusted by the way George would go around Charles's apartment in the Alcázar half-dressed. He also accused the duke of trying to undermine the match and being in league with the French. George had also fallen out with the papal nuncio in Madrid, telling him that unless the Vatican proved more cooperative negotiations would only proceed with a drawn sword held over the heads of British Catholics.

There were even hints of a falling out between Charles and George as they responded differently to their predicament – George becoming angrier, Charles more frightened. But what they could agree on, was that a combination of Spanish inertia and the worsening crisis facing Charles's sister and her husband Frederick had left the negotiations in a state of diplomatic purgatory. They found themselves officially ignored while being constantly monitored. Nothing they could say or do seemed to produce a decisive response. They were, in short, trapped and could see no means of escape. This was the news they had communicated secretly to James, that had 'strucken' him so forcefully.

The king responded by telling them to accept whatever terms would secure their quick release. On 7 July, Charles duly agreed to the conditions set by the Vatican and the Spanish, including a pledge on his own and James's behalf that no laws 'employed against

Roman Catholics in England, Scotland and Ireland' would be observed and that 'perpetual toleration' would be permitted 'in private homes'.

The announcement produced a mood of euphoria in Madrid, with three days of fireworks and fiestas to celebrate the liberation of British Catholics after nearly a century of oppression.

A departure date of late August was set, and in the meantime everyone carried on with a desultory performance of nuptial expect-ation. Even in their letters to James, Charles and George wrote as though the wedding was going ahead. The reason was revealed in a short note written days before their scheduled departure. Unusually, it was penned by Charles, George lying sick with a severe fever, and was presumably conveyed to James via a messenger he did not normally use. 'You are betrayed in your bedchamber,' the prince announced starkly, as a result of which the Spanish ambassador in London, Hinojosa, had somehow got hold of all the letters they had written to him.

A few days later, George, recovering from his illness, wrote to James.

The tone is abject. He informs the king that his 'humble heart' is ready to 'consider my own defects and unworthiness and how fruitless a servant I have been'. He lists his failings and regrets: that the 'great business' of the match had achieved so little 'for yours, your son's and the whole nation's honour', that his absence from the king's company continued, and that they had been forced to give away so much to the Spanish.

On 1 September, George sent another note, his final from Madrid, written without Charles's knowledge, to reassure James of 'his perfect recovery' from his sickness, and revealing that 'my heart and very soul dance for joy' at their imminent reunion, 'from sadness to mirth, nay from hell to heaven', his thoughts being 'only bent of having my dear Dad and master's legs soon in my arms'.

They were at the Escorial, the royal palace-cum-monastery. Charles was out hunting with King Philip in the surrounding foot-hills, their final expedition. Philip had suggested a further day's delay as arrangements were not yet in place for him to escort the prince to Valsaín, the royal summer lodge just outside Segovia, for their formal farewells. Charles politely demurred. So arrangements were made for Charles and George to take their official leave later that day.

Before departing, Charles signed the documents that appointed Philip to act as proxy in the prince's forthcoming marriage to the infanta, which was to take place within ten days of the pope ratifying the deal. Philip also presented Charles with a magnificent portrait by Titian of his great-grandfather Charles V, the Holy Roman Emperor. It was a profound and generous acknowledgement not only of the prince's artistic taste, but of the Spanish king's hopes for a union. The picture beautifully captured Philip's lineage and expectations, depicting the figure who had through marriage as well as conquest helped unite the Habsburg dominions, and suggesting that, were the Stuarts to join such a bloodline, it would close a rift that had begun with the divorce of Henry VIII from Katherine of Aragon, and was now threatening to tear Europe apart.

On an outcrop of rock in the grounds of the Escorial, at a spot subsequently commemorated by a tall, undecorated '*columna del adiós*' (the pillar of farewell), Charles and George took their leave of Philip. Heading for Segovia, they stopped at the Valsaín lodge for a meal. A gun salute welcomed them into the city later that afternoon, and they were given a tour, which like most royal tours involved visits to factories as well as palaces – in this case a mint, where Charles beheld a large gold coin being made to be presented to him as a gift from the city's burghers. At the castle, there was a set of arms combining those of England and Castile, in honour of another and long-forgotten Spanish match, between King Henry III of Castile and Catherine of Lancaster, the daughter of John of Gaunt.

The formalities dispensed with, Charles sat down to write two letters, one of thanks and reassurance to Philip, the other a note to Sir John Digby at the House of the Seven Chimneys, who was to remain to clear up the mess left behind. The ambassador was commanded 'not to deliver my proxy', the letter which was needed to allow the wedding to go ahead in his absence. Those five words brought to an ignominious end all the efforts of the last decade and the past few months of adventure and angst.

On 18 September 1623, George and Charles sailed for England. It had taken a little over six months to turn a romantic escapade designed to sweep the infanta off her feet into a squalid fiasco mired in turgid diplomacy.

Fool's Coats

When George's father-in-law the Earl of Rutland was sent to Santander to pick up George and Charles, he was welcomed by Archie Armstrong. The king's fool announced he had given his new 'fool's coat' to Charles, his old one to George, and 'when I come to England, I will have fool's coats for you all'.

It was that mood of mockery and humiliation that on 5 October 1623 welcomed them home at Plymouth, following a rough voyage. Allowing themselves only a short rest, they set off for London as fast as they could on post-horses, making such haste 'that few followed them'. They became lost around Guildford, with some thirty miles to go. Coming to the village of Godalming, they stopped at a house for refreshments. Paying in Spanish gold, the 'gentle-woman' who served them, one Mrs Wyatt, guessed who Charles must be, and boasted the first kiss the prince gave since his return to home shores. As they were leaving, a poor woman who had seen him at Mrs Wyatt's home asked to kiss his hand. When he offered it, she clung on to it. Puzzled by her reaction, Charles asked her to let go, but she 'desired him first to promise he never to go again to Spain'.

The news reached London at three in the morning. A servant shook London's lord mayor awake to tell him of the prince's approach, and the mayor went personally to break the news to the king, who was staying at Theobalds. The city's sergeants dashed madly about town 'raising up the constables and other officers, who raised up every household'. By 7 a.m., despite persistent rain, bonfires were being set alight at almost every door. The young lawyer, Simonds D'Ewes, wandering around the city in amazement, counted more than three hundred fires between Whitehall and Temple Bar, the City's western entrance – a distance of a few hundred yards.

Reaching London Bridge, George and Charles found George Abbot, the Archbishop of Canterbury, waiting for them in the drizzle. Abbot had complained as far back as 1614 that the king and prince had become 'enchanted by the false, fraudulent, and siren-like songs of Spain', but restrained himself from gloating, as he welcomed the two soaked adventurers into Lambeth Palace, his home on the south bank of the Thames, opposite the Palace of Westminster. The couple then took the archbishop's barge to York House, George's riverside residence, where they had breakfast. The duke's watergate, the entrance to the house facing the river, became crowded with dignitaries, allies and enemies alike, the 'press of people' becoming 'so great that no man could get in or out'. After an absence of six months, many could not believe George and Charles were back, and wanted to see them with their own eyes, having been 'deceived so often' by false reports.

Elsewhere in the kingdom, the scepticism was maintained – at least that was the explanation for the absence of celebrations outside the capital. But in London, the bonfires 'seemed to turn the City into one flame'. Carts carrying firewood had their loads tipped onto the street and set alight, and sometimes the carts were thrown onto the flames too. Shops were shut, a holiday was declared, bells were rung and there was 'mirth and jollity', particularly among the ten or so condemned prisoners due to be executed that morning who 'were all saved and set free'. There were street parties, 'with all manner of provisions, setting out whole hogsheads of wine and butts of sack'. The tower of St Paul's Cathedral was festooned with torches, while inside the xenophobic words of Psalm 114 became 'a new anthem', celebrating 'when Israel came out of Egypt, and the house of Jacob from among the barbarous people'.

'I have not heard of more demonstrations of public joy than were here and every where from the highest to the lowest,' noted John Chamberlain. 'The only thing to be lamented,' the young, earnestly puritanical D'Ewes added, 'was the great excess and drunkenness of this day, the two usual faults of Englishmen upon any good hap.'

As desperate ambassadors and dignitaries continued to shoulder their way into York House, George and Charles left by carriage, heading for Royston in Hertfordshire, where James was nursing his gout. As they drove along the Strand, crowds gathered to cheer them, George enjoying the moment, bareheaded and bowing to them, while the more reserved Charles kept his hat on, but waved and smiled.

The prince was impatient, even desperate, to see his father, and at Charing Cross told the driver not to go via the City, which had become choked by the fires, but head off up St Martin's Lane, at that time little more than a muddy lane heading north. Whipped on by the coachman, they hurtled through puddles, and, as they approached a flooded stretch of road, a shout was heard: 'for God's sake to beware and stay a little'. It was a local miller's boy, who warned the coachman he was entering 'a dangerous deep place'. The coachman slowed, and the boy 'guided them safely through' – another providential deliverance.

James, meanwhile, raced south from Royston to meet them at Theobalds. He was waiting for them as they came up the drive. As their coach pulled up at the bottom of the steps, the king flew down to them, and they ran up to him, the three meeting in the middle 'where the Prince and the Duke being on their knees, the King fell on their necks and they all wept'. There was 'ecstasy of joy on the Prince's return, which has cured the King', wrote Sir Edward Conway, the king's secretary. 'The embraces and familiarities between him, the Prince, and Buckingham, are just the same as though they had not been an hour absent.'

The three retired to the king's bedchamber. Attempts to overhear the discussion proved inconclusive. 'They that attended at the door sometime heard a still voice, and then a loud; sometime they laughed, and sometime they chafed, and noted such variety as they could not guess what the close might prove.' The three emerged later for supper, the king appearing to 'take all well'. He announced that 'he liked not to marry his son with a portion of his daughter's tears', meaning that he was not prepared to submit Charles to a dishonourable match for Elizabeth's sake.

Across the country, confusion reigned. The day after the reunion, the Privy Council announced that 'the marriage goes on just as before the Prince went to Spain; it is to be consummated by proxy before Christmas, and the Infanta to come in March'. The king also dispatched a letter to Digby. The perplexed English ambassador had been left in Madrid with a proxy that Charles had ordered him to rescind, and which the council in England was now declaring would be 'consummated' by Christmas. James tried to clarify, writing in terms that suggested the marriage would go ahead as planned, but only after Digby had secured King Philip's 'clear' agreement to ensuring the 'restitution of the Palatinate and electoral dignity of our son-in-law' – in other words that Charles's sister Elizabeth and her husband Frederick be allowed to return to his ancestral lands in Germany. This requirement, the king airily added, had always been 'understood and expected' as a condition of the marriage, and implied it was entirely achievable.

Meanwhile, the news-mongers were getting mixed signals from government officials and nothing from the royal household. Some assumed the match negotiations were finished. One diarist had heard that the infanta had decided to enter a monastery rather than marry the prince. Others assumed that the fact that the prince and duke had returned empty-handed simply meant that the marriage was delayed.

Hinojosa and Coloma made their way towards Royston in the hope of congratulating the prince on his homecoming, but in an apparent snub found themselves diverted to a village ten miles short of their destination, where they were to await further instructions in a local inn.

'Matters are still kept so secret that we know not what to judge of the match,' complained the well-placed Chamberlain. The week following Charles and George's return, and after a prolonged absence due to illness, James had gone to London and held secret meetings with the Spanish, and soon after it was noted that orders were being issued for various Jesuits held on sedition charges to be freed.

George seemed to be as powerful as ever, his 'carriage in all the business' being 'much applauded and commended' as 'brave and resolute'. But his falling out with his Spanish counterpart, Olivares, was also widely reported. Would this change the king's attitude to him or the Spanish? Perhaps it was nothing more than posturing; the 'Northern and Southern favourites' – George and Olivares – were bound to 'look proudly one upon another, when they met in the same cockpit'.

Bedraggled members of the entourage who had sailed with the prince from Santander did not reach the capital until three days after the prince, and were barely noticed by the revellers who had welcomed George and Charles. Among them was another Spanish ambassador, Diego Hurtado de Mendoza, who was to join Hinojosa and Coloma in the increasingly cramped embassy in Holborn. He was followed a month later by a fourth member of staff. Though he came from Brussels, Diego de Mexía was 'another Spaniard', Chamberlain caustically noted; 'it seems they mean to hold a council table here'.

A deadly incident heightened the mood of confusion and foreboding. On the evening of Sunday 26 October, three weeks after the prince's return, 300 worshippers gathered in the upper storey of a large garret adjoining the French embassy in Blackfriars to attend an evening service given by a Jesuit priest. During the sermon, the floor gave way, collapsing through the room beneath into the building's basement, killing the preacher, another priest and ninety of the congregation. Within days, the streets were littered with ballads and pamphlets reporting what came to be known as the 'Fatal Vesper'.

Puritan writers were eager to seize upon the incident as an apt and providential demonstration of the weakness of the theological foundations of Catholicism. By way of evidence, some even pointed out that there had been no fatalities in similar incidents of floors collapsing in Protestant churches. It was also noted that, by the New Style 'Romish calendar', which had been in use on the Continent since 1582, 26 October was 5 November – the anniversary of the infamous Gunpowder Plot of 1605, when Catholic insurgents had tried to blow up the Houses of Parliament.

There was a twist to the story that unsettled the critics' religious complacency. It turned out that a number of the casualties of the Fatal Vesper had been Protestants, drawn by the mood of religious toleration. This aspect of the incident involved confronting the most sensitive matters of official policy, matters that had become ever more delicate since the prince's return. A pamphlet containing a lurid account of the Blackfriars incident was rushed out the week after it took place, but was 'called in' – that is, censored – for touching on such delicate matters. Another pamphlet, titled *Something Written by occasion of that fatal and memorable accident in Blackfriars*, managed to escape official attention. It openly declared the 'memorable accident' to be the result of the king's 'lenitive courses' towards

Catholics. It noted how, as a result, 'the papists grew of late so audaciously bold, that they durst even boast again of the king's pardon and grace, and tell us to our faces, we are heretics, and for nothing but the fire, and to be consumed to cinders'.

The king took little interest in these matters, instead revelling at having George and Charles back with him. '"Welcome home" is still the only business at Court,' a councillor noted impatiently. The world had to wait as the king clutched possessively to his two sweet boys.

As the weeks passed, it became clear that all was not well. Tensions began to build over James's persistence with the marriage. Despite all the humiliations the Spanish had inflicted on his son, James would not countenance any kind of retaliation. He clung tightly to the idea that Spain would help restore the Palatinate. He would not listen to his two boys' insistence that such hopes were futile. They had spoken to the Spanish king, they had negotiated with Olivares, they knew that Spain would never threaten war with the Holy Roman Empire over the Palatinate; they had heard from the *valido*'s own lips that it was a 'maxim of state that the king of Spain must never fight against the Emperor'.

The king made a show of welcoming the Spanish ambassadors who had arrived since Charles's return. A somewhat chaotic reception was laid on for them at Whitehall, where they were received by James in his privy chamber. After a brief meeting, he escorted them 'by the way of the Stone-gallery' to meet Charles. They presented the prince with a letter from King Philip, apparently urging the prince to proceed with the match for the sake of peace and religious toleration as well as to requite the passionate love he had expressed for the infanta. Charles received it coolly, with a 'Spanish gravity' that contrasted with his enthusiastic wooing of the infanta in Madrid, and with 'no more capping nor courtesy than must needs'.

These overtures were followed up, at James's insistence, with a great feast for the ambassadors, hosted by George at York House. Paid for by £300 from the royal exchequer, it was a splendid affair. A Spanish account illustrated by an engraving showed James and Charles seated at one end of a table beneath a canopy bearing the royal coat of arms, with the Spanish ambassadors either side of them, and courtiers crowded all around. The meal began with an antipasto of cold meats followed by twelve pheasants piled in a dish and no fewer than 480 partridges and 'as many quails', and concluded with a masque and a selection of sweetmeats.

All was not as it seemed, however. John Chamberlain observed that George had arranged the event 'rather *pro forma* than *ex animo*' – out of duty rather than conviction. He did not attend the feast in person, though he may have appeared in the masque, which he had commissioned from his loyal servant John Maynard. The text does not survive, but the theme was Charles's homecoming, his arrival back in England from Madrid represented as a deliverance in a way that seemed calculated to insult the Spanish guests of honour.

It was also noted around this time how those who had been among Charles's entourage during the Madrid escapade had begun to 'speak liberally' of their 'course usage and entertainment' in Spain, where they had found nothing but 'penury and proud beggary, besides all other discourtesy'.

In November, James's loyal servant Thomas Erskine revealed to his kinsman the Earl of Mar the toll the turmoil had taken on the king's health: 'both of his gout and I think, as many other so, of his mind likewise. I can write no more what will be the conclusion of the match. You can not imagine how the world is possessed of the vexation that his majesty has in his mind. It may come that young folks shall have their world, I know not if that will be first for your lordship and me.'

ACT III

The Greatest Villain in the World

The Honey and the Sting

The mission to Madrid had been a disaster. George had been away from court for months, opening a space at James's side for rivals to fill. He had been frolicking in the Spanish sunshine while England had endured one of the worst summers in years. And he had returned having accomplished nothing, expecting 'malice and revenge', leaving the prince humiliated and George's allies alienated.

Yet his reception had been rapturous. He was 'much applauded and commended' for his actions in Madrid, and the decision to come back empty-handed was regarded as 'brave and resolute'. Even Thomas Erskine, who latterly had admitted to having 'little cause to like well of Buckingham's love and affection to myself', felt he could not but 'wish him well and love him the better of his behaviour and carriage at this time', which the earl perversely thought had brought honour rather than opprobrium to Charles and the kingdom.

As George leafed through the letters of support pouring into York House, he noticed one from his old mentor Francis Bacon. Since plummeting from power in 1621, Bacon had been living in exile, suffering from poor health and depression, riding 'at anchor all your Grace's absence', as he put it to George, and as a result his 'cables are now quite worn'. 'My Lord, do some good work upon me,' he implored, 'that I may end my days in comfort, which nevertheless cannot be complete except you put me in some way to do your noble self service.'

Times were 'stirring', he warned George in another letter, so full of 'dissimulation, falsehood, baseness and envy in the world, and so many idle clocks going in men's heads'. It made him grieve that he could not be at George's elbow, 'that I might give you some of the fruits of the careful advice, modest liberty, and true information of a friend that loveth your Lordship as I do'.

George was responsive. Although he had maintained an image of resolve and confidence since returning to England, Spain had left a bewildering and contradictory set of impressions: envy at the confidence and opulence of Philip's court; love of the glorious beauty, austere elegance and teasing reserve of Spanish arts, architecture and etiquette – the Alcázar, the Escorial, the glimpses of the infanta on the Paseo del Prado; disgust at the poverty and ugliness of peasant life; contempt for and alarm at the malicious workings of the Catholic authorities; amazement at their influence over the most powerful monarch in Europe; fascination at coming up against his Spanish equal and opposite, Philip's formidable *valido*, Olivares; the feeling of fear and excitement at engaging in the seductive charm, rampant bullying, magical thinking and demonic deception that make up the process of negotiation – George a witch, Olivares the devil.

George sent off a quick if typically convoluted reply to Bacon, mixing up the original maritime metaphor so that he could allude to the 'country fruits' of advice that had first cemented their relationship: 'The assurance of your love makes me easily believe your joy at my return,' he wrote, 'and if I may be so happy, as by the credit of my place to supply the decay of your cables, I shall account it one of the special fruits thereof.'

It was not long before Bacon was at George's door, clutching a sheaf of notes. The former Lord Chancellor cut a pathetic figure, like a lost dog returning to his master, trembling with expectation, weak with illness and neglect. Exile had been like living in darkness, he said. Just six years ago, when the king and George had been in Scotland, James had left Bacon the keys of the kingdom. He had been living in the very home that George now occupied, York House, which Bacon had enlarged and embellished as a concrete symbol of his status. Now he was forced to live in his cramped chambers in Gray's Inn, the lawyers' enclave just a short walk away, in a state 'I cannot call health but rather sickness, and more dangerous than felt.'

He had not given up, though. From the darkness had emerged a succession of books – masterpieces, some of them, on politics, religion and most notably natural philosophy, setting out the concep-tual foundations of modern science. George had been bombarded with them; one even made its way to Madrid. He had received them with polite gratitude and bafflement, but nothing much had resulted. Nevertheless, while he had gently rebuffed Bacon's pleas for restitution, hopes had been kept alive. The previous year, for example, George had arranged for him to be allowed once more within 'the verge', the twelve-mile zone around the court which those who had lost the king's favour were forbidden to enter. Now he was back at York House, albeit as guest rather than host.

Reflecting the sensitivities surrounding the subject matter, and the importance he attached to the advice he was seeking, George insisted their meeting – Bacon grandiosely called it a 'conference' – be kept secret. The favourite needed to be able to discuss candidly his situation, his confused feelings, his perilous position, both reliant on the king, but now at odds with him. His response to the Madrid escapade was anger towards the Spanish, but it was unclear perhaps even to George whether such feelings were the result of personal pique or political conviction. To his peers, he was still the king's catamite. His opinions were ignored, except by those who out of necessity of employment or rank had to take notice of them. His ambitions were seen as self-serving and resented by those who already possessed the titles and estates he had sought. But there was more to him than that, and he needed to show it. He had once expressed doubts – 'disgusts', as they were described – concerning the Spanish match in the earliest days of the negotiations, but had gone along with it for the sake of the king, and been caught up in the romance. Now the disgusts were revived. The Madrid escapade had demonstrated that the match would be a disaster, for Charles, for the kingdom and for Europe.

Bacon seemed to recognize all this. He marvelled at the duke's position, that he had come home 'with so fair a reputation'. But he warned it would 'vanish like a dream' unless he 'do some remark-able act to fix it and bind it in'. He quoted a Spanish proverb: 'He that tieth not a knot upon his threads looses his stitch.'

What remarkable act, then, would tie the knot, fix and bind his reputation as a leading political as well as courtly figure, a man of national consequence rather than just a royal plaything? 'I that live in darkness cannot propound,' Bacon claimed, but it boiled down to a decision over the match: either he should force it through, or end it. Both options were dangerous. One meant alienating the people, the other undermining the king, and if he did not take the 'king's way' he might lose his own way.

Bacon also warned him about his position in a court that was becoming increasingly factious. Three groups were 'considerable in this state': 'papists' who hated George; Protestants, including Puritans, whose 'love' was 'yet but green' – unripe, in other words; and 'particular great persons' – he was probably thinking of the likes of the earls of Arundel and Pembroke – 'which are most of them reconciled enemies or discontented friends', so, not to be trusted. There was also 'a great many that will magnify you and make use of you for the breaking of the match or putting the realm into a war', but who as soon as the business was done, or if it failed, would 'return to their old bias'.

So what to do?

One suggestion was to persuade the king to call a Parliament. Bacon had been a victim of the 1621 session, the impeachment by his peers in the House of Lords leading to his downfall. So he was naturally cautious. He held it 'fit' to summon one, 'when there have passed some more visible demonstrations of your power with the King, and your constancy in the way you are in: before, not'. In other words, he should not openly call for a new Parliament until he could show that he was able to align the king's will to Parliament's, because it would be much more difficult to achieve the reverse.

He ended his advice with one other matter, 'tender to be spoken of': George's relationship with Charles. While he should keep close to the prince, he should be sure it would not result in the king finding himself 'the more solitary'.

Overall, George should remain aloof from the arguments and alliances that would flare up as tensions intensified. 'It is good to carry yourself fair,' Bacon said. Do not 'trust too far nor apply too much but keep a good distance'. George should play his own game, 'showing yourself to have, as the bee hath, both of the honey and of the sting'.

The English Junta

George reacted to Bacon's carefully drafted advice with typical brashness, adopting some of his ideas while almost carelessly discarding others. He made an attempt to keep the king happy by taking part in the busy exchange of letters with Philip of Spain which James insisted on maintaining. But he was realistic and blunt enough to tell the king that all efforts at appeasing the Spanish were probably futile, and that his reputation was being 'taken away by the Spaniards'. He also publicly declared his support for the Hispanophobes, provocatively telling a 'Flemish gentleman' accompanying an envoy of the Spanish Netherlands that he marvelled 'how such worthy gentlemen could tolerate the Spanish yoke'.

The prince joined in, telling his father that he felt he could no longer trust the Spanish. 'Do you want me to go to war, in my twilight years, and force me to break with Spain?' a distraught James asked, tears streaming down his cheeks.

Meanwhile, George set about putting together a political coalition in support of an anti-Spanish policy. It was hard work. In December 1623, Bacon noted, perhaps with a touch of told-you-so, that 'you march bravely, but methinks you do not draw up your troops'.

George began by turning his charms on William Herbert, the Earl of Pembroke and current Lord Chamberlain. Herbert was a popular parliamentary figure and prominent opponent of a Spanish match. However, the Baynard's Castle conspirator who had introduced George to court back in 1615 had become resentful of his protégé's rise through the ranks. Now he found himself exposed to the full force of George's charm. At first he resisted, but with Charles's encouragement, he eventually became 'reconciled'.

George adopted a similar approach with other leading members of the anti-Spanish clique. Henry Wriothesley, the Earl of Southampton, Shakespeare's patron, had been exiled following a heated row with George in the House of Lords which nearly came to blows. Wriothesley had subsequently been arrested on charges of 'mischievous intrigues with members of the Commons'. George now welcomed him back into favour, and the grateful earl became a prominent champion of the prince and the favourite's policies. Henry de Vere, the Earl of Oxford, a veteran soldier who had fought for James's son-in-law to save the Palatinate, had languished in the Tower for twenty months following an imbroglio involving one of George's relatives; his release was now secured, and George backed his marriage to the highly eligible Lady Diana Cecil, from a family with close ties to the Villiers clan. Oxford wrote in fulsome gratitude to George, accepting that he was now bound to the favourite 'in a perpetual acknowledgement'. George also persuaded the king to receive William Fiennes, Lord Saye, after he had fallen out of favour for protesting against the king's use of extra-parliamentary levies to raise money to support his daughter Elizabeth in the Hague.

Where the honey had been applied to these magnates, a little more of the sting was required with others. John Williams, the Lord Keeper, was like so many enemies a former ally – a 'discontented friend', as Bacon put it. An ambitious, restless, bumptious figure, he was liked by James for his wit and erudition, and had strong parliamentary connections. However, he was strongly pro-Spanish, and blamed George for the failure of the match.

George responded by staging an encounter with Williams in the Shield Gallery at Whitehall, at which he showed the Lord Keeper to be 'dead in his affections'. As well as the favourite's displeasure, rumours began to circulate that Williams might be asked to surrender the great seal of state, making him a lord keeper with nothing to keep. In face of the unrelenting pressure Williams began to yield, and, by early February 1624, George was able to tell his chaplain that a reconciliation had been achieved.

James would have been aware of these manoeuvres, and had suspicions about their purpose, but George seemed oblivious of the dangers. The man he had once described as 'my maker, my friend, my father, my all' became almost peripheral to his plans, as he focused his attention on Charles. The friendship of James's two 'sweet boys', forged in the heat of the Madrid negotiations, had now become stronger than ever: George helping to give Charles a princely bearing and assertiveness that surprised and impressed the court, Charles giving George's ideas and interventions a legitimacy that even the king was loath to challenge.

'They are very closely united', the Venetian ambassador noted, fearing that these 'two young men' might 'come off badly in opposing the obstinate will of a very crafty King and the powerful arts of the most sagacious Spaniards'.

A select group of privy councillors, identified with dark irony by the Spanish term 'junta', began to form around the pair. They met regularly and in secret, discussing ways of dealing with both the match and the Palatinate crisis. As packets of diplomatic correspondence passed between London and Madrid, continuing what many now saw as a delusional negotiation, Charles and George began to push for the recall of Parliament. They argued that the popularity that they had attracted since their return from Madrid would encourage the House of Commons to put the Spanish under serious pressure, perhaps enough to get concessions on the Palatinate, and, if that failed, a vote for the tax rises needed to support its military recovery.

The junta convened on several occasions in late November and early December to thrash out the issues, and by mid-December they had managed to secure a majority in favour. George then went to James, who was still languishing in the country, complaining of feeling ill and old. The favourite persuaded him to come to Whitehall. He arrived 'against his will', and during a series of meetings held in complete secrecy, Charles, George and their supporters set about persuading him of the benefits of a new Parliament, presumably on the grounds that it might wring further concessions from the Spanish, which in turn might revive efforts to conclude the match. Somehow, eventually, they got him to relent, and he returned to the country.

While he remained away, Charles summoned another meeting of the junta, to call for a vote on whether to continue with negotiations over the match. During a first round, five councillors came out in favour of continuing with the Spanish. Four abstained. Three voted against, including Charles – under the influence of George, rivals claimed, as he 'engrosses the Prince's favour so far as to exclude all others'. Charles forced another vote, having managed to swing some of the abstaining 'neuters' to his side, but was shocked to find that William Herbert, now supposedly an ally, refused to shift from the fence, 'alleging that if the Spaniard performed the conditions agreed on, he saw not how the King in honour could fall from the conclusion'.

'What passed is not known,' reported the usually well-informed John Chamberlain. The 'variety and uncertainty of reports and surmises' had left him clueless.

It was noted, however, how much the French were now in favour. Perhaps the sister of the French king Louis XIII, Henrietta Maria, though just fourteen years old, and also a Catholic, offered more promising prospects as a marriage partner for Charles. An ambassador arrived from Paris, making his entry into London 'very magnificently with all his retinue in good order and with store of torchlight which gave the more lustre to all his long show and to his own bravery, indeed very rich and gallant'. He had brought gifts of horses, dogs and hawks from the French king, which had raised an ailing James from his gouty pain and lethargy. The hawks were said to 'fly at anything' – kites, crows, magpies, whatever came in their way – and the king was eager to try them out.

The growing rift between the king and his sweet boys, his growing efforts to avoid confrontation or decision, his desire to stay in the country and enjoy his French hawks and his English hounds, emphasized what Bacon had feared: the king's isolation. James felt too weak to stand up to either the Spanish or his son and favourite. He was handing out wild concessions to both, desperate to maintain their approval, but instead earning their indifference.

Rather than opening up a dangerous gap between the favourite and the king, these developments had the unexpected effect of revealing to James how badly he needed his George. In late December, he poured intense, pathetic feelings into a letter addressed to his 'only sweet and dear child', a salutation recalling their romantic correspondence during the early years of their relationship.

In an extraordinary declaration of deep and sincere feeling, the widower king fantasized about how the coming festivities might mark a new start in their relationship, how he and his Steenie 'may make at this Christmas a new marriage, ever to be kept hereafter'.

'For God so love me as I desire only to live in this world for your sake, and that I had rather live banished in any part of the earth with you than live a sorrowful widow's life without you,' the king wrote, in his jittery hand. 'And so God bless you, my sweet child and wife, and grant that ye may ever be a comfort to your dear dad and husband.'

A Secret Matter

Thursday, 12 February 1624, had been appointed the day of the official opening of the new Parliament, but at the last minute it was postponed by royal command until after the weekend. A heavy snowfall and freezing temperatures were blamed, though no one was sure if this was the real reason. The Venetian ambassador wondered if it was a precautionary measure, because of security fears.

Despite the conditions, Ludovick Stuart, Duke of Lennox and Richmond, the Lord High Steward of James's household, had turned up at 8 a.m. at New Palace Yard, the entrance to Parliament, to find it packed with more than two hundred shivering MPs who had learned of the postponement too late. Stuart was the king's cousin and son of Esmé Stuart, the first royal favourite, and one of the few survivors of the Scottish retinue that had accompanied James to England in 1603. He had remained a loyal and constant presence in the royal household, and now as High Steward was in charge of the parliamentary ceremonials. Since so many MPs were already there, he thought he would set up a table in the outer room of the Commons' chamber, and start to swear in the members, reaching more than a hundred before realizing the rest would freeze, so deputing sixteen volunteers to speed things up.

It was to be Ludovick's last official engagement. Four days later, the day of Parliament's postponed opening, as James was putting on his robes of state and crowds gathered in Whitehall for the royal procession to the Palace of Westminster, news broke that Ludovick had died unexpectedly that morning of a fit of apoplexy. James was grief-stricken, and postponed Parliament once again, delaying it to the following week.

On 19 February, the ceremonies finally went ahead, the king setting off for Westminster in a chariot lined with purple velvet, drawn by six horses, Charles following on horseback. Members of the Commons awaited the king's arrival in the Painted Chamber.

Lionel Cranfield, the Lord Treasurer, was making some welcoming remarks when a large section of plaster fell from the ceiling. Memories of the Gunpowder Plot to blow up James's first Parliament were still fresh enough to prompt cries of 'Treason!' and 'Traitors!', sending members scrambling for the door, spreading such confusion that cloaks, hats and even weapons were abandoned.

By the time the king arrived, order had been restored, and the MPs were summoned to the bar of the House of Lords' chamber to hear his opening speech.

Looking tired and ill, James delivered a rambling address, full of laboured similes and convoluted language. St Paul had said Christ was the spouse of his Church and she his wife, said the ageing widower. Similarly, Parliament was James's wife, and the people the Commons represented were his children. It is the part of a good husband, he continued, to procure and maintain the love of his wife, which is done by two means: by continual cherishing of her, and communicating the secrets of his labours so he can have her best advice about what is to be done upon extraordinary occasions. And here was such an extraordinary occasion, 'which is that of which you have often heard, the match of my son'. He had spent 'much time with great cost' in the negotiation of a treaty with Spain, he superfluously announced, for the 'advancement of my state and children, and procuring the general peace of Christendom'. The treaty having been agreed in its generalities, he had allowed Charles to go to Madrid with George to deal with the particularities. But when they got there, they found the treaty so 'raw, as if it had almost never been treated of', and this had given the Spanish an 'easy way to evade' an agreement.

This was the reason Charles and the duke had returned from Madrid empty-handed, and why, before proceeding with further negotiations, he wanted to seek Parliament's 'assistance to advise me what is best and fittest for me to do for the good of the commonwealth and the advancement of religion, and the good of me, my son and grandchildren of the Palatinate, and of our estates'.

After years of James treating Parliament as a tiresome constitutional formality, the MPs were amazed and flattered to be asked their opinion – on anything, let alone 'a secret matter', as James called it, 'of as great importance as can be to my state and the estate of my children'. They also interpreted James's remarks about the Spanish to be evidence that, for the first time since he had signed the treaty of 1604 ending hostilities, he was in a mood to break off relations. The king had openly acknowledged Spanish 'deceit', according to the MP John Pym. James had 'showed his dislike of the Spaniard', Simonds D'Ewes reported. Chamberlain thought he had confessed to being 'deluded in the treaty of the match', and on that basis was referring the matter 'wholly' to Parliament.

But James had not been quite as emphatic as those opinions suggested. He had also made it quite clear – in fact, it was one of very few areas of the speech expressed with clarity – that he did not see himself as 'bound' or in 'any way engaged' by the advice Parliament chose to offer, but remained 'free to follow' whatever he considered to be 'best advised'. He also declared that 'very fair and full promises to have satisfaction in my demands' had been received from the Spanish, suggesting that he was far from ready to give up on them.

Nevertheless, Parliament's advice had been sought, and so the details would be forthcoming in helping it reach an informed opinion. James did not have the time to brief the lords and honourable members himself, but referred them to his son and his favourite, 'who shall relate to you all the particulars'.

The Banqueting House

George stood at one end of the great hall, next to a table. The Secretary of State, George Calvert, was at his side, nursing a portfolio of documents. Charles was sitting next to him, and George leaned casually, or perhaps protectively, on the back of his chair. They watched the crowds gather in the opulence of the new Banqueting House, London's first Baroque building, a gleaming edifice the shape of a cut emerald, set among the dingy medieval structures of the old Palace of Whitehall.

It was three in the afternoon on 24 February 1624. Officers of state and senior earls sat next to the prince at the table, and on either side the bishops, judges and more junior barons were crammed onto benches. The MPs were packed six deep onto scaffolds that lined the walls. There was such a crush, some members of the Privy Council had been told there would be no room for them. James Hamilton, who had been hastily appointed Lord High Steward following the death of Ludovick Stuart, was standing at the door, checking the guest list.

Francis Bacon had compared ambition to choler – the humour that burns in the stomach and stings the throat, but which also 'maketh men active, earnest, full of alacrity, and stirring'. This was the humour that had driven George from his humble origins to become the king's most trusted servant and beloved companion. But in Madrid it had become blocked, and when ambition is blocked, it sours, becoming 'malign and venomous'.

Perhaps James had recognized this. Perhaps this was why he had endured his beloved Steenie turning his attentions away from him, even against him. Because, as Bacon warned, those who are thwarted in their ambitions become 'secretly discontent, and look upon men and matters with an evil eye, and are best pleased when things go backwards', whereas those who find 'the way open for their rising, and still get forward' are 'rather busy than dangerous'. The ambition still burned strongly in the favourite, surged through every duct of his body. It had achieved the seduction of the king and his heir, but had needed a new outlet, which had now been found: the seduction of Parliament.

As George watched the MPs jostling for space, he could feel confident that they would behave themselves. Several supportive members prominent in earlier Parliaments had been re-elected, the likes of Sir Edwin Sandys, a friend of the Earl of Southampton, and Sir John Eliot, a Cornish magistrate whom George had made Vice Admiral of Devon. Secretaries Calvert and Conway, who were MPs as well as government officials, could be relied upon to keep George and other members of the king's inner circle informed of developments in the lobby. Sir Edward Coke, who had stirred up so much trouble in 1621, was there, but despite all the fuss over the patents, he had actually helped insulate George from being directly implicated. He also owed George £2,000, which should help keep him in line.

The duke struck a characteristically confident pose, light catching the glinting jewels and silken sheen of his lordly robes. Many were prepared to congratulate him for bringing their prince safely back from Spain, and waited in excited anticipation for what he and the prince had to tell them about their adventure. But others beheld him with a 'sour eye'. They blamed him not just for the Madrid fiasco, but for contributing to the collapse of the last Parliament in 1621. It seemed a measure of the man's arrogance that, having been a prime mover in recent disasters, he should now be given the chance to account for them.

George's tactic in the face of hostility was a disarming humility. He began by apologizing in advance for failing to express himself as well as might be expected, as he had never spoken to so grave and learned an assembly before. He then turned to Secretary Calvert and asked him to read out a letter. It was from the king to Digby, England's ambassador in Spain, sent a few months before their departure to Madrid, which set out the diplomatic quandary they faced over the marriage treaty.

The MPs were entranced. This was secret diplomatic correspondence being shared with a body denied access to the most anodyne domestic government papers. In 1621 they had been castigated for even daring to discuss the Spanish match. But that was just a beginning. George, his points bolstered by the occasional intervention from Charles, went on to tell them a personal tale of the slights and deceptions that the Spanish had inflicted upon the two of them in Madrid. An enthralling story unfolded of his clandestine meetings in coaches and gardens, of efforts by panels of divines to convert Charles, of traps laid out to humiliate them both. Snatches of their most private conversations were shared: 'We must be friends and part all the world between us,' Olivares had said – a great offer by them that would 'swallow all', George caustically noted. 'Let us make a match presently and not call for the assistance of the Pope,' the king's duplicitous *valido* had apparently whispered into the prince's ear. Convert to Catholicism and he could consummate his marriage in days. Charles had protested – he would never convert! Then Olivares had accepted that a dispensation must be sought from the pope. George saw the letter that Olivares had drafted to the Vatican, which was 'cold and slack'. He had asked to add a postscript, putting the English point of view, but was refused.

George told the MPs about the constant prevarications, of the efforts by the Spanish to clog the treaty with new conditions, of the growing realization that they were trying to deny the match by delaying it. The MPs were taken into the streets of Madrid, where Charles was allowed only 'a sight of his mistress', this beautiful young princess, dazzling and delectable in the hot Spanish sunshine. But then the Spanish snatched her away! For four or five days Charles was not allowed to see the woman he had travelled a thousand miles to woo. Deal plainly, George had told Olivares: he wanted to know if it was true that the prince would not be allowed to see his bride until the dispensation came. Olivares had confessed as much, saying that the infanta had already been 'prejudiced in her honour' by allowing herself to be seen in the street.

At last, a visit with her had been allowed, but one stifled by formalities, with Charles unable to speak freely to her, the Spanish arguing that they did not know whether to treat him as a suitor or a visitor.

George then took his audience through the final, disastrous stages of the negotiations. Repeatedly, Charles and George had asked about the Palatinate, the ancestral lands of Charles's brother-in-law Frederick, seized by Spain's own allies; but the Spanish refused to address the matter. George also threw suspicion on Ambassador Digby, who just a few weeks before Parliament had assembled had been recalled from Madrid and was now under house arrest in his London home. The evidence now pointed to him having made reckless promises to the Spanish king in order to keep hopes of the match alive.

MPs, for so many years shunned by James's government, could barely believe their ears. Things that 'never came hitherto to any men's knowledge' had been publicly and generously shared, one of them noted.

The reception George received for these revelations was rapturous. In the space of an afternoon, he had transformed himself from a spoilt minion to 'Preserver of the Nation', from a creature of the royal bedchamber to the 'Darling of the Multitude', from rival to saviour of the people's beloved prince.

Transcripts of the duke's 'Relation' quickly began to circulate

London and beyond, and within days the printing presses around St Paul's were churning out copies of his vivid account of the 'Spanish Labyrinth' for popular consumption, widening his rehabilitation. The duke had become a British saint, 'St George on Horseback – let the Dragon take heed, that stood in his way'. He was lauded as a 'noble, wise, and a generous prince' whose status and wealth were just reward for his 'faithful service' in protecting Charles in Madrid. He was a champion of ordinary people who enjoyed their 'general love' as well as the 'affection and heart of the King and Prince'. A man once treated with political suspicion was now unable to 'go or ride or stand in his gates, for press of people to behold him'.

Even the libellers, who had until now relentlessly lampooned him in their bawdy satires, came out in support, one poem addressed to James celebrating George for having:

> . . . done more
> Than twenty of thy favourites before
> Give him but force his own head to maintain
> And like brave Scipio he will sack proud Spain.

The appreciative and patriotic mood extended into the House of Commons, where the MPs began to debate with the utmost gravity the king's request for advice on his foreign policy. One member wrote of the excitement they felt in discussing 'a cause of the greatest weight that ever he knew within these walls'. Another urged the House not to be 'slow to apply a remedy' to the corruption and duplicity the duke had identified. 'Let our principal care now be *salus republicae*' – the welfare of the state. 'If we go on, we shall be caught in a net, the poorest and basest way of being destroyed.' They should advise the king, 'humbly', to break off his treaties with the Spanish, to do so speedily, and to commit 'really and roundly' to assisting Protestant allies on the Continent 'by a diversive war'. The religious tone began to intensify. One MP, alluding to an obscure section of the Book of Numbers, likened Parliament to Mount Pisgah, where Balaam said he could not cure the people God had blessed. The prince's return was 'like Noah's dove that brought news of the floods abated'.

Sir John Eliot, seen as an ally of the duke, got up to speak. Eyes might be expected to roll. His previous intervention following George's presentation of the 'Spanish Labyrinth' had been typically bombastic, an appeal to assert ancient parliamentary privileges that seemed designed more to draw attention to himself and to reignite the battles of James's previous Parliaments than to advance proceedings.

This time he excelled himself. It was the time to do rather than speak, he pronounced. There must be a quick resolution to break off all treaties. 'War only will secure and repair us.'

Countless Difficulties

While Parliament wallowed in its new-found sense of importance, the government, now apparently firmly in the hands of Charles and George, began to reshape James's foreign policy.

The vigilant Venetian ambassador noticed that Henry Rich, one of George's allies, had turned up in Paris. 'I cannot find that he has any orders except to listen,' he reported to his masters in Venice, and what he had heard was that the powerful dowager queen Marie de' Medici was apparently 'well disposed' to the idea of Charles marrying her daughter, Henrietta Maria. Though substituting one Catholic princess with another presented 'countless difficulties', France was in ferocious competition with Spain for European dominance, and perhaps that leverage would make the Bourbon king's diminutive fourteen-year-old sister a potent weapon.

As the diplomatic machinations continued, fears of a Catholic backlash, perhaps fomented by Spanish spies, began to intensify. The Privy Council ordered the City authorities in London to make an 'exact and secret' search of alehouses and other lodgings on the pretext of trying to recover goods stolen from the Palace of Whitehall. All 'suspicious persons who cannot give a good account of themselves' were to be reported to the council.

James, meanwhile, lingered at Theobalds, claiming to be indisposed by 'a fierce rheum and cough'. He refused to have anything to do with parliamentary affairs – even to meet government officials. George tartly pointed out to him how he found time 'to speak with the King of Spain's instruments, though not with your own subjects'.

Though he had previously chided and teased James, George now began to adopt a more openly critical tone. As the weeks passed, it became increasingly bitter. He decried the king's 'unfavourable interpretation' of his speech to the joint Houses, which James had described as crude and 'Catonic', referring to the Roman censor Cato the Elder. Having in the past indulged the king's many ailments, on this occasion he dismissed his illness as hypochondria, noting that the same afternoon James had claimed to be falling sick he had been riding in the fields around Theobalds.

Though his 'rheum' may not have been particularly serious, the king did seem to be in the grip of a debilitating melancholia. He seemed 'practically lost', according to the Venetian ambassador. Racked with indecision, 'he now protests, now weeps, but finally gives in' to whoever he sees.

The French ambassador wrote of him 'descending deeper and deeper into folly every day, sometime swearing and calling upon God, heaven and the angels, at other times weeping, then laughing, and finally pretending illness in order to play upon the pity of those who urge him to generous actions and to show them that sickness renders him incapable of deciding anything, demanding only repose and, indeed, the tomb'. He had developed a strange obsession with some Spanish asses that he had heard were available for sale in the Low Countries, deciding with a resolve he had failed to show in any matter of state that he must import them. His moods became as twitchy as his body, producing unexpected explosions of anger and tremors of mortifying anxiety. And relations with George inevitably began to fray, as the invigorated favourite tried to goad the resentful and awkward monarch into action. James could be mawkishly tenacious towards him one moment, sulky or paranoiac, even hostile the next. He accurately suspected that George was looking 'more to the rising sun' than to his 'maker' – more to Charles than James – and carped at what he saw as the strutting poise Charles had adopted since his return from Madrid, sneering at it as 'a little too popular'. When the Spanish ambassadors came to complain about the insulting remarks George had made about the King of Spain, James could not bring himself even to defend him, but told them to take the matter up with Parliament.

James's isolation seemed to intensify by the day: his squirming impatience with the demands made upon him, his need to escape his officials and take refuge in the country, his restless rides through the forests and chases of Hertfordshire or Cambridgeshire. He pondered on what had happened to his two 'sweet boys' since their return. His George had become another George, no longer his Steenie. The lustre of his charisma and energy was tarnished now it was no longer focused on the king, but aimed in other directions, towards Parliament and people, activism and innovation.

The Forger of Every Mischief

As the king moped in the countryside, a joint committee of both Houses of Parliament continued to ponder its official response to the king's invitation to advise on the Spanish match. George was voted in as a member, while Charles, now thriving in his role as an enthusiastic member of the House of Lords and parliamentary activist, hovered respectfully on the fringes. According to the Venetian ambassador, 'there was no lack of divers opinions as well probably as of divers passions' among the committee members as they debated on what they should say, and intense wrangling broke out between militant MPs and more moderate Lords on matters of religion and the economic impact of war.

Charles, who seemed to have forgotten his bashfulness, seized the moment. Addressing the committee in a 'prudent, friendly and most praiseworthy' manner, and with George there to urge him on, he 'worked wonders' in getting agreement on what might be said to his father, and pledged eternal gratitude for the support he was getting. He even ventured into the House of Commons. It was his first time, as the chamber was usually considered forbidden territory for royals. But he was welcomed, and he listened attentively as they deliberated the evidence he and George had presented.

Reinforcing the bond of trust, Charles released more confidential documents to back up what George had said in his Banqueting House speech. These showed that it was the Spanish who had initiated the idea of the prince marrying the infanta in 1614, and they who had been responsible for the breakdown in relations. He also produced a letter he had written to his father from Madrid to refute allegations of a cowardly plan to 'steal away from Spain through fear' when it became clear he and George were trapped there. The letter showed that, far from trying to slip off back to England, Charles had accepted his predicament as a Spanish prisoner, telling his father 'to think no more' of him as a son, but consider him 'lost'. He had urged the king to focus all his affections and the kingdom's prospects upon his sister Elizabeth, the exiled queen in the Hague, and her children, who would now become the heirs of the Stuart line.

Efforts were made to keep James engaged with the parliamentary deliberations. George went to Theobalds to tell him of the latest thinking, but James maintained his surly and uncooperative mood, refusing to commit himself to anything that might bring his long-cherished role as mediator and peacemaker to an end. All he would say was that he felt no obligation to follow whatever was proposed – if anything, he was inclined to ignore or reject it.

Back in Westminster, the committee tried to ignore James's recalcitrance. There was, by now, general agreement on what the advice should be: that, for the sake of the Palatinate, the king should break decisively with Spain and that, in return, Parliament would pledge to raise the funds needed to put the country on a war footing.

On the morning of Friday 5 March, there was a hint of nervousness in the Commons as the committee reported its deliberations to the House. Sir Isaac Wake, the representative for Oxford University and a noted Puritan academic, girded loins by reporting the seizure of letters coming from Rome which showed that the Spanish king had no intention of letting the Palatinate return to Protestant hands. While he was in the midst of speaking, Wake was interrupted by the Attorney General and sergeant-at-arms, carrying a message from the duke with news that the king would make himself available that afternoon to receive Parliament's advice at Theobalds.

Delegates were swiftly chosen and duly dispatched. After a nervous two-hour coach journey, they arrived at Theobalds in the late afternoon. The Archbishop of Canterbury, George Abbot, appointed to act as spokesman, presented their findings to James. The advice was clear and succinct: the alliance with Spain could 'not any longer be continued' without the loss of 'the honour of your majesty, the safety of your people, the welfare of your children and posterity', and so must be ended.

Initially, James seemed ready to accept the advice. He thanked the members of both Houses for their advice in 'this great business' given by 'unanimous consent'. He had heard that there were MPs who had 'cast jealousies and doubts between me and my people', and was pleased to learn that the parliamentary committee had 'quelled those motions, which otherwise might have hindered the happy agreement' between king and Parliament that he hoped to reach.

But, but, but: James, at fifty-seven years of age, considered himself to be an old king, and an old king must be allowed to express doubts. After all his efforts to maintain peace, becoming embroiled in war was madness. Resorting to a typically misogynistic image, he explained that belligerence was so far from his nature that unless it was 'as some say merrily of women, *malum necessarium*', a necessary evil, he would not consider it. And since improved offers were still arriving from Spain on the restoration of the Palatinate, he remained hopeful of a peaceful settlement. Furthermore, though he accepted that he had 'craved' Parliament's advice, his first consideration in deciding between war and peace must still be his conscience and honour. Then there was the issue of money. If he was to commit to war, assurances must first be made that it would be properly financed.

I am old now, he repeated, and 'like Moses beholding the Promised Land from a high mountain' he hoped to glimpse the Palatinate restored before death caught up with him – but, he added, that did not mean it would be right to go to war over it, as it was 'an unchristian thing to seek that by blood which may be had by peace'.

As he proceeded, his mood darkened. No king, he claimed, had received less help from Parliaments than he. This had left his own necessities 'too well known' – his personal debts and extraordinary expenses. And these 'disabilities' had been made worse by Charles's visit to Madrid, the sending of ambassadors to negotiate treaties, the maintenance of Elizabeth and her reckless husband Frederick in the Hague, and a 'great debt' he owed the King of Denmark, 'which I am not yet able to pay'. Furthermore, he had to take into account the lack of support from Protestant princes and states on the Continent, who were 'all poor, wrecked and disheartened'. And as if that were not bad enough, war would disrupt trade, which would decimate customs duties, one of his few reliable sources of revenue. And even if Parliament voted through new taxes, it would take time to collect them, forcing him to borrow more money, at rates of interest that would 'eat up a great part of them'.

Nevertheless, despite this litany, he thanked them again, and felt reassured of their love for him, because it was the heart that 'opens the purse' and not the purse that opens the heart. It was therefore up to them to appoint treasurers to work out the costs of what they proposed, and how they would pay for it. If they could promise the means to make war then . . . well, he still would not make a commitment. In a string of conditional clauses that left even learned heads spinning, he asserted the 'peculiar prerogatives' that made matters of war and peace his to determine, but seemed to promise that he would consult Parliament on any treaties leading to war – not so Parliament could vote on them, but because being backed by a parliamentary promise to prepare and pay for war, it would give him more leverage to sue for peace.

The despondent and confused delegates were left to go back to London and pick through the archbishop's notes. The MP Edward Nicholas, an ally of George, despaired. The king appeared to have dismissed the warnings Charles and George had given about Spanish duplicity. 'The papists began to brag,' he lamented, and Archbishop Abbot was left so discouraged that he absented himself from the House of Lords the following morning to take to his sickbed.

The queasy archbishop managed to make his way to Westminster later in the day to attend a conference of both Houses chaired by Charles. The aim was to craft a new version of the king's answer to Parliament's advice, with 'amendments' to bring it closer to what he should have said.

The prince took the new draft to James, who was so exhausted by the whole business that he accepted it. On Monday, the revised answer to Parliament's advice was read out to MPs, and copies were distributed among the members so they could study it.

The following week, the Chancellor of the Exchequer delivered a report on the royal debt. It provoked uproar. The total was nearly

£700,000. The enormity of the figure spread a mood of dismay and anger through the chamber. Efforts were made to calm the House. 'Let us not lay all the blame upon the king,' said Benjamin Rudyard. 'We have had our own heats and passions,' he reminded them, and wittily warned that if they complained too much, 'we may blow up ourselves without gunpowder, even with our own breaths'. Edwin Sandys, the Earl of Southampton's man and now an ally of George, took a more hard-line approach. There was no greater enemy to action than delay, he said. James had asked their advice, and they had given it. 'Let us say to the King,' he suggested, 'Sir, if your Majesty will declare yourself in pursuit of our advice, we will assist your Majesty with our persons and fortunes.'

The negotiations continued. 'Matters go on uncertainly,' Chamberlain reported. 'The King's speeches needing interpreta-tions, and the Houses being as wary and suspicious as though dealing with enemies'. 'Every day brings its novelty,' observed the Venetian ambassador, noting how James had become 'variable, tricky, inscrut-able, determined upon peace, dominated by fear only and the forger of every mischief.' MPs 'fear his Majesty's nature', and it seemed likely that he was on the verge of dismissing Parliament so he could 'return to the vomit of his feeble negotiations'.

Eventually, James's patience ran out. No one was listening to him, and 'when Jupiter speaks he should have his thunder'. If Parliament wanted him to consider its advice, then it would have to pay. He named his price: £900,000 – a fantastic figure that would impose a crippling burden of tax on a fragile economy. Charles and George 'turned pale' when they heard it, according to the Venetian ambassador. 'The prince was exceedingly perplexed, and spoke not a word that night, and Buckingham wept,' a government official observed. In an effort to get the king to withdraw the demand, George wiped his face and entered the royal bedchamber. 'Shut in there' by the prince, he knelt before the king, asking for some 'milder explanation' for his demands. But he was rebuffed.

The following day, in an act of almost suicidal defiance, George sent the king a letter threatening to end their relationship. A distance had grown between them, he wrote. He yearned to wait upon the king more often, but James was going 'two ways, and myself only one'. This had resulted in 'so many disputes' that 'till you be once resolved, I think it is of more comfort and ease to you and safer for me that I now abide away'.

The endless negotiations came to a sudden halt, and silence descended on the proceedings. Then, a few day later, an MP friendly to George noted that 'the wind has turned'. On 19 March, Sir Benjamin Rudyard, a moderate and measured member of the anti-Spanish camp, came up with a compromise. 'The king in his wisdom knows that generals dwell too much in the air,' he told the House of Commons, so the best way to reassure him that Parliament would pay for any immediate threat of breaking with Spain was to work out the costs themselves. He had a figure ready: around £300,000 to repulse any attempt by the Spanish to invade, with a commitment for ongoing costs in the event of war.

In what seems to have been an orchestrated manoeuvre, Sir Thomas Edmondes, the treasurer of the royal household, and effectively acting as a royal spokesman, got up and mentioned a similar figure as acceptable. Despite the obvious makings of a deal, MPs had built up such a head of steam that it took two days of heated debate before a resolution along the lines Sir Benjamin had originally suggested could be passed. It was then put to the House of Lords to be presented as a joint 'proposition' to James.

On Sunday 21 March, an agreement of sorts was finally reached. An ailing James, along with the prince, the duke, delegations from both Houses of Parliament and 'an infinite assembly of people', attended an open-air sermon delivered by the Archbishop of Canterbury in Whitehall on the theme of the nature of divine love. The dignitaries and delegates then repaired to James's bedchamber in order to hear George's 'justification' for the remarks he had given in his Banqueting House speech concerning the King of Spain, and James responding with a 'full and royal acquittal, approbation and commendation of the duke'.

The aim was to reinforce George's position at the apex of the new policy, and as the fulcrum in the seemingly closer relationship now emerging between king and Parliament. The king gave reassurances of his trust in George, declaring himself 'unworthy' of such a servant if he did not trust him. In a striking image, he commended the favourite for having run his head 'into the yoke with the people'.

Over the following two days, Parliament drew up a 'proclamation' to present to the king setting out what had been agreed on the 'great matter' of tax and Spain, securing a unanimous vote in favour in both Houses. Only one awkward earl abstained, 'although the Prince and the Lords had laboured him much to the contrary' – George's obstinate father-in-law the Earl of Rutland.

Finally, on 23 March, just before the recess for Easter, a 'resolution' was read out in the Commons and proclaimed across the city and beyond that the king was going to break with Spain – unleashing a night of carnivalesque revels not seen since the prince and duke had returned from Madrid, celebrated with bonfires in the streets. As had become customary, crowds of unruly apprentices gathered outside Exeter House, the Spanish embassy in Holborn, and threw stones at the windows.

A Game at Chess

On 5 August 1624 crowds packed the Globe, Shakespeare's theatre, for the premiere of a play to be performed by the King's Men called *A Game at Chess*, by Thomas Middleton. The conceit for the play was clever: the characters were chess pieces, the stage a chessboard, and the drama was the playing out of the game. But it was hardly sufficient to explain the interest.

The draw, it turned out, was another kind of game, a guessing game.

In the opening 'Induction', the ghost of St Ignatius of Loyola, founder of the Jesuit order, was to be seen centre stage looking around in wonder, asking how he had managed to find a place that has escaped his 'designs' and 'institutions' – escaped Catholicism, in other words. 'I thought they'd spread over the World by this time.'

His servant, Error, lies at his feet, and he kicks him awake. 'What have you done?' Error demands to know. He had been enjoying a dream of 'the bravest setting for a game' that 'had ever my eye fixed on'. 'Game? What game?' Ignatius asks.

> *Error:* The noblest Game of all, A Game at Chess,
> Betwixt our side, and the White House, the men set
> In their just order, ready to go to it.

Listening to these lines, noting that Ignatius was dressed in black Catholic vestments, a London audience would soon begin to catch on to what was happening. This was an allegory of some sort. The 'Black House' was Catholic Spain, making the 'White House' Protestant Britain.

Right from the start, the script invited the audience to puzzle over hidden messages. Ignatius's first words were: 'What Angle of the world is this?' – as well as a corner, an angle could refer to the tribe that first inhabited England. There was a fat bishop – surely Marc Antonio de Dominis, Archbishop of Spalato, the sophisticates would have noted. The reforming Catholic archbishop had been welcomed to England by King James in 1616 and was famous for his corpulence and greed. Just two years before the play's premiere, in 1622, he had been found to be in secret contact with the Vatican in Rome. He had returned there soon after, chests of hoarded wealth confiscated from him as he tried to make his escape.

One of the most controversial clues came in a bawdy scene towards the end of the play. The Black Knight asks his servant, the Black Pawn, to fetch his 'chair of ease' and mentions the 'foul flaw in the bottom of my bum'. This, as everyone from the groundlings up would have realized, must surely be a reference to James's old friend Ambassador Gondomar, famed for his influence over the king, as well as an anal fistula.

There was the White King, the White Knight, and the White 'Duke' – the term used for a rook. Given how few dukes there were in England, these identifications were easy: James was the king, obviously, making the duke George, with Charles the knight, a suitable designation given the prince's recent adventure in Spain. There was also a Black 'Duke', described as 'an olive-faced ganymede' – surely Olivares, King Philip's *valido*. This would obviously make Philip IV the Black King.

But the identification game got more complicated with other characters. Who was the White Queen? James's wife, Anne of Denmark, had been dead for five years. Could this be Elizabeth, Charles's sister, the 'Winter Queen' exiled in the Hague with her German husband Frederick? Someone thought mention of a 'lost piece' could refer to the Palatinate, the lands seized from Frederick by Catholic forces.

Then the Black Knight, describing himself as 'the master-piece of the play', decides he will 'entrap the White Knight with false allurements' and 'entice him to our black House' – further hints that the play, in part at least, is about Charles's escapade in Madrid. In which case, the references to a 'universal monarchy' must be to Spanish ambitions to conquer all Europe for the Habsburgs and Catholicism.

Even more sensational was the character of the White King's Pawn, whose doublet is snatched away to reveal black beneath. Who was this? An English traitor? Speculation focused on Lionel Cranfield, deposed as Lord Treasurer earlier that year. Others, though, wondered if the Pawn might be John Digby, England's ambassador suspected of going native in Madrid.

'This vulgar pasquin,' the scandalized MP Sir John Holles called the play in a letter to the disgraced Robert Carr, James's former favourite, now exiled to Hertfordshire, 'already thrice acted with extraordinary applause.' He claimed to have been 'invited' by someone else to go – he would not normally attend such 'facetious' comedies. So he rowed to the playhouse, and found it to be 'so thronged' that 'by scores' members of the public were being turned away 'for want of place'.

Squeezing into his seat, Holles joined in the guessing game, identifying 'a representation of all our Spanish traffic, where Gondomar his litter, his open chair for the ease of that fistulated part, Spalato appeared on stage'. The message, as far as he was concerned, was that 'all the Christian world' was going to be brought 'under Rome' when it came to religious confession, and under Spain when it came to worldly rule.

However he also noted specific references to Charles's Madrid adventure, pointing out how the prince made 'full discovery' of all the 'knaveries' of Gondomar and Olivares, which were 'by the prince pitched into the bag, and so the play ends'. It was, Holles concluded, 'more wittily penned than wisely staged'.

Tumbling out of the Globe into the stews and brothels of Southwark, heads would have been light and spinning with the seditiousness of it all. It was hard to imagine how such a play had even been staged – a play about kings and dukes, religion and foreign policy, supposedly prohibited subjects for the public theatres. In 1620, James had issued a proclamation forbidding 'men to speak of matters of state, either of this kingdom or any other place, upon pain of his majesty's high displeasure'. This production was flagrantly dealing with such matters, yet must have been passed by the official censors. It was all, as one of the characters in the play acknowledges, 'immeasurably politic'.

Some speculated that the 'gamesters' must have the protection of a senior government figure, otherwise surely they would not have dared 'charge thus princes' actions, ministers', nay their intents'. As a correspondent writing to William Trumbull, the English agent in Brussels, pointed out, if such a play had been staged a year before, 'then had everyman been hanged for it'. How had the King's Men, James's own acting company, got away with it? 'Not without leave from the higher powers, I mean the P and D' – the prince and the duke, Charles and George. The two had seen the play, and even though it suggested they had been duped by the Spanish, they had 'by report laughed heartily at it'.

Humiliatingly, James's 'first notice' of the play came nine days after it had opened, when Hinojosa and Coloma, the Spanish ambassadors, had come to him to complain about the lampooning of their distinguished predecessor Gondomar. How could this have happened, the king wanted to know, 'while so many ministers of his own are thereabouts and cannot but have heard of it?' A messenger was sent to summon Middleton, but the playwright did not appear, nor did he three days later when the 'principal actors' were interrogated. Furious that they had managed to stage such a 'scandalous comedy', the king demanded to see the 'perfect copy' of the play script carrying the endorsement of Sir Henry Herbert, Master of the Revels, who acted as the royal censor. Wrong-footed by the actors presenting confirmation that the play had been 'allowed' by Herbert, all James could do was deliver a 'round and sharp reproof' of his 'high displeasure' and instruct them to close the production down immediately.

Hobgoblins

Life for the Spanish embassy staff was miserable. As well as having to endure mockery and even physical attacks, their mission had stalled. Serious negotiations over the match had all but ceased, access to James had become limited, and well-paid informants and supporters, scared off by the growing mood of hostility, had begun to slope away.

Yet, despite the setbacks and provocations, they had not only refused to break off relations, but had increased their diplomatic activity.

For what the British had not realized was that Spain was terrified of war. Philip's treasury was in an even more parlous state than James's. Expert as well as popular opinion imagined that the royal coffers were bursting with bullion, annually replenished by an inexhaustible stream of silver coming from the New World. But working depleted mines, administering unruly colonies and protecting the fabled *flota*, or treasure fleet, was proving to be increasingly costly, while inflation was eating away at the value of the bounty. As a result, the annual amount delivered from South America to Cádiz had more than halved in value since the beginning of the century to below 1 million ducats, and was continuing to fall. Meanwhile, the annual cost of maintaining the opulence that had so impressed George and Charles in Madrid had risen to as much as 9 million ducats.

So, the embassy staff were under strict orders to keep the talks with James going. In the game of diplomatic chess, they needed to secure not checkmate so much as stalemate. And to do that it became clear that they needed to remove one particular piece from the board: the White Duke, George Villiers.

Their first attempt had come soon after Parliament had been summoned in the spring of 1624. Despite efforts by Charles and George to limit the Spaniards' access to the king, they managed to slip him a note. It requested a private audience with the latest member of the embassy staff, François de Carondelet. Known to the English as Don Francesco, Carondelet was Archdeacon of Cambrai, a well-known outpost of English Catholic agitation. A man of great charm as well as guile, he had been brought in by the Spanish as a special envoy specifically to turn James against the favourite.

Don Francesco was invited to Theobalds while Charles and George were distracted by the parliamentary negotiations in

London. The envoy arrived late in the evening on the appointed day, but James, fearful of staff loyal to the prince and duke getting wind of the meeting, would not receive him, and he was told to spend the night in the guest quarters.

A Catholic servant woke Francesco at dawn the following day, before the rest of the staff had risen, and escorted him via the back passages of the mansion to James's apartment. There he was received by the king's ever-loyal Scottish servant Thomas Erskine, who showed him into the royal bedchamber, then took up position outside the door to prevent eavesdropping.

Given the risk both were running in meeting in secret, James was expecting Francesco to deliver generous new terms that would confound his critics and revive hopes for the match. He had heard that Gondomar's former confessor, Friar Diego Lafuente, known as 'Father Maestro', had arrived in London a few days earlier direct from Rome carrying, it was assumed, a new dispensation from the pope. But Francesco had to confess he was empty-handed. Father Maestro had been attacked in France en route to England, and all his papers stolen, allegedly by men suspected of working for George. Had those papers arrived, Francesco told James, then he might have been able to report on 'several matters which would have pleased and interested' the king.

Instead, he was there to inform him of a plot by a cabal within James's own government to put an end to the Spanish match by marrying Charles to the French princess Henrietta Maria. When James denied that the French had even been engaged in official negotiations, Francesco informed him that a proposal of marriage had already been sent on George's authority. Noting James's confusion, the envoy pressed the point that this was yet another example of the duke exceeding his authority. The king had become a captive of his favourite, he boldly suggested, pointedly comparing him to John II and Francis I, two French monarchs who had found themselves imprisoned by their own subjects. Parliament, he said, was meeting for the sole purpose of serving the duke's interests, noting that the MPs who spoke most viciously about James's foreign dealings seemed to be those closest to the duke. 'The only thing one heard was that the king had grown old, and that it would be a great happiness if the prince reigned instead,' Francesco claimed. The duke had talked openly of Charles taking the throne, with James being forced to retire from royal duties to one of his country houses.

According to Francesco's own report on the meeting, James's response to these sensational charges was at first bewilderment, then an outburst of fury, directed not at Francesco, but at George. He told the Spaniard that he had suspected the duke of wanting to make himself 'popular' – one of the worst charges he could level – and pledged that if he discovered what Francesco had said was true, George would lose his head over it.

Two days later, with Charles and George still preoccupied by the new session of Parliament, Father Maestro himself arrived at Theobalds and was secretly shown to the royal apartments. His presence was noted by a royal secretary, who was known to act as George's 'sentinel', but the secretary was sent away while the king held a three-hour private meeting with his visitor.

Maestro continued the denunciation of George, and was encouraged to see that James's attitude continued to harden. If any of this was true, the king told the envoy, then 'Buckingham was the greatest villain in the world, a greater traitor than Judas, for Judas had only had charge of the purse, while he had trusted Buckingham with his life and honour'.

While the envoys worked on the king, damaging reports began to leak out about George's behaviour while he was in Spain: his insolent manner, his engaging in 'obscene things' and 'immodest gesticulations and wanton tricks'; his lying to Olivares and using 'frequent threatenings' against the pope's representatives.

The most specific and scandalous charge, which became the 'table talk in all England', was that he had 'attempted the chastity' of Olivares's wife, and 'cheated with a diseased strumpet laid in his bed'. The allegations were as plausible as they were thrilling, drawing on the duke's powerful erotic charge and wayward reputation.

At around the same time, a courtier noticed the sudden re-appearance among the king's entourage of a comely young gallant called Arthur Brett. In 1622, Brett had been appointed one of James's grooms of the bedchamber. Noting the king's interest in the young man, and fearing the emergence of a rival just as he was preparing to leave for Madrid with the prince, George had moved quickly to have Brett exiled to France. Now he was back 'without the Duke of Buckingham's consent', and was attempting to find his way into the king's favour.

Brett's brother-in-law and patron was Lionel Cranfield, Lord Treasurer since 1621 and the figure later suspected of being represented by the pawn in *A Game at Chess*. Cranfield was a leading member of the pro-Spanish clique and a powerful critic of Parliament's growing enthusiasm for war. The connection was enough to persuade George to take action. While James was secretly receiving Spanish envoys in Theobalds, Cranfield found himself under investigation in Westminster for his 'late conduct in Parliament'. The campaign intensified over the coming weeks, and, despite James's half-hearted efforts to save his embattled treasurer, and Cranfield's own vigorous defence of himself, it soon became apparent that he was going to sink the same way as Francis Bacon: impeached by his own peers.

'Gnawn with perplexity' by the swirling rumours and loss of his Lord Treasurer, James's feelings finally erupted on Friday 23 April, St George's Day – the day the king awarded the ancient chivalric Order of the Garter, but also the anniversary of his making the young, vigorous, charming cupbearer George Villiers a knight.

A royal carriage waited at the gatehouse of St James's Palace to take the king, accompanied by Charles and George, to Windsor, where the Garter ceremony was to take place. But just as they were about to depart, James instructed George to perform a 'slight errand', which meant he would be unable to accompany them. Sensing a snub, George asked what was wrong, at which point James burst into tears and declared himself the unhappiest man alive, treated with ingratitude by those dearest to him.

With the scene unfolding in public, in front of servants and lords shifting uneasily in their livery and robes, George stood at the carriage door and began to weep. He protested his innocence and demanded to know the charges made against him. But the king closed the door on him and commanded his coachman to drive off, leaving George to watch the carriage disappear into St James's Park.

The dejected duke walked to nearby Wallingford House, where he took to his bedchamber and refused to talk to anybody.

Later that day, he was visited by John Williams, the slippery

Lord Keeper and leading member of the pro-Spanish clique. The duke having browbeaten him into offering his support earlier in the year, the Lord Keeper had come as a friend to give him some advice.

Williams was initially rebuffed, but after 'much ado', managed to gain admittance to George's room. The dejected duke was lying on a couch 'in that immovable posture, that he would neither rise up, nor speak'. Williams, who was also Bishop of Lincoln, might have been expected to say some words of religious consolation. But the Lord Keeper was there to give George a sermon. The snub he had just received from the king was 'God's direct hand' stirring him 'at this pinch of extremity' into rescuing his relationship with the king, which was close to collapse. It was vital he act quickly, Williams claimed, before the breach became permanent. 'For the danger was that some would thrust themselves in, to push on his majesty to break utterly with the Parliament, and the next degree of their hope was upon that dissolution to see his grace committed to the Tower, and then God knows what would follow.' He would not say who was trying to 'thrust themselves in', only urged George into action. 'Make haste for Windsor,' the Lord Keeper said. Show himself to the king 'before supper was ended', lavish his royal highness 'with all amiable addresses' and stay by his side night or day.

The speech apparently had its intended effect. According to the dubiously self-serving account Williams gave his biographer, George roused himself, raced off to Windsor to be with the king, and stayed by James's side 'as inseparable as his shadow'.

A few days later, Charles came to Williams, and thanked him for giving George the 'warning for his safety'. But the prince promised the Lord Keeper 'greater thanks' if he would 'spread open this black contrivance' to which he had alluded when he had been with George. Who was plotting to lure his father into breaking with Parliament and imprisoning the duke?

Williams trod carefully. He claimed only to know that 'some in the Spanish ambassador's house have been preparing mischief'. Otherwise, the 'curtain of privacy is drawn before the picture that I cannot guess the colours'. Charles was unconvinced by the noncommittal reply. 'No counsellor in this kingdom' was better acquainted with the Spanish than the Lord Keeper, the prince pointed out. Williams tried to hide behind his own imagery, claiming not to know 'what misshapen creature' was being drawn, and that it was impossible to find out because the prince and duke had 'made it a crime' to visit the artists' studio, the Spanish embassy. Charles's tone became more threatening. 'Before we part,' he said – and he did not mean just for the day – Williams should 'keep not from me how you came to know or imagine' the 'high misdemeanours or perhaps disloyalty' the Spanish agents claimed the duke had committed against the king. 'I would hear you to that point,' the prince insisted with sinister courtesy, 'that I may compare it with other parcels of my intelligence.'

Fearful of suffering the same fate as his fallen colleague Lord Treasurer Cranfield, Williams relented. He admitted that he and the Spanish envoy Don Francesco had become 'pleasant together', and would regularly meet in a tavern in Mark Lane, an area near the Tower of London known for its alehouses and brothels. There, the envoy had met one of 'our English Beauties', a thoughtful woman who demanded to be 'courted with news and occurrences at home and abroad, as well as with gifts'. Williams claimed that all he had done was bribe her to tell him all that the 'paramour' Francesco had said to her. That was the 'dark lantern' that had brought these deeds to light, and – artfully diverting the issue from one of loyalty to one of piety – if there was any imputation that by consorting with a prostitute he had committed a sin, then he was 'not ashamed to enquire of a Delilah to resolve a riddle'.

Charles enquired no more into the matter, but sensing he was in danger, Williams decided he would make further efforts to find out what the Spaniards were up to and inform on them to the prince.

Thanks to his conversations with Don Francesco in the taverns of Mark Lane, Williams had learned of an English Catholic priest 'who was dearer to Francesco than his own confessor'. So he hired a 'pursuivant', or kidnapper, one Captain Toothbie, and instructed him to snatch Francesco's friend from his lodgings in Drury Lane and hold him in hiding. Francesco went 'wild' when he heard that the priest had been taken. With anti-Catholic sentiment running so high during the sitting of Parliament, he knew 'how hard it would be to save his life'. So he sent a note to Williams, begging for help. 'With a seeming unwillingness,' the Lord Keeper agreed to receive him, telling him to come to his house at eleven that night by the back door of his garden 'where a servant should receive him'.

When the Spaniard arrived at the bishop's home, he was brought up to the gallery, where Williams awaited him. The Lord Keeper patiently listened as the envoy 'passionately implored' him to secure the priest's freedom. 'Would you have me run such a hazard to set a priest at liberty, a dead man by our statutes, when the eye of Parliament is so vigilant upon the breach of justice?' Williams asked. 'My lord,' Francesco apparently replied, accenting his words with 'passionate gesture', 'let not this parliament trouble you; I can tell you, if you have not heard it, that it is upon expiration.' When pressed for details, Francesco finally confessed to Williams his efforts to turn the king against the duke.

After the envoy had left, Williams 'retired to his own thoughts, and poured the whole conference out of his memory into his papers, as if Francesco had stood by to dictate every line'. He revealed what the Spanish ambassadors had been trying to do, how they had manipulated James to plant 'hobgoblins' of suspicion in his mind. He saw no sleep that night, he claimed, nor stirred out of the room. He emerged at seven the following morning, and woke one of his servants, who made a fair copy, which Williams took to St James's Palace and presented to a bleary Charles, boasting that he had caught 'the viper and her brood in a box'.

Meanwhile, there were signs that the viper's poison was beginning to have its effect. George's brief absence from the king's side during the St George's Day celebrations had allowed the two most senior Spanish ambassadors, Hinojosa and Coloma, to meet the king privately. Out of 'zeal & particular care of his person', they promised James to reveal 'a very great conjuration against his person and royal dignity'. At the beginning of the Parliament, George had 'consulted certain lords of the arguments and means which were to be taken touching the breaking and dissolving of the treaties of the Palatinate and the Match'. Apparently George had said to them that if the king could not 'accommodate himself to their counsels' he would be given 'a house of pleasure whither he might retire himself to his sports, in regard that the Prince had now years sufficient to, and parts answerable for the government of the Kingdom'.

The king's response to the ambassadors' revelations was unexpectedly emphatic. He drew up a list òf questions or 'interrogatories' for his ministers and councillors, including George, to answer under oath. Charles managed to obtain a copy, and sent them to George in advance, reassuring him that he would 'incur no danger in this' just as long as he cooperated. 'My advice to you is,' the prince wrote to his 'sweet heart', 'that you do not oppose, or show yourself discontented, at the King's course herein.'

The interrogations were to take place at Theobalds a week after the emotional confrontation between the king and the favourite on St George's Day. Taking leave of his wife Kate and mother Mary, George told them he would return either 'as he was born' with all his titles and status, all that he had achieved confiscated, 'or having vanquished his enemies'.

Accounts of what happened vary wildly. The Spanish ambassadors, presumably eager to portray a man defeated by their efforts, reported to their masters in Madrid that George had been kept on his knees by a furious James for two hours, as the king castigated him for acting so imperiously in his dealings with Parliament. And when Charles came to George's defence, James slapped him down.

Other accounts capture a more emotional encounter, the king veering between rancour and despair. Having confronted George with the ambassadors' charges, he echoed Caesar on the steps of the Senate, saying: 'Ah, Steenie, Steenie. Wilt thou kill me?' George retorted that the plot of which he was accused – that he intended to 'retire' the king to his hunting grounds in Theobalds so that Charles could rule – would surely be known by the prince, 'whose filial piety would rise against it'. And even if the prince had not known, then the 'affection of the people to his Majesty' would mean they would 'tear in pieces any who attempted it'. Confronted by George's emphatic denial, James apparently backed down, saying that had he really believed the ambassadors' accusations, he would never have mentioned them. But George was not placated. Exercising the principle that attack is the best form of defence, he demanded a full enquiry to exonerate what he had done, and threatened to drag Parliament into the investigation. James, frightened of escalating an issue that had already got out of hand, decided on another course.

The king summoned the rest of his privy councillors before him and, with a copy of the ambassadors' testimony to hand, examined them one by one. He then made them swear on the Bible, which he held, to the innocence and loyalty of the duke. This they all did, and in the absence of any solid evidence presented by the ambassadors, the matter appeared to be settled.

Still, suspicions lurked. The hobgoblins were still at play in the king's head. They pointed out to him that men who were George's dependents were bound to acquit their patron, and that to confess that the duke had engaged in treasonable actions raised the issue of why they had not mentioned this before.

George responded with a written vindication of his actions, in which he poured scorn on the notion that he had exercised overweening power, pointing out that the Madrid escapade had been suggested by Charles and endorsed by the king, and that the summoning of Parliament was the king's absolute prerogative. He also noted that the privy councillors who had earlier been receptive to Spanish advances had since voted unanimously to reject them, and that the breakdown of relations was not a result of the British being bellicose, but of the Spanish being deceitful.

The duke also provided a stout defence of a resurgent Parliament, arguing that 'our greatest and wisest kings' had long referred treaties, marriages, declarations of war and matter of religion 'to the consultations of their parliaments'. Those who undervalued this 'high court do but expose their own judgments to censure and contempt, not knowing that Parliaments, as they are the honour and support, so they are the handmaids and creatures of our kings, inspired, formed and governed by their power'.

George's transformation into a vigorous champion and figurehead of Parliament had taken a heavy toll on his relationship with James. They did not talk or write to each other as they had done before. Every political act by the favourite was taken as a slight by the king, while every equivocal action by the king seemed like an attack on the favourite.

And yet without Steenie, James seemed bereft. Writing in secret code, the Venetian ambassador reported that the 'exhalation' of so much 'extreme passion' had led to James having 'perverse' feelings towards the favourite. 'His mind is ulcerated and full of poison,' he wrote.

Then, in mid-May 1624, George fell ill.

To Ride Away an Ague

George's health had always been fragile. He fell ill regularly and particularly at times of intense strain. He had also inherited his mother's hypochondriac tendencies, and like her was keen to explore unorthodox medical practices in the hope of finding relief for various chronic and acute ailments.

On this occasion George was treated by James's own physician, Sir Theodore Turquet de Mayerne, whose prestige and seniority as a licensed member of London's College of Physicians disguised his earlier membership of a banned circle of alchemists in Paris. On 10 May 1624, Mayerne attended George at Wallingford House, diagnosing a case of tertian ague (malaria) and jaundice, noting the evacuation of bile the colour of saffron. Mayerne was so alarmed, he reported to the king that he feared for George's life.

The onset of the illness was so sudden and serious, rumours quickly spread that the duke had been poisoned. Pustules and blains were said to have broken out all over his body. The finger of suspicion quickly turned towards the Spanish ambassadors, though some speculated that he had been given something while he was in Madrid, 'which now begins to work upon him'. Reports from Paris suggested that Olivares, George's Spanish nemesis, had hired an Irish captain to do the deed, a man who was 'the greatest monster for such ill deeds that ever was in this world'. The Venetian ambassador, however, was more matter-of-fact, suggesting that recent political attacks on the duke had taken their toll, his illness 'possibly arising from mental distress' which 'may grow worse'.

By mid-May, George was well enough to be carried by litter to St James's Palace, Charles's London residence, for a council meeting. But the constant bloodlettings had made him so weak, he could barely stand, and he was still being described as dangerously ill a week later.

On 25 May, James came to London to take George with him to Greenwich, the palace on the banks of the Thames downstream of London, in the hope that cleaner air would be restorative. However, no sooner had they arrived than George suffered a serious relapse, and had to be taken back to Wallingford House. A distraught

James followed him there, and spent three hours at his side. Over the following days, the king sent him food parcels to build his strength – cherries to start with, then the eyes, tongue and testicles of a deer he had hunted in Eltham Park. The king 'hath shown great tenderness over him', one government official noted, sensing that the suddenness and seriousness of the illness had reminded the king that he might lose his favourite, and producing a shift in his feelings for George.

The duke's illness did not hold back the press of parliamentary business, and the scrum of MPs, officials and suitors wanting to get access to him became so intense James ordered that a guard be placed around the house. Spanish supporters took this as evidence that the duke had gone mad, like his brother, while the anti-Spanish clique saw it as a sign that the king had placed him under house arrest.

Confounding both parties, George slipped out of London and headed for New Hall, his house in Essex. From there he wrote a letter to James that was to change everything.

He had earlier promised the king that he would join him at Theobalds as soon as he was well enough to travel, so he began with an apology for going 'many miles from you another way, and consequently from myself, all my perfect joys and pleasures chiefly, nay solely, consisting in attending your person'. Writing in an 'unsteady and weak' hand, he explained that, despite the extraordinary care and watchful eye the king had placed over him, he had found himself too close to the court at Wallingford House to recuperate. Theobalds was too hot and lacked the facilities to accommodate a sick patient, so he had decided to come to New Hall because the air was as good as any in England 'to ride away an ague'.

George candidly noted the recent absence of the king's favour. But illness had brought them close again, and 'I find you still one and the same dear and indulgent master you were ever to me.' Subtly alluding to James's jealousy of his recent 'popularity', he pointed out that he so naturally loved the king, and, upon such good experience and knowledge adored all his other parts, that if all the world was set on one side of a divide, and James alone on another, 'I should, to obey and please you, displease, nay despise' the many in favour of the one; 'and this shall be ever my popularity'.

No more was needed for all the feelings that James had bottled up to burst forth. A flurry of solicitous missives arrived at New Hall from Theobalds, recalling the fervour and affection of his letters to Madrid.

'Alas, sweet heart,' James wrote, the letter George had sent caused his 'heart to bleed'; he could take no pleasure in Theobalds without him. With forlorn expectations, he begged him to come the following night, because it would be a great comfort to him, 'and thou and thy cunts may see me hunt the buck', he added, manly vulgarity combining with flirtatious innuendo.

Of course George was too ill to go, but on the hunting field of James's imagination he frolicked with his favourite in the letters that followed. 'Blessing, blessing, blessing', began one; 'Blessing, blessing, blessing on thy heart-roots', began another. He tried to entice George to Theobalds with news of the fine kennel of hounds bred by Tom Badger, the Royal Master of the Dogs, which prompted a tender digression into George's marital bed, which had yet to produce a son: he and his wife Kate might soon have a well-bred litter of their own, pretty little girls and well-shaped boys, all of them 'run together in a lump'.

The letters are full of advice about his health and welfare. James admonishes him for relying too much on the 'drugs'. George must 'bid the drugs adieu this day'. He is told to 'take the air discreetly and peace and peace'. 'For God's sake and mine, keep thyself very warm'. He is desperate for George's company. 'Put thy park at Beaulieu to an end,' he implores, referring to New Hall by its historic name, 'and love me still and still'; the repetition of repetition in the letters becomes like an incantation of solace.

George responds teasingly, his replies containing hints of heroic forbearance and pathetic vulnerability, each arousing the strange combination of carnal and protective impulses that fired the king's affections to a higher pitch. James repeatedly tells him not to reply to his letters because it will put too much of a strain on him. But George protests that the strength of his feelings means he cannot stop himself. In one letter, it is ingenuity that enables him to 'write no answer' to a recent missive, as he recruits Kate to write it for him, getting her to sign her name alongside Steenie's. In another, dictated to his secretary, he is compelled to seize the quill and, ignoring his secretary's protests and James's orders, demands, perhaps suggestively, that 'now and then' he should be allowed to address the king 'with my own hand'.

Fluctuations between frailty and recovery increase the anticipation. Despite the 'highness' of his urine – its smell, a conventional measure of health – and the yellowness of his skin, the 'sweet cordial' of James's solicitation, as well as the 'seasonable drawing of blood', arouses George's hopes of their reunion on the hunting field. He pledges to get better so he can ride at the king's side and break a recent run of bad luck chasing the stag, then he ends the letter abruptly, feeling 'faintish'.

As George regained his strength, more letters flew in from the king, but fewer replies were sent by return, provoking James's impatience and fervour. Eventually, a date was set for their reunion at Theobalds. Before setting off, George penned one of his most fulsome and eloquent expressions of love and appreciation. Apologizing for his silence, he explains that 'a hundred answers' to the king had been made up in his mind, but none offered an adequate response, 'for kinder letters never servant received from master'. He was so grateful that the king had shown himself 'in a style of such good fellowship, with expressions of more care than servants have of masters, than physicians have of their patients (which hath largely appeared to me in sickness and in health), of more tenderness than fathers have of children, of more friendship than between equals, of more affection than between lovers in the best kind, man and wife; what can I return? Nothing but silence.' His language is unable to describe what he feels, especially considering what he is trying to say, and to whom it must be said. But if he must speak, he would be 'saucy' – impertinent, as well as wanton – to say what he owes the man who means so much to him.

He arouses anticipation of the ending of his self-imposed exile by imagining their imminent reunion. 'I begin my journey tomorrow,' he writes. He would ride to Theobalds, where Charles would meet him. The two will spend the day in the park, Charles chasing 'hinds and does', George, too weak to hunt, surveying the 'trees, walks, ponds, and deer'. The next day they would lay themselves at the king's feet, and 'there crave your blessing'. They would not discuss controversies – Spanish ambassadors, military preparations, parliamentary popularity – but rather speak of the pleasures of Theobalds Park, 'to the best of man, though not of the kind of man, yet made by man, more than man, like a man, both artificial man, and my most natural sovereign, who by innumerable favours hath made me'.

The Price of a Princess

George made his formal return to court in mid-June 1624, nearly a month after falling ill. Though 'received and embraced by His Majesty with all good testimonies of welcome', one courtier noted how ill he looked: 'much discoloured and lean with sickness'.

The duke returned to find the political world in a curious state of limbo. Having finally passed a subsidy bill into law, Parliament had been suspended by the king on 29 May. James, in captious mood, had airily announced that provisions in the preamble of the subsidy bill had been 'made without his advice and contrary to his interests', which he would alter by adding marginal notes – surely, some MPs mumbled, a constitutional violation. The king also 'slighted the subsidy gift' by pointing out there was nothing in it for him – meaning the paying off of his personal debts. He hoped that during the next session, expected that winter, he would be remembered. With that, after all the raucousness and passion, the chambers of the Palace of Westminster had been allowed to fall silent.

The Spanish envoys, meanwhile, were still in their embassy, and, according to the Venetian ambassador, still busy trying to prove George's treachery to the king. Their latest effort was to present James with books about the dangers of Parliaments deposing kings, and an Italian gazette reporting a story published in Germany apparently confirming their claim that the duke had sabotaged the Spanish match with the aim of marrying his own daughter, Mal, to James's grandson, Frederick the younger, son of Elizabeth and Frederick, Count Palatine. They clamoured for another audience, but James did not want to put himself or his revived relationship with George under any further strain, so they were rebuffed.

Hinojosa, the chief ambassador, left England on 26 June, two months after he and Coloma presented to the king their allegations against George. His departure was a humiliating affair. Rather than the usual royal audience and exchange of gifts, he had to slip away in coaches hired using his own money, and was bundled onto a merchant ship flying English colours. He was accused of leaving a 'foul stink behind him in Exeter House', according to one jubilant Protestant commentator, 'which at parting seems he made no more esteem of them than a jakes' – a lavatory. 'All the furniture, all the rooms of the house, so beastly abused that we wish him here again with his Spanish troop to thrust their noses into it.'

Throughout, John Digby had been languishing under house arrest following his recall from Madrid. While recuperating, George had helped draft charges against England's former ambassador, and the Privy Council had conducted an enquiry, but its conclusions, while critical of Digby, were inconclusive. Digby continued to campaign for an open hearing or trial, and on the day George returned to court, the royal secretaries were still handling his complaints about their foot-dragging. With Parliament suspended, and the king about to embark on his summer progress, and all manner of delaying tactics being used to stall Digby's case (such as delivering official documents unsigned, making them legally inadmissible), he was becoming frantic. Even a request to visit his sick mother was interpreted as a ruse to solicit support and make trouble, so permission was only granted on condition that he go 'as privately as conveniently as you may'. By July his position looked so helpless, he was having to contemplate utter defeat and seek a reconciliation with George.

The other main threat to George's position, Lionel Cranfield, had been safely confined to prison for the duration of the duke's illness. The king, who remained supportive of his deposed Lord Treasurer and eager to see him rehabilitated, had agreed to his release, but accepted his exile to beyond 'the verge'.

The efforts of Cranfield's brother-in-law, the pretender Arthur Brett, to win the king's favour also came to nothing. While George languished in New Hall, Brett made a last, desperate effort to gain

James's attention, presenting himself 'on the sudden' while the king was out hunting in Waltham Forest. He reportedly laid a hand on the king's stirrup, 'whereat the king was much offended and, spurring away, commanded the Earl of Warwick to forbid his coming any more into his presence'. A few days later, a royal warrant was issued for his arrest, and he found himself thrown into a cell in the Fleet, a wretched prison situated in the City, on the banks of the stinking Fleet River.

With all immediate threats neutralized if not defeated, George set about re-establishing himself at court. He paid off all his doctors, adding a hefty £50 bonus in thanks for their efforts, and told his staff at Burley-on-the-Hill, a venue with warm memories for George and James, to order in venison, game and fish, and delicacies such as muskmelons and Colchester oysters, in preparation for a feast to celebrate his return to health. His vigour and ambition surging back into his wasted body, he was eager to forge ahead with the political strategy he had put together with Charles, and which during his illness, despite the prince's efforts, had become stalled by James's inertia.

With Spanish ties now decisively if not yet formally broken, the focus switched to sealing a match between Charles and the French princess, Henrietta Maria. George was also wanting to negotiate a military alliance with France to help retake the Palatinate and ultimately challenge the grip of the Habsburg Holy Roman Emperor and Spanish king over Europe.

Early signs were encouraging. The current French ambassador, the Comte de Tillières, considered by the British to be 'too much Jesuited to be a friend or furtherer of this match', was recalled by King Louis and replaced by the Marquis d'Effiat, a close friend of Cardinal Richelieu with a more pragmatic approach to foreign policy. George went out of his way to give the marquis a warm welcome, arranging for him to be feasted at Windsor and New Hall.

At Windsor, George took Effiat to one side and told him a secret that was to change the tone of the negotiations. With breathtaking and apparently suicidal candour, he revealed that if the French match were to fail, it would not only have huge ramifications for the balance of European power, it would result in George's personal ruin. He even asked the ambassador if Louis XIII would offer him protection in that event. Effiat responded sympathetically by suggesting that his future was similarly on the line.

George's disclosure might be interpreted as a huge diplomatic blunder, since it made him dependent on Effiat. If the French increased their demands, they would know that any threats from George of withdrawing his support would be empty, because of the personal as well as political consequences. But his frankness had another effect. By taking Effiat into his confidence, he not only established his sincerity, but raised the stakes of the negotiations, suggesting that failure would lead to James breaking decisively with France in favour of Spain, resulting in a potentially overwhelming shift of the European balance of power in favour of the Habsburgs.

Effiat was among the honoured guests at George's thanksgiving feast for his return to health, held in late July 1624 at Burley-on-the-Hill. As usual, the banquet was followed by a masque. Written by John Maynard, who had been commissioned the previous year to produce the masque celebrating Charles's return from Spain, it set a suitably triumphal and optimistic tone for the forthcoming negotiations.

They proved to be tough. In late June, George received a visit from the secretary of Count Mansfeld, a German mercenary who had been hired to lead a mission to retake the Palatinate. After visiting London earlier in the year to negotiate terms, Mansfeld had gone to Paris to explore the idea of a joint Anglo-French mission, as French involvement would allow easier access to the Palatinate via Lorraine, on France's eastern border with the German empire. However, his secretary reported to George that the count was being held 'as half a prisoner', with the French refusing to make a commitment until the marriage between Charles and Henrietta Maria had been concluded. Apparently the French king did not want to 'buy war at the price of the princess'.

At the same time, Louis XIII was eager to show that he could demand similar terms for his sister as the Spanish had for the infanta. He insisted that for the marriage to proceed, James would have to suspend penal laws against English Catholics, the demand that had so infuriated Parliament during the death throes of the Spanish negotiations.

Despite these setbacks, George, with a combination of doggedness and flair that had been missing from James's desultory efforts, pushed forward. He certainly managed to win over the French ambassador. Effiat described him to King Louis as 'the unchallenged ruler of England', James loving him 'so deeply that he let him do what he liked and saw everything through his eyes'. Charles, too, 'looked on him as the sole source of his happiness and contentment', while members of the government 'were all Buckingham's creatures and held their places only during his good pleasure'. Despite George's scandalous liaison with Louis's wife, Anne of Austria, the previous year (or perhaps because the true identity of the periwigged interloper had never been discovered), the French king was clearly impressed, and began to write to George directly, addressing him as '*mon cousin*'.

After a long, hot summer of negotiation, a settlement seemed to be in sight. Though the French refused a formal military alliance with Britain, they volunteered to help pay for Mansfeld's expeditionary mission to recover the Palatinate. On religion – the marrying of the Protestant Charles to the Catholic Henrietta Maria – a fragile compromise was reached under which James would sign an agreement – the French called it an *Ecrit Particulier* – promising Catholic toleration, but on the basis that it would remain secret, to avoid provoking parliamentary and public outrage.

Throughout the negotiations, George maintained a lively correspondence with James, cajoling and reassuring him on a process with which the king was only reluctantly engaged. There are glimpses of the tenderness that had been rekindled during George's long illness, James lavishing him with gifts of foods such as Barbary melons, pheasant eggs and sugared beans, to help preserve his health. George even started to refer to the king teasingly as his 'sow' and 'sowship', sensing that his place in James's heart was so secure that he could safely compare the king to a female pig. At the risk of reprising the charges made by the Spanish ambassadors that he had been plotting for James's overthrow in favour of Charles, he urged him for his wellbeing to spend more time at Theobalds, where he had 'new trees to plant, new ridings too make' as well as hawking, cards and golf to enjoy.

But George's letters also hint at a growing impatience that his hard work was not being taken seriously. The king's attitude was evident in a note sent by his own secretary to a councillor, which reported that, despite evidence that the French 'really desire the match', James did not want to have further dealings with Effiat as their meetings had already 'taken up all the time the King can spare from hunting'. At one difficult point during the negotiations James had taunted George about the delays, saying to him, 'where is your glorious match with France, and your royal frank *monsieur*?'

Only one letter during this period addressed more personal issues, referring back to the old business of the mental health of George's elder brother, John. In October, while the French marriage negotiations were at their most intense, John's reluctant bride, Frances, the daughter of Lady Hatton, had given birth to a son. At the time the child would have been conceived, Frances had been living away from her husband. James himself had given his blessing to a temporary separation. It had followed an incident two years before when John had broken into a room near Wallingford House and 'beat down the glass windows with his bare fists and, all bloodied, cried out to the people that passed by that he was a Catholic and would spend his blood in the cause'. It was therefore widely believed that the child was not her husband's but that of a former suitor, Sir Robert Howard, a member of the powerful pro-Spanish Howard family, which was hostile to George. Frances nevertheless insisted the boy was legitimate, putting George in a difficult position, as John was the duke's heir, which meant that this bastard scion of the Howard clan was second in line to inherit George's estates and titles, as he was yet to have a son of his own with Kate.

As a result of the strain of the situation, John, who had been stable since the incident at Wallingford House, had 'fallen back to his old bias and worse', as John Chamberlain put it. An exasperated George confided to James of the 'witchcraft' that had taken hold of his beloved brother, and his feeling of an obligation to stay in London because he could not leave him 'in the midst of his troubles'.

Despite these family distractions, negotiations continued through the summer and into autumn, and by November 1624 were close to a settlement. From the far-off perspective of Dorchester, the merchant William Whiteway had been following events closely. 'There was great speech at this time of the marriage of the Prince with the King of France's sister,' he had reported in June. In July, he heard that the 'drum went about London' as troops were drafted for the fight to restore the Palatinate, and was excited to note in early November that Count Mansfeld had arrived back in England, and had 'forthwith 12,000 men bound for him in England', and another 10,000 in Scotland. 'In our town,' Whiteway noted, 'were taken up 14 lusty fellows.' On the 16th of that month, he had 'news that the Prince's match with France was concluded' as well as a false rumour that 'the Duke of Buckingham was created Prince of Tipperary, a place in Ireland'. Five days later, 'the King commanded Bonfires, ringing of bells, discharging of ordinance at London for the conclusion of the French match', while 'the Prince of Tipperary' prepared to fetch the French princess. Prince Charles had also borrowed £35,000 from the City of London to spruce up his palace and wardrobe and John Chamberlain went to St Paul's to hear the organ play for two hours on its 'loudest pipes' – 'God grant it may prove worth all this noise,' he added.

An English agent crossed the North Sea to deliver the news of the match to Charles's sister and brother-in-law, Elizabeth and Frederick, exiled in the Hague. 'They were exceedingly delighted and it has revived their hopes,' a local envoy reported. For the first time since Frederick lost his German lands, James appeared ready to take action.

Not everyone was convinced. 'The nuptials are already so far advanced that it would seem nothing could hinder them more,' a newly appointed Venetian ambassador reported. But Rome had yet to deliver its dispensation – an essential condition for the French – 'and', he added, switching into coded writing, 'the king and Parliament could alone urge this pretext for breaking off'.

The ambassador attached a copy, also in code, of an undertaking signed by Count Mansfeld, which, 'in consideration of the levies granted by the King of Great Britain under his command', obliged him to promise to 'do nothing to harm the king's friends and allies', in particular 'the King of Spain and the Infanta Isabella' – the Spanish king's aunt and the governor of the Spanish Netherlands. Instead, James had instructed Mansfeld to employ his troops solely 'for the recovery of the states of the Prince Palatine'. If he did otherwise, 'he will justly incur his Majesty's disfavour and forfeit his position and pay'.

A formal event was organized for the signing of the treaty for the French match, but James, suffering another attack of gout, claimed that the pain in his fingers was so severe he could not put his hand to it, so it was stamped instead. He absented himself from the subsequent state banquet welcoming the French emissaries, and took to his bed, Charles acting in his place.

Soon after, George had a meeting with the new Venetian ambassador at which he spilled out his plans and ambitions. Even through the filters of deciphering and translation, his excitement shines through the dispatch sent home, as does his grasp of the huge complexities of European diplomacy and warfare. He beheld the Continent's mottled map, smudged with so many religions and realms, with a fresh clarity, and wanted to build a broad alliance, a spectrum that stretched from Venice to Sweden, from Catholics to Calvinists, from obscure confederacies such as the Grey League, to the great powers such as Britain and France, that would challenge the German and Spanish empires of the Habsburgs. If everyone played their part, he told the ambassador, their enemies, and in particular Spain – the kingdom that had humiliated him and the prince – would never 'recover from the blow'.

The diplomatic wrangling was not yet over, however, and in January 1625, Mansfeld's army found itself stuck at Dover, detained by ongoing negotiations over how it should be deployed. His men, a ramshackle collection of tramps and convicts pressed into service, became ever more restive as money and supplies began to run short. Soldiers were reported to be plundering surrounding villages and towns 'as though in an enemy's country'. Local authorities were having to declare martial law to maintain order. Men found breaking into houses were hanged to set an example.

Finally, on 31 January 1625, thanks in part to an emergency supply of cash from George's own pocket, the rampage was quelled and the fleet set sail.

The original plan was that it would land at Calais. From there, Mansfeld's army would march south to the French province of Lorraine and turn east towards central Germany, to engage directly with the imperial troops holding the Palatinate lands along the

Rhine. But, raising in British eyes 'strange doubts' about the French king's commitment to the project, Louis had abruptly announced that he would not allow Mansfeld's troops to cross French soil. This was apparently because the French had come to learn of the secret limitations James had set on Mansfeld's mission, which they took to show a worrying lack of commitment on his part.

So, Mansfeld was instead forced to head across the North Sea and land his troops in the Dutch Republic. The fleet approached Vlissingen – or Flushing, as the British called it – an inlet marking the border between the Spanish Netherlands and the Dutch Republic. Its arrival surprised the Dutch, who were unable to garrison the huge influx of troops. As a result, many of the ships were forced to sail further north, where a severe frost prevented them from landing. Disease had by now got hold of the weakened men, and they began to die in their hundreds. Bloated bodies were thrown overboard and began to wash ashore, forcing locals to dig burial pits to dispose of them.

As James's secretary put it, the Mansfeld mission had become a 'perplexed work'. Reports of the debacle were widely circulated back in Britain, and doubts began to spread about the whole enterprise. Dangerous and unpredictable forces had been unleashed. Among the English parliamentarians whose taxes were supposed to pay for the venture, the braggadocio kindled by George gave way to a more protective, insular mood. 'If we may live quietly at home, we shall not greatly care how the world goes abroad,' a glum Chamberlain observed.

The fortified city of Breda lies on the Dutch border with modern Belgium. In 1625, it was an outpost of the Protestant Dutch Republic, which was struggling to retain its independence from the Catholic Spanish Netherlands. The previous year, as part of the same strategic effort that had led to the seizing of the Palatinate, the city had come under attack from a Belgian–Italian force led by the formidable Spanish commander, Ambrogio Spinola. By early 1625 it had come close to surrender – threatening a devastating, even decisive blow to the Dutch, potentially trapping Mansfeld's army and ending all hopes of retaking the Palatinate. As it was only a few miles from where the remnants of Mansfeld's bedraggled army had assembled, and as the Dutch were offering supplies and weapons in return for assistance, it made sense to deploy in defence of the weakening city.

'Now is the time to help the good cause,' Mansfeld wrote to George, urging him to agree to the plan, and to provide more funds.

While he awaited confirmation, Mansfeld decided to march towards the city. By the time he reached the outskirts, George's reply had arrived. It was accompanied by orders from James addressed to the six English colonels recruited to lead the British contingent of Mansfeld's army. It seems both documents were unsealed at the same time. James's orders forbade his officers from becoming involved in Breda. George told Mansfeld he could go wherever and do whatever 'in his judgment' he thought best. Mansfeld and the colonels compared the two apparently contra-dictory orders, and, 'not with a little amazement', noted that they were written on the same date and by the same hand: that of the king's secretary.

The confusion was to have devastating consequences. The marooned troops began to 'die like dogs' as supplies once again ran short. One man found his plight so desperate, he cut his own throat so he would 'suffer no more'. Being 'pressed men', forcibly conscripted rather than volunteers, there were concerns that their treatment would 'breed a great cry' back home if their dreadful predicament became known.

When he heard the news, fury and frustration poured out of George. He feared the 'ill satisfaction' of Parliament, were it to be reassembled to raise more money. He bemoaned the 'good cause' being set 'further back', complained of 'the loss of time and the unfruitful expense of money', much of it his own. All the hard work that had gone into the mission was 'made vain' and his judge-ment had been 'infinitely charged' – he did not specify who by, but his very reticence was an obvious clue that he meant James.

Around the same time, the papal dispensation for Charles's marriage to Henrietta Maria arrived, apparently clearing the way for the wedding to go ahead. Plans had been discussed for George to go to Paris to escort her back to England. George had even arranged for his carriages to be sent to Dover for shipping over to France.

In the midst of all this, James's dogged obstinacy was suddenly and mysteriously revived. His bone of contention was the papal dispensation. It now included conditions not previously agreed, prompting James to threaten to break off the entire negotiation. The situation had become so volatile, George had to pretend to shun Effiat, referring the French ambassador directly to the king. He did, however, send a message to his friend Conway, the royal secretary, in 'blind ink' for him to read before the ambassador's audience, no doubt to brief him on what Effiat could say to mollify the king. In the event, Effiat 'encountered a severe storm' during which James, with unusual decisiveness, made it clear that he was prepared to go no further with the negotiations and considered them to be at a close.

Meanwhile, agents arriving in London from Spain and Brussels were getting a very different reception. It was noted how welcoming James was being, how he was treating them with 'graciousness', and appearing receptive to their pleas to reopen peace negotiations. He told them that he wished to 'remain at peace' with both Madrid and Flanders.

Confirming suspicions that a concerted effort was underway to undermine the anti-Spanish policy, George also discovered that Sir Walter Aston, who had taken over the ambassadorial role from John Digby in Madrid, had been lobbying Philip IV to send James's old friend Gondomar back to London. George responded by sending Aston a menacing letter, reminding him that Gondomar was 'the instrument to abuse my master, the Prince, and the state, and if now, by your means, the King should be fetched on again upon a new treaty, the blame would light upon you'.

Rumours swirled of yet another breach in relations between George and James, with Charles positioned uneasily between the two. There was disquiet 'in every direction' at the rumoured return of Gondomar, and it was noted that 'the Duke of Buckingham more than anyone else ought to take double precautions for his own salvation', as any 'renewal of confidence or relations with the Spaniards' was bound to lead to 'his fall'. Gondomar himself seemed almost to be taunting George from afar. He wrote a letter to the duke proclaiming that he was coming only to 'procure peace', and appointed as 'the field of our battle' the gallery in York House overlooking the Thames 'where I hope your excellency shall see that the Earl of Gondomar is an honest man, and that he hath been, is, and ever will be, a faithful and true servant and friend'.

William Whiteway, the Dorchester merchant whose business as an international wool trader meant he had good contacts on the Continent, had been monitoring developments with growing alarm. He reported in the opening days of March 1625 that 'the state of businesses' was beginning to 'alter at our Court' with the French match 'at a stand' and the Spaniards once more making overtures. 'Gondomar,' he confidently reported, 'is coming into England to treat with the king.'

It was as if all the struggles of the past year, begun with George's rallying cry to Parliament, had come to nothing.

What an Age We Do Live In

In late February, James, who had been restlessly touring his hunting lodges in Hertfordshire and Cambridgeshire, 'retired for fresh air and quietness to his manor at Theobald'. His ongoing ailments and the clamour of foreign affairs had crippled and exhausted him.

Restored a little by the tranquil surroundings, he sent a message to London begging George to join him. Charles was already there, but it was George he wanted. Despite recent tensions over the diplomatic wrangling, the lonely widower needed some pampering, and he could not abide being long without the favourite's company. Charles wrote to George of the king's impatience, saying he would 'take no pleasure' at Theobalds if he was not there.

'Dear Dad,' a frantically busy George replied, 'I cannot come tonight.' Depriving himself of the 'comfort and my heart's ease' of being with the king, gave him 'nothing but trouble and vexation'. But business detained him, including meetings, arranged at James's insistence, with the Spanish agents who had recently arrived in London. 'Tomorrow, without fail, I will wait of you,' he promised, and would bring 'the cunts', his mother Mary and wife Kate. He signed off affectionately, using the curious and intimate language of gratitude so characteristic of his letters, offering his 'humble thanks' to the king 'for not only clothing my outside, but filling me in, and with such precious bits as was only fit for you'.

The king's mood was further lowered by news of the death of yet another of his old Scottish friends: James, second Marquis of Hamilton, who had succeeded Ludovick Stuart as Lord High Steward, and now followed him into the grave. He had died on 2 March of 'pestilent fever, as is supposed'. His body had swelled 'immeasurably' after he died, it was reported. Following a post-mortem, physicians ascribed the swelling to some 'malign or venomous humour of the small pox or such like that might lie hid'. Others ascribed it to poison. The king was distressed to hear talk of a Catholic priest securing a deathbed conversion, though few took it seriously. As another Scottish noble observed, Hamilton had been 'more subject to his pleasures and the company of women than to priests'.

Over the days that followed, the king's gout became more troublesome, forcing him to take to his bed. He became gripped by a deep melancholy, weighed down by feelings of mortality and the 'apprehension of danger'. News of his condition began to spread through the medical world, and physicians began to gather at his bedside, eager to cure him.

James had an official team of medics licensed to practise by the College of Physicians and hand-picked by the king's chief physician, Sir Theodore Mayerne. But despite their eminence and learning, the king had never been particularly impressed by them. As they endeavoured to treat him, he would become restless and impatient, 'cursing' them for pretending 'any physic could be wholesome that was so troublesome'. Doctors, who made a lucrative living by dispensing elaborate medicines as well as advice, were known to be enthusiastic with their interventions, particularly when the client was rich. Now James found himself overwhelmed by them.

A range of treatments were prescribed in the *Pharmacopoeia Londinensis*, the official list of medicines published by the College of Physicians, for gout. Several took the form of oils, massaged into the skin. *Oleum Latericium Phylosophorum* – literally, 'Oil of Philosophers' Brick' – was one of the novel 'chemical' remedies thought to be particularly effective. It comprised fragments of brick pulverized and then heated, before being mixed with oil. It was a 'sovereign remedy' for the gout, apparently, as well as all other afflictions of the joints and nerves. *Unguentum e Nicotiana* or 'Ointment of Tobacco' was also recommended, though given James's famous disapproval of the weed, now being imported in bulk from the British colony in Virginia, the doctors may have tactfully looked for alternatives.

On 8 March, his health took a turn for the worse as he was struck by an attack of the tertian ague – malaria.

Malaria was a familiar disease at the time, its symptoms readily identifiable. They took the form of intermittent fevers that occurred as 'fits' every forty-eight hours (a 'tertian' ague) or seventy-two hours ('quartan'). Each fit comprised a succession of distinct phases. During the first 'cold' phase, the patient would shake violently, and sometimes experience a pricking sensation all over the skin. During the second, 'hot' phase, the pulse and breathing would suddenly accelerate. The shaking and pricking might intensify, and might culminate with vomiting. It was noted that any urine passed during this phase would usually be cloudy. In the final phase, the fever would subside, and the patient would begin to sweat copiously.

This distinctive pattern was understood to result from an imbalance of the humours, which might typically be produced by the excessive consumption of certain foods, such as unripe fruit and raw oysters, and overexertion, in particular too much hunting, swimming or tennis. Treatment therefore relied on trying to restore balance by purging excess fluids. This demanded prompt and often drastic measures, as the humours (and, James seemed to believe, the doctors) became increasingly corrupted the longer they were allowed to linger.

Various methods of purging were available, from the use of expectorants and laxatives to scarification and 'cupping' – incising the skin in the area of the body where the corrupt humours were thought to have accumulated, followed by the application of hot cups to the wounds, which would draw blood out as they cooled.

In the case of a tertian fever, a 'remollitive clyster' (enema) was a first line of attack, injected into the rectum to cleanse the bowel of any 'rotten and stinking choler'. Then a 'loosing' or 'purging' syrup or electuary (a medicinal paste) might be administered orally. These medicines were extremely complex to make and had varying effects. The *Pharmacopoeia Londinensis* suggested several purging electuaries for cases such as James's. 'Diacassia cum Manna', for example, contained such ingredients as violet flowers and damask prunes mixed with tamarind and candied peel, and worked 'gently and without trouble'. More difficult cases might demand the use of a *Confectio Hamech*, comprising a long list of ingredients, including senna, rhubarb, the astringent fruit myrobalan and the toxic herb wormwood, which 'purged very violently, and is not safe given alone'.

'A tertian in the spring is physic for a king,' James's servants would have intoned merrily, but he found the physicians' ministrations unendurable. Chamberlain noted that 'if he would suffer himself to be ordered and governed by physical rules' – the physicians' instructions – the sickness would proceed 'without any manner of danger'. The Venetian ambassador echoed the sentiment: 'His majesty's tertian fever continues but as the last attack diminished the mischief, the physicians consider that he will soon be completely recovered. His impatience and irregularities do him more harm than the sickness.'

Around this time, the 'cunts' turned up, Mary bringing with her a doctor called John Remington. Mary and George spent lavishly on physicians and medicines, and the countess held strong opinions on the best remedies in a market heavily populated by mystics, wise-women and empirics. Her scepticism of orthodox medicine was not misplaced. The doctors' own claims to competency rested on slender theoretical foundations and generally poor outcomes. Even William Harvey, now celebrated as one of the greatest medical scientists of modern times, peddled remedies that can only be described as quackery.

Earlier that year, in the aftermath of his own prolonged illness, George had sent an abashed letter to James admitting to spending £400 – at least twenty times the price of a conventional consultation – to acquire a treatment developed by an alchemist. 'I have never given credit to those that undertake to have the Philosophers' Stone,' he wrote, alluding to the fabled alchemical substance that was supposed to be the elixir of life, but apparently the alchemist – dubbed by the duke 'my devil' – had managed to extract a compound that would preserve the king from sickness, so he felt compelled to give him some support.

Remington was not a member of the College of Physicians. He was a humble country doctor from the Essex market town of

Dunmow, where he had built up a respectable practice treating local dignitaries. New Hall, where George had gone to recover from his protracted illness of the previous year, was included in Remington's rounds, and Mary had ordered from him a herbal 'posset ale' as part of her son's treatment.

Mayerne, the king's chief physician, was abroad at the time James contracted his fever. He had attended Prince Henry during his fatal illness, and on the basis of that experience had drawn up a detailed list of instructions for treating members of the royal family. His first and main command (ignoring his own dubious origins as a medic) was that no laymen or unlicensed doctors should be given access to the patient. 'Cranks and triflers, the fraudulent parasites of the great' must be excluded at all costs. Only the heads of the profession 'whose number is very small and select', must be admitted, the royal 'physicians-in-ordinary' who made up the king's medical team.

The number at Theobalds was certainly select, but not so small. Deputizing for Mayerne was the seventy-year-old president of the College of Physicians, Dr Henry Atkins. He had been a trusted royal medic since James had succeeded to the English throne, sent to Scotland in 1604 to ensure the safe delivery of the sickly Charles to London. Atkins was joined by several more junior but highly experienced doctors, including a young Dr David Beton, who would not become a full fellow of the college until 1629; Dr Alexander Ramsey, who had studied in Basel in 1617; Dr James Chambers, a Scottish academic; and Dr John Craig, made a college fellow in 1616 and possibly the longest-serving of James's physicians – all of them Scots. The other English members of the contingent included Dr Matthew Lister, a 'censor' of the College of Physicians responsible for policing medical practice throughout London, Dr John Moore and Dr William Harvey, who would go on to become Charles's most devoted physician, as well as the discoverer of the circulation of the blood. Sir William Paddy, another veteran as long-standing as Dr Atkins, and an ex-president of the college, was also due any day.

In all, at least nine medics would be in attendance during the king's illness, amounting to nearly a third of the total number licensed to practise in London.

For all their eminence, not all of these royal doctors had un-blemished records, medical or otherwise. Sir William Paddy was rumoured to have been caught naked in his consulting rooms with one of his female patients, while Dr Moore, as part of a campaign to be accepted as a fellow of the College of Physicians, had given a £20 'gift' to President Atkins, which other members of the college's ruling body took to be a bribe. He was also suspected of being a Catholic, which had led to the Archbishop of Canterbury banning him from practising.

Nevertheless, they were all more or less in agreement on how to treat the king, and began to work in shifts to keep an eye on him as the 'fits' of feverish attacks began to take on their familiar pattern. A day or two into the illness, hopes were already high that the ague had more or less run its course. The king seemed to be approaching his third attack, which one of his Scottish courtiers thought would 'do him good and no harm', as the copious sweating would help rebalance his distempered humours.

George was at Theobalds on 11 March, and the king was well enough to play cards with him. Around this time, Remington began to prepare the medicine the duke and Mary had instructed him to bring. It was made to the doctor's own secret recipe, and was said to be based on mithridate, an elaborate antidote usually made to an ancient recipe comprising as many as fifty ingredients. It came in two forms: a potion for drinking and a treacle that was applied to the skin using a plaster. James was told that it was highly recom-mended, having been used successfully to treat feverish attacks suffered not only by George the previous year, but by Robert Rich, the Earl of Warwick, and Henry Carew, the Earl of Totnes, both close to the Villiers clan.

George had by now installed himself in a private room near the king's bedchamber, where the plaster, a strip of leather, was prepared by being slathered with the treacly mithridate. George and his mother then took the plaster, together with the potion, to the king's bedside.

The doctors were not particularly concerned with the king's condition at that moment, and, despite Mayerne's instructions, loath to interfere with an intervention by the royal favourite. So they left Mary to instruct Archibald Hay, the king's surgeon, to apply the plaster to the king's abdomen and wrists. Nothing much happened, and over the next few days he seemed to be on the road to recovery. On 16 March, the royal secretary Conway could report that the king's latest fit was 'less intemperate than the rest, and hath left more clearness and cheerfulness in his looks than the former'. On 18 March, the Venetian ambassador noted that 'his Majesty's tertian fever continues but, as the last attack diminished the mischief, the physicians consider that he will soon be completely recovered'. A fit the following day was so mild, many assumed it would be the last.

The king was well enough to receive a translation of a book 'reflecting' on the Holy Roman Emperor, the King of Spain, and infanta, 'out of a recent work on the whole proceeding relating to the Palatinate, that His Majesty may judge how far it will coincide with any relation that he may be induced to put forth'. It had been sent to him by John Murray, recently made Earl of Annandale, deputed by the king to stamp Gondomar's letters of safe conduct, and who a few days later would receive £300 for performing a mysterious 'secret service' on the king's behalf.

Whether George had a chance to see the patient's reading material is unclear, as he went to deal with pressing business in London, leaving Mary at the king's bedside to keep him comfortable and entertained. The duke was back at Theobalds by Monday 21 March, thirteen days into the illness, when the king seemed well enough to get out of bed.

James had managed to walk a short distance the day before, but had felt a 'heaviness at his heart', and returned to bed. Despite the signs of improvement, he was still anxious, insisting to the bemused physicians that the next fit would surely be worse because the previous one had been so mild.

At about 4 p.m. that Monday, George and his 'folks', including his mother, came into the sickroom with the plaster and potion that had been applied the week before. At the time, James was being attended by doctors Harvey, Beton, Craig, Lister and Ramsey – a formidable group. Soon after, they were joined by Dr Moore, apparently at the behest of Mary and George. Dr Beton was surprised and a bit put out to see Moore there, as he was 'no sworn physician to the king'.

Charcoal portrait of George, sketched by Peter Paul Rubens during his visit to Paris in May 1625.

Henry Frederick, Prince of Wales, Charles's older brother, by Isaac Oliver, c.1612

Charles when he was Duke of York, by Robert Peake the Elder, c.1612, around the time of Henry's death.

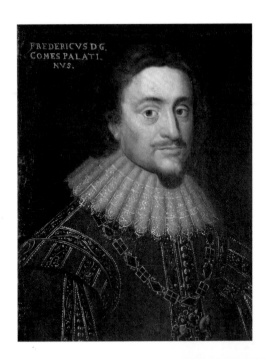

Frederick, Count Palatine
and King of Bohemia.

Elizabeth, Frederick's wife
and Charles's sister, the
'Winter Queen'.

Conde de Gondomar, Spanish ambassador and close friend of James.

Infanta Maria of Spain, Charles's
first fiancée.

Philip III, King of Spain and
Maria's father.

Anne of Austria, wife of Louis XIII
of France and Maria's sister.

Don Gaspar de Guzmán, Conde-Duque
de Olivares and Philip IV's *valido*.

Endymion Porter, George's Spanish
secretary, by Van Dyck.

Sir John Eliot, MP for Cornwall,
Vice Admiral of Devon.

Supper with James, engraving by Melchior Tavernier, 1623–4, showing
James as guest of the Spanish ambassador Mendoza at the height of tensions
between James, George and Charles.

Henrietta Maria,
Charles's French queen,
by Van Dyck, *c.*1632.

Dr William Harvey,
who attended James in his
final hours and became
Charles's most trusted
physician.

Sketch for equestrian portrait of George commissioned from
Peter Paul Rubens in 1625. The finished painting, which hung at
York House, was destroyed by fire in 1949.

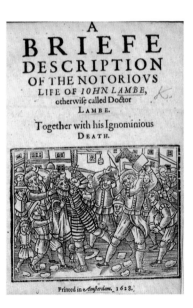

Title page of *A Briefe Description of the Notorious Life of John Lambe*, 1628, an engraving depicting Lambe's death.

Van Dyck's 1630 family portrait of Charles, Henrietta Maria, their children and pets, known as the 'great peece'.

In violation of Mayerne's instructions, Moore was allowed to remain and the other doctors looked on as George personally administered a dose of Remington's mysterious potion. Some of the physicians were worried that the king might be entering the 'prohibited time', the three-hour period in the lead-up to an expected fit when the use of medicines was considered to be dangerous, but they apparently stifled their concerns. Only Dr Lister was brave enough to speak up, saying the king should 'forebear' the treatment, but he was ignored. Doctors Lister, Harvey and Beton then left the room.

Those remaining watched as the king's barber-surgeon Archibald Hay once again adjusted the king's nightgown to expose his abdomen. He then pressed the plaster onto the side of his stomach, and onto his wrists. George gave the patient another sip of the potion.

The king started to suffer a violent fit. His symptoms were later described as panting, raving, swooning. His pulse became irregular. He was offered a third helping of the potion, but it was refused. Dr Craig went to George's room and in front of the duke and Mary made some 'plain speeches' complaining about what they had done. Craig was dismissed from court. Henry Gibb, one of his grooms of the bedchamber, also registered a protest. At midnight, the king told Gibb to take the plaster off.

The following day, Tuesday 22 March, a fortnight into the illness, Lord Keeper John Williams rushed to Theobalds. He had just heard the alarming news that the king's sickness had suddenly become 'dangerous to death'. Dr Chambers, who had been absent since the previous Saturday, also arrived, and was shocked to see the transformation in the king's condition. James was given some broth, which produced a bowel movement considered to be of 'large benefit'. He relapsed into a deep sleep. He revived a little later that day, and a small communion service was held in the room, James sharing the sacrament with Charles, George and other members of court, who beheld the ceremony in tears that mixed 'comfort and grief'.

Around this time a delegation of the doctors went to see Charles, and asked that only they be allowed to treat James. Their request was ignored.

That night, Chambers and Ramsey, two of James's Scottish doctors, were left in charge. Chambers heard James muttering about the treatment he had received, describing the potion George had given him as making him 'burn and roast'. It was supposed to be a posset of gillyflower, a soothing medicine. 'Will you murder me and slay me?' the king had apparently said.

The following days were a blur of frantic efforts by the physicians to treat the king's sudden and catastrophic decline. Fits were now lasting twenty hours, and when they abated the king's pulse slowed dramatically. An 'uncertain change' was noted in his urine, which indicated 'an obscure and hidden malignity'. Purges were dispensed to try to emit the rotting humours, which resulted in a copious bout of diarrhoea, during which the king produced 'burned, bilious, and putrid things'. His speech began to fail, his tongue and throat swelled and, unable to drink, he suffered a violent thirst. Scabs were noticed on his tongue.

In the midst of this melee, two foreign agents, unimaginatively codenamed 'X' and 'XX', dispatched letters to their spymaster, Jean Baptiste Van Male, based in Brussels, the capital of the Spanish Netherlands. They had both somehow managed to penetrate the royal bedchamber at Theobalds, and were at the king's side throughout his illness. X reported the 'strange tragedies' he had witnessed involving 'plasters and potions', which had brought the king close to death. XX was even more concerned, declaring that he feared for 'all Christendom' because 'the duke hath the absolute power and possession of the prince' and, if James should die, he would 'endeavour the ruin' of not just the Habsburgs but 'all Catholic princes'.

XX also enclosed a letter written 'late at night' from Theobalds relating the events of Monday 21 March. According to the anonymous correspondent, the king had been suffering 'an ordinary ague and his fits lessening by fair degrees' when the duke, either to treat it or 'for a worse end', did 'force the king to make a plaster on his stomach and a scurvy drink inwards without so much as acquainting any one doctor therewith though 8 were in the house'. As a result, 'that night he was one hour dead, and two hours more senseless, not knowing anybody'. The letter reported that Dr Craig had accused the duke of having as good as given the king 'poison', provoking a furious denial from the favourite, who consulted James Ley, a former judge who was at Theobalds, about bringing legal action against the doctor. George also 'prevailed' on Charles – whose presence throughout the king's illness went curiously unnoticed by others – to have Craig and the recalcitrant groom Henry Gibb thrown into gaol. The duke, it was also noted, had used the royal stamp, which the king had with him at the time because he was too weak to sign official documents, to authorize a warrant 'to stay the Count of Gondomar from coming hither'.

'Fie upon this time what an age we do live in,' XX had lamented.

On Friday 25 March, the elderly Sir William Paddy arrived, and, on seeing the king, pronounced there was nothing more the physicians could do for him other than pray. After a crisis meeting the following day, the physicians handed over the king's care to George Abbot, the Archbishop of Canterbury, and John Williams. By dawn on Sunday, it was clear that the end was close. The king indicated that he wanted his old friend Williams to lead the prayers. 'Come, Lord Jesu, come quickly', the bishop whispered several times, as the king's breathing became more irregular. James's soul 'began to retreat more inward and so by degrees he took less notice of external things'. Just before noon on Sunday, 27 March 1625, with 'lords and servants kneeling on one side, his archbishops, bishops and other of his chaplains on the other side of his bed, without pangs or convulsions at all, Solomon slept'.

Within a quarter of an hour members of the Privy Council, who had rushed up from London, had met and pronounced Charles king. A hurriedly improvised ceremony was staged at the main entrance of the house, the traditional place to mark the crossing of a great personal and national threshold. There, the new monarch was proclaimed by the Knight Marshal. Secretary Conway dictated the resounding declaration: 'That whereas it has pleased God to take to his mercy our most gracious sovereign King James of famous memory, we proclaim Prince Charles his rightful and indubitable heir to the kingdom of England, Scotland, France and Ireland.' Flustered by the significance and pace of events, the unfortunate Knight Marshal, who was repeating Conway's words, declared Charles the 'rightful and dubitable heir'. A potentially excruciating gaffe was more likely to have produced smiles rather than embarrassment, because, for the first time in nearly eighty years, the English throne was passing directly from father to son. The ideal of primogeniture, the fragile underpinning of hereditary monarchy, had been fulfilled.

The instant the ceremony was completed, James Howell, who had been with Charles and George in Madrid, jumped onto his horse and set off for London to break the news. He arrived to find the City gates shut, apparently in response to the news of the king's death, and was annoyed to find that someone had managed to get there before him. Charles and George departed soon after in the king's carriage, reaching St James's Palace some time mid-afternoon. George was put in a room 'as near to the king as conveniency might be'. After they had refreshed themselves, they went to St Paul's Cathedral, where Bishop Laud was to give evensong. Laud was given the news just as the service was about to start.

'I ascended the pulpit, much troubled, and in a very melancholy moment,' Laud recorded in his diary. An effective preacher, he began to speak no doubt eloquently about the loss of a beloved sovereign, but found he was interrupted by loud sobs. Looking down into the congregation, he could see they were coming from the Duke of Buckingham, and perhaps out of sympathy for his friend and patron, as well as respect, he 'broke off' his sermon in the middle.

Recovering himself, George later went to Charles's chamber 'and continued with him alone in very private and serious discourse for more than two hours' while the rest of the palace, exhausted by the day's events, slept.

Those lying awake in the new king's antechamber, listening to the faint murmurings of the two men through the door, might have marvelled that Charles was 'so much favouring' James's favourite. As George's biographer, Sir Henry Wotton noted, the state of a favourite is usually 'at best tenant-at-will, and rarely transmitted'. His honours and status do not usually survive his patron. Jealousies and rivalries that have built up over the years might be expected to be unleashed by the change in regime. Yet George was already as comfortably ensconced in the new king's bedchamber as he had been in the old. Indeed, some who listened might have wondered who was more in command.

Charles's succession was proclaimed that night at Whitehall and Cheapside, but celebrations were muted by a persistent drizzle – weather suited, noted the political writer James Howell, to the 'cloudy' mood of the times. The realm, Howell wrote to his father some weeks later, had been left in a precarious state, with the new king 'engaged in a war with a potent prince, the people by long desuetude unapt for arms, the fleet-royal in quarter repair, himself without a queen, his sister without a country, the crown pitifully laden with debts, and the purse of the state lightly ballasted'. He nevertheless hoped that God will 'make him emerge, and pull this island out of all the plunges, and preserve us from worser times'.

Not everyone was pessimistic. Chamberlain found a short elegy that he thought he should share with his friend in Holland, Dudley Carleton, though perhaps more out of hope than conviction. It played on the well-known association of the appearance of comets with historic events:

> Q. Can a king die, and we no Comet see?
> Tell me, Astrologers, how can this be?

> A. Heaven's Beacons burn but to give Alarm
> Unto a State of some ensuing harm.
> The Angels carrying up our blessed King
> Did still with Musique his sweet Requiem sing.
> No Innovation being to be heard
> Why should Heaven summon men unto their guard?
> His Spirit was redoubled on his Son
> And that was seen at his Assumption.

Act IV

We the Commons

Poisonous Applications

His charcoal moving across the paper in graceful arcs and sweeps, Peter Paul Rubens put the finishing touches to his sketch of George, being careful to capture the lively frizz of the duke's long hair. He paid close attention to his eyebrows, delicately delineating each strand to emphasize their shape, and finished off the moustache with touches of a tawny-red chalk to catch the colouring. He tinted the lips with the same colour, giving them the sort of full, rounded quality that came to be known as 'Rubenesque'.

The irises of the eyes, which looked slightly askance at him, were filled in with cross-hatching and a light smudging of the chalk. A circle was drawn around them to give them definition. Rubens picked up a pen, dipped it into an inkwell, and marked a sharp punctuation point in the centre of each eye, bringing a startling intensity to the duke's gaze.

The sketch was to form the basis of two new commissions from George for an equestrian portrait that would become the centre-piece of the main reception room in York House, and a 'plafond' or ceiling painting, for his bedchamber.

Rubens had already been given a commission to work on pictures to decorate the new Banqueting House in London, but there had been a dispute over the quality of the work he had produced, which turned out to be by his studio staff rather than his own hand. He had been forced to take it back and offer a replacement. Here was his chance to redeem himself.

George had seen Rubens's work in Madrid, including a magnificent portrait of the Duke of Lerma in full armour mounted on a white steed, a military treatment which captured with vivid intensity the subject's majestic confidence and power. That was the sort of quality the artist was now expected to reproduce for George. The plafond was to represent George's astonishing social ascent using a classical theme. He would be featured in an almost Christ-like pose being conducted up to a temple in the heavens by Mercury and Minerva, with the figure of Envy pulling at his ankle, and a lion representing Anger threatening to bite his foot. A considerable fee of £500 had been agreed for the works – nearly twice the price the almost bankrupt duke had paid for Titian's *Ecce Homo*.

Rubens was seated with a bandaged foot, a cobbler having wrenched it fitting a boot. As he sketched they talked. He was a diplomat and politician as well as a sought-after artist, a devout Catholic who acted as a confidential advisor and agent of Archduchess Isabella, governor of the Spanish Netherlands and aunt of Philip IV of Spain. A meeting with George provided him with a chance to size up a significant political figure, and one of the archduchess's main antagonists.

They talked about the need for peace between religions as well as nations, Rubens later recalling the duke as showing a 'laudable zeal' for the 'interests of Christianity'. Rubens had heard the military threats that had accompanied James's final weeks, and expressed the hope that, now Charles was securely installed on the throne, his father's more peaceful approach to diplomacy might be revived, focused on preventing rather than stirring up war, the 'scourge from Heaven'.

Yet from behind the easel, the shrewd eye of the artist could see little to reassure him. George's expression has both a relaxed and threatening quality to it, a suggestion of what Rubens later characterized as 'caprice and arrogance'. The hint of a smile could be misleading, as an upward curve at the corners of the mouth was exaggerated by the flick of the long whiskers of his moustache. He emanated a vitality that teetered between the tragic and the heroic, the mercurial resolve of a man who had everything and nothing to lose. 'He seems to me forced by his own daring either to triumph or to die gloriously,' Rubens would recall.[*]

---

[*] The paintings, which ended up in the collection of the Earl of Jersey at Osterley Park, were destroyed in a warehouse fire in 1949. The chalk-and-ink sketch is in the collection of Albertina Museum in Vienna.

It was May 1625, Paris in the spring. Rubens had been summoned from his Antwerp studio by the formidable French queen mother, Marie de' Medici, to deliver fifteen of twenty-four paintings she had commissioned for the Palais du Luxembourg. They had been due a few months later, but she had insisted on them being installed early, even though some were unfinished, as she wanted them in place for the marriage by proxy of her daughter, Henrietta Maria, to Charles.

George was there for the same occasion, and was due to take the bride back to meet her groom in London as soon as the celebrations were over. The betrothal, a small affair involving just members of the royal family and English ambassadors, had taken place in the Louvre on 28 April 1625 (8 May in France, which used Europe's New Style calendar), a month and a day after James's death.

The wedding itself had been on 1 May (11 May), with Charles de Lorraine, the Protestant Duc de Chevreuse and a distant cousin of Charles, acting as the king's proxy. The princess had dressed in a lavish gown of gold and silver thread decorated with diamonds and fleurs-de-lis, the fabric making the train so heavy it took three women to carry it. In the late afternoon, Henrietta Maria had been led from the archbishop's palace along an arcade raised on pillars and swathed in satin to the great west door of Notre Dame, where Chevreuse, in a black velvet suit with slashed sleeves, was waiting for her on a specially erected stage. The ceremony was conducted in the open, with Cardinal de la Rochefoucauld presiding, intoning a liturgy acceptable to both sides. Onlookers, including the English ambassadors, could admire a demonstration of ecumenical toleration, a Catholic princess, god-daughter of the pope, exchanging vows with the representative of one of Europe's most powerful Protestant figures. But as soon as the ceremony was over, Henrietta Maria and her entourage disappeared through the doors into the church for a private mass, leaving the proxy groom and English ambassadors to stand outside.

As celebrations to mark the wedding had begun in Paris, London was in mourning for the death of King James.

The late king had lain in state in Denmark House for a month, his body 'seared and wrapped in lead' inside a sumptuous coffin filled with 'odours and spices' to cover the smell of putrefaction, and decorated with purple velvet, 'the handles, nails, and all other iron-work about it being richly hatched with gold'. A life-size effigy dressed in state robes had been placed on top of the coffin, the painted, wooden head bearing James's crown laid on a purple velvet cushion. Despite Protestant disapproval of idol worship, the effigy became a holy relic for the thousands of members of the public who poured into the chamber of sorrows to pay their respects.

George, meanwhile, had suffered another collapse in his mental as well as physical health, suffering from an 'impostume' or purulent cyst that 'broke in his head' and made him 'somewhat crazy'. He became so weak, he had to be carried around the streets in a chair. Whether it was grief or remorse, it was intense. The royal secretary Conway saw him become 'sorrow itself': if 'grief and sickness not shorten his days as friends fear it will', it seemed possible he might commit suicide. Charles tried to console the duke, promising to be an even more gracious master than his father. At one point, he even showed a hint of impatience, suggesting that if George were to show any more anguish, it would be to suggest 'want of confidence' in the new king.

While George lingered in his sickbed, rumours that James had been poisoned began to circulate. The Venetian ambassador had heard the whispers of 'poisonous applications', and thought the 'common people' would want to enquire into them. At least one newsletter reported Dr Craig's expulsion from the king's bedside. But the allegations were vague and drowned out by an outpouring of sermons and eulogies. One, a complex work by the celebrated poet Hugh Holland, was addressed to George, calling on him 'to help us in our weeping', and wondered how one who bore 'the name of George the Dragon-killer' had failed to kill the 'dragon-fever' that had taken the king. It was strange that James should have died of a mild 'tertian', but in the end Holland blamed the royal doctors, who 'for the Crowned head' had 'no physic' – at least, none that worked.

The funeral took place on 7 May. As many as nine thousand people dressed in black, at royal expense, assembled for the event. Even on an occasion calling for a tone of restrained solemnity, the emphasis was on splendour: £28,000 – nearly double the entire budget for Elizabeth I's funeral and monument – had been spent on cloth alone. Charles had to borrow £60,000 from City merchants to cover the costs.

The heavy coffin was carried from Denmark House to Westminster Abbey in a magnificent funeral chariot with 'pillars, rails, valence and fringes', covered with a large pall of velvet with 'deep' fringes of gold and silk.

The procession was enormous and somewhat disorganized. It was led by 300 'poor men in gowns', who followed servants of the royal household, 'door-keepers, pot-scourers, turnbroaches' – spit turners – 'bell-ringers, watermen' and so on, followed by tradesmen, 'arras-makers, gilders, potters, cutlers, fruiterers, ale-brewers' and 'provision-makers-extraordinary', followed by 'grooms of all offices', followed by yeomen, followed by officers of London's lord mayor, followed by the 'blanch-lion pursuivant-at-armes-extraordinary', in escalating order of precedence through the ranks of burghers, mayors and ambassadors, knights, barons and earls, culminating with the hearse, followed by the 'chief mourner' Charles, supported by the earls of Arundel and Rutland, George's father-in-law.

The cortege trundled along the Strand as the crowds watched in respectful silence. It turned down into Whitehall at Charing Cross, passing the Banqueting House and coming to a halt at the great west door of Westminster Abbey. The coffin was taken from the hearse and conveyed by the pall-bearers up the soaring Gothic nave to the altar, where the 'offer for the defunct', the receiving of the body, was performed. Charles then retired, and a two-hour sermon was given by Lord Keeper Williams. Entitled 'Great Britain's Solomon', the text was the eleventh chapter of the first book of Kings, which tells the story of Solomon's funeral.

George, barely recovered from his sickness, was an uncharacteristically restrained presence, unnoticed by official and ambassadorial accounts of the event, walking alone behind the king and his entourage, leading James's favourite steed, the usually vivacious duke weighed down by his drizzle-soaked mourning clothes.[*]

---

[*] It is possible George did not even attend the funeral. There is mention of a 'master of the horse' in the cortege, who it has been assumed was the duke, but he may have been Thomas Howard, who served Charles in that capacity when he was the Prince of Wales.

Later that day, he was visited by his old friend Sir George Goring, who had just arrived from Paris with news about the proxy marriage celebrations underway in France. Henrietta Maria, he told George, had announced that she would come to London the following week.

George's response was a violent switch in mood. His illness and melancholy vanished, along with other pressing business, such as planning for Charles's coronation, dealing with the intricacies of summoning a new Parliament and putting the navy on a war footing. Regret and hesitancy were replaced by impetuosity and brio as he announced he would leave for Paris immediately to collect the queen.

During James's final weeks, when the old king was trying to reopen negotiations with the Spanish, George had made preparations for a formal state visit to France. He had already ordered a magnificent wardrobe, including a rich, white satin and velvet suit covered with diamonds and, for more formal occasions, a purple satin jacket embroidered with pearls. He had arranged for an entourage comprising 160 musicians and a 200-strong team of labourers, cooks, footmen, gentlemen, grooms, pages and huntsmen, all clothed in new livery, along with twenty-two watermen, wearing 'skycollared' taffeta tunics bearing anchors and George's arms in gold thread. He had already dispatched to Dover his coach, upholstered in rich velvet and decorated with gold lace.

The duke now moved so swiftly that even these preparations could not be completed in time and had to be abandoned. Instead, recapturing the spirit of the 'venturous knights' who had left for Madrid two years earlier, he left London with just three trusted associates, Goring among them, and a few servants. They sailed from Dover on 12 May, a good wind taking them across the Channel in just four hours. Seized by an extravagant, generous mood, he tipped the master and crew of the ship £70 for the quick crossing, and in a gallant gesture that must have aroused local excitement, gave £30 to the wife and daughter of the postmaster in Boulogne, a belated gift for their help when he and the prince had passed through two years earlier disguised as Tom and John Smith.

George and his company galloped to Paris, arriving two days later. He stayed (at his own expense – running to as much as £200 a day) at the home of the Duc de Chevreuse, Charles's proxy at the wedding. The French duke was well placed to introduce George formally to King Louis, and to overcome any awkwardness that might arise from his disguised visit in 1623. Furthermore, Marie de Rohan, the twenty-four-year-old Duchesse de Chevreuse (and mistress of England's ambassador in France, Henry Rich, the dashing Earl of Holland) was a lady-in-waiting to Anne of Austria, the French queen.

George's formal introduction to Parisian society caused a sensation few Englishmen have matched before or since. Overcome by a manic, almost wild exuberance, he dazzled the French nobility, flourishing in the courtly milieu of gallantry and extravagance later immortalized in Alexandre Dumas's *Three Musketeers*. Dressed in his diamond-studded white suit, George was 'the best made man in the world, with the finest looks', gushed a member of Anne of Austria's household. The daughter of Anne's secretary thought he had a 'great soul' as well as a beautiful face, and noted how he seemed to embody lofty and noble thoughts, scintillatingly combined with dangerous and shameful desires. He filled the ladies of the court with joy, 'and something more than joy', provoking envy among the court gallants, and jealousy among the husbands. The Comte de Brienne reflected the mood, noting sourly how the Duke of Buckingham absolutely shone, dancing with 'great applause' while rivals were made to look on. He should restrain himself, thought the count: be more respectful and less vain.

Vain or not, *tout le monde* wanted to emulate him. In the capital of European style and sophistication, the English hunting cap the duke wore proved to be such a hit that before long every man at court was to be seen wearing one, the style becoming known as *un boukinkan*. Everyone seemed to fall in love with him, yearned to be near him, wanted to please him. At one of the many masques laid on for his entertainment, he danced with his usual energy and grace, but in the process lost one of the diamonds from his suit. To his delight, it was restored to him the following morning.

The one person who did not submit to his charms was Henrietta Maria. During his visit two years before, he and Charles had glimpsed her through the tresses of their periwigs as she rehearsed a ballet with her sister-in-law Anne of Austria. It was like 'a stolen taste of something that provoketh the appetite', as George's friend and biographer Sir Henry Wotton put it salaciously. Now she was fifteen years old, pious, strong-willed and reserved, with looks that were subject to close scrutiny and divided opinion. One of her relatives cruelly described the shock of Henrietta's failure to match up to her portraits, the reality being 'short, with long, dry hands, uneven shoulders, and teeth sticking out of her mouth like fangs'. However, even the relative had to concede that she had 'very beautiful eyes, a regular nose, and a delightful colouring in her face'.

Despite his ability to speak her language, and a sympathy for Catholic rites and culture, George's efforts to win her over were rebuffed. She missed a meeting with the duke in favour of greeting a cardinal who was visiting Paris. When George questioned her priorities, she told him she was merely displaying the courtesy due to an emissary of the pope. There had been optimistic efforts to get her to accept a French translation of the Anglican Book of Common Prayer as a gift, but she had shown no interest in engaging with the religion of her new home. Instead, she prepared for her departure in a mood of frosty compliance, choosing a large retinue of familiar ladies-in-waiting, advisors and confessors to insulate her from the foreign, heretical world into which she was about to be immersed.

George would not allow her haughtiness to dampen his mood. He gorged on the city's ability to cater for the most refined tastes and basic appetites, thriving on the sense of adventure and lack of responsibility. As well as commissioning his portrait from Rubens, he made regular visits to the Duc de Chevreuse's barber to have his hair curled and his beard and moustache trimmed, a service he found so pleasing he paid £100 to take one of the barber's assistants back to England. He also visited the formal gardens of the Tuileries with his gardener John Tradescant, who had arrived some days after him with a cart carrying 'my lord's stuff and trunks', and they bought exotic plants for the ever-expanding Villiers estates back home.

Reflecting his surging confidence, George also decided to approach the king's chief minister, Cardinal Richelieu, about his plan to create a league of nations, Catholic as well as Protestant, capable of taking on the Habsburg empires of Spain and the Holy Roman Emperor.

The cool, sophisticated *eminence rouge* was a very different character to the bumptious duke – restrained where George was exuberant, scholarly and calculating where George was self-taught and instinctive. Richelieu's eyes, pulled down by their sloping lids, his arched eyebrows, aquiline nose and pursed lips gave an impression of sharpness and focus as he listened politely to George's grandiose plan. France now shared with Britain concerns that gave them common cause, George told the cardinal. For example, just as Britain was trying to save the Palatinate in Germany, so France had its own concerns over the port of Genoa in northern Italy, and the Valtelline, a state on the Swiss border that commanded the passes connecting Germany to northern Italy. Both were in Habsburg hands, and being used by Philip of Spain to send troops into Germany in support of the emperor.

George proposed Britain and France join together with other states across the Continent and its religious divide to form a grand military alliance capable of challenging Habsburg dominance. Denmark, Sweden, the Dutch Republic, Venice, and several embattled states in Germany were all ready to sign up, he claimed. Great fleets of British ships were in place in Plymouth and Portsmouth to attack the coasts of Spain and the Spanish Netherlands. They could land British armies in Flanders which, with the aid of the famous French cavalry, could capture Dunkirk, link up with Count Mansfeld, and recover Artois, the region of Flanders that France had ceded to the Spanish Netherlands. With Habsburg forces facing a battle on two fronts, the Palatinate would be liberated, and France would control the Alpine passes into southern Germany, severely weakening imperial and Spanish efforts to encircle France's easterly and southerly land borders.

The restrained Richelieu listened to George's epic geopolitical vision with polite consideration, but, with Jesuitical precision and clarity, dismissed it. He was prepared to support Mansfeld's troops in Holland for a further six months, but that was all. He had other issues to contend with. Just before George's arrival in Paris, a Huguenot leader, the Duc de Soubise, had led a Protestant revolt at La Rochelle, one of France's strategic Atlantic ports. The rebels were occupying Ré, an island which lay at the opening of the harbour, allowing them to blockade the port. Soubise, Richelieu might have coolly noted, had been welcomed in London when he visited in 1622, and no doubt many of his British co-religionists still supported him and his mutinous forces in a misguided belief that they shared common cause. Religious differences between kings Louis and Charles, in other words, could not be ignored.

In an effort to distance himself from Soubise and keep the focus on his plans for an anti-Habsburg league, George insisted the situation in La Rochelle was not about religion, but Spanish efforts to stir up trouble. Richelieu dismissed the idea, making it clear that all the evidence pointed to this being another outbreak of the wars of religion that had been tearing at France for over half a century. And while they were still underway, he could not afford to stir up hostilities abroad by having a formal military alliance with the British.

King James's taunts about the capricious French might have echoed in George's mind: 'where is your glorious match with France, and your royal frank, *monsieur*?'

Anne of Austria

George's love life was a subject of constant speculation. His wife Kate had to endure endless rumours about his sexual antics, rooms falling silent when she walked in, lewd songs echoing through the London streets. In a letter she wrote to George while he was with Charles in Madrid, she described herself to him as 'that happy woman to enjoy you from all other women', as if he needed reminding. She was also aware that she lacked the beauty of so many of her husband's admirers. Should she die, she once told him, he would surely have 'a finer and a handsomer, but never a lovinger wife than your poor Kate is'. She had never sought to measure herself by an ability to dance a flirtatious pirouette or cast a coquettish look; she knew that what she brought to their relationship was pedigree and pragmatism.

In France, however, George's responsibilities to her, and to their daughter Mal, seemed far away, as a mood of wild, self-destructive recklessness seemed to overcome him. This manifested itself in his efforts to gain access to the French queen, Anne of Austria, continuing the pursuit begun during his visit to Paris with Charles.

His persistence was provoked by more than Anne's famous grace and beauty. She was an enemy of Cardinal Richelieu, whom she found interfering, as well as sister of Philip IV of Spain and Charles's former fiancée, the Infanta Maria. Just as he had been drawn to the wife of Olivares in Spain, George evidently found the same yearnings for sexual revenge and conquest surging in response to the frustrations of his negotiations with Richelieu.

However, what George did not realize was that he was under surveillance. Richelieu had appointed an agent, Nicolas de Bautru, to follow him during his visit. A report of his findings surfaced in the nineteenth century, revealing the extraordinary combination of determination, ingenuity and burlesque that went into George's efforts to get close to the queen.

Madame de Chevreuse, the wife of his host the duke, was Anne's lady-in-waiting, and agreed to act as his go-between. With her own reputation for infidelity well known, he found he was able to have regular private audiences with the duchess under the pretence of being her lover, whereas in reality she was his confidante. And she demanded a high price for her help. Not only was he already making a large contribution to her household costs, but in return for securing an encounter with Anne, it was said the duchess demanded a diamond necklace and a loan of 2,000 gold coins.

George's antics of 1623 had resulted in Anne being banned by the king from having any private contact with men in her apartments. So George needed a less direct route to the queen's affections. His campaign of seduction, which seemed consciously designed to re-enact the masquerades of courtly romance, began with a midday 'collation', staged for the queen at the Duchesse de Chevreuse's home.

As would be expected, Anne arrived in her carriage to find herself received by a group of footmen dressed in her hosts' livery. 'With inconceivable temerity,' one of the servants stepped forward to let down the carriage step, usually the function of a royal flunkey. As the queen stepped out of the carriage, the servant laid his hand on the royal ankle. Glancing down to see who would dare take such a liberty with the royal person, she found herself staring into the face of the Duke of Buckingham. That afternoon, when she was walking in the gardens of the Chevreuse residence, one of the gardeners approached her with fruits and flowers – again the duke, who this time 'dared to utter a compliment' which was seen to make her blush. Later, he appeared as a fortune teller, and by means of this disguise spoke twice to her, the first time nudging her arm, the second time appearing to tell her fortune, which aroused such confusion in the queen that the Duchesse de Chevreuse made signs to George to back off.

When it came to the evening's masque ball, attended by Richelieu and the king, George appeared yet again, now disguised as a devil, dancing twice in a 'ballet of the demons'. At the climax of the 'gorgeous pageant', a group of noblemen disguised as emperors, sultans and moguls of exotic lands, from Tartary to Peru, approached the queen to pay homage to her 'beauty and merit'. This time George was the Grand Mogul, having taken the role from the Duke of Guise, who had been persuaded to surrender his costume and act as the Grand Mogul's sword-bearer in return for a loan of 3,000 gold coins. Some of the guests noted that the Grand Mogul's costume, a 'blaze of jewels', included diamonds from the English crown, 'which, through an excess of foolish confidence, the King of Great Britain had allowed his favourite to bring away with him to France', the spy Bautru noted. Later, just before the foreign potentates were about to unmask themselves before the king, the dukes of Buckingham and Chevreuse had to cram themselves into a nearby closet so they could swap costumes, the Duchesse de Chevreuse acting as lookout.

'Since that evening,' Bautru's report continued, 'no day has passed that the Duke of Buckingham has not incognito and by the connivance of the duchess seen the queen and sometimes spoken to her.'

The duke's antics culminated with an almost comically flamboyant as well as hair-raisingly dangerous effort to reach the queen's private apartment in the Louvre Palace. He had requested a secret interview with the queen at which he could deliver direct into her hands a letter 'related to the means of bringing about the downfall of Cardinal Richelieu'. This implicated her in a plot against the king's powerful chief minister, and Bautru, aware of the effect of reporting this to his master, tactfully put her indiscretion down to her Spanish temperament. Being 'accustomed no doubt to the chivalric and adventurous gallantry' of that kingdom, she 'saw in these demonstrations only a subject to divert her mind,' Bautru insisted. And certainly the fantastical method dreamed up by the Duchesse de Chevreuse to smuggle George into the queen's apartment would seem to confirm he was right, because by this time romantic gallantry had turned into melodramatic farce, complete with stage tricks and cross-dressing.

According to an ancient superstition, the ghost of a white lady would be seen wandering through the Louvre just before the death of a monarch. It was rumoured that she had appeared around the time of George's visit, though the news had been kept from the king so as not to alarm him. It was therefore decided that George would steal into the palace wearing a black cloak, beneath which he would be dressed as the white lady. If he was discovered by a member of staff, he could manifest himself as the ghost and, during the resulting confusion, make his escape.

As though preparing for a masked ball, George put on his elaborate disguise in his rooms at the Chevreuse residence. He donned a 'white and fantastically shaped robe, painted with black tears', with a representation of the face of death painted on the front and the back. A 'pellicle' or film made of gold leaf coated with soft, white wax contrived by an 'ingenious mechanician' was then laid over his face, with holes for the eyes, nose and mouth. He put on a cap 'equally fantastical as the other parts of his dress', enveloped himself in an ample black cloak, covered his face with a black velvet veil and put on a sombrero.

In the dead of night, he and the Duchesse de Chevreuse set out into the silent streets of the city, heading for the Louvre. A secret knock opened a rear door to the palace, where a 'confidential servant' of the duchess had been waiting for his mistress and the mysterious guest, introduced as an Italian astrologer. George was then conducted up secret staircases and through dark passages, 'to which, for a long time back, none have had access' but the 'creatures' of the duchess.

George and the duchess reached the queen's chamber undetected to find her alone. Her lady-in-waiting, 'Mademoiselle de Flotte', had been sent away on a 'pretence'. When George took off his cloak to reveal his costume, Anne 'jested graciously' at its laughable effect, which, according to Richelieu's spy, left the duke's *amour propre* – his self-esteem – 'wounded'. The queen, 'perceiving the pain she had caused him, gave him, by way of compensation, her hand to kiss'. George presented her with the 'confidential letter' that had been the pretext for his visit, and he and the queen withdrew to a nearby 'oratory' to read it, leaving the duchess to wait in the queen's chamber. The door to the oratory was left half open, but the mischievous duchess closed it.

From an antechamber came a loud knock, apparently a warning signal from the queen's valet that the king was approaching. George tumbled out of the chapel, threw on his cloak, and escaped 'like a thief', leaving the duchess behind. 'In his hurry and confusion his hat fell off and his cloak flew open, and being seen for a moment in his apparition dress by some of the lower servants, caused them not a little terror.' The panic led to Richelieu being summoned, who arrived to find the queen's apartments in a state of 'much agitation and confusion', the servants asserting that they had seen the ghostly white lady.

By late May 1625, arrangements for Henrietta Maria's much-delayed departure from Paris were in the final stages, and in early June a fleet of ships which had been riding at anchor off the coast of Kent since 8 May, was dispatched for Boulogne. The new 'Queen of England', escorted by her brother King Louis, left Paris in the evening of 22 May 'amid shouts of applause and a countless throng of people, accompanied by the guards, by the people of the city, by Buckingham, by the other English and by all her suite'. The French king, suffering from a bad cold, parted company with the convoy at Compiègne to head for his hunting lodge at Fontainebleau, while Henrietta Maria and George continued on towards Boulogne.

At Amiens, about eighty miles from the coast, they were joined by Queen Anne and the queen mother. Here they lodged in a house on the banks of the River Somme, and Marie de' Medici took to her sickbed, having caught her son's cold. The queens' presence caused a stir that reached far beyond the limits of the modest, provincial

French city. In London, Sir Henry Mildmay had heard of the historical conjunction of the 'three queens' so close to the English Channel, and begged Charles for permission to go and pay his respects, but was denied leave from the frantic preparations for Henrietta Maria's arrival.

Anne now flouted the king's orders against her venturing out unescorted and decided to go for an evening stroll in the gardens, which ran alongside the river. With difficulty, she got hold of the keys from the captain of the guard and, together with the Duchesse de Chevreuse and a 'little court' of other women, and her equerry, left the house. There, in the gardens, they found George, and Anne and he walked together for a while. As the evening light faded, Anne somehow managed to become detached from her entourage as she and George turned down a path leading to a pergola, which hid them from view. After a while, she cried out for her equerry, who came running to find her flustered but unharmed. There was no sign of the duke, who had disappeared into the dusk.

In London, a lack of news and the constant delays meant that 'commotion was general everywhere', feeding wild rumours that the long-awaited marriage had been stopped. So when in the final days of May news arrived that Henrietta Maria's journey to Boulogne was imminent, it was greeted with relief and a frenzy of activity. Charles's baggage was hurriedly dispatched to the coast, along with 'cavaliers and ladies' who were to act as a royal escort. George's sister Susan and mother Mary were sent across to Boulogne, while a number of other countesses and baronesses, plus the 'Duchesses of Richmond and Lennox with a numerous train of ladies', booked accommodation in Dover and Greenwich, where the king and his new queen were expected to stay some days.

Messages flew across the Channel urging the new queen to hurry along. Charles told her 'not to stay anywhere, but to come straight to him'. It would not be the first of his instructions that she chose to ignore.

Charles reached Dover on 4 June, fretting about his bride's arrival. His secretary sent an urgent message to George telling him not to come 'until he can bring the queen to his hand'. The king had apparently spent two hours sitting on a balcony at his lodgings, staring out across the Channel, wondering whether he should cross to meet his wife at Boulogne. 'Reasons against the King's passing to Boulogne,' wrote his secretary tersely: 'the precedent an abasing of the Kings of England; concessions to be feared from the Papists' importunities; necessity for holding the Parliament; and possible danger from his Majesty's putting himself in the power of another King'. No one wanted a repeat of what had happened when he was a prince in Spain.

Reluctant to leave her sick mother, Henrietta lingered in Amiens, but was eventually cajoled into continuing to Boulogne with her brother Gaston, Duc d'Orléans, the only member of her immediate family to accompany her. As she was about to depart, her mother gave her a letter of advice, written by one of her priests. It told her to give thanks to God for being called into the world to serve a great and glorious purpose, and explained that she was being sent into a country of heretics to help relieve the Catholics of their oppressions and to use her charity to try and bring the unfortunate English back to the true faith. She must love and honour her husband, the letter insisted, but in a way that suggested it to be a secondary duty, as a means of securing his conversion.

On the morning of 6 June, Henrietta and her brother prepared to leave Amiens. Anne came in her carriage to see the party off, accompanied by Louise-Marguerite de Lorraine, one of the queen's senior ladies-in-waiting. George came to kiss Anne's gown, screening himself with the carriage curtains so he could have a private moment with her. Louise-Marguerite, sitting alongside, saw the depth of their feelings, and, despite a reputation as a court gossip, reassured the queen that she would say nothing to the king about what she had witnessed.

The party set off on its long journey, reaching Boulogne three days later. Henrietta arrived reportedly 'in good health and very merry'. At 5 p.m. she was seen on the beach, gazing across the Channel towards her new homeland, standing so near to the water that the sea 'was bold to kiss her feet'.

That evening she was introduced to George's mother and sister, with Sir Toby Matthew, a Catholic convert (and son of the strongly Protestant Archbishop of York) acting as their interpreter. They found Henrietta to be more mature than expected, Sir Toby poetically describing her as sitting 'upon the very skirts of womanhood'.

He observed 'nobleness and goodness' in her countenance, but also 'a little remnant of sadness, which the fresh wound of parting from the Queen Mother might have made'. She was 'not afraid of her own shadow', he noted, and was impressed to learn that she and her brother Gaston had ventured out of the harbour in a dinghy, despite signs of a storm brewing over the Channel. He perceptively wondered if she 'might carry some steel about her'.

Later that day, the weather deteriorated sharply, and plans for a quick departure were abandoned. As winds and seaspray lashed the coast, a small boat, battered by the tempest, struggled into Boulogne harbour with the latest dispatches from London. George claimed that amongst the correspondence was a letter from Charles that needed to be taken directly to the queen mother.

Rushing to Amiens, George found Marie de' Medici still convalescing. He discussed with her the pressing matter he claimed to be the reason for his unexpected reappearance. He then asked to see Anne of Austria, who was also in bed 'and almost alone'. His request caused such consternation among the queen's ladies-in-waiting that they insisted upon the queen mother being consulted first. Marie seemed to have no objection: he had just come to see her in bed, so why not the queen? Discretion prevented the ladies-in-waiting from pointing out the age difference between the fifty-year-old queen mother and the twenty-four-year-old queen, so they were forced to relent.

George was reluctantly shown into Anne's bedchamber, which was now crammed with all the 'princesses and ladies' that could be found, summoned to ensure the interloper behaved. George seemed unconcerned by the audience. He knelt next to the bed, but one of the ladies-in-waiting 'had him up quickly', insisting he should use a chair. He refused, claiming that it was the English custom to kneel before a queen. He said 'the most tender things in the world' to her, but she asked him to leave – though, it was noted, 'without perhaps being very angry'. He did so, and after glimpsing her again the next morning 'in presence of all the court', set off back to Boulogne.

By Sunday 12 June, the storm had cleared. A fleet of twenty British ships had gathered off shore ready to escort the queen to Dover. George, with Henrietta Maria, his mother and sister, boarded the flagship the *Prince Royal*. The flotilla set sail that morning, heading into choppy seas.

And So the Devil Go with Them

Since King James's death, Britain had undergone what one of Charles's servants called a 'great earthquake'. A mood of disorientation prevailed. The official tone was reassuring. 'In his reverence to so good a Father,' Charles had confirmed all the late king's acts 'and in his favour to his ministers all his choices'. Members of the government were told that for the time being their jobs were safe.

However, it soon became clear that changes were afoot. Officials were put on probation. With a steely resolve few had expected, Charles told one 'amazed' minister, a prominent Spanish supporter, to conform to the new regime's anti-Spanish stance or lose his office 'sooner than you are aware'.

George was made first gentleman of the royal bedchamber, receiving the golden key, 'the emblem of his office, so that he can, whenever he pleases and at any hour, enter that chamber as well as any other part of the palace occupied by His Majesty'. Fresh elections had been announced for a new Parliament, due to assemble in May 1625. Gondomar's safe passage was formally revoked. And at an extraordinary meeting with the Privy Council, the king made his ministers swear to the three things James supposedly recommended before his death: a ban on any further negotiations with the Spaniards, the preparation of the royal navy for war, and the hastening of the French marriage.

Charles also established a more disciplined courtly culture. 'Whoever may have business with him must never approach him by indirect ways,' an agent from Tuscany reported back to his master. No more creeping about by 'back stairs or private doors leading to his apartments'; no more bribing of 'retainers or grooms of the Chambers, as was done in the lifetime of his father'. From now on, all approaches were to be by 'public rooms' and on days of the week set apart for that purpose. A precise and rigid timetable for the day was enforced, starting with a 'very early rising for prayers', followed by 'exercises, audiences, business, eating and sleeping'.

There was a slackening of interest in the sports so beloved by his father, Charles commanding the return to their previous uses of the 'remote parks and chases' that James had used for hunting. Court became more austere. The debauched banquets had stopped, informality in address and attire was frowned upon. There was even talk of Kit Villiers being banished from Charles's entourage, as the king 'would have no drunkards of his bed-chamber'.

Speculation was also rife about the sort of government that Charles would lead. He seemed ready to play a more active part in daily affairs than his father, but through a cabinet of close ad-visors, led by George, rather than a full Privy Council.

The orderliness left a favourable impression on the Venetian ambassador. 'He professes constancy in religion, sincerity in action and that he will not have recourse to subterfuges in his dealings,' he reported.

A breath of fresh air at court, then, but outside it was foul. London had been hit by plague. It was rumoured to have started in the same house and on the same day of the year as the previous outbreak, which had coincided with James's succession. Bills of mortality, posted on church doors, listed the deaths of parishioners and were lengthening by the week. Charles's first Parliament, essen-tial to raising the funds needed to provide military support for Mansfeld's efforts to retake the Palatinate and for the proposed anti-Habsburg league, was indefinitely delayed.

The king's nuptials were also disrupted. The sickness had spread to all areas of London and into the suburbs, and there were fears it might reach the king's palace at Greenwich. Four hundred and one Londoners had died the week the queen was due to arrive. Adding to the tally of bad news were reports that besieged Breda, the outpost of the Dutch Republic on the border with the Spanish Netherlands, had finally succumbed to Spanish attack. In such doleful circumstances, there was no jollity at the marriage, one Cambridge don observed.

Henrietta's twelve-hour Channel crossing had been rough, the queen among those suffering badly from seasickness. It was late in the evening by the time Dover harbour was reached, the fleet's firing of its guns in salute a damp squib in the desultory conditions.

The passengers disembarked to discover that Charles was not there to greet them, but in nearby Canterbury, where the accommodation was more comfortable. Henrietta was to spend her first night in Dover Castle, a cold, dank medieval fortress perched on the top of the cliffs overlooking the harbour. The bed she was offered was said not to be fit for a servant, let alone a queen, while her disgruntled retinue found themselves being farmed out to rougher quarters in the surrounding countryside. The English ambassadors in Paris had promised her an earthly paradise, but she had found herself in a primitive hovel.

Charles arrived at ten the following morning, while Henrietta was at breakfast. He waited for her in the presence chamber. She 'made short work' of her meal, and went down to meet him, falling to her knees and pledging in French that she had 'come to your Majesty's country to be at your service and command'. She kissed his hand, but Charles lifted her up and 'wrapped her up in his arms, and kissed her with many kisses'. He tried to say a few words to her, but his stammer made him bashful, so he stared at her shoes. Henrietta assumed he was checking to see if she was wearing heels, and lifted her skirts so he could see that 'I stand upon my own feet . . . This is how high I am, neither higher nor lower.' She came up to his shoulder – a pleasing comparison, it was agreed, flattering the king's diminutive stature.

Following introductions to her extensive entourage, which included several Catholic bishops, they shared a lunch of pheasant and venison. Her confessor stood at her side throughout, telling her to watch what she ate, it being the eve of the feast of St John the Baptist (according to the French calendar, rather than the English one), during which she would be required to fast.

As they were preparing to leave for Canterbury, where they would spend their first night, the strain of the formalities briefly gave way. After the queen had climbed into the carriage with the king, Henrietta's female companion piled in after her. Charles was extremely sensitive about who was allowed close to him, and the surprise appearance of the interloper caused him to shrink away and shout at her to get out. This provoked an outburst from the queen, who insisted she remain. The French ambassadors hurriedly intervened, crowding round the coach door to explain that it was customary for the queen to have an attendant with her, especially when she was surrounded by people of a different religion and language. Charles eventually relented, but with bad grace.

They reached Canterbury in time for supper. The queen went early to the marital bed, Charles following some time later. Servants saw him bolting the seven doors leading into the suite, allowing only two valets to stay to undress him. Once they had finished, they too were told to leave.

The royal couple lay in until seven the following morning, when the king emerged 'very jocund', a mood he maintained as the couple made their way back towards London.

On Friday 17 June, they reached the capital, sailing in along the Thames, a huge flotilla in their wake, crowds, thinned by the plague and the relentless rain, lining the shores. Plans for the royal couple to remain at Greenwich had been shelved. Delays had already led to the cancellation of Charles's first Parliament three times, and the king insisted it must now go ahead, as planned.

Lord Keeper Williams, responsible for helping to organize the parliamentary session, had been worried about the plague. He reported to Charles's secretary that an infected broker had recently brought the disease from the City to Westminster. 'Searchers', hired to monitor the plague's spread, were scouring the vicinity of Whitehall, dressed in protective clothing, with nosegays dangling under their nostrils. They were concerned that the victim, now dead, had given the disease to the six relatives who shared a house near the palace, and were infecting local inhabitants. Williams revealed that a very sick woman had the night before been carried in a coach in a 'very suspicious' fashion 'in the very way and passage of his Majesty to the House of Parliament'. Williams begged the king to 'come no nearer than Greenwich', but if he insisted on entering Westminster, asked George to persuade him to do so 'in the most private manner that can be devised and to avoid with all possible diligence all concourse of people'.

Undaunted by the risks, Charles appeared the following afternoon before both Houses of Parliament, dressed in full regalia, including the robes and crown of state. This was presumptuous, as he had yet to be formally crowned – 'a very ancient, sacred and weighty ceremony', as Lord Keeper Williams had reminded him. Some wondered if he was trying to avoid taking the coronation oaths to uphold the English law, religion and welfare of his subjects, so he could 'remain more absolute'.

As always, the parliamentary session began with prayers, which caused consternation among members of Henrietta's entourage invited to attend as royal guests. To avoid having to listen to the heretical babbling, her bishops got up to leave. But in a gesture perhaps calculated to reassure the most strongly Protestant Members of Parliament, Charles called for the chamber doors to be locked, 'and so enforced the popish lords to be present, some whereof kneeled down, some stood upright, and one did nothing but cross himself'.

The king then told the assembly that, being 'unfit for much speaking' – a reference to the 'deficit and impediment of his tongue' – he would keep his speech short. His brevity concentrated a stark message: that, while his father may have been 'too slack to begin so just and so glorious a work' as to break with Spain and fight to regain the Palatinate, Parliament itself had agreed to it, and must now help pay for it. 'I hope in God that you will go on to maintain it as freely as you were willing to advise my father to it.'

The following week, the 'ceremony of the formal proclamation' of the royal marriage took place in Whitehall Palace, witnessed by the Duc de Chevreuse and other French nobles. 'Nothing could be more splendid than this festival,' wrote one observer. But a sour note was introduced. For the first time since his succession to the throne, Charles had agreed to dine in public with his French guests. Henrietta, however, declined her invitation to attend, preferring to eat in her own apartment for reasons left unexplained. She was also absent from a banquet at York House hosted by George, which featured as its centrepiece a six-foot-long sturgeon caught in the Thames.

Meanwhile, the mood in the House of Commons was turning hostile; a prince 'bred up' in Parliament and a favourite hailed as its champion suddenly found themselves its enemy. MPs were disgruntled that Charles had put their lives at risk by summoning them to the epicentre of a deadly sickness, and became desperate to escape the capital's noxious airs. Suspicions were also growing that the king had granted secret concessions to the Catholics in order to secure the marriage. Members began to wonder about the benefits of the French match over the Spanish one.

In this hostile environment, George tried to cajole the Commons into granting a new subsidy. Two were offered, worth perhaps £140,000. On 8 July, the king sent a message to the Commons, pleading for more, and providing a detailed list of costs already incurred, many of which had been paid for by the king and duke out of their own pockets: £20,000 by the king on the navy, more than £44,000 by the duke, with costs running at £200,000.

The next day the Commons responded by ordering that 'no new matter should be received into the House, and to send to the Lords to know when they would be ready to adjourn'. During James's reign, they had been banging on the chamber doors to be let in, and fought equally hard to stay there. Now they were pleading to be let out. Charles eventually agreed, and arrangements were made for them to reconvene in late summer in the safer environs of Oxford.

In the interlude of political calm, George started work on mounting a strike against Spain. The scale and ambition of the plan was breathtaking. It would avenge the humiliations of the Palatinate and the Spanish match, as well as solve Charles's money problems. He would assemble a fleet at Plymouth to blockade the Spanish port of Cádiz and attack the *flota*, the Spanish treasure fleet that took advantage of seasonal winds to carry silver and other precious commodities from the Americas. Ships and soldiers were ordered to make for Plymouth and await orders, while details of the plans were kept secret. 'The din of preparation is heard, but where is the thunderbolt to fall?' asked an Italian agent.

Soon, a fleet comprising twelve naval ships, twenty armed merchantmen and fifty barges was ready at Plymouth, along with an army of restless conscripts, surly with hunger and boredom. The pressure to send them on their way was building, but lack of funds was hampering efforts to ensure they sailed with sufficient supplies for a dangerous and potentially lengthy campaign.

George was eager to lead the mission. When James had made the son of a landlocked county with no naval experience Lord Admiral, it had exposed him to a certain amount of ridicule, and he wanted to prove himself. But his friends, including the MP and Vice Admiral of Devon, John Eliot, persuaded him not to go. He was needed in England, they told him, to continue efforts to build an anti-Habsburg league. Indeed, his activism had produced some progress on that front, with several countries, including Holland, Denmark and Sweden, agreeing to attend a conference to discuss the matter in the Hague.

Instead George appointed Sir Edward Cecil as the fleet's commander. Though no seaman, he was a veteran soldier with experience of fighting the Spanish and had been a member of the Council of War set up the previous year to plan military operations. He had also championed Charles and George's policy, impressed that they had 'resolved to stand staunchly for the good of their country and to be revenged of the falsehood of the Spanish'.

The Spanish were making moves of their own, though. George's supporters found news of Gondomar, the Spanish envoy, taking up residence at the French court, 'not easy to contemplate with a quiet mind'. Sinister rumours were circulating of a Scottish earl and an Irish earl, both living in Brussels and fighting on the Spanish side, returning secretly to their homelands to foment rebellion and mount an attack on London.

Hostilities had already broken out on the domestic front. The king's relationship with the queen and her entourage had failed to improve and by summer looked close to collapse. The issue over Henrietta's refusal to ride with her husband without her retinue of ladies had reached levels of petty vindictiveness, with Charles choosing to travel in smaller coaches, so her companions could not fit in.

In the face of all efforts to coerce her, Henrietta proved to be impressively indomitable, and neither the twenty-four-year-old Charles nor the thirty-three-year-old George could work out how to handle the sixteen-year-old princess. George counselled patience and kindness, as both agreed 'it was not in her nature' to be so difficult, but the work of 'ill instruments' – or the *monsieurs* as they were now known, her entourage of French nobles and priests.

While she was staying at Hampton Court, and Charles had left for the royal manor in Oatlands, George decided to talk to her. Comte de Tillières, the former ambassador accused of being 'too much Jesuited to be a friend' and now one of the leading *monsieurs*, was in attendance that day. He had built up a powerful dislike of George during the marriage negotiations in Paris, which was reflected in his record of the encounter. He accused the favourite of menacing Henrietta with threats, of telling her he would make her 'the most unhappy woman in the world' if she did not submit to her king. Whatever was said, it upset the French, who were confounded when, the next day, 'the same person, no longer remembering his speech, or wrongly imagining his offences to be courtesies, came to beg her to accept his wife, his sister and niece as ladies-in-waiting'. Henrietta tartly observed that England's famous Queen Elizabeth had only had two ladies to attend her, and she already had three. Another three would be greedy. As a concession, she agreed to leave the decision in the hands of the ambassadors in her train, who, after consulting one of their bishops, reached the inevitable conclusion that no English ladies should be allowed in Henrietta's immediate circle, a result which George was duly forced to accept.

Plague was now everywhere. The court, which had been chasing around the country to avoid it, was apparently spreading it. The agent of the Grand Duke of Tuscany reported that 5,000 people had succumbed in the last week of July 1625 alone. 'The magistrates, in desperation, have abandoned every care; every one does what he pleases, and the houses of merchants who have left London are broken into and robbed.' 'As for me,' the agent added in a personal aside, 'I sit with my boots on, ready for flight, which besides the cost is a source of great perturbation of the mind.'

In late July, the students and dons of Oxford were, by royal command, told to vacate their rooms to make way for the parliamentarians, who were assembling for a new session. The plague moved in too, so Charles's hopes of clearing the air after the last meeting in London were dashed.

The king gave a short opening address to both Houses on

4 August 1625 in the grand setting of Christ Church college. He
described himself as, like them, a member of parliament, and
repeated the message he had delivered in London that they had
voted for the break with Spain, and must now pay for the consequences.

Removing to a lecture theatre in the university's Divinity School,
which now acted as their debating chamber, the MPs continued to
discuss their own grievances while ignoring the king's demands.
They set about investigating what had happened to the money
already voted through. 'The king's estate, like a ship, has a great
leak,' one MP complained. 'A kingdom can never be well governed
where unskillful and unfitting men are placed in great offices,' said
another.

With each speech, the focus of discontent began to solidify
into the form of the duke. George wanted to defend himself, but
by convention could not enter the Commons' chamber uninvited.
So, as the session of 5 August drew to a close, his loyal instrument
Sir George Goring got to his feet and introduced a motion asking
that the duke be asked to attend the House and address its
concerns.

On 9 August, George came before the restive parliamentarians
and delivered his response to the criticisms. He reminded them
'that I had the honour to be applauded by you', and that it was
their 'counsels and resolutions' which had led to the royal government's current policies. He then went on to list his achievements
since the previous year: the liberation of the Alpine passes of
Valtellina, which had previously been in Spanish control; Spain
having to fight on a new front in Italy; the kings of Sweden and
Denmark committing to the anti-Habsburg league. He listed all the
parliamentarians' complaints, and dealt with them succinctly. He
recalled the death of King James – about which, the Commons'
reporter observed, he spoke 'fetchingly, his eyes and his tongue
witnessing it' – and the funeral, and his journey to France, and all
the other contingencies that had interrupted the government's plans
and increased its costs. And he urged them again to sustain what
they had started, and not to delay, but have a 'care and regard of
the season and of your own healths', because 'if you lose time, your
money cannot purchase it'.

On this occasion, his charm was not so effective. The following day, Charles sent a message to the Commons via the chancellor, reminding them that his affairs 'require a speedy match' before winter set in and the plague reached the fleet and army at Plymouth. This prompted two days of debate, culminating with John Glanville, a Plymouth MP and Devonshire lawyer, declaring that the House of Commons would vote through 'all necessary supply to his most excellent Majesty' when 'convenient' and in 'a parliamentary way, freely and dutifully' – in other words, at a time of its own, rather than the king's choosing. It was a devastating refusal of Charles's pleas of urgency.

Sir Edward Villiers, George's elder half-brother, now a Leicestershire MP, made a lame effort to support calls for more immediate action, but he was too late. Black Rod, the parliamentary usher, was at the door with news that the king had issued orders that Parliament be dissolved.

Charles's administration stumbled on through the following months. In October, the fleet at Plymouth, already depleted by the constant delays, was dispatched to Cádiz. John Glanville was sent as the mission's secretary – in revenge, it was said, for his declaration in Parliament.

Soon after, George went to the Hague, where the main actors in his proposed anti-Habsburg league were to meet. The negotiations, 'prosecuted with heat', resulted in an agreement with the Dutch and Danish, but hardly the pan-European operation that was needed to take on such formidable opposition. The French wanted nothing to do with it.

George arrived home in early December to the chilling news that ships from the fleet sent to Cádiz had been seen straggling into the southern ports of England and Ireland, their hulls leaking and their crews starving and diseased. It turned out that they had been caught up in winter storms as they were making their way to Spain. Prevented from intercepting the treasure fleet, some of the ships diverted straight to Cádiz to mount an attack, but a series of tactical blunders culminated with the troops being withdrawn after they became drunk on looted wine. It was a devastating end to a bad year. The world was 'out of tune in every way', lamented an ailing John Chamberlain.

Pageant provides a good distraction at times of national crisis, but Charles's English coronation, belatedly held on 2 February 1626, nearly a year after his father's death, was barely noticeable. Continuing outbreaks of plague and lack of money meant a low-key affair, without crowds or cavalcades. Not even Charles's queen would come. Nothing could prevail upon Henrietta to attend what her confessors, and even the professors of the Sorbonne, unanimously agreed to be a heretical rite.

After weeks of wrangling, it was suggested that the crowning could be performed in the French manner, outside the doors of the abbey, with the religious service conducted privately after, but this was rejected by the English, partly out of ceremonial dogmatism, partly because of the relentless wet weather. In the end, it became clear the queen would not participate, nor even spectate, despite being offered a closed box with curtains screening her from the congregation.

So George acted as Charles's consort that day, travelling with him by royal barge up the Thames. They were supposed to land at the steps of the riverside house of Sir Robert Cotton, which had been expensively refurbished and carpeted for the occasion. His house was also packed with 'ladies and gentlewomen'. Cotton had invited 'to see their sovereign and his followers pass through the garden into the palace at Westminster, where they were to put on their robes'. But the barge overshot the steps and landed instead at the stairs leading to the back yard of Westminster Palace. According to one of Cotton's guests, who had joined his host to watch the king arrive, the palace steps were 'dirty and inconvenient', their 'incommodity increased by the royal barge's dashing into ground and sticking fast a little before it touched the causeway'. Some wondered if this was a snub against Cotton, who was supposedly responsible for an incendiary speech given the previous year in which George had been compared to an earlier royal favourite who had brought 'misery to the kingdom' and 'poverty to the king'.

Notwithstanding the barge's lurching arrival, Charles was seen leaping out 'lightly' upon the landing stage, George following after him. They went into Westminster Hall, where the robing ceremony was to take place on a wooden scaffold raised in the middle of the hall. A fascinated spectator standing next to the stairs leading up to it watched how Charles and George 'came close together' as they ascended the steps. George offered his hand to the king, but Charles instead put his hand under the duke's arm. 'I have more need to help you than you have to help me,' Charles was overheard to say affectionately, perhaps referring to the Cádiz fiasco.

And so, king and companion, as husband and substitute wife, processed to Westminster Abbey for the main ceremony. George knelt before the king to present him with the ancient regalia and place the spurs on his heels. After the anointing, Charles stood to be hailed by his subjects, but was met with a moment's awkward silence, until one of the lords shouted out 'God bless the king!', and everyone else joined in.

A few days later, another Parliament opened, and once again Charles's estrangement from his wife was painfully prominent. She would not accompany him on the official procession to Westminster, but instead watched the ceremony from a room in the palace gate, a 'convenient stronghold' on Whitehall.

George suggested she would get a better view watching from his mother's apartment elsewhere in the palace complex. Tillières, Henrietta's chaperon, was suspicious about this, suggesting it was an attempt by the duke to show to Members of Parliament that she was on good terms with the duke and his mother the countess. Initially, the queen agreed, but, according to Tillières's account, the journey involved walking across a muddy and wet garden, so she declined the duke's invitation, saying the conditions would spoil her dress and coiffure. This was duly communicated to the king, who took it as another snub. And so, while the mounted escort stood in the rain waiting for the pageantry to begin, and the MPs and Lords sat in the Painted Chamber waiting for the king's arrival, the quarrel escalated, until Charles declared that he would cancel the entire event if she did not do as he commanded.

Henrietta relented, and stood alongside Mary, Countess of Buckingham, as the desultory parade passed by. They watched together as George struggled with the bridle on his horse, which had started to come loose. After two attempts at a fix, it fell off, causing the duke to plunge onto the wet cobbles along with the plume of feathers decorating the horse's head, a humiliation which was 'by many reputed ominous'.

As the wet, miserable spring of 1626 merged into a sodden summer, morale in the royal household hit its nadir. In July, Henrietta decided she would go into retreat at Denmark House, the former home of James's wife, Anne of Denmark, and now the home of the queen's French entourage. As part of a 'special season of devotion', she also decided to undertake a pilgrimage to Tyburn, London's place of execution, where many Catholics had met their deaths on charges of treason. She reportedly walked through the streets barefoot, her confessor egging her on as he rode alongside in a coach. When she reached the execution site, she knelt at the foot of the gallows, and prayed for Henry Garnett, a Jesuit hanged, drawn and quartered for his involvement in the Gunpowder Plot.

Such antics had left Charles despairing, and increasingly determined to be rid of the interfering French. He wrote to George, addressing him using James's pet name 'Steenie', that 'necessity urges me to vent myself to you in this particular, for grief is eased being told to a friend'. He commanded George to 'advertise to my mother-in-law', Marie de' Medici, 'that I must remove all those instruments that are causes of unkindness between her daughter and me, few or none of the servants being free of this fault in one kind or other'. An ambassador extraordinary was duly dispatched to Paris, arousing considerable curiosity.

A few weeks later the king and queen were in London. Though pockets of the plague persisted across the capital, they had come for the betrothal of George's three-year-old daughter Mary, James's beloved 'grandchild' Mal, to the seven-year-old Charles Herbert. Herbert's uncle was William Herbert, Earl of Pembroke, George's one-time sponsor and more recent rival. It was a match designed to entwine the Villiers line with that of an ancient branch of the Anglo-Welsh nobility, to be consummated once Mary had reached maturity.

On the afternoon of 31 July, Charles appeared in the queen's apartment. According to one account, he found her with 'some Frenchmen her servants unreverently dancing and cavorting in her presence'; according to another she was suffering from toothache. Either way, he took her by the hand and led her to his lodgings, where he ordered all his servants to leave, and locked the door. In what was turning out to be a coordinated manoeuvre, one of the king's secretaries together with the yeomen of the guard started to round up Henrietta's entourage, the women howling and lamenting 'as if they had been going' to their 'execution'.

As this was going on, Charles revealed to Henrietta that he was sending all her servants and companions back to France. Her distress was alarming. She burst into tears and pleaded with Charles to relent in a manner that would have 'moved stones to pity'. She became angry, screaming at him 'loud enough to split rocks'. She begged that he at least let her say goodbye to them, but he refused. Then she ran at the window, and beat her fists against the panes of glass until they smashed and her hands bled.

It was to no avail. Charles sent a letter to 'Steenie' commanding the duke to 'send all the French away tomorrow' by any means necessary, driving them off 'like so many wild beasts' if required, 'and so the devil go with them'.

All Goes Backward

As the bitter winter of 1625 set in, Sir John Eliot, Vice Admiral of Devon, stood on the cliffs overlooking Plymouth Sound, watching in despair as the fleet sent a few weeks earlier to attack Cádiz straggled back into port.

The horror of the disaster had first appeared on the horizon on 9 December. Ghostly hulks started to drift into harbour, bodies being tipped over the gunwales as they approached. A hundred or so ragged, diseased soldiers appeared in the town, the mayor forced to buy them clothing, accommodation and firewood out of his own pocket, 'without which they would have perished'.

Two weeks later, Eliot wrote to the king's secretary. Ships were still arriving, and the vice admiral had been touring the taverns and billets, listening to the fractured and confused accounts of what had happened. One Captain Bolles, 'who has died since', told of the 'scarcity and corruption of the provisions', producing appalling mortality among the troops. 'Yesterday seven fell down in the streets,' Eliot wrote. 'The rest are weak, and unless there be a present supply of clothes there is little hope to recover them.'

The situation would not improve. By Christmas, thirty-one ships had made their way back to Plymouth, out of ninety that had set sail, the remainder either lost at sea, or forced to shelter in ports as far away as Ireland. A picture emerged of a farcical mission poorly planned and badly executed, resulting in a humiliating with-drawal from Cádiz before serious contact with the enemy had even begun.

A sense of gloom descended upon the country. John Chamberlain struggled to capture the mood in one of his letters. 'All goes backward,' he lamented, 'both in our wealth, valour, honour, and reputation.' It was clear that 'God blesses nothing we take in hand', whereas in Queen Elizabeth's time 'all things did flourish'. There were those that complained of matters being 'ill managed', he added, who 'glance and aim at somebody for misleading and carrying his rider awry'. He dared not name him, even in a personal letter, but everybody knew that 'somebody' to be George Villiers. Chamberlain's image was of the favourite as a bucking and bolting horse who was carrying his king, as well as the kingdom, to a terrible fall. This was a perception now shared by John Eliot.

The vice admiral had long been a friend and supporter of George. According to at least one source, they first met on the Continent in 1609, when George was touring Europe with his older brother. In 1618, George had nominated him for a knighthood and made him acting Vice Admiral of Devon. By the early 1620s, Eliot was considered by both court and Parliament as 'powerful with the Duke' as well as 'affectionate to the public', a useful combin-ation.

George and Sir John were of a similar age and background, both coming from the ranks of England's minor gentry. However, in temperament, they could not have been more different. While George's ambitions were boundless, Eliot's were more provincial. He served as a local magistrate and the MP for his Cornish birth-place, St Germans near Plymouth, where he continued to live. As vice admiral, his primary duties were the local administration of the navy, pressing men from the district for military service, boarding ships at Plymouth and Falmouth to check their goods, surveying wrecks, and organizing vessels to police the Atlantic approaches to the Channel, which were then prone to attacks by pirates.

Where George admired audaciousness and impulsiveness, Eliot, despite a sometimes explosive temper, saw himself as cautious and conservative. George made it his maxim to find 'new ways' to explore 'old courses'. Eliot was suspicious of novelty, and looked to precedents from the past rather than opportunities in the future to justify his political convictions. This made him a staunch champion of the supremacy of the Crown in national affairs, a defender of the royal prerogative as well as parliamentary privilege. 'No man may dispute against it,' he argued in Parliament, 'it being an inseparable adjunct to regality.'

As a public figure, he was seen as pompous, naive and a bit of a windbag. But he was respected as a man of conscience and conviction who could be trusted. He also had some awareness of his flaws and battled to correct them. As a teenager, he had attacked a neighbour who had criticized him to his father, inflicting a minor wound with his sword. He immediately showed such remorse that his victim forgave him, and became a close and lifelong friend.

Eliot had been loyal to George, too, happily accepting the favourite as his overlord and supporting his policies in Parliament. Once, while serving a spell in prison for an argument over the ownership of a pirate's bounty, he had even refused an offer of early release, because he would answer only to George, who at the time was in Madrid with Charles.

When he was released following George's return in 1623, he had vigorously supported the favourite's project for an anti-Habsburg war, serving on several parliamentary committees involved in putting the country on a war footing, and championing a sharp military response to Spanish duplicity, regardless of the financial consequences. 'A sudden pain,' he declared, was better 'than a continued grief'.

But the sight of the shattered fleet returning to port, and the horrific aftermath of billeting hundreds of diseased and starving soldiers, produced in Sir John a profound sense of betrayal. Despite voting for George's war and perhaps having some culpability for its failure, the conviction grew that a terrible mistake had been made, and that the favourite must be held responsible for it.

The Knot Draws Near

In London, desperate appeals for money were coming in on a daily basis. The treasury could not even afford to pay the wages of the sick and miserable seamen and soldiers gathered in Plymouth, which meant they could not be discharged, forcing local ratepayers to pay for their upkeep. Unrest was spreading, and unless it could be staunched, a terrible reckoning was expected.

Henrietta Maria's dowry of £120,000, though much smaller than had been expected from the Spanish match, had gone some way to meeting military costs, but it was now all spent, and George, with Charles's agreement, was reduced to trying to pawn the English Crown Jewels in the Hague in his efforts to stave off imminent bankruptcy. The jewels had been valued at £300,000, but the offers he received were so paltry he had been forced to bring them back home and negotiate a more modest loan of £100,000 from London merchants.

The shortfall made a recall of Parliament inevitable, and writs were issued for fresh elections. In an effort to ensure a more co-operative session, Charles and George revived the feudal custom of 'pricking' potential troublemakers – appointing them as sheriffs, who by tradition were confined to their counties while in office and so prevented from attending Parliament in Westminster. Several prominent critics were successfully removed this way, but such heavy-handed electoral interference only succeeded in stirring up resistance among those who were allowed to stand, among them Sir John Eliot.

Opposition was poorly organized, however. Owen Wynn, a legal clerk, noted that the 'many great and active spirits' who had been agitating against George were in need of 'a good director'. So, Sir John, despite a perception that he was still loyal to George, appears to have decided to adopt the role.

On 15 January 1626, as the official opening of the new Parliament approached, Eliot drew up a list of detailed 'instructions to his agent' in London. The agent's identity is unknown, but it was someone well enough connected to have access to the court, the chamber of the Privy Council and the Royal Exchange, London's meeting place for merchants and bankers. He was also in a position to make discreet enquiries of such figures as Philip Burlamachi, a powerful merchant who was central to the government's efforts to finance ongoing military costs. This agent was expected to send daily reports back to Eliot in Cornwall, addressing them to one 'Ab. Jennens'.

Meanwhile, and presumably with the help of this agent's reports, Eliot was involved in drawing up a planning document entitled 'Perticular misdemeanours of the Duke' for the forthcoming Parliament. It began by declaring that George was 'vicious ergo not fit to be so near a king', and set out charges that might be brought against him.

The plan was to adopt the same process that had led to the downfall of George's mentor, Francis Bacon. The House of Commons would effectively act as the prosecutors for an impeachment case heard by the House of Lords. However, George was a far more formidable figure than even the former Lord Chancellor. He not only had the support of a huge network of dependents but the backing of an apparently submissive king. Bringing down such a figure called for testimony and evidence of such compelling credibility that not even Charles could ignore it.

Several lines of attack were explored in the document: George's 'juggling' in matters of religion, his attack on prominent government figures (including his 'horrible oppression' of Francis Bacon), rumours of his sexual antics with various women of court, his threatening behaviour towards Henrietta Maria, as alleged by the French ambassador.

The document also alluded to George's 'foul and unchristian-like carriage' towards King James during his final hours.

Garbled and confused rumours linking George to poisoning had been circulating since the previous year. In November 1625, a north-country cattle drover called Christopher Hogg, returning from a long journey to a fair in Norfolk, had run into a 'man clothed in black seeming to be a minister'. The man asked 'what news there was in the south', and Hogg told him that the Duke of Buckingham, along with his father-in-law, the Earl of Rutland, had been committed to the Tower of London for attempting to poison Charles.

Hogg's interrogator turned out to be a Northumberland clerk named Martin Danby, who reported what he had heard to a local magistrate. The magistrate had the unfortunate drover arrested and questioned. Protesting that he was only a 'poor labourer' who had been hired 'to drive and look to the cattle he had in charge', Hogg eventually confirmed what he had told Danby, and a report was sent to both George and Rutland. George did not respond, but on 26 December, the furious earl wrote from Belvoir Castle to the royal secretary, demanding that the king be made aware of the 'aspersions' being cast against him and his son-in-law, protesting that if he had ever had a 'thought to hurt his majesty, sweet Jesus will damn him perpetually'.

Eliot's contacts and agent had managed to dig up some of these stories. They had also discovered, presumably from a source within the court, that George had administered a 'posset and plaster' to James when he was 'almost recovered' from his tertian ague, with the result that the king 'never looked cheerful but said he was killed'. The protests and expulsion of Dr Craig and Henry Gibb, the royal groom, were also mentioned.

Yet despite an abundance of suspicions, there was little evidence to back them up, let alone witnesses prepared to testify in public.

Charles opened Parliament on 6 February 1626, generously embracing the right of members to review 'the great, weighty, and difficult affairs of the Kingdom', but reminding them of his resolve 'to confine this meeting to a short time'. In other words, if they did not produce a tax bill promptly, they could expect to be smartly dismissed.

The initial response was muted, the following days spent in dealing with procedural matters. Then, on 10 February, following a series of motions relating to charitable gifts, elections and committees, John Eliot got to his feet.

Shattering the administrative mood, he recalled the failures and horrors of their last Parliament, and what the current one might do to correct them. He began by reminding the honourable members that they had unfinished business. When they had last met, in the Divinity School at Oxford with plague raging outside, they had passed two subsidy bills, yet before they had even begun to discuss other matters, they had been dismissed. 'The business it is we *should* come for, the country's business, the public care, the common good, the general affairs of king and kingdom: not the mere satisfaction of any private ends or hopes' – *that* business had, Eliot claimed, 'overslipped us'.

'I am for supply,' he told his fellow MPs, but not just the supply of money to the royal coffers. There were other deficits to consider, 'supply in government, supply in justice, supply in reformation, supply in aid of our long-neglected grievances'. And these were the supplies that the Commons must attend to first.

'Methinks I hear some courtier saying to me: you go now too far,' Sir John speculated. But he had barely begun. He went on to complain about how the money the last Parliament had given to the king had not been properly accounted for, how 'so much wrong' had been done to his majesty which had been 'unpunished', how the military and financial losses that the country had sustained had been casually disregarded, 'losses abroad, losses at home, losses to our friends, losses to ourselves!'

Reaching the highest pitch of indignation, even despair, he implored the Speaker, as representative of his fellow MPs, to 'cast your eyes about' and behold the terrible state the country is in. 'Our honour is ruined, our ships are sunk, our men perished; not by the sword, not by the enemy, not by chance, but, as the strongest predictions had discerned and made it apparent beforehand, by those we trust.

'I could lose myself in this complaint,' Eliot confessed, 'the miseries, the calamities' he had witnessed having 'so strong an apprehension on me'. As a result, he believed the House should make 'no mention, no overtures, nor motion' to any other matter before these grievances had been addressed.

A combination of hesitancy and shock seemed to pass through the House. Even Christopher Wandesford, the measured, prudent member for Richmond in Yorkshire, and quite probably one of Eliot's conspirators in drawing up charges against the duke, was caught by surprise. The motion was 'made too soon', he advised, giving the excuse that many members were yet to arrive for the session. He also suggested that 'grave bodies', meaning sensible ones, 'must go slowly'.

Eliot's motion was discarded, business continuing almost as though nothing had happened. A mood of caution settled on the House, as it contemplated with a mixture of fear and excitement the momentous, possibly disastrous confrontation to come.

Commenting on the debacle, Amerigo Salvetti, the Florentine agent in London, resorted to a well-known Tuscan saying: 'The knot draws near the teeth of the comb.'

Common Fame

George's behaviour in the early weeks of the Parliament showed a blissful lack of awareness of the trouble that was brewing. He attended the House of Lords sporadically, his main contribution being a proposal to set up an academy 'to take care of the breeding and education of the children of the nobility and gentry of worth of this kingdom'. It was an idea that he had first proposed two years before, having secured James's agreement to call it 'King James's Academy, Society Heroic, or College of Honour'. But a lack of money and political backing meant nothing had come of the scheme. His peers probably took it as a sign of social insecurity – an attempt to institutionalize his own dizzying rise in rank, to prove that there was a quick and artificial way of bypassing generations of breeding.

The proposal may have reflected his continuing struggles to set an acceptable tone for his rare public appearances. Somehow, the lords from the established ancient families seemed able to carry their grandeur with ease. He, on the other hand, had a habit of attracting ridicule. A simple trip, for example, to the house of a local grandee around the time of the opening of the new Parliament turned into a farcical production. He decided to go 'carried on men's shoulders' in a 'Spanish chair or hand litter', drawing the taunts of a 'rabble of boys', his ostentation 'much spoken of and thought more than needed' by polite society.

There was a similar air of vulgar and reckless bravado surrounding his foreign dealings. Following the expulsion of Henrietta Maria's entourage, relations with the French had come under severe strain, and he had sent his friend Henry Rich, the Earl of Holland, back to Paris as his envoy to try and patch things up. However, he had also instructed Rich to sound out Anne of Austria's feelings for him. Holland obliged, reporting back that he had 'been a careful spy' of the French queen's 'intentions and affections towards you'. The news was not encouraging. 'I find many things to be feared, and none to be assured of a safe and real welcome' should the duke try to visit her in France. King Louis 'continues in his suspects, making (as they say) very often discourses of it, and is willing to hear villains say that she hath infinite affections, you imagine which way'.

Nevertheless, in a summary garbled by his efforts at discretion, Rich suggested that Anne might be receptive, ready even to 'do things to destroy her fortune rather than want satisfaction in her mind' – news which Rich acknowledged would make the duke 'the most happy unhappy man alive'. As for what action to take, 'do what you will', he wrote. 'I dare not advise you. To come is dangerous. Not to come is unfortunate.'

Perhaps George's greatest vulnerability, though, was greed. As with his striving for imperial grandeur and unobtainable women, it seemed to be a symptom of insecurity, a conviction that his status could only be secured by exhibiting a degree of wealth obtainable only through epic borrowing and expropriation. Extravagant gestures of generosity, such as personally paying for the relief of pressed sailors and soldiers, came to be seen by him as the currency of esteem. But it demanded a relentless and addictive quest for money, one that was to begin his undoing.

One of the bones of contention between the British and the French was the seizure of shipping in the Channel on the pretext of piracy. Among the ships that had been taken by the English was the *St Pierre* of Le Havre, found to be carrying a haul of gold, silver, cochineal (an expensive scarlet dye) and jewels – assumed to be Spanish goods and therefore subject to confiscation. The capture had caused uproar among merchants, because in reprisal the French had started confiscating English cargo. The Court of the Admiralty responded by ordering that the *St Pierre* be released and the ship set sail. But George overruled the court, commanding that it be stopped and returned to port, apparently with the aim of confiscating the booty.

This rash intervention proved to be a serious tactical error. Sir John Eliot had managed to get himself appointed onto a Commons committee investigating merchants' complaints, and witnesses had presented evidence that the staying of the ship had been ordered by the Lord Admiral on his own authority, rather than the king's. The Commons was by convention not allowed to enquire into royal matters, but it could investigate private individuals, and it ruled that George had acted in that capacity.

Eliot seized the opportunity. On 1 March 1626, he boldly demanded that the duke 'may be sent for as a delinquent' to be questioned by the House.

Days passed, and George did not respond.

On 11 March, members of the king's Council of War filed into the House of Commons, having been summoned to account for the spending of taxes raised in James's time. They refused to answer the MPs' questions, one claiming the king had 'expressly forbidden them to give any account'. This was taken as an insult to the House, and a mutinous mood set in. Eliot then brought up the matter of the *St Pierre*, claiming the duke had 'too slightly apprehended' the gravity of the problem. 'This is a great grievance and abuse' of the people, he proclaimed, and demanded that the House hold a vote on the matter. After lunch, the vote was taken, and Eliot's motion was only narrowly lost by 127 to 133, following a last-minute intervention by the Chancellor of the Exchequer.

Then Dr Samuel Turner got to his feet. He was a physician who had treated Charles's mother, Anne of Denmark, during her final illness. This was his first term in Parliament, and virtually his maiden speech.

There is no official record of what he said – it is only thanks to letters and private journals that his speech has been preserved. Whether he had planned to speak that day, or was encouraged by the narrowness of Eliot's defeat, his intervention would prove momentous.

Turner announced that it was time for the '*causa generalissima*' of current woes to be identified, and that 'common fame' – in other words public reputation – 'presents one man to be this cause': 'that great man, the Duke of Buckingham'. It was the first time that George had been identified in this way. Turner summarized six areas for which the duke should be called to account: for the recent wranglings over shipping in the 'Narrow Seas' or Channel; for squandering taxpayers' money; for the 'engrossing of offices of state and trust into his hands; for conferring the same on his kindred'; for fostering Catholicism (notably his mother's); for selling honours and titles and for the military fiasco in Cádiz.

The following day, the royal secretary, Sir Edward Conway, wrote in furious indignation to George. The secretary declared Turner a 'slave', a 'vile and base person', 'loathesomely offensive', false, base and, for good measure, vile again. No penalty was sufficient to give the duke 'satisfaction or revenge' for what Turner had said about him, nevertheless 'such offences must not pass unmarked or unpunished'.

But vilifying Turner, or indeed Eliot, would not help, because – as George had just learned – there was a much more substantial figure hiding in the shadows who, it seems, was behind the sudden outpouring of abuse.

The Bottomless Bagg

In early March 1626, George received a letter from Sir James Bagg, the corrupt but wily MP for East Looe in Cornwall, who had volunteered to act as the duke's agent in the West Country. Bagg, known locally as the 'bottomless bag' for his capacity to take bribes, had long been a jealous rival of John Eliot's for George's attention and patronage, and had been quick to exploit the growing antagonism between his fellow Cornish MP and the favourite.

As part of these efforts, Bagg had been enquiring into the parliamentary attacks against the duke, and in his letter to George he revealed a breakthrough in his investigation. Far from being a spontaneous expression of popular discontent, he had discovered that the campaign was being secretly orchestrated by a powerful cabal, 'maliciously without cause intending your ruin'. Their leader, according to Bagg, was George's former champion, occasional ally and now chief rival, William Herbert, Earl of Pembroke. The late Queen Anne of Denmark had warned Herbert and the other Baynard's Castle conspirators of George becoming 'beholden to none but himself' and a 'plague' to those 'that labour for him', and Herbert had evidently decided the time had come to do something about it.

Bagg had learned through one of Pembroke's deputies in Cornwall how the earl had secretly used his position as the county's lord lieutenant to get at least five MPs elected to the new Parliament who were prepared to act against George. Not all their names were known, but he was almost certain that Dr Samuel Turner was one of them, having been selected at the last minute for a seat conveniently vacated by a servant of the earl's. Bagg also implicated Sir John Eliot in the plot, warning George that he had been 'in a distraction how to divide himself betwixt Your Grace and the Earl of Pembroke'.

Herbert was Charles's Lord Chamberlain. He was also considered by many to be the 'only honest hearted man' left at court, and had considerable support from other members of the nobility, particularly those ancient families who resented George's rise to a rank superior to theirs. This made the earl a formidable enemy. Following the advice of his mentor, Francis Bacon, George duly responded by applying the honey rather than the sting. He arranged for the king to promote the earl to Lord Steward, with his brother Philip, the Earl of Montgomery, taking over William's old post of Lord Chamberlain. This gave the Herberts almost complete control over the royal household.

Meanwhile, Turner was to receive the sting. On 15 March, four days after the MP's speech, a letter from the king was read out to the Commons which fulminated at Turner's 'seditious' words against the 'honour and government' of the king. 'This his Majesty says is an example that he can no ways suffer,' particularly when it impugned the reputation of one 'so near to him'. Turner must therefore face justice, which will be delivered at the king's own hands if not by the House.

As the Commons Journal noted, the letter was met with a 'long silence', after which the matter was referred to a committee.

By the following day, the MPs had recovered their tongues. Turner protested that he had spoken 'not for any particular ends but out of loyalty and sincerity for the good of his country'. He pointed out that 'common fame' had been used as the basis for charging prominent figures before, as in the time of Henry VI, when it had successfully led to an overmighty member of court being brought to justice. In a letter delivered to the House a few days later, Turner further claimed that the accusations he had levelled were just a selection 'out of many' expressed by public opinion, and that he had only reported them to stop an endless consideration of 'grievances in abstractions' and out of 'duty and public service to my country'.

Turner's talk of public rather than royal service and duty to country rather than king produced a profound sense of unease at court. Could this be evidence that the popular mood had turned hostile to the favourite and, by extension, to the king? In search of reassurance, courtiers began to challenge the Commons' claim to represent popular grievance. One tract by a 'plain countryman', conveniently discovered in the pocket of a 'paralytic poor man' found dead on the road to London, declared that 'we the Commons' – the real people rather than their supposed silken-tongued repre-sentatives filling the benches in Parliament – found the charges against George ludicrous. An anonymous letter circulating court saw the House of Commons as being overrun with a corrupt and unaccountable elite of 'meddling and busy persons', 'covetous land-lords', 'recusants and papists', 'puritans', 'malcontents', 'king-haters' and 'lawyers in general', whose sole objective was 'the debasing of this free monarchy' through 'the duke's side'.

Charles's response was to summon both Houses of Parliament to a meeting on 29 March. His chosen venue was the Banqueting House, where George had delivered his speech about the 'Spanish Labyrinth' following their return from Madrid. The king thanked the Lords for their 'care' but, turning to the MPs, was 'sorry that I may not justly give you the same thanks but that I must tell you that I am come here to show you some errors and, as I may term them, unparliamentary proceedings'.

The following day, at a joint meeting of the Lords and Commons in the Painted Chamber in Westminster, George stood up to reply to the accusations made against him. He chose not to use the sort of defensive or scolding tone adopted by Charles, but rather set out in a calm, reasonable, even humble way his responses to the individual charges, and a full account of the military costs of ongoing efforts to win back the Palatinate. Addressing the MPs, he also reminded them of the importance of that international emergency. 'Gentlemen,' he told them, 'it is no time to pick quarrels one with another; we have enemies enough abroad', making it all the more necessary 'to be well united at home'.

But the Commons were not so easily placated. Turner, having provided the fuse, had by now stepped back, leaving Eliot and other more seasoned hands to set it alight. Work began on a 'remonstrance' to formally set out the grievances against the duke, while discussions began about a generous supply bill to dissuade Charles from dismissing the House. This effectively put a price of three subsidies and three fifteenths on the duke's head. Charles's predictable response was that he would not submit under duress.

And so the wrangling continued day after day, the MPs persisting with their investigations, Charles maintaining his defence of the duke. However, as Turner's original charges were debated and adapted, anxiety began to build about the notion of 'common fame' as the basis for prosecuting them. George himself had described it as a 'subtle' concept, amounting to little more than rumour and gossip. Furthermore, the Lords had ruled it out as grounds for impeachment in 1614, declaring that it provided insufficient grounds for charging one of their members.

Concerned that the case against the duke was weakening, a committee of twelve members, most of them experienced lawyers, was appointed to 'consider of the businesses concerning the Duke of Buckingham and to reduce it into form and search and prepare such precedents as they see fit'. A motion was also passed to subject the matter of common fame to a full debate.

The debate took place the following day, a Friday. The MPs fretted about what common fame meant, what distinguished it from rumour and gossip, some pointing out that it was not considered adequate in cases heard before a grand jury, others arguing that it had been used successfully before, and could be used again. As the arguments continued, the lawyers took over, their speeches scattered with Latin epigrams.

Eventually, after 'long debate', they voted to accept common fame as an adequate basis upon which to proceed, but only after exposing the unsettling weaknesses of using it to bring down such a powerful man. And in a mood of apprehension about the difficulties ahead, they broke for the weekend.

The Forerunner of Revenge

On 18 April 1626, Rubens was at his lavishly appointed, Italianate palazzo in Antwerp, working on the paintings George had commissioned in Paris. His assistants had produced a sketch for the equestrian portrait, which had been presented to the duke for approval. It showed George mounted on a rearing horse, dressed in shining armour, with a red velvet cape flapping from his shoulders. Cowering beneath him, among reeds, were a bearded Poseidon, god of the sea, and a sea nymph dressed in pearls. Overhead fluttered the winged figure of Fame, who had removed his trumpet from his mouth to exhale a blast of wind to fill the sails of a fleet of ships moored in the background. Though the rendering of the duke's face was still rudimentary, a lot of effort had gone into working out the essential elements, notably the composition, the palette, and the appearance of the clothing.

Rubens decided to take a break from his work and go for a walk down towards the cathedral. Passing through the thriving markets of a city enjoying its golden age, he arrived at the Plantin-Moretus house, the workshop of a leading printer and publisher in Antwerp's book market, which he visited regularly. It had a shop attached, offering books recently produced by the printshop as well as other publishers in the Spanish Netherlands. The shelves were filled with the latest works on religion, war, medicine, exploration and scandal. He liked to pretend that he had little interest in the scandal. Earlier that year he had sent a friend a 'highly infamous' and highly sought-after example, not to titillate, but because, he claimed, its rarity was reassuring evidence of such 'libellous publications' being hard to come by, which explained why 'they have very little vogue'.

As Rubens browsed the titles, two recent publications caught his eye. One, apparently printed in Oxford, was a miscellany of quotes attributed to 'Mercury' and Machiavelli, supposedly by an English author called Richard Thunderstruck. The other was a pamphlet with the verbose Latin title: *Prodromus Vindictae in Ducem Buckinghamiae, pro virulenta caede potentissimi Magnae Britanniae Regis IACOBI, nec-non Marchionis Hamiltonii, ac aliorum virorum Principum* – 'The Forerunner of Revenge upon the Duke of Buckingham for poisoning the most powerful James, King of Great Britain, as well as the Marquis Hamilton and other nobles'. Intrigued, Rubens bought a copy to find out more about the man he was in the midst of painting. He paid 1 florin and 6 stivers for two copies of each publication.

Antwerp was then a centre of Habsburg propaganda, the shelves heaving with anti-Protestant, anti-Dutch, and anti-British pamphlets. Many had the sort of sensational title emblazoned across the frontispiece of the work attacking the Duke of Buckingham. However, most were anonymous or attributed to obviously fake names like 'Richard Thunderstruck'. The cover page of *The Forerunner of Revenge*, in contrast, proudly proclaimed that its sensational allegations were 'Discovered by M. George Eglisham, Scot', adding with surely suicidal specificity, 'one of King James's physicians for his Majesty's person for more than ten years'.

Eglisham was a colourful figure, fairly well known as the author of various works of poetry, astrological medicine and theology that had earned him the nicknames 'Windbag' and 'Ass's Fart'. As *The Forerunner* made clear, he considered himself of blue-blooded if not aristocratic breeding, being descended from the Lundy family of Fife, members of the magnificently titled lairds of Balgonie, and through them distantly related to the Hamiltons, one of Scotland's most illustrious families, who in turn boasted ties to the royal Stuarts. *The Forerunner* proudly boasted that the author had been brought up with James Hamilton, son and heir of John, first Marquis of Hamilton, and a close friend of King James. In his and James's 'young years', John had lain his right hand upon his son's head, and a left hand upon Eglisham's, as he presented both boys to the king to kiss the royal hand, 'recommending me unto his Majesty's favour'.

In the early 1600s, Eglisham and the young Hamilton parted company, the latter following the king to England, where he would inherit his father's title. Eglisham went to the Continent, where he enrolled at the Scots College in Louvain (or Leuven), one of several well-known 'training camps' for Catholic spies and insurgents. By 1604 he was back in Britain, working in Rotherham as a tutor to the children of a former magistrate and his Catholic wife.

By 1616, Eglisham was declaring himself 'Doctoris Medici Regii', royal physician. He had probably acquired the title through James Hamilton, now a marquis and an important figure in James's household. Despite the royal connection, Eglisham had struggled to establish a successful medical practice in London, having failed to acquire a licence from the College of Physicians, probably because of suspicions about his religion. This had forced him to support himself by investing in various dubious business ventures, including an attempt to corner the production of gold leaf for luxury items such as book-bindings and furniture.

Reflecting the fringe existence of a Catholic living in London at the time, Eglisham had married one Elizabeth Downes 'in the Clink', a gaol in Southwark, where the Catholic priest they chose to officiate was imprisoned. They had a daughter, and moved into an apartment in Bacon House, named after Sir Nicholas Bacon, Francis's father and Lord Keeper during Elizabeth I's reign. But by the mid-1620s he was in financial trouble, the gold leaf venture coming under parliamentary scrutiny alongside many of the Villiers patents in 1621, and soon he was being sued by his creditors. He was also accused of counterfeiting coins with one Edward Yates, a 'villain', 'pirate' and 'mountebank', and of living with Yates 'at bed and at board', a phrase suggesting a sexual relationship.

Until this time, Eglisham had no connection with the Duke of Buckingham, beyond the association with dubious royal patents. But, as Rubens was to read in lurid detail in *The Forerunner*, all that had changed in the spring of 1625, when he was called to the sickbed of his dying childhood friend, James, Marquis of Hamilton.

The marquis was in a dreadful state, suffering a violent fever and constantly vomiting. Eglisham tried to treat him, but it soon became clear that nothing could be done.

Eglisham described the terrifying transformation of Hamilton's body following his death two days later. The mouth and nose began 'foaming blood mixed with froth'. The body started to swell 'in such sort that his thighs were as big as six times their natural proportion, his belly became as big as the belly of an ox, his arms as big as the natural quantities of his thighs, his neck so broad as his shoulders, his cheeks over the top of his nose, that his nose could not be seen or distinguished, the skin of his forehead over his eyes'. His hair began to fall out if it was touched 'as easily as if one had pulled hay out of an heap of hay'. His torso and arms were covered with blisters as big as fists 'of six diverse colours, full of waters of the same colours, some white, some black, some red, some yellow, some green, some blue'. When a post-mortem was performed on his internal organs, the liver was found to be green, his stomach purple 'with a blueish clammy matter adhering to the sides of it'.

Servants flocking to the side of their dead master shouted that he had been poisoned, and 'that it was a thing not to be suffered'.

A 'jury' of physicians was sent for to pronounce on the cause of death. Eglisham recalled the reaction of one of them, Dr John Moore, a fellow Scot, when he drew back the cloth covering the corpse. 'At the sight thereof Doctor Moore lifting up both his hands and his hat and his eyes to the heavens astonished, said "Jesus bless me, I never saw the like. I cannot know him, I cannot distinguish a face upon him."' One of the other doctors remarked on similarities with the condition of the body of Henry Wriothesley, Earl of Southampton, who had died under mysterious circumstances in Holland the previous November.

Seeing the amazement of his fellow doctors, Dr Lister, a censor of the College of Physicians, and known to be 'one of my Lord of Buckingham's creatures', drew each of them aside 'and whispered them in the ear to silence them, whereupon many went away without speaking one word'.

There was never any doubt in Eglisham's mind that his friend had been murdered and that the duke was responsible. The motive was clear, and went back to 1622, when Hamilton first learned of George's plans to marry his niece, Mary, the daughter of his beloved sister Susan, to Hamilton's son and heir, also called James.

The betrothal followed the familiar Villiers pattern of entrapment, though this time with the variation that the reluctant party was the groom, and that the bride was just ten years old.

When George had first suggested such a match, he had been rebuffed for the familiar reason that his family was too common. His father was 'obscure amongst gentlemen', and his mother, the countess, had been a mere 'serving woman'. Nothing is prouder 'than baser blood when it doth rise aloft', Eglisham noted, which is why the duke had the audacity to attempt, through a match with the Hamiltons, an intermingling with 'the blood royal both of England and Scotland'. There was even speculation that his objective was for his offspring to claim a line to the throne.

Snobbery was perhaps the greatest obstacle to George fulfilling his ambitions, and the greatest provocation to achieving them. It had motivated the Earl of Rutland's attempts to stop George marrying Kate, and had almost defeated efforts to find brides for his brothers John and Kit. He was not about to let this new attempt by a stiff-necked Scot thwart him.

On Sunday, 16 June 1622, Hamilton and his son James the younger had been 'urged' by a member of the royal household to come 'in all haste' to Greenwich Palace, where the king and court were in residence. Mystified by the summons, they arrived 'a little before supper' to be told that the younger Hamilton, who was just three days shy of his sixteenth birthday, was to marry George's ten-year-old niece Mary, the wedding to take place after the meal.

The announcement having been made by the king before the whole court, the older Hamilton had no option but to agree to the ceremony going ahead. Young James Hamilton and Mary were duly married later that evening in the king's apartment – one of 'diverse young alliances and unripe marriages' to be made around this time, observed a disapproving John Chamberlain. Eglisham claimed that, to make the nuptials 'more authentic', George had later that night 'caused his niece to be laid a-bed with the marquis's son for a short time in the king's chamber, and in his Majesty's presence, albeit the bride was yet innubile.

'Many were astonished at the sudden news,' Eglisham continued, 'all the marquis's friends fretting thereat, and some writing unto him very scornful letters for the same.' However, Hamilton took consolation in the thought that, since the marriage had not yet been properly consummated, it could still be annulled, and trusted an opportunity to 'untie that knot which Buckingham had urged the king to tie upon his son' would arise before Mary reached sexual maturity. Meanwhile, he would send his son 'beyond the seas' to ensure no further contact between the couple was possible.

However, his plans were thwarted by George arranging for the groom to be promoted to the position of gentleman of Charles's bedchamber. The young Hamilton was now effectively trapped at court, only able to venture abroad when he was appointed to the entourage that joined Charles and George in Spain during the Madrid escapade.

Matters had reached a head early in 1625, when Mary, approaching thirteen, had become 'nubile', and efforts were underway by the Villiers clan to force a consummation. In the end, according to Eglisham, George's relations resorted to kidnapping the young man – a credible accusation given previous behaviour.

When Hamilton went to George to demand access to his son, an altercation resulted during which George accused the marquis of 'speaking disdainfully of him and his house'. Hamilton dismissively replied that he could not recall saying anything against the duke, prompting George to point out that he had 'scorned the notion of matching with my house, which I made unto you', to which the marquis replied that 'it became not the duke to speak to him in that fashion'. The French ambassador attempted to intercede, but George was enraged by the marquis's slight.

Eglisham affirmed what even some of George's friends would privately acknowledge (the king included): that he could be 'wonderfully vindictive' when roused, his 'malice insatiable'. Hamilton responded to his altercation with the favourite by taking immediate precautions to protect himself. The giving of gifts of food was one of the most important forms of courtly exchange, and soon after the breakdown of relations, Hamilton insisted that everything received from George's extensive network of allies and associates at court must first be tasted by one of his servants. Then, in late

February, two of them, 'one belonging to his wine cellar, and another to his kitchen', fell sick and died. Two days later, Hamilton joined them.

For Eglisham, this was clear evidence of poisoning, reinforced by his own toxicological observations about the extraordinary manner and aftermath of Hamilton's death. Infectious illness produces buboes, carbuncles and spots, he argued, not fluid-filled blisters and a 'huge uniform swelling'. In fact, these were effects neither he nor any of the other physicians who saw the marquis's corpse had witnessed before, except in dogs given poisons experimentally 'to try the forces of some antidotes'.

And as for George, 'when my Lord Marquis's body was to be transported from Whitehall to his house at Bishopsgate', Eglisham noted that the duke had accompanied the cortege 'muffed and furred in his coach, giving out that he was sick for sorrow of my Lord Marquis's death'. But as soon as he returned to his house, 'he triumphed and domineered with his faction so excessively, as if he had gained some great victory, and the next day coming to the King put on a most lamentable and mournful countenance for the death of the Marquis of Hamilton'.

Rubens had himself noted George's 'caprice and arrogance', and no doubt considered Eglisham's accusations concerning the death of Hamilton to be plausible. This must have added credibility to the even more sensational allegations made in the next section of the pamphlet, in which the author set out his accusation that George's next victim was the man who had made him: King James.

Great Matters of Weight

On Monday, 24 April 1626, a member of Charles's court received a secret letter about the current state of affairs in the House of Commons and its battle with George: it noted that there was 'some thing now on foot, which at the least makes a noise'.

In fact, what was afoot was an attempt to muffle the noise. As members arrived for that day's session, John Glanville MP, chair of the Committee of Twelve set up the previous Friday to investigate the case against George, made a short announcement. Over the weekend, he had become aware of 'some great matters of weight' which, 'if they shall be publicly now examined, may, by the notifying thereof hinder the service and ends of the House'. He therefore proposed that the committee's further deliberations should be conducted in private.

Several MPs objected. Sir John Lowther, one of George's loyalists, led the protests, arguing that the rest of the House would be 'blinded' by such secrecy, allowing members of the committee to 'take what they will' from their deliberations. He lost the vote, but as a concession, the committee agreed that members could attend the hearings just as long as they did not intervene or take notes.

The committee duly met that afternoon, Lowther among the spectators. The venue was the Court of Wards, a cramped room down a flight of steps leading from the lobby of the Commons' chamber. The stairwell was a favourite and rowdy haunt of members' servants, but today, as Lowther descended the stairs, he found it to be full of distinguished physicians.

Flouting the ban on taking notes, Lowther jotted down that day's proceedings, his fragmented and sometimes illegible scribbles providing the only written record by an MP of what happened that momentous afternoon.

Since James's death, the doctors who had attended his final hours had remained silent. None dared speak out for fear of implicating himself in the mismanagement of their illustrious patient's treatment. However, copies of Eglisham's tract in English had started to arrive in London, around the time Rubens had first seen the Latin edition in Antwerp – 'in the very nick', as one contemporary put it, of Parliament's deliberations. Whether in bundles already stored in a secret warehouse in London for a concerted campaign, or in a more haphazard fashion by Catholic supporters and agents, it was being 'industriously scattered up and down in the streets of the City of London', in the Royal Exchange, the precincts of St Paul's Cathedral, Westminster Hall, in alehouses, churches and playhouses.

Besides the vivid details about Hamilton's death, it contained a sensational – but to those with any knowledge of the events, credible – account of James's final hours. It reported how, on the Monday before his death, the duke gave the king some 'white powder' mixed with wine, after which James became 'immediately worse and worse, falling into many soundings and pains, and violent fluxes of the belly'. It told of how George's mother Mary had applied a plaster to 'the king's heart and breast', resulting in him growing short of breath and suffering 'in great agony'.

It also mentioned that the physicians, who were absent at dinner when these interventions were made, returned to their patient to find a lingering 'offensive smell' left by the plaster. This had made them believe 'something to be about the king hurtful to him, and searched what it could be, and exclaimed that the king was poisoned.

'Then Buckingham entering,' Eglisham's tract continued, 'he commanded the physicians out of the room, caused one to be committed prisoner to his own chamber, and another to remove from court, quarrelled with others of the king's servants in the sick king's own presence, so far that he offered to draw his sword against them in the king's sight.'

Some of these allegations were already known to the committee members, thanks to the work of Sir John Eliot's London agent. However, Eglisham's account also contained an incriminating new charge: that, following the king's death, the duke had forced the physicians who attended the king to sign 'a testimony that the powder which he gave the king was a good and safe medicine'.

In his introduction to *The Forerunner to Revenge*, Eglisham had implored Parliament to investigate his claims, since only 'the whole body of a Parliament' had the power to 'lay hold upon him'. The committee at least was up for the job. Besides Eliot, it included several MPs with grudges against George and patrons who were his enemies. John Glanville, well known as one of England's top lawyers, had been pressed by George into acting as secretary during the disastrous Cádiz escapade, seemingly in revenge for obstructing a subsidy bill during the previous Parliament. The mission had reduced his family to poverty; it had forced him to endure weeks of severe seasickness, which ended with him being marooned in Ireland, and only just managing to get back to London in time for the new parliamentary session. Other members included Edward Herbert, a kinsman of George's rival William, the Earl of Pembroke, who appeared to be orchestrating the duke's downfall, and Christopher Wandesford, a childhood friend and mouthpiece of Sir Thomas Wentworth, a member of a powerful family and a well-connected government critic who had been 'pricked' by George to become a sheriff, preventing him from standing for election.

As the twelve took their seats in the committee chamber, the doctors were brought in one at a time to give their testimony, Lowther watching from the side, scribbling surreptitiously in his notebook.

Eight doctors had agreed to testify to the committee, including many of the team who dealt with James during his final hours. But several key figures were missing, notably Sir William Paddy, who had arrived at the king's bedside two days before his death, Henry Gibb, the royal groom who had been dismissed for trying to obstruct George's interventions, and perhaps most crucially the mysterious 'doctor from Dunmow', John Remington, who had supplied the medicine George and his mother had used.

Despite the absences, the testimony given over the following two days was sensational. With varying degrees of cooperation, depending on their closeness to Charles and George, and subject to their desperate efforts to exonerate themselves while implicating their opponents, they all agreed that the substance of Eglisham's account was true: that a plaster and potion had been administered to the king at a vital stage in his recovery, and that he had subsequently suffered a sharp deterioration in his condition. Furthermore, none of them had been told in advance what had been in the medicine, let alone witnessed the making of it.

Not everyone was prepared to disapprove of the use of the duke's medicine. Chief among George's supporters was William Harvey. Harvey has been hailed the Isaac Newton of medical science, his discovery of the circulation of the blood revolutionizing medicine's view of how the body works. He would also go on to become a trusted personal doctor of Charles. At the time of James's death, he was one of James's 'sworn physicians', and in attendance through most of the king's final illness.

Harvey was a cold fish, a dedicated anatomist and a royalist. Charles's patronage was central to his scientific ambitions – he received deer foetuses from the royal parks for his dissections – and he responded to the poisoning accusations with a kind of languid confidence that suggested he knew the charges against George would never stick. He had been at the king's bedside during the crucial final days, and witnessed most of the main events, including the administering of the plaster and potion. When asked of his medical views concerning the duke's intervention, he accepted that he was unable to give one as the ingredients were 'not known'. Nevertheless, he 'gave way to it, thinking it could do no harm'. He thought it 'not against his opinion nor consultation' since the king 'desired it'. Harvey saw no reason to suspect the duke's claim that it was a medicine he had himself used in the past. James 'took diverse things', the doctor pointed out.

Archibald Hay, James's surgeon and now in Charles's service, backed up the tenor of Harvey's testimony, though with less assurance. He accepted he had applied the plaster, but was vague as to whether he had taken it off. 'No physician disliked it,' he insisted, though he later admitted some were 'not content'. As to its ingredients, Hay claimed that it had first been 'tasted' by John Baker, one of the duke's servants. He thought that Baker, a barber, had mixed the 'posset' or potion in the duke's chamber. None of the medics tasted it before it was given to the king, as far as he knew, but he saw the king 'taste of it'. He obviously found it unpleasant, as Hay had then mixed it with gillyflower, a clove-scented plant, to make it more palatable.

As for the ingredients, Hay confirmed what some of the other doctors had presumed, that there was a compound in a 'box' that was the basis of both the plaster and the potion. Hay guessed that it was probably a 'treacle or mithridate', one of the highly elaborate concoctions used by doctors to treat various illnesses, including fevers. Two of Charles's physicians-in-ordinary agreed, David Beton saying that 'the smell of it was like some treacle composition', while Matthew Lister identified its smell as similar to 'London Treacle', a local and widely used remedy. However, other doctors were not so sure: Alexander Ramsey and Henry Atkins, the two Scottish doctors who were first to give evidence, denied that they could identify it.

Despite the differences, they all confirmed Eglisham's claim that, soon after James's death, they had been told to endorse a recipe for the medicine the duke and his mother had used, which showed it to be made up of harmless ingredients. They also identified John Moore, alongside Sir William Paddy, as the doctor who had presented it to them.

Moore's testimony to the committee was a confusing story about writing a letter to the 'maker' of the medicine asking for its ingredients, and receiving a reply identifying it as London Treacle with 'juice of citrons'. Following the complaints from the other physicians concerning its use, a 'note was made at Sir William Paddy's instance that it was not hurtful' – presumably mentioning the recipe that the doctors endorsed. But Moore could supply no evidence that either the contents of the letter or Sir William Paddy's 'note' identified the potion's ingredients.

The generally consistent picture that was emerging took a sinister and strange turn on the final day of submissions. It began with a report from committee member Christopher Wandesford, who had been given permission to leave the House to interview witnesses. He had talked to James's other surgeon, Gilbert Primrose, who confirmed that James had felt 'much worse' after the application of the plaster. Furthermore, 'a little before the king died' James had produced 'a great deal of black matter' with a 'very noisome' stench. It had emerged 'without purging' – in other words, spontaneously.

The committee then interviewed Robert Ramsey, a mysterious figure with an even more mysterious story. Ramsey reported several exchanges the previous month with an Irishman called Piers Butler, some sort of magician claiming to have 'strange faculties'. Butler said he had connections with the duke, and had discovered earlier that month that one Rennish – perhaps John Remington, the Doctor of Dunmow – had set to work 'to distill the spirit of toads', an ingredient associated with witchcraft:

> Round about the cauldron go;
> In the poison'd entrails throw.
> Toad, that under cold stone
> Days and nights has thirty-one
> Swelter'd venom sleeping got,
> Boil thou first i' the charmed pot.
>
> (*Macbeth*, Act IV, sc. i)

Bemused by Ramsey's testimony, the committee turned without further ado to its final witness, John Craig, the Scottish doctor who had been excluded from court by George for his protests at James's treatment.

Exile had given Craig the leisure to reconsider his highly vulnerable position. At first he seemed to make light of what had happened, confirming that the unauthorized plaster had been used on the king, but claimed that 'it was quickly removed', and that the attending physicians 'saw no effect of any hurt done by it'. However, under further examination, he did admit that when it was applied a second time, the king 'did dislike the laying on of the plasters and it did heat him more', in other words, produce feverish symptoms.

He confirmed that he was the doctor Eglisham had mentioned being excluded from court, but claimed he never said the words attributed to him, specifically that the medicine given to James by George 'was as bad as poison'.

Much of this was already familiar to the committee members, but Craig then let slip a crucial and shocking new detail: he revealed that, at the height of the crisis, he and another (unnamed) doctor had gone to Charles, 'to desire him that he would advise the Lord Duke to remit all to the care of the physicians'.

Until this moment, no one had even considered the whereabouts of the heir, still less speculated what he knew of George's antics. Indeed, the official record and the committee's witnesses had been altogether silent about Charles's involvement in the final hours of his father's life.

Perhaps it had not been surprising to discover that the king was close to his father's sickroom. But it had occurred to no one that he had known, even been consulted about the unfolding medical drama. Deadly questions seared the lips: Why had he failed to intervene? Why had he not insisted that his father's treatment be left to the physicians? Why had he ignored the doctors' pleas that medical protocol be followed – a protocol that had been developed in response to the mysterious death of his own brother, Prince Henry? What answer could there be to such questions that did not beg even more alarming ones? Had he turned a blind eye? Could it even be that he had conspired with George?

What about the testimony of all the other doctors? How come

none of them had mentioned this? What, for example, about William Harvey, who had witnessed the plaster being applied? He must have known of Craig's attempt to appeal to Charles. Yet he had remained silent on the matter. Those on the committee with links to Harvey's medical rivals may have been aware of how close he now was to Charles – a view that would be confirmed just a few weeks after he appeared before the committee, when he received a gift from the king of £100 for his 'pains and attendance about the person of his Majesty's late dear father, of happy memory, in time of his sickness'. Just a few months after that, he would also receive the curious and potentially incriminating award of a royal pardon, granting him immunity for past crimes.

Such thoughts had to be expunged, however – or at least suppressed. Any hint that the king was going to be brought into the affair risked Parliament's instant dismissal, charges of treason and a fresh harvest from Tyburn's tree.

And yet, the thoughts must have been insistent – the bond between Charles and the duke following their return from Madrid, which they had seen for themselves when George had stood at the prince's shoulder and told them of the 'Spanish Labyrinth'. Then there was the rupture between James and George in the following months, and George's seamless transition from being favourite of the father to becoming favourite of the son. There was Charles's obvious and growing dependency on George; his youth, his impressionability, his reluctance to speak for himself – the multiplicity of indications that he was yet another to be ensnared in George's 'magic thraldom'.

The day following Craig's testimony, John Glanville, the committee chair, revealed to the whole House the 'substance of proof' or findings of their investigation. The conclusion was coy but nevertheless incendiary: that the plaster and potion had been 'applied at prohibited times', when the king was vulnerable to new fits if the wrong kind of medicine was used. They asserted that this had been 'done by the direction of the duke', that the treatment had been applied twice, that it had made the king's condition worse and that on the third attempt, was refused by James. Furthermore, as Eglisham had claimed, doctors Paddy and Moore had presented the other physicians with a 'bill' claiming that it listed the ingredients of the duke's medicine, which they had endorsed even though none of them were in a position to confirm that it was the true recipe.

'The opinion of the committee,' Glanville concluded, was that these allegations should be 'annexed to the duke's charge' as a 'transcendent presumption of dangerous consequence'.

A Silly Piece of Malice

The doctors' testimony touched a nerve. Charles ordered that Alexander Ramsey, the first physician to appear before the committee, be put under house arrest. At the same time, an order was issued for the apprehension of Piers Butler, the Irish mountebank who had linked George with the mixing of poisonous potions. Butler appears to have fled for the coast, presumably with the intention of escaping to the Continent or Ireland, and pursuivants were sent to Kent, Bristol and Chester to find him.

Little is known about Butler. He claimed to be related to the earls of Ossory and Ormond, and a man named Piers Butler with those connections had been in contact with George on several occasions the previous year, seeking a knighthood from the king. He may have been the 'devil' George had mentioned hiring for a princely sum in a letter written to King James around 1624. George had told James of this devil's ability to mix an antidote that would 'preserve you from all sickness ever hereafter'. It was made out of a 'towrd', which could be a corruption of toad, as mentioned in the testimony Robert Ramsey gave to the Committee of Twelve. But as well as being one of George's clients, Butler also seemed to be one of his enemies. He had been seen in a cellar tavern near Denmark House bragging that he had a bullet with which 'he should have killed the Duke of Buckingham'.

Whatever his relationship to George, he was clearly identified as a liability at a vulnerable time for the duke, so considerable effort and expense was made to apprehend him. It seems he escaped, leaving behind unsettling corroboration of an association voiced by Eglisham that George was 'infamous for his frequent consultations with the ringleaders of witches'.

Attempts were also underway to track down the source of Eglisham's tract. Charles's security apparatus was bereft of any secret intelligence or leads, so had to rely on a clue contained in the book itself. Eglisham had mentioned 'a paper found in King Street', the thoroughfare connecting the palaces of Westminster and Whitehall, that contained a list of George's enemies. The paper, he revealed, had been discovered by Anne Lyon, who came from a noble Scottish family with connections to the Marquis of Hamilton. She had handed the paper over to the marquis, who found not only his own name on the list, but that of Eglisham.

Charles instructed Henry Wotton, an old friend of George's and now provost of Eton College, to investigate this claim. Wotton wrote a few days later to George to announce his findings, enclosing a copy of his report. 'I have seen many defamatory and libellous things of this nature, abroad and at home, though for the most part always without truth, yet oftentimes contrived with some credibility,' he explained in the covering letter. 'But this appeareth in the whole contexture utterly void of both.' He had found Anne Lyon living in Windsor with a sister and 'a gentlewoman of her attendance'. Arriving with a copy of Eglisham's tract, and worried that the 'somewhat harsh and umbrageous' nature of his business might make her reluctant to talk, he 'laboured to take from her all manner of shadow touching herself'. However, he had no need for concern, because when he showed Anne the passage in *The Forerunner* mentioning her, she was so furious at being 'traduced for a witness of this foul defamation' that she was happy to tell him everything she knew.

As with so many details in Eglisham's pamphlet, this one turned out to be more or less accurate. The paper had been found by a 'carman' called Smith, who had given it to the footman of Anne's mother, who had brought it to Anne. She described it as 'half a sheet of paper laid double by the length, and in it was written in a scribbled hand the names of a number (above a dozen) of the Privy Council'. There was no mention of poison, though she had seen signs of some additional words 'which were scraped out'.

The Marquis of Hamilton was one of those listed, and written next to his name was the curious entry 'Dr. Eglisham to embalm him'. As the marquis had been away at that time, Anne Lyon had initially shown it to Alexander Heatley, secretary to Ludovick Stuart, the Duke of Lennox. Heatley did not think it was necessary to trouble his lordship with the matter as he thought it was probably a list of names drawn up by a lawyer, presenting a case to one of the government's courts or councils. Anne then showed it to a servant of the marquis, who gave it to Hamilton, who simply put it in his pocket. 'Whereby may appear to any reasonable creature,' Wotton concluded, 'what a silly piece of malice this was.'

Dissolution

'The arraignment of the Duke of Buckingham occupies the exclusive attention of the House of Commons,' Amerigo Salvetti wrote on 28 April 1626, in his weekly report to his Florentine masters. 'The excitement grows daily as new and important complaints are brought forward. The Members sit twice a day to expedite the business in hand.'

On 1 May, the MPs' high-stakes deliberations were interrupted by the arrival of a thirteen-year-old boy at the entrance to the chamber. It was George Digby, the son and heir of John Digby, Earl of Bristol, with a petition on behalf of his father.

Still under house arrest, ex-Spanish ambassador Digby was now demanding that either he be released and allowed to take his place in the House of Lords or tried for his supposed offences. The young Digby's petition claimed that the 'honour and good name' of his father had been 'much wronged by many sinister aspersions cast upon him by the Duke of Buckingham', and he pleaded with the MPs in their 'high wisdom' to give his father 'satisfaction'.

The same day, the vilified duke was just down the corridor, in the House of Lords. With an air of neutral interest, he watched as John Digby knelt at the bar of the Lords' chamber. The government's Attorney General began to read out the charges against him when Digby got to his feet and turned to George. 'I accuse that man the Duke of Buckingham of high treason,' he cried, 'and will prove it.'

In the hush that followed, nervous eyes turned on George, who was sitting just a few feet away. The recent tide of criticism had taken a toll on him. The Venetian ambassador had an audience with him in mid-May and noticed a 'pallor of his face' that betrayed 'deep uneasiness at the embarrassments in which he finds himself'. While George still spoke of his affairs with 'temperate vigour', the ambassador could see his mind was 'tossed by a thousand agitations', and he was nervous whether Charles would be able to uphold his authority 'in order to counteract the activities of the parliamentarians'.

Now faced by his principle accuser, in the House of Lords, George managed to maintain an appearance of unruffled calmness, allowing Digby to speak, and pledging not to interrupt him, because 'he has been his friend'.

A furious denunciation followed, beginning with the former ambassador's account of Charles and George's unexpected arrival at the House of the Seven Chimneys. It was the duke who had lured Charles there, Digby claimed, having promised the Spanish that the heir could be converted to Catholicism, 'the which conversion he endeavoured to procure by all means possible'. It was the duke who had worked his occult 'power' on the young Spanish king Philip 'for the procuring of favours and offices, which he bestowed upon base and unworthy persons, for the recompense and hire of his lust'. And it was the duke's behaviour that had in the end 'so incensed the king of Spain and his ministers, as they would admit of no reconciliation nor further dealing with him'.

Then came the bombshell, timed to cause George as much damage as possible. A few days before the start of James's final, fatal illness, the king had asked Digby to return to London so he could 'hear him against the said duke' concerning the collapse of the Spanish match negotiations. But George had learned of the summons, 'and not long after, his blessed majesty sickened and died'.

The final accusation brought George to his feet. How dare Digby 'touch upon the late king's death', the duke shouted, and threatened that if he did not 'prove it, then he may have *lex talionis*' – the law of retaliation, an eye for an eye.

A mood of awkward confusion descended on the House. The

Lords had been expecting to deal with Charles's charges against the former ambassador, but now had a countercharge to consider. After some discussion, it was decided that the king's charges should take precedence, but Digby protested that this would effectively stop his case from being heard.

In a characteristically abrupt and disconcerting change of mood, George suggested a compromise: that both cases be heard at the same time. The intervention seemed to calm frayed nerves, and the House reverted to procedural consultations to consider how this might be done.

Meanwhile, it was decided that Digby should be 'committed in the Gentleman-usher's House', though with the concession that he would have 'access of friends to be permitted to come unto him' to help him prepare his defence. As he was taken away, in a burst of 'angry passion' Digby demanded to know why George was not being treated in the 'same manner'.

The following day, the finalized list of charges drawn up by the Committee of Twelve was presented to the House of Commons. Twelve of the charges were already known and had been debated, covering everything from corruption to extortion. Now they were joined by a thirteenth. It was carefully worded, carrying the merest 'whisper of poison', as the Tuscan agent put it. It was that the duke did 'unduly cause and procure certain plasters, and a certain drink or potion to be provided for the use of his said majesty', which were applied 'without the direction or privity of his said late majesty's physicians, not prepared by any of his majesty's sworn apothecaries or surgeons, but compounded of several ingredients to them unknown'.

On the same day, a letter from Charles was read out in the Lords. His continuing loyalty to the favourite was obvious from the opening sentences. He knew 'more than any man' of George's 'sincere carriage', and dismissed Digby's suit as an attempt to silence the duke, as he was to be the main witness in the charges the king had brought against Digby. He urged the Lords to 'put a difference' between his charges against the 'delinquent' Digby, and Digby's charges against George and 'not to equal them by a proceeding *pari passu*' – side by side. He also commanded them 'not to match the imprisonment of the one and the other, as the Earl of Bristol desired, the ground being so different and unequal'.

Despite the intervention, the attack on the duke had by now achieved a momentum that not even Charles could stop. On 3 May, the Commons passed a motion to send a delegation to the House of Lords at the earliest opportunity to present the thirteen charges it had drawn up, and to demand the duke's impeachment. Eight MPs, selected from among the Committee of the Twelve, were duly appointed to deliver the evidence. Given the magnitude of the task, it was agreed that they would be accompanied by a further twelve 'assistants'. Over the following week, as other parliamentary business continued around them, the delegates practised and polished what they would say. By 6 May, each had been allotted his role: Dudley Digges to introduce the charges, Christopher Wandesford to argue the case regarding the 'certain Plaisters, and a certain Drink' administered by the duke, and John Eliot to provide a conclusion.

Meanwhile, in the House of Lords, matters surrounding Digby's trial were escalating. With an eye on the poisoning allegations, Digby had introduced a new piece of evidence. It concerned a conversation between George and the Marquis of Hamilton just before the marquis's death. Apparently, the duke had discussed with Hamilton a plan to have Digby committed to the Tower to prevent him telling King James about the duke's role in the collapse of the Spanish match. On 8 May, George stood up to respond to the allegation. While condemning the use of 'my dead friend' the marquis 'who cannot answer for himself', he accepted that the allegation was essentially correct, simply adding that his comments had not been made 'out of any malice' towards Digby, but because even if the ex-ambassador 'had been my brother, considering his carriage in this business, I should have thought the Tower the fittest lodging for him'.

Later that morning, a message arrived from the Commons to the Lords asking for a 'conference'. With anxieties surrounding their most powerful member growing, the Lords agreed to 'admit a meeting but not a conference'. In other words, they would sit and listen, but they would not discuss.

At 2 p.m., delegations from both Houses met in the Painted

Chamber, eight Lords – including George's enemy William Herbert, Earl of Pembroke – facing twelve MPs and their eight assistants, carrying a thick bundle of papers.

Dudley Digges introduced the proceedings with an elaborate analogy. Recalling the work of his father Thomas, a famous astronomer, he compared the king to the sun, the great offices of state to the planets, and George to the 'blazing star' that had appeared in the constellation Cassiopeia in 1572, an apparition that had caused consternation, presaging, it was believed, a disturbance to the cosmic order. 'Such a prodigious comet the Commons takes this Duke of Buckingham to be,' Digges proclaimed, 'against whom, and his irregular ways, there are, by learned gentlemen, legal articles of charge to be delivered to your Lordships, which I am generally first commanded to lay open.'

The charges duly followed, listed by Digges and his colleagues, in an outpouring of conjecture and evidence running to 30,000 words on paper and many hours in a hot and increasingly tense chamber. They culminated with Christopher Wandesford introducing the thirteenth charge. He was nervous, later conceding to his fellow MPs that George, who was in the room but sitting apart from the Lords' delegation, listened to the charge 'with more confidence than I could deliver it'.

Stiffening his resolve, Wandesford asserted that the duke, 'contrary to his duty, and the tender respect which he ought to have had of his majesty's most sacred person', had administered medicines to a sick James which had 'a strange smell, and an invective quality, striking the malignity of the disease inward' causing 'great distempers, as droughts, raving, fainting, an intermitting pulse', as well as other 'strange effects', which ultimately led to the king's death. Quoting learned opinion, Wandesford added 'that if one that is no physician or surgeon undertake a cure, and the party die under his hands, this is felony', in other words, the most serious sort of crime. He wondered if what George had done was 'a fatal error in judgment only', or 'something else'. In reply, the MP cited the story of Julius Caesar, provocatively quoting the famous words used in Shakespeare's play, when Caesar's friend Brutus assassinates his leader: '*Et tu, Brute?*'

Sir John Eliot provided the conclusion. He had lost none of his fury and disgust at the behaviour of his former patron. Arousing profound discomfort among members of the Lords' delegation, he compared Villiers to Sejanus, the corrupt favourite of the Roman Emperor Tiberius, and the subject of a controversial play by Ben Jonson which depicted him as a rapacious royal catamite who used poison to kill off his enemies.

As the official record of the event noted with a brevity lacking in the MPs' submission: 'Sir Dudley Digges, having made the Prologue, and Sir John Eliot the Epilogue, in the impeachment of the duke, they were both by the King's command committed to the Tower.'

In the Commons there was uproar. The MPs pledged that while their colleagues were imprisoned, all proceedings would be broken off, and with cries of 'rise, rise', the chamber emptied. The following day the members gathered in silence, not even allowing the Speaker to read out the order of the day. Then John Wylde, the MP for Droitwich, stood to deliver a speech. In an almost funereal tone, he lamented the loss to the Commons of 'two whose excellent parts and indefatigable labours are fresh in our memories'. He claimed that the arrests had put in danger the 'broad charter of our great inheritance gained with so great cost, so often confirmed' – Magna Carta, the bulwark of personal liberty and political rights. After he had sat down, the silence continued until Dudley Carleton, the king's vice chamberlain, stood to justify what Charles had done.

Carleton's speech, which began with rambling remarks about his youthful experiences at sea, drew a hostile response. Ignoring angry interruptions, he revealed the reason for the arrests. It was not Digges's characterization of the duke as a 'prodigious comet' threatening to destroy the settled order of the political cosmos, nor even Eliot's description of the favourite as 'full of collusion and deceit'. 'The cause,' Carleton said, 'is a high offence the king takes at certain scandals and words passed in that speech touching the end of the last king which was inferred as hastened by a drink and plaster.' Under interrogation, both Eliot and Digges had refused to repudiate what they had said. Indeed, Digges had made things worse. In an outburst perhaps provoked by his interrogators, he told them he had nothing more to say about James's medical treatment 'in regard of' – in order not to damage – 'the King's Honour'. This implied that he believed Charles was in some way implicated. Digges had subsequently and vehemently denied this, but five witnesses attested otherwise, and, as far as Carleton was concerned, a failure to acknowledge the king's innocence was as bad as proclaiming that he was 'not worthy to wear the crown' – a treasonous charge.

This was why the two MPs had to remain in detention. It was why the House should take heed: if it continued to take such 'tumultuary licence' in debating the matter, it might find itself abolished, like representative assemblies elsewhere in Europe.

Yet even as Carleton tried to intimidate Parliament at Westminster, a mood of desperation and fear had set in at the king's palace in Whitehall. The state of the treasury was by now worse than ever. The clamour from creditors, officials and suppliers had become deafening. Thousands of unpaid sailors and soldiers who had returned from failed military adventures had started to migrate to London. Southwark had become so overrun with them that the Privy Council was forced to close the Globe Theatre to prevent it becoming a focus for 'riotous action', and to give local magistrates time to gather the officers they would need 'for the suppressing of any insolences or mutinous intentions'.

The night of the MPs' arrests, Charles was overheard in the royal bedchamber in a state of despair. 'What more can I do?' he asked George. 'I have in a manner lost the love of my subjects. What woulds't thou have me do?'

George would not relent. His confidence seemed bolstered rather than weakened by the attacks. He would have the king defy the scoundrels. Having been accused of taking on too many offices, Charles must offer him another. Though he lacked a university education and freely admitted to being no scholar, it emerged he was to be nominated as the next chancellor of the University of Cambridge, a royal appointment. The provocative announcement caused yet more uproar. The university dons resisted fiercely. But, with what has coyly been described as a 'less than scrupulous counting of votes', their objections were overcome.

Leaving his enemies aghast, George then delivered to the House of Lords an answer to the impeachment charges that dextrously made them almost impossible to prosecute without mounting a direct attack on the king.

The duke began in a familiar tone of disarming humility. He accepted that he may have been 'raised to honour and fortunes' beyond his merit, but hoped that he would be able to restore the good opinion of his critics. He then gave each of the charges the Commons had brought against him the dignity of a considered response, explaining his actions and challenging his accusers, while throughout reminding their lordships that all he had done was at the command and with the knowledge of the king.

George then concluded with a legalistic point invoking memories of the fall of his predecessor, Robert Carr. He reminded their lordships that he had received a general pardon from King James, which had been reconfirmed by Charles 'at the time of his most happy inauguration and coronation'. He had even brought along a copy of the document, helpfully pointing out that it bore the great seal. So, even if he was guilty of any of the crimes he was accused of, he was immune from prosecution.

A few days later, on 12 June, the Commons received a copy of George's replies. It was referred to a subcommittee while discussions continued about a remonstrance against the arrest of Eliot and Digges. A letter was also sent by the king threatening the dissolution of Parliament if a subsidy bill was not passed within the week.

At three that afternoon, the windows of the Commons' chamber were rattled by gusts of wind and a sudden and violent downpour of rain and hail. Those unfortunate enough to be caught outside in the precincts of the Palace of Westminster noticed the strange 'turbulency of the waters' of the Thames, and a mist rising up in a great whorl 'like the smoke issuing out of a furnace'. It was noted that this storm had 'bent itself towards York House', George's Thames-side residence, 'beating against the stairs and wall thereof' before it 'ascended higher and higher till it quite vanished away'.

Two days later, a delegation went to the king with a copy of the remonstrance that had occupied the Commons since the arrest of Eliot and Digges. Charles said he would respond the following day, which he did with a summons of MPs to the House of Lords. There, one of the king's officials announced that Parliament was immediately dissolved.

An MP who had kept a diary of the session's momentous events ended his final entry for the Parliament of 1626 with a Latin aphorism: *Sic abeant omnes et cessat gloria regni.* 'So they may go away, and all the glory of the kingdom ceases.'

The Devil and the Duke

Like all of London's theatres, the Fortune Playhouse was situated just outside the City's walls, beyond the reach of the authorities. Rebuilt in 1621 following a fire, it had been considered one of London's more refined as well as most commercially successful open-air venues, the profits generated by its owner, Edward Alleyn, going towards the founding of a school in Dulwich. By the summer of 1628, it had fallen into decline, drawing a rabble of apprentices and 'apple wives', beggarly street sellers. Just two years before, a crowd of cashiered sailors had run riot there, refusing to stop in the king's name as they 'cared not for the king, for the king paid them no wages'.

On Friday, 13 July 1628, Dr John Lambe, recently turned eighty, joined the jostling crowd to see the Fortune's latest production. He was a sinister and by now notorious figure in London, mentioned in *The Forerunner of Revenge* as one of the 'ringleaders of witches' Eglisham claimed George Villiers had 'frequently consulted'. He had a long history as a mystic, quack and sexual predator. In 1622 he had been arrested on a historic charge of attempting 'to disable, make infirm and consume the body and strength' of a young pupil, and for having 'invoked and entertained evil spirits'. He was remanded in Worcester Castle awaiting trial, where forty fellow inmates subsequently died under mysterious circumstances. He was then transferred back to the capital, to the King's Bench prison, where a relatively relaxed regime allowed him to set up in practice as a medic and fortune teller, attracting a string of visitors, some of them high-ranking women. This financed a lavish lifestyle, which included a suite of two rooms furnished with keyboard instruments. In 1623 he was indicted for the rape of an eleven-year-old girl, who had been sent to his prison cell with a basket of herbs. He was tried and sentenced to be hanged. However, in the summer of 1624, the Lord Chief Justice intervened, apparently on behalf of the king. The evidence was reviewed, and on the basis of perceived weaknesses in the case, he was issued a royal pardon and took up residence in a house next to Parliament.

This is when Lambe's name became associated with George. Around the time of his release, the scandal surrounding the pregnancy of Frances, the estranged wife of George's brother John, was captivating the court. Among the rumours in circulation was 'an imputation laid on her that with powders and potions she did intoxicate her husband's brains, and practised somewhat in that kind upon the Duke of Buckingham'. This had apparently been 'confessed by one Lambe a notorious old rascal'. George had ordered an investigation, at which witnesses claimed that Frances had been seen going to Lambe's house dressed in 'the habit of a maid servant, with a basket on her arm', where her lover, the brother of the Earl of Suffolk and the presumed father of her child, awaited her.

Though the association would suggest that George was at odds with Lambe, over the following months the link with the Villiers family seemed to hint at an alliance. In 1627, it was reported that George's mother, Mary, 'solicitous to know what would become of her son', had consulted Lambe about George's future. Peering into a crystal ball, he claimed to see 'a big, fat man, with a reddish face, brown beard, an iron arm, and a long dagger'.

By the time John Lambe was making his way to the Fortune Playhouse that summer day of 1628, his name was well enough established as an associate of the duke for the two to be linked in a number of popular songs, one satirizing George's riposte to the charges brought against him by the Commons:

> Nor shall you ever prove, by magic charms
> I wrought the king's affection, or his harms,
> Or that I need Lambe's philtres to incite
> Chaste ladies to give my foul lust delight.

The pair may even have been the subject of a 'scurvy book', since lost, entitled *The Devil and the Duke*, which had caused 'much inquisition in Paul's Churchyard', the location of London's booksellers.

So when Lambe took his seat in one of the galleries overlooking the one-penny 'groundlings' in the theatre yard, many were aware of his notoriety and his association with the duke.

Whatever play was put on that day, it generated a surly mood, and as the audience was filing out into Golding Lane some 'boys of the town and other unruly people' decided to follow Lambe as he made his way back towards the City.

Heading along Chiswell Street towards Moorfields, the doctor became concerned for his safety and took refuge in a tavern near the City walls, where he stayed until about 9 p.m., hoping to lay low until the mob dispersed. He emerged to find the crowd still there and, hiring a group of sailors for protection, made his way through Moorgate and down Coleman Street. Reaching Lothbury, the street of coppersmiths and chandlers, the crowd had become even more menacing, so he took refuge across the junction in the Windmill tavern, an old converted synagogue on the corner of Old Jewry. While he was sheltering there, the building came under attack, and the landlord forced him back onto the street, where he found his escort of sailors had deserted him. Now terrified for his life, he set off down Old Jewry and briefly managed to take refuge in the house of a lawyer. The mob threatened to tear the building down unless he was ejected, and he found himself once again on the street. The crowd fell upon him 'with stones and cudgels and other weapons'. The constables had by then been alerted, but either chose not to intervene or arrived too late.

He was found lying unconscious on the cobbles. His 'skull was broken' and one of his eyes 'hung out of his head'. His body was 'bruised and wounded so much, that no part was left to receive a wound'. He was carried down to the Poultry Compter, the sheriff's prison at the end of Old Jewry, where he died early the following morning, a 'wretched life' ended by 'a miserable & strange death'. His pockets were searched, showing he was carrying several knives, a nightcap braided with gold thread, 40 shillings, a crystal ball and a collection of miniatures, including one of the gaoler of Frances Howard, the wife of Robert Carr and perpetrator of the Overbury poisoning.

The official response to the death was outrage. The king summoned the lord mayor to Whitehall and demanded those responsible be punished. When the authorities failed to produce the culprits, several constables were arrested and gaoled for neglect of duty, but quickly bailed so they could take part in the hunt for the ringleaders.

While these investigations were underway, handwritten notes appeared nailed to signposts and doors around Coleman Street:

> Let Charles and George do what they can,
> Yet George shall die like Doctor Lambe.

The Scrivener's Tale

A few hundred yards from where John Lambe fell, John Felton, one of the many unpaid soldiers in the capital, was nursing his grievances and a wounded hand. Having made his way to London from Portsmouth, he had been forced to take mean lodgings in the house of Thomas Foot, a servant to the warden of the nearby Fleet prison. The Fleet had bad associations for Felton. His father, once a successful pursuivant and bailiff based in rural Suffolk, had died there, ruined by unemployment and debt.

One of nine children with precarious prospects, Felton had signed up for soldiering some time in the mid-1620s, and had taken part in the Cádiz fiasco of 1626. Following the defeat and scattering of the fleet, he had ended up in Ireland.

By June 1627, Felton had made his way back to England where he learned that Buckingham was preparing to lead a new expedition to attack the port city of La Rochelle. Relations with the French had deteriorated sharply after the expulsion of Queen Henrietta Maria's entourage, and in a gesture of Protestant solidarity the duke had ordered a mission to relieve Huguenots who had become besieged in the city by forces loyal to King Louis. As with Cádiz, the mission had been a disaster; arriving with a second wave of ships and soldiers, Felton had taken part in an attack that ended in horrific slaughter and ignominious withdrawal.

Since coming to London, the soldier had begun to suffer from a paralysing 'melancholy', his sleep interrupted 'by dreams of fighting', a condition for which he blamed the mission's figurehead, the Duke of Buckingham. Adding to his resentment was a claim to £80 of backpay, and a conviction that the duke had cheated him out of a captaincy in favour of one of his minions.

Around the time of John Lambe's death, Felton had started to look for a scrivener, or professional scribe, to write petitions about his grievances so he could present them to the Privy Council. Elizabeth Josselyn, who shared his lodgings, was the wife of a stationer, so perhaps she recommended George Willoughby, who was based in nearby Holborn.

Scriveners were enjoying a boom in demand for their services. In January 1628, Charles had summoned yet another Parliament in his ongoing yet futile efforts to raise money for his regime's military adventures. The MPs were proving as defiant as they had been in 1626, promising a generous subsidy, but also producing a steady stream of remonstrances and demands that disgruntled citizens, increasingly despondent about the state of national affairs, were eager to read. Printing such tracts, or the flurry of scurrilous poems and songs that were produced in response to them, was difficult without attracting the attention of the authorities, so a lively black market had sprung up in copies produced by hand. Willoughby was an enterprising and enthusiastic supplier, supplementing legitimate and less exciting work by transcribing a range of illicit texts, including a copy of the ditty nailed to signposts in Coleman Street predicting the duke's demise following John Lambe's murder.

Felton arrived at Willoughby's shop to find him busy transcribing the Commons' latest remonstrance. The document had originally been delivered to Charles at a joint meeting of both Houses of Parliament held at the Banqueting House on 17 June 1628. News of its damning indictment of the duke had spread quickly through the city, producing a strange outburst of popular exultation, with a ringing of bells and lighting of bonfires that 'equalled those at his majesty's coming from Spain' in 1623. The king had responded by issuing a proclamation that dismissed yet again the allegations made against the favourite. He also ordered that the thirteen articles brought against George by the previous Parliament be struck from the official record.

Felton, it emerged, was something of a connoisseur of prohibited literature, having seen a copy of Eglisham's *Forerunner of Revenge*. He

asked Willoughby if he could borrow the scrivener's copy of the
MPs' remonstrance to read. Despite the dangers of putting a paper
bearing his own imprint into the hands of a stranger, Willoughby
agreed. Tucking it into his jacket, Felton went off to study it in a
tavern on Shoe Lane, round the corner from his lodgings.

The effect was revelatory. It awoke a feeling that George was
not only responsible for Felton's personal problems, but a dangerous
tyrant at the heart of government who had undermined the consti-
tution and thrown the kingdom into disarray. A messianic conviction
overcame the traumatized ex-soldier, commanding him to take
action, not just on his own account, but for the sake of the nation.
For the next few weeks he underwent a period of fasting and prayer,
during which he reflected on his feelings, wondering if he was being
lured by a 'temptation from the devil'. Then on Sunday, 18 August
1628, he concluded that the time had come to act.

The following morning, Felton rose and dressed, carefully
fastening into his hatband a passage copied from a popular work
of moral guidance, which argued that a man who was not willing
to sacrifice his life for the honour of God, his king and his country
was 'cowardly and base'. He went to visit his mother and sister,
who lived nearby, to borrow some money. He told them that he
was returning to Portsmouth because the duke was visiting the port
to review a fleet being prepared for another mission to La Rochelle,
and he intended to confront him about the matter of his missing
pay. He then went to a cutler near Tower Hill, where he bought a
tenpenny dagger.

I Am the Man

Southwick House, a small mansion built among the ruins of a
monastic abbey, overlooked the beautiful wooded countryside of
south Hampshire. Since late July 1628, as the fleet gathered in
nearby Portsmouth, it had been Charles's home. George had been
expected to join the king, but was detained in London, frantically
dealing with organizing the Rochelle relief mission that he hoped
would redeem his military reputation. Everything was on the line.
He had pledged to lead the expedition himself, had replaced key

members of the Admiralty in the hope of improving management of the ramshackle fleet, ordered deserters to be hanged, mortgaged his property, even raised £1,500 by selling the buttons off his best pearl suit, all, as he put it, 'for the use of His Majesty's Navy'.

On 6 August, George wrote to Charles that he was still having problems victualling the ships; 'I dare not come from hence,' he wrote, until he had seen the matter 'despatched, being of such importance'. Finally, by 12 August he was ready to leave, and set off for Southwick, arriving two days later.

After a brief reunion with Charles, he rushed off to Portsmouth, setting up quarters in the Greyhound Inn. It was already packed with members of his staff, along with his wife Kate, who was pregnant with their fourth child, and the French Huguenot leader Benjamin de Rohan, Duc de Soubise. Frantic final preparations kept George occupied, which included with typical aplomb the provision of ten pieces of tapestry to decorate his cabin in the fleet's flagship and a tent for his personal use.

On 17 August, George set off for Southwick for a pre-arranged meeting with the king, but found his coach surrounded by hundreds of sailors demanding to be paid. One leaned into the coach and tried to pull him from his seat. George responded by leaping out, grabbing his assailant, and dragging him back to the Greyhound, where he was locked up in a room to be dealt with later.

News of the emergency reached Southwick, and a courtier saw Charles waiting anxiously at the window of his chamber for 'a whole hour', gazing across the downs for a sight of George's coach. When it was finally spotted, Charles's entourage 'all left the king, lords and all', and rushed 'down into the base court to meet him, as if he was the greatest prince in the world'.

Following his meeting with a relieved king, George returned to the Greyhound Inn to find his attacker had been released for fear of reprisals. George demanded his recapture, which was achieved a few days later. However, when he was seized, fellow mariners surrounded the prisoner's escort, threatening to free him, whereupon George with 'divers of his followers, colonels, captains and others, went on horseback and, having their swords drawn, rode down the street and drove all the mariners before them'. A furious battle ensued during which two of the mariners were killed and many others wounded. The duke finally captured the ringleader and took him to a gibbet by the shore, where he was hanged.

The violent reprisal, while typical of military discipline, poisoned the already aggrieved mood among the troops, and a sense of unease descended on the town.

On 22 August, George wrote despondently to his friend John Pennington that he had begun to feel that 'no happy success' could be expected of the mission 'without an especial blessing from God'. He took to his bed, remaining indisposed for the rest of the day until Charles arrived from Southwick. They met for a while, and when the king took his leave, George, it was noted, embraced Charles 'in a very unusual and passionate manner'.

By the following morning, however, George's mood had improved, and he bounded down to the inn's parlour full of energy. Negotiations had been underway with the French king over the fate of La Rochelle, and according to Soubise the threat of another English attack had led to the siege of the city being lifted. George was so delighted that he danced a jig for joy. He snatched a quick breakfast before calling for his horse so he could break the happy news to the king at Southwick.

As George made to leave, he walked from the parlour into the hallway, where he stopped to talk to one of his colonels. After they had spoken, the colonel bowed, and George reciprocated. As he stood, a man leaned over the colonel's shoulder and thrust a knife into George's left breast 'clean through a rib'. George staggered back, crying 'villain!' He pulled the dagger from his chest and reached for his sword, but a swoon overcame him, causing him to stumble. The press of people around prevented him from falling, until, in the melee, someone realized what had happened, and started to yell for help. The crowd pulled away, and George's limp body dropped to the floor.

The breakfast things were swept off the parlour table, and a group lifted the duke onto it. Others rushed off to apprehend the assassin. Kate, who had stayed in bed, was drawn from her room by the noise. She called for a friend, and came onto the gallery overlooking the parlour. Gazing down, she saw her dying thirty-five-year-old husband spread out on the table beneath her, blood seeping from his mouth.

In the confusion, John Felton had managed to escape into the inn's kitchens. The panicking crowds in the parlour and hall suspected the assassin to have been an agent of King Louis, and began to shout 'Frenchman! Frenchman!' Mistaking their cries for his name, he drew his sword and stepped forward, proclaiming with a heroic flourish that would make his victim proud: 'I am the man!'

Sad Affliction's Darksome Night

One of Charles's grooms came 'boldly' to the king while he was at prayers to break the news of George's assassination. Charles apparently said nothing. He continued with his devotions, and then withdrew to his bedchamber. He did not come out for two days. Across the downs came the sound of peals of bells, and of the 'base multitude' drinking healths to the duke's assassin, their cries of jubilation a bitter rebuke to Charles's loyalty and love.

In London, the Tuscan agent Salvetti reported that 'the news of this fatal blow has spread rapidly over the whole kingdom, and, if I may express myself frankly, the appearances of satisfaction are almost universal'. George's mother, Mary, was said to have taken the news calmly, having had powerful presentiments of the tragedy that was to befall her beloved son.

George's body was conducted back to the capital with due ceremony. He laid in state in Wallingford House for nearly a month, though how many visited to pay their respects goes unrecorded. He was buried at Westminster Abbey on 22 September, under the cover of dark to avoid raucous crowds disturbing the ceremony. Charles had called for a lavish monument to be raised in his memory, but it was considered tactless at a time of economic austerity, and the funds were diverted to paying off some of George's creditors.

John Felton was tortured, tried, and finally executed on 22 November. While the dust began to settle on George's simple gravestone in Westminster Abbey, Felton was hailed a patriotic hero, even a Protestant martyr, who:

> With zeal and justice arm'd, hath in truth won
> The prize of patriot to a British son.

The longer term effect of the duke's death on Charles and his regime was profound. The king withdrew from the political fray, preferring to govern through small committees, and occupying the rest of his time indulging in the passion of his childhood, collecting objets d'art.

The loss of a rival for Charles's affections gradually aroused fresh feelings in Henrietta Maria. A courtier noted that, following George's death, relations between the king and queen grew to 'such a degree of kindness as he would imagine him a wooer again, and her gladder to receive his caresses'. The increase in affection had a corresponding effect on the couple's fertility. After five barren years, a son was born on 29 May 1630, and christened Charles. Six children would follow, Van Dyck capturing the new mood of domestic intimacy in a painting known as the 'great peece', showing Charles with his sons, dogs and wife. The king looks out at the viewer with a tired but contented expression, while his wife glances at him with convincing fondness and the younger Charles rests his hands on his father's knee.

During the period that became known as the Personal Rule, Charles tried to reign without Parliament, but events eventually forced its recall in 1640 and the rancour that had arisen during the 1620s quickly re-established itself: MPs were told to raise taxes, taxes were not forthcoming unless grievances were met, Parliament was dismissed, until, finally, Parliament refused to be dismissed and civil war broke out.

By 1648, Charles had been cornered by parliamentary forces on the Isle of Wight. He was captured and imprisoned there while MPs pondered the charges he should face. To the surprise of the Venetian ambassador, the focus was not on the supposed tyrannies of his Personal Rule, nor his role in provoking civil war. Instead, 'old and almost forgotten charges' were dragged up, principal among them that 'his Majesty hastened the death of his father by poison', or that George had 'attempted it with his consent'. Though this was not the formal basis of his trial and execution in January the following year, it was a reminder of what had put the king and his Parliament at such deadly odds.

In one of the many editions of the *Eikon Basilike*, a memoir attributed to King Charles I and published following his death, he portrayed himself, like Felton, as a martyr:

> And as the unmov'd rock outbraves
> The boisterous winds and raging waves;
> So triumph I, and shine more bright
> In sad affliction's darksome night.

George would receive no such uplifting elegy, at least not in the months following his death. Instead, the man once hailed as St George on Horseback became the subject of relentless satire and scorn. He was described as poisoning the court and kingdom as well as the late king. He had exploited Charles's 'yielding nature', and become heady with the 'favourite's honey' while the 'vital powers' of others was 'by poison wasted'. On and on it went, in the form of diatribes and dialogues between the duke and John Lambe; letters to his mother from Hell; a sometimes witty, often lewd outpouring of pent-up invective:

> Of honour, power, and pleasure, thou mightst be
> To all the world a just Epitome.
> Yet thou, even thou, like other Men art dead,
> And to th'infernal shade thy spirit's fled.

A few years later, after the anger had been allowed to dissipate, a single, sharply observed and beautifully crafted epitaph was published. It painted a more balanced portrait, which, despite its brevity, is more revealing than the atrocity that now hangs in the home of the current Prince of Wales. It was written by James Shirley, a playwright, poet, and contemporary of George's:

> Here lies the best and worst of Fate,
> Two kings' delight, the people's hate,
> The courtiers' star, the kingdom's eye,
> A man to draw an Angel by.
> Fear's despiser, Villiers' glory,
> The Great man's volume, all time's story.

Epilogue

I first encountered the accusation that George Villiers had a hand in King James's death while researching *The Herbalist*, a book about the seventeenth-century apothecary Nicholas Culpeper. Part of that story concerned the king's physician, Dr William Harvey, and I was intrigued by his relaxed attitude to the treatment of his patient in his final hours, particularly when I discovered that, just after James's death, Charles had awarded Harvey both a pension and a general pardon.

Historians of the period have generally adopted Harvey's attitude, dismissing the accusations of the Commons' Committee of Twelve as politically driven. Nevertheless, I decided to send a dossier of evidence to John Henry, Professor of Accident and Emergency Medicine at Imperial College, London. Henry was a world-renowned toxicologist who helped solve several notorious poisonings, including that of the Russian dissident Alexander Litvinenko, murdered using radioactive polonium-210 in 2006. I received no response and thought no more of it.

Six months later, and a month or so after *The Herbalist* was published, the phone rang. 'He was probably poisoned,' Professor Henry announced, with barely any preamble. And he knew the likely toxin. I asked him how sure he was. Not beyond all reasonable doubt, he replied, but certainly on the balance of probabilities.

A curious figure, John Henry was the son of an Irish GP based in London. He followed his father into the medical profession, and while studying at King's College in London, noticed a strange rash on his body. He asked one of his tutors about it, and was assured there was nothing to worry about. He decided to run his own tests, which revealed that he had a rare condition called Henoch-Schönlein purpura. As well as producing a rash, the disease attacks other parts of the body, including the kidneys. In 1968, while on a trip through Italy, he developed a throat infection, and was treated with a powerful antibiotic. Two years later, it was discovered that the treatment had destroyed one of his weakened kidneys. Told he did not have long to live, he was forced to give up medicine as a profession and undergo dialysis twice a week.

A kidney transplant in 1976 allowed Henry to restart his medical career, and his attentions turned to clinical pharmacology. As experience had shown him, the well-known medical adage 'the dosage makes the poison' applies also to the circumstance. A compound that acts as a medicine at one time can be toxic in another. An antibiotic that can save the life of one patient can threaten the life of another.

Henry rose to become a consultant in accident and emergency medicine, and was a founder of the pioneering poisons unit at Guy's Hospital. But the effects of his condition forced his retirement in 2004, the year I contacted him about King James. In April 2007, his transplanted kidney failed, forcing its removal; he died of internal bleeding weeks later.

Direct but affable in manner, Professor Henry was rigorously forensic when it came to his work, celebrated for his flashes of diagnostic brilliance. When a scaffolder was admitted to hospital with a broken leg, Henry recognized from his reddened conjunctivas (the lining of the eyelids) that the cause of his accident was probably related to cannabis use. Similarly, the green tinge of another patient's urine sample revealed that her drink had probably been spiked with a powerful sedative. Henry came to international attention for suggesting the facial lesions suffered by the Ukrainian politician Viktor Yushchenko were the result of consuming food laced with dioxin, and for helping to identify the poison given to Alexander Litvinenko as radioactive polonium-210.

Professor Henry was also eager to find medical explanations for historical events. For example, after I contacted him about King James, he suggested an investigation into the Salem witch trials. He hypothesized that the women accused of demonic possession shared a hereditary disease common in the close-knit communities of East Anglia, from where many of the New England colonists originally came.

Henry was not a conventional rationalist in the mould of a

Sherlock Holmes, however. In 1959 he became a 'numerary celibate member' of Opus Dei, the Catholic order founded in 1928 and made notorious by Dan Brown in *The Da Vinci Code*. He met the movement's founder, St Josemaría Escrivá, in 1972 while he was undergoing dialysis, and attributed the success of the subsequent kidney transplant not just to medical science but to the saint's intercession.

An Irish Catholic living in London in the latter decades of the twentieth century would have found it hard to ignore the reverberations of the religious and political eruptions that shaped the reign of James and Charles Stuart four centuries before. The Troubles still raged in Northern Ireland and London was a regular target for IRA bombs – a legacy of colonial policies shaped by the Stuart regime. Every Bonfire Night, the sight of children with a ragged sack fashioned into a roughly human shape, asking for a 'penny for the Guy', provided a reminder of Guy Fawkes's 'powder plot' to blow up the Houses of Parliament in 1605.

So, was the death of King James just nature taking its course, or a product of the political forces shaping those poisonous times? Was it *opus Dei*, or *opus hominis*?

At one level, it seems more than likely that George Villiers, assisted by his mother, was James's killer if not his murderer. His insistence on interfering with the king's treatment at a vital point in the patient's recovery from a familiar disease seems to have helped the king into his grave, whether intentionally or not.

However, on the basis of the medical evidence, Professor Henry was clear it was probably murder, and he identified aconite as the likely poison, derived from a genus of plant known as wolfsbane or monkshood. Recent medical research conducted in Asia (where derivatives of aconite are used in a variety of treatments) has shown the compound's deadly action and effects. It was also well known in the seventeenth century, herbals such as Culpeper's containing numerous antidotes to treat accidental poisoning.

Aconite certainly seems to explain the mysterious symptoms James suffered in his final hours, and poison was very much a weapon of the age, coursing through the veins of a corrupt body politic. And, thanks to James's timely illness and the duke's intimate access to the royal person, George had both the opportunity and means to use it. But what of motive? Why would he have murdered the man who had made him?

Eglisham's suggestion was that Buckingham wanted to unite the Villiers line with the Hamiltons so that his future grandchildren would be in line to inherit the throne, a theory easy to dismiss as overwrought. However, it does not appear to be the motive that was in the minds of the Committee of Twelve MPs when they were interrogating the doctors and formulating their impeachment charges.

They had a far simpler explanation as to why George had 'hastened' the king's death. He was acting with Charles, the two of them conspiring to clear the way to realizing the more majestic, stately conception of monarchy they had dreamed up during and following their adventure to Madrid – a conception that James had obstructed, and Charles would so catastrophically realize.

Bibliography

Akrigg, G. P. V., *Jacobean Pageant, or The Court of King James I*, Cambridge, MA: Harvard University Press, 1962

Anon., *A Briefe Description of the Notorious Life of Iohn Lambe*, Amsterdam [London]: 1628

—— *Cabala Sive Scrinia Sacra*, 3rd edn, London: 1691

—— *Eikōn basilikē*, London: 1649, Wing, 2nd edn, 1994

—— 'Secret Anecdotes of the French Police', *Monthly Chronicle*, 4 (1839), pp. 534–48

—— *Something Written by Occasion*, London: 1623

—— *A True Relation and Iournall*, London: William Barret, 1623

Bacon, Francis, and James Spedding (ed.), *The Letters and the Life of Francis Bacon*, vol. 6, London: Longman, Green, Longman and Roberts, 1861

Bacon, Francis, and Michael Kiernan (ed.), *The Essayes or Counsels, Civill and Morall*, Oxford: Clarendon Press, 1985

Ball, Thomas, *The Life of the Renowned Doctor Preston*, ed. E. W. Harcourt, Oxford: Parker and Co., 1885

Baker, Philip (ed.), *Proceedings in Parliament 1624: The House of Commons*, British History Online http://www.british-history.ac.uk/no-series/proceedings-1624-parl. 2015

Beasley, A. W., 'The Disability of James VI and I', *Seventeenth Century*, 10 (1995), pp. 151–62

Beaumont, Edward Thomas, *The Beaumonts in History, A.D. 850–1850*, Oxford: 1929

Bellany, Alastair, 'The murder of John Lambe: crowd violence, court scandal and popular politics in early seventeenth-century England', *Past & Present*, 200 (2008), pp. 37–76

—— and Thomas Cogswell, *The Murder of King James I*, New Haven; London: Yale University Press, 2015, Kindle edition

Bergeron, David Moore, *King James and Letters of Homoerotic Desire*, Iowa City: University of Iowa Press, 1999

Bevington, David M., Lars Engle, Katharine Eisaman Maus, and Eric Rasmussen (eds), *English Renaissance Drama*, London: W. W. Norton, 2002

Bidwell, William B., and Maija Jansson, *Proceedings in Parliament 1625*, London: Yale University Press, 1987

—— *Proceedings in Parliament, 1626*, London: Yale University Press, 1992

Birch, Thomas (ed.), *The Court and Times of Charles the First*, 2 vols, London: H. Colburn, 1848

Birch, Thomas, and Robert Folkestone Williams (eds), *The Court and Times of Charles the First*, I, London: H. Colburn, 1848

Bireley, Robert, S.J., *Religion and Politics in the Age of the Counterreformation*, Chapel Hill: UNC Press Books, 2012

Brotton, Jerry, 'Buying the Renaissance: Prince Charles's Art Purchases in Madrid, 1623', in Alexander Samson (ed.), *The Spanish Match: Prince Charles's Journey to Madrid, 1623*, Aldershot: Ashgate Publishing Ltd, 2006, pp. 9–26

Burke, Marcus B., and Peter Cherry, *Collections of Paintings in Madrid, 1601–1755, Parts 1 and 2*, Los Angeles: Getty Publications, 1997

Butler, Martin, 'Jonson's Folio and the Politics of Patronage', *Criticism*, 35.3 (1993), pp. 377–90

Carlton, Charles, *Charles I, the Personal Monarch*, London: Routledge, 1995

Casaubon, Isaac [attrib.], *Corona Regia*, ed. Winfried Schleiner, trans. Tyler Fyotek, Geneva: Droz, 2010

Cecil, William, *Scrinia Ceciliana*, London: Henry Bennet, 1663

Chadwick, Hubert, S.J., 'The Scots College, Douai, 1580–1613', *English Historical Review*, 56 (1941), pp. 571–85

Chamberlain, John, and Norman Egbert McClure, *The Letters of John Chamberlain*, Philadelphia: American Philosophical Society, 1939

Charles, Victoria, *Anthony Van Dyck*, Parkstone International, 2011

Clark, Gregory, 'The Condition of the Working Class in England, 1209–2004', *Journal of Political Economy*, 113 (2005), pp. 1307–40

Coast, David, 'Rumor and "Common Fame": the Impeachment of the Duke of Buckingham and Public Opinion in Early Stuart England', *Journal of British Studies*, 55 (2016), pp. 241–67

Cogswell, Thomas, *The Blessed Revolution*, Cambridge: Cambridge University Press, 2005

Cokayne, George Edward, *The Complete Peerage of England, Scotland, Ireland, Great Britain, and the United Kingdom, Extant, Extinct, or Dormant*, vol. 6, London: 1895

Cornwallis, Jane, *The Private Correspondence of Jane Lady Cornwallis, 1613–1644*, London: S. and J. Bentley, Wilson and Fley, 1842

Cross, Robert, 'Pretense and Perception in the Spanish Match, or History in a Fake Beard', *Journal of Interdisciplinary History*, 37 (2007), pp. 563–83

Cuddy, Neil, 'The Revival of the Entourage: the Bedchamber of James I, 1603–1625', in David Starkey, *The English Court from the Wars of the Roses to the Civil War*, London: Longman, 1987, pp. 173–91

Culpeper, Nicholas, *Pharmacopoeia Londinensis*, London: 1653

Cuming, Geoffrey J., 'The Life and Works of Anthony Cade, B.D., Vicar of Billesdon, 1599–1639', *Transactions of the Leicestershire Archaeological and Historical Society*, 45 (1970), pp. 39–56

D'Ewes, Simonds, *The Autobiography and Correspondence of Sir Simonds D'Ewes, Bart., during the Reigns of James I and Charles I*, ed. James Orchard Halliwell, London: 1845

—— *The Diary of Sir Simonds D'Ewes (1622–1624)*, ed. Elisabeth Bourcier, Ann Arbor, MI: University of Michigan, 1974

Earle, John, *Micro-Cosmographie*, London: 1628

Eglisham, George, *Prodromus Vindictæ in Ducem Buckinghamiæ, Pro Virulenta Cæde Potentissimi Magnæ Britanniæ Regis Jacobi*, 1626

—— *The Forerunner of Reuenge, Vpon the Duke of Buckingham, for the Poysoning of . . . King Iames . . . and the Lord Marquis of Hamilton, and Others of the Nobilitie*, Franckfort: 1626

Elliott, J. H., *Imperial Spain 1469–1716*, London: Penguin, 2002

Ellis, Henry (ed.), *Original Letters, Illustrative of English History*, second series, London: Harding, Triphook and Lepard, 1825

Forster, John, *Sir John Eliot*, 2 vols, London: Chapman and Hall, 1872

Gardiner, Samuel Rawson, 'Facts and Fictions About the Duke of Buckingham's Mother', *Notes and Queries*, 4th series, VII, 179 (1871), pp. 469–71

—— 'Notes by Sir James Bagg on the Parliament of 1626', *Notes and Queries*, 4th series, X (1872), pp. 325–6

—— *History of England*, vol. 3, London: 1907

Goldstein, Leba M., 'The Life and Death of John Lambe', *Guildhall Studies in London History*, 4 (1979), pp. 19–32

Goodman, Godfrey, *The Court of King James the First*, ed. J. S. Brewer, London: Bentley, 1839

H., W. [Haydon, William], *The True Picture and Relation of Prince Henry*, Leiden: William Christian, 1634

Hacket, John, *Scrinia Reserata*, London: 1693

Halliwell, James Orchard, *Letters of the Kings of England*, vol. 2, London: Henry Colburn, 1848

Harington, H., *Nugæ Antiquæ*, London: 1804

Healy, Simon, 'Oh, What a Lovely War? War, Taxation, and Public Opinion in England, 1624–29', *Canadian Journal of History*, 38 (2003), pp. 439–66

Held, Julius S., 'Rubens's Sketch of Buckingham Rediscovered', *The Burlington Magazine*, 118.881 (1976), pp. 547–51

Heylyn, Peter, *Aulicus Coquinariæ*, London: 1650

Hirst, Derek, *The Representative of the People?* Cambridge: Cambridge University Press, 2005

Hoefer, Ferdinand (ed.), *Nouvelle Biographie Générale*, Paris: Fermin Didot, 1862

Holland, Hugh, *Cypres Garland*, London: Simon Waterson, 1625

Holles, John, *Letters of John Holles 1587–1637*, ed. P. R. Seldon, Nottingham: Thornton Society, 1983

Holmes, Frederick F., *The Sickly Stuarts*, Stroud: Sutton Publishing Limited, 2003

Holstun, James, '"God Bless Thee, Little David!" John Felton and his Allies', *ELH*, 59.3 (1992), pp. 513–52

Hoskins, W. G., 'The Deserted Villages of Leicestershire', *Transactions of the Leicestershire Archaeological and Historical Society*, 22.4 (1941), pp. 242–64

Howard-Hill, T. H., 'Political Interpretations of Middleton's "A Game at Chess" (1624)', *The Yearbook of English Studies*, 21 (1991), pp. 274–85

Howell, James, *Epistolæ Ho-Elinæ*, 9th edn, London: 1726

Hulme, Harold, *The Life of Sir John Eliot*, London: George Allen & Unwin, 1957

Jaffé, Michael, 'Van Dyck's "Venus and Adonis"', *Burlington Magazine*, 132.1051 (1990), pp. 696–703

James, VI of Scotland and I of England, *Letters of King James VI and I*, ed. G. P. V. Akrigg, London: University of California Press, 1984

Jardine, Lisa, and Alan Stewart, *Hostage to Fortune: the Troubled Life of Francis Bacon*, London: Phoenix Giant, 1999

Juhala, A. L., 'The Household and Court of King James VI of Scotland, 1567–1603', (doctoral thesis), University of Edinburgh, 2000

Keevil, J. J., 'The Illness of Charles, Duke of Albany (Charles I), From

1600 to 1612', *Journal of the History of Medicine and Allied Sciences*, 9 (1954), pp. 407–19

Keynes, G., *The Life of William Harvey*, Oxford: Clarendon Press, 1966

Kindleberger, Charles P., 'The Economic Crisis of 1619 to 1623', *Journal of Economic History*, 51 (1991), pp. 149–75

La Porte, de, P., *Mémoires: Contenant Plusieurs Particularités Des Regnes De Louis XIII et Louis XIV*, Geneva: 1755

Laud, William, *The History of the Troubles and Tryal of William Laud*, ed. Henry Wharton, London: 1695

Leveneur, Tanneguy, *Mémoires Inédits Du Comte Leveneur De Tillières*, ed. Célestin Hippeau, Paris: 1863

Lockyer, Roger, *Buckingham, The Life and Political Career of George Villiers, First Duke of Buckingham, 1592–1628*, London: Routledge, 2014

Long, W. H., *The Oglander Memoirs*, London: Reeves and Turner, 1888

Luciani, Vincent, 'Bacon and Machiavelli', *Italica*, 24.1 (1947), pp. 26–40

MacDonald, Michael, *Mystical Bedlam*, Cambridge: Cambridge University Press, 1981

Martin, Gregory, 'Rubens and Buckingham's "Fayrie Ile"', *Burlington Magazine*, 108.765 (1966), pp. 613–18

Memegalos, Florene S., *George Goring (1608–1657)*, Aldershot: Ashgate Publishing, 2013

Michaud, Joseph-François, and Jean-Joseph-François Poujoulat, *Nouvelle Collection des Mémoires Pour Servir À L'histoire De France*', vol. 5, Paris: 1838 http://gallica.bnf.fr/ark:/12148/bpt6k30902r

Middleton, Thomas, *A Game at Chess as it was acted nine days together at the Globe . . .* London: 1625

Minor, Margaret Sinclair, 'Female Peers during the Reign of James I' (doctoral thesis), Kent State University, 1986

Moote, A. Lloyd, *Louis XIII, the Just*, Berkeley: University of California Press, 1989

Nicholas, Edward, *Proceedings and Debates of the House of Commons, in 1620 and 1621*, London: Clarendon Press, 1766

Nichols, John, *The History and Antiquities of the County of Leicester*, vol. 2, Wakefield: S. R. Publishers, in association with Leicestershire County Council, 1971

—— *The Processes of King James the First*, London: Society of Antiquaries, 1828

Oldys, William, and Thomas Park, *The Harleian Miscellany*. London: 1808

Osborne, F., and J. Pitcher and L. Potter (eds), *The True Tragicomedy Formerly Acted at Court: A Play*, New York: Garland, 1983

Paisey, David, 'Supper with James I in a Paris Print for a Spanish Grandee', *Print Quarterly*, 22.1 (2005), pp. 45–54

Parker, L. A., 'The Depopulation Returns for Leicestershire in 1607', *Transactions of the Leicestershire Archaeological and Historical Society*, 23.2 (1947), pp. 231–89

Payne, Helen Margaret, 'Aristocratic Women and the Jacobean Court, 1603–1625' (doctoral thesis), Royal Holloway, University of London, 2001

Peters, T. et al., 'The Nature of King James VI/I's Medical Conditions: New Approaches to the Diagnosis', *History of Psychiatry*, 23.3 (2012), pp. 277–90

Petitot, Claude-Bernard, *Collection des Mémoires Relatifs à l'histoire de France*, vol. 35, Paris: 1824, http://gallica.bnf.fr/ark:/12148/bpt6k36311h

Peuchet, Jacques, *Mémoires Tirés des Archives de la Police de Paris*, vol. 1, Paris: 1838, http://gallica.bnf.fr/ark:/12148/bpt6k64771m/f51.image

Plowden, Alison, *Henrietta Maria: Charles I's Indomitable Queen*, Stroud: Sutton Publishing, 2001

Porter, Endymion, *Life and Letters of Mr Endymion Porter*, ed. Dorothea Townshend, London: T. Fisher Unwin, 1897

Pursell, Brennan C., 'James I, Gondomar and the Dissolution of the Parliament of 1621', *History*, 85.279 (2000), pp. 428–45

Quarmby, Kevin A., *The Disguised Ruler in Shakespeare and his Contemporaries*, London: Routledge, 2016

Ransome, David R., 'The Parliamentary Papers of Nicholas Ferrar, 1624', *Camden Fifth Series*, 7 (1996), pp. 3–104

Redworth, Glyn, 'Of Pimps and Princes: Three Unpublished Letters from James I and the Prince of Wales Relating to the Spanish Match', *Historical Journal*, 37 (1994), pp. 401–09

—— *The Prince and the Infanta: the Cultural Politics of the Spanish Match*, New Haven and London: Yale University Press, 2003

Ruigh, Robert E., *The Parliament of 1624*, London: Harvard University Press, 1971

Russell, Conrad, 'The Foreign Policy Debate in the House of Commons in 1621', *Historical Journal*, 20 (1977), pp. 289–309

Salvetti, Amerigo, and Henry Duncan Skrine, *The Manuscripts of Henry Duncan Skrine*, London: HMSO, 1887

Sanderson, William, *A Compleat History of the Lives and Reigns of Mary Queen of Scotland, and of her Son and Successor, James the Sixth*, London: 1656

Schreiber, Roy E., *The First Carlisle*, Philadelphia: American Philosophical Society, 1984

Scott, Walter, *Secret History of the Court of James the First*, Edinburgh: J. Ballantyne, 1811

Sharpe, Kevin, *The Personal Rule of Charles I*, New Haven: Yale University Press, 1996

Shirley, James, *The Dramatic Words and Poems of John Shirley*, ed. William Gifford and Alexander Dyce, 6 vols, London: John Murray, 1833

Smith, Logan Pearsall, *The Life and Letters of Sir Henry Wotton*, Oxford: Clarendon Press, 1907

Somerset, Anne, *Unnatural Murder: Poison at the Court of James I*, London: Weidenfeld & Nicolson, 1997

Stewart, Alan, *The Cradle King*, London: Chatto & Windus, 2003

Strong, Roy, *Henry, Prince of Wales and England's Lost Renaissance*, London: Pimlico, 2000

Trevor-Roper, Hugh Redwald, *Europe's Physician*, London: Yale University Press, 2006

Van Zanden, J. L., Eltjo Buringh, and Maarten Bosker, 'The Rise and Decline of European Parliaments, 1188–1789', *Economic History Review*, 65 (2012), pp. 835–61

Vautor, Thomas, *The First Set*, London: 1619

Verweij, S., 'Booke, Go Thy Wayes', *Huntington Library Quarterly*, 77 (2014), pp. 111–31

Walsham, Alexandra, '"The fatall vesper": providentialism and anti-popery in late Jacobean London', *Past & Present*, 144 (1994), pp. 36–87

Weldon, Anthony, *The Court and Character of King James*, London: 1650

Whiteway, William, and Thomas D. Murphy, 'The Diary of William Whiteway of Dorchester', (doctoral thesis), Yale University, 1939

Wilson, Arthur, *The History of Great Britain, Being the Life and Reign of King James the First*, London: 1653

Wotton, Henry, *A Short View of the Life and Death of George Villiers*, London: 1642

—— *Reliquiae Wottonianae*, 3rd edn, London: 1672

Wright, Pam, 'A Change in Direction', in David Starkey et al. (eds), *The English Court from the Wars of the Roses to the Civil War*, London: Longman, 1987, pp. 147–72

Notes

Prologue

3 **The sexual charisma** . . . Shirley, 1833, vol. 6, p. 449; Cogswell, 2005, p. 84.

Act I: Christ Had His John and I Have My George

The King's Way

7 **In the early seventeenth century** . . . Earle, 1628, sig. C4.

7 **These were the prospects facing George Villiers.** TNA C 3/293/104, 'Vyllyeres v Vyllyeres' (undated, mutilated); TNA C 2/ Eliz/U3/32, 'Villiers v Villiers', 1599.

8 **Mary had no land or wealth of her own to fall back on.** Beaumont, 1929.

8 **This was a practice his family** . . . Parker, 1947, pp. 239–40; Nichols, 1795, vol. 2, p. 195.

9 **George's roguish uncle** . . . Hoskins, 1941, p. 261.

9 **Mary was evidently impressed with the glamorous visitor.**
Gardiner, 1871; Lockyer, 2014, p. 8.

9 **John had what was politely termed 'giddiness of the head'**
. . . Wilson, 1653, p. 147; Lockyer, 2014, p. 116. George's illness is
implied in Mary's Lenten letter to him: Bodleian, Tanner MS
74/194, quoted in Minor, 1986, p. 111.

9 **Like his older brother** . . . Lockyer, 2014, p. 8.

10 **Though she remained** . . . Wotton, 1672, p. 209; Lockyer, 2014,
p. 10.

10 **This showed that George senior owed over £2,500** . . .
Bodleian MSS.Eng.hist./c.477/f112. For historical estimates of
craftsmen's income, see Clark, 2005, table A2.

10 **For example, she decided to hire a personal musician** . . .
See Vautor, 1619.

11 **To prepare George** . . . Cuming, 1970.

The Malcontent

11 **The King's Men were booked** . . . http://www.bbc.co.uk/
programmes/articles/4TzvnDHl4btXXxxnZwG5bSM/shakespeare-
s-company-visit-leicester [accessed 1 Dec 2016]. A payment of 40
shillings is recorded in the accounts of the city's chamberlain. The
entry is subsequently crossed out, so perhaps the fee was paid by
someone else (a local benefactor), or a dispute led to Leicester's
chamberlain refusing to pay, or the production was cancelled.

12 **The change of regime** . . . See Wright, 1987.

12 **In 1584 a narrative poem** . . . Stewart, 2003, p. 51 ff. For circulation
of the poem in England as well as Scotland, see Verweij, 2014.

13 **James's attitude towards Esmé** . . . 'Border Papers, Volume 1:
May 1582', in *Calendar of Border Papers*: Vol. 1, 1560–95, ed. Joseph
Bain (London, 1894), pp. 81–4.

13 **Christopher Marlowe made a sly allusion to Esmé** . . .
Bevington et al., 2002, p. 351 ff.

13 **'swum from France' to 'smile'** . . . Christopher Marlowe, *Edward
II*, Act I, sc. i, 39.

13 **'minions' and 'ganymedes'** . . . Christopher Marlowe, *Edward II*,
Act I, sc. iv, 390–3, 181.

13 **Since James's arrival in England** . . . Cuddy, 1987.

13 **The new version of *The Malcontent*** . . . For a discussion on the
political meanings of *The Malcontent* as they might have been
perceived at the time, see Quarmby, 2016, chapter 2.

13 **The play began with a warning** . . . John Marston, *The Malcontent* [Prologue]; Act I, sc. ii, 5–10; 'The Induction', 95; Act III, sc. i, 48, 78; Act I, sc. v, 20–3.

All We Here Sit in Darkness

15 **William Feilding, the son of a Warwickshire gentleman** . . . *DNB*, Feilding, William, first Earl of Denbigh (*c*.1587–1643); Warwickshire County Records Office, CR 2017/F29.

15 **Sir William Reynor was in his eighties** . . . Bodleian MS.Eng. hist./c.477/f112; Reynor's name is also spelled Reyner, Raynor and Rayner.

15 **Though some suspected** . . . Wotton, 1672, pp. 208–9.

16 **Unfortunately for her** . . . TNA STAC 8/12/8.

16 **Sir William was in no condition** . . . TNA PROB 11/108/376.

16 **She had powerful connections.** http://www. historyofparliamentonline.org/volume/1604–1629/member/holcroft-sir-thomas-1557–1620 [accessed 1 Dec 2016].

16 **Drawing on these links** . . . The details of the case are to be found in the proceedings of the Court of Chancery (TNA C 2/JasI/R1/43) and the Star Chamber (TNA STAC 8/12/8). A full and colourful account of the episode appears in an undated newsletter of the Keyworth and District Local History Society, drawing on a newspaper cutting in the society's archives dated 12 Sep 1925, entitled: 'Old Notts. Marriage Romances', by R. W. Marston of High Barnet. http://www.keyworth-history.org.uk/about/newsletter/wanton-wench.htm [accessed 1 Dec 2016].

17 **Sir Thomas Compton was quite unlike** . . . Wilson, 1653, pp. 147–8.

17 **Mary, a shrewd judge of men** . . . Edward Hasted, 'Parishes: Erith', in *The History and Topographical Survey of the County of Kent: Volume 2* (Canterbury, 1797), pp. 227–63; Heylyn, 1650, p. 166; Cokayne, 1895, p. 71.

18 **Meanwhile, Mary's efforts** . . . Wotton, 1672, p. 209.

18 **While his conversative qualities began to flourish** . . . Lockyer, 2014, p. 10.

18 **She had been consulting** . . . See for example: Bodleian MS Ashmole 239, f16ov.

19 **George would remain at Goadby** . . . Wotton, 1672, p. 209; Lockyer, 2014, p. 10; Holles, 1983, vol. 2, p. 297.

Debateable Lands

22 **Young hopefuls would mill around** . . . Akrigg, 1962, p. 397.

22 **Mild interest was aroused** . . . Wilson, 1653, p. 79.

23 **Ann's older sister, Elizabeth,** . . . Bodleian MS.Eng.hist./c.480/ fols.105–47.

23 **Whatever the obstacles, Ann and George** . . . Weldon, 1650, p. 28.

23 **The argument over the match** . . . Sir John Graham's name is variously referred to as Grimes, Grahme, or Greames.

23 **Hailing from the gloriously named 'debateable lands'** . . . Samuel Lewis, 'Faifley – Fifeshire', in *A Topographical Dictionary of Scotland* (London, 1846), pp. 411–28; Wotton, 1672, p. 209; Cuddy, 1987.

Apethorpe

24 **King James was a restless spirit.** Stewart, 2003, p. 75.

25 **These progresses came like a plague** . . . Nichols, 1828, vol. 3, p. 98.

25 **One of James's favourite places** . . . *DNB*, Sir Anthony Mildmay (*c*.1549–1617), in Sir Walter Mildmay (1520/21–1589).

25 **Apethorpe was one of those distinctively English** . . . Nichols, 1828, vol. 3, pp. 97–8.

26 **The Danish king was infamous** . . . Harington, 1804, p. 353.

27 **It was 4 August** . . . 'Apethorpe', in *An Inventory of the Historical Monuments in the County of Northamptonshire*, vol. 6, London: HMSO, 1984, pp. 1–16.

27 **Furthermore, the demands on cupbearers were daunting.** Cuddy, 1987, p. 194.

27 **First impressions of the royal presence** . . . Weldon, 1650, p. 55; Stewart, 2003, p. 172.

28 **The impetuous act** . . . Sanderson, 1656, p. 466; Heylyn, 1650, p. 158.

28 **George now became the focus of fierce curiosity** . . . Bergeron, 1999, p. 102.

29 **Thomas Erskine** . . . Juhala, 2000, p. 119; Stewart, 2003, pp. 265–6.

30 **Revealing his weakness and dependence** . . . Bergeron, 1999, pp. 80–4.

30 **George was spotted at a horse race at Newmarket.** Nichols, 1828, vol. 3, p. 38; D'Ewes, 1845, p. 86.

Baynard's Castle

31 **The public mood** . . . *DNB*, Henry Frederick, Prince of Wales (1594–1612).

32 **'the beauty of both sexes'** . . . This is the description given for the character of the Earl of Somerset, identifiable as Carr, in Francis Osborne's play *The True Tragicomedy Formerly Acted at Court*, written in the 1650s, though not published until 1983. See Osborne et al., 1983.

32 **'Wondrously in a little time'** . . . Stewart, 2003, p. 257 ff; Thomas Wyatt, 'Mine own John Poyntz', *c.*1536.

33 **As his wealth and status had risen** . . . Harington, 1804, p. 396.

34 **The ringleaders were William Herbert** . . . *DNB*, Herbert, William, third Earl of Pembroke (1580–1630).

34 **The strategy this secret cabal** . . . John Rushworth, 'Historical Collections: 1627 (part 1 of 2)', in *Historical Collections of Private Passages of State*: Volume 1, 1618–29 (London, 1721), p. 461.

34 **With the king distracted** . . . Weldon, 1650, p. 84; Nichols, 1828, vol. 3, pp. 255–6.

35 **Together, Goring and his fellow master fools** . . . Scott, 1811, pp. 398–403.

35 **For Twelfth Night** . . . Chamberlain and McClure, 1939, vol. 1, p. 561; Lockyer, 2014, pp. 17–18.

35 **'Ben's plays are works** . . . Butler, 1993, p. 377.

35 **The masque opened in an alchemical workshop** . . . Nichols, 1828, vol. 3, pp. 30–7.

36 **And George, everyone could agree** . . . Nichols, 1828, vol. 3, p. 256; Lockyer, 2014, pp. 236, 33.

37 **Dance demonstrated George's charms** . . . Wotton, 1672, p. 209.

37 **James was smitten.** Wilson, 1653, p. 40.

St George's Day

37 **In the early months of 1615** . . . Leveneur, 1863, p. 14; Lockyer, 2014, p. 16.

37 **With Carr placated** . . . *DNB*, Anne [Anna, Anne of Denmark], Queen of England, Scotland, and Ireland (1574–1619).

38 **Fortunately, Anne did not care** . . . John Rushworth, 'Historical Collections: 1627 (part 1 of 2)', in *Historical Collections of Private Passages*

of State: Volume 1, 1618–29 (London, 1721), pp. 422–89. *British History Online* http://www.british-history.ac.uk/rushworth-papers/vol1/pp422–89 [accessed 9 Nov 2016].

38 **Heavy snow fell** . . . Nichols, vol. 3, p. 38.

39 **'Notwithstanding this,'** . . . John Rushworth, 'Historical Collections: 1627 (part 1 of 2)', in *Historical Collections of Private Passages of State*, vol. 1, 1618–29 (London, 1721), pp. 422–89. British History Online http://www.british-history.ac.uk/rushworth-papers/vol1/pp422–89 [accessed 9 Nov 2016]. Abbot's use of the word 'instant' has been changed to 'insistent'.

40 **Then the queen rallied** . . . *CSPV*, 19 Dec 1618 [New Style], item 658; Payne, 2001, p. 66.

40 **Anne then rose from her bed** . . . Goodman, 1839, v. I, p. 224. Both James and Charles suffered from apparently congenital ailments that have been the subject of much medical speculation but which are hard to identify, given the discretion courtiers needed to use when describing the health of a royal. See Holmes, 2003, Beasley, 1995, and Peters et al., 2012.

41 **After the ceremony was over** . . . John Rushworth, 'Historical Collections: 1627 (part 1 of 2)', in *Historical Collections of Private Passages of State*: Volume 1, 1618–29 (London, 1721), pp. 422–89. British History Online http://www.british-history.ac.uk/rushworth-papers/vol1/pp.422–89 [accessed 23 Sep 2016].

The Matter of the Garter

42 **John Holles, an experienced observer of courtly affairs** . . . Holles, 1983, vol. 1, p. 66; Weldon, 1650, p. 28.

42 **As the day of the investiture approached** . . . Nichols, 1828, vol. 3, p. 91; Chamberlain and McClure, 1939, vol. 1, p. 597.

43 **For more than a year** . . . Birch, 1848, vol. 1, p. 337.

44 **In July 1615** . . . Weldon, 1650, p. 29.

44 **Around this time** . . . Nichols, 1828, vol. 3, p. 100.

45 **May suggested to George** . . . Weldon, 1650, p. 30.

46 **The strange performance** . . . Stewart, 2003, p. 269.

46 **Some time in August** . . . Weldon, 1650, p. 30. Only Weldon mentions Gotly, its modern location is unknown, however. Some (e.g. Lockyer) assume that Weldon was referring to Goadby Marwood, but that was hundreds of miles away from the course of James's progress at this time. Nichols shows that Gotly was likely to have been a stop-off between Purbeck and Lulworth, both West Country

locations. Lockyer, 2014, p. 22; Nichols, 1828, vol. 3, pp. 97–8.

47 **Many years later . . .** Bergeron, 1999, p. 179.

47 **Carr was now estranged . . .** Weldon, 1650, p. 29.

48 **Reflecting some time later . . .** Bergeron, 1999, p. 180; Stewart, 2003, p. 176.

49 **Some could not keep up, some fell; Nicholas Brett . . .** Nichols, 1828, vol. 3, p. 100.

50 **As these ancient bonding rituals . . .** Somerset, 1997, pp. 287–8; *DNB*, Sir Ralph Winwood (1562/63–1617); http://www.historyofparliamentonline.org/volume/1604–1629/member/winwood-sir-ralph-1563-1617 [accessed 1 Dec 2016].

50 **Two contemporary accounts . . .** Bergeron, 1999, p. 96.

51 **Then suddenly George's rise faltered.** Lockyer, 2014, p. 27.

51 **Then George recovered and rallied.** Nichols, 1828, vol. 3, p. 138.

Neither a God nor an Angel

52 **On 2 May 1616 . . .** Jardine and Stewart, 1999, p. 464; *DNB*, Francis Bacon, Viscount St Alban (1561–1626).

52 **Bacon's initial contact . . .** Jardine and Stewart, 1999, pp. 373–4.

53 **George intuitively grasped . . .** Bergeron, 1999, pp. 106–7.

54 **Bacon, whose snobbery . . .** Jardine and Stewart, 1999, p. 388.

54 **The title was conferred at Woodstock . . .** Lockyer, 2014, p. 27.

55 **The following month . . .** Bergeron, 1999, p. 104.

Keeper of the Seal

56 **In an address . . .** Bergeron, 1999, p. 113.

56 **He became particularly attached . . .** Minor, 1986, p. 93; Howell, 1726, p. 116; TNA SP 14/89 f50.

56 **But James enjoyed her company.** Nichols, 1828, vol. 3, p. 175; Chamberlain and McClure, 1939, vol. 2, p. 141.

57 **James and George left London . . .** Stewart, 2003, p. 284 ff.

58 **Memories of the kidnapping . . .** Nichols, 1828, vol. 3, p. 327.

58 **From London came Bacon's . . .** Jardine and Stewart, 1999, p. 398.

59 **Some were not so approving.** Weldon, 1650, p. 41.

60 **Sir Francis wrote to George . . .** Jardine and Stewart, 1999, pp. 401–5.

62 **This devastatingly calm** . . . Luciani, 1947, p. 30.

62 **Bacon moved quickly to redeem himself.** Jardine and Stewart, 1999, p. 410.

62 **By this point** . . . Bacon and Spedding, 1861, p. 248.

63 **A few days later** . . . Jardine and Stewart, 1999, p. 412.

64 **Weldon noted with admiration** . . . Weldon, 1650, pp. 41–2.

64 **Sir Edward Coke was given back** . . . Lockyer, 2014, p. 44; Jardine and Stewart, 1999, p. 421.

Made or Marred

64 **By the late 1610s** . . . MacDonald, 1981, pp. 21, 256; Lockyer, 2014, p. 57.

65 **The greatest obstacle** . . . TNA SP 14/113 f78v; Chamberlain and McClure, 1939, vol. 2, pp. 296–7; Goodman, 1839, pp. 189–92.

66 **The reason for the king's enthusiasm** . . . Jaffé, 1990.

67 **George used the windfall** . . . Lockyer, 2014, pp. 62–4.

67 **Following the nuptials** . . . Bergeron, 1999, p. 149.

67 **For James, the title of 'dear dad'** . . . Bergeron, 1999, p. 150; Lockyer, 2014, p. 120.

67 **And so the rise** . . . Ball, 1885, p. 153.

Wickedest Things

68 **In the late 1610s** . . . Casaubon, 2010, pp. 16, 35, 77, 81, 83.

69 **Simonds D'Ewes recorded his shock** . . . D'Ewes, 1974, pp. 92–3; Stewart, 2003, pp. 278–9.

69 **Above in the skies** . . . Chamberlain and McClure, 1939, vol. 2, p. 52.

69 **Heaven bless King James our joy** . . . ESL, L10.

70 **'You are a new-risen star** . . . Cecil, 1663, p. 44.

70 **For example, he had arranged for a distant relation** . . . http://www.historyofparliamentonline.org/volume/1604-1629/member/mompesson-giles-1584-1651; http://www.historyof parliamentonline.org/volume/1604-1629/member/villiers-sir-edward-1585-1626 [accessed 26 Jan 2017].

71 **Hail, happy genius** . . . Jardine and Stewart, 1999, p. 442.

Poor George Villiers

71 **That winter, while Bacon . . .** Chamberlain and McClure, 1939, vol. 2, p. 337; Kindleberger, 1991.

72 **A combination of factors . . .** Van Zanden et al., 2012; Hirst, 2005, pp. 104–5, http://www.historyofparliamentonline.org/volume/1604–1629/survey/i-nature-functions-and-remit-house-commons [accessed 1 Dec 2016].

73 **If any institution . . .** For the size of the Parliament, see: http://www.historyofparliamentonline.org/volume/1604-1629/survey/ii-membership [accessed 1 Dec 2016]; Stewart, 2003, p. 208.

73 **Bacon was James's representative . . .** Oldys and Park, 1808, p. 12.

74 **Complaining bitterly . . .** Chamberlain and McClure, 1939, vol. 2, p. 351.

75 **The performance might be thought . . .** Hacket, 1693, p. 49.

76 **Foreign observers . . .** Lockyer, 2014, pp. 98–9.

76 **'Swim with the tide' . . .** Hacket, 1693, p. 50; 'House of Commons Journal Volume 1: 13 March 1621', in *Journal of the House of Commons*: Volume 1, 1547–1629 (London, 1802), pp. 551–3.

76 **Charges of corruption . . .** British History Online http://www.british-history.ac.uk/commons-jrnl/vol1/pp551–53 [accessed 27 Aug 2016]; 'House of Commons Journal Volume 1: 15 March 1621', in *Journal of the House of Commons*: Volume 1, 1547–1629 (London, 1802), pp. 554–6. British History Online http://www.british-history.ac.uk/commons-jrnl/vol1/pp554–6 [accessed 14 Jun 2016].

76 **Bacon wrote to George . . .** Jardine and Stewart, 1999, pp. 451, 464–5.

77 **Within this sty a hog doth lie . . .** ESL, Mii3.

Act II: Two Venturous Knights

The Favourite and the Fountain

81 **In 1611, a factory in Florence . . .** Strong, 2000, pp. 149–50.

82 **Charles could not have been more different . . .** Strong, 2000, p. 6; Keevil, 1954, p. 415.

82 **Then Prince Henry had fallen ill.** H [Haydon], 1634, p. 33 ff; Strong, 2000, p. 166.

83 **But where James had harboured jealousies . . .** Carlton, 1995, pp. 10, 20.

84 **Once again, Charles found himself eclipsed.** James, VI of Scotland and I of England, 1984, p. 367; Chamberlain and McClure, 1939, vol. 2, p. 29.

84 **The second incident . . .** *CSPD*, 14 Mar 1616, item 14; *CSPD*, 31 May 1616, item 40; Carlton, 1995, p. 24.

A Masque on Twelfth Night

85 **In 1616, Francis Bacon . . .** Cecil, 1663, p. 66.

85 **A turning point . . .** TNA SP 14/113 f78v.

85 **Since the ambassador's arrival in England in 1613 . . .** Redworth, 2003, p. 28.

86 **In response to the king's growing affection . . .** Lockyer, 2014, p. 71; Redworth, 2003, pp. 40–1. Lockyer says that George never received a pension; the *DNB* entry on Gondomar suggests otherwise.

87 **Now that Gondomar's embassy . . .** Nichols, 1828, vol. 3, p. 500. This seems to have been misdated by Nichols, who suggests the masque was performed a year later.

87 **It began a little inauspiciously . . .** *CSPV*, 24 Jan 1618 [NS], item 188.

88 **Up until this stage . . .** Chamberlain and McClure, 1939, vol. 2, p. 128.

89 **Charles wrote in desperation . . .** Nichols, 1828, vol. 3, pp. 484–5.

90 **George did so by staging . . .** Birch, 1848, vol. 2, p. 78.

The Spanish Match

91 **Then, in 1617, Anne had aroused shock . . .** *CSPV*, 9 Oct 1615 [NS], item 54; *CSPV*, 8 Sep 1617 [NS], item 14.

91 **One explanation for the volte-face . . .** Payne, 2001, pp. 72, 237.

91 **The queen's opposition to the Spanish match . . .** *CSPV*, 19 Dec 1618 [NS], item 658.

92 **Convinced that he too was about to follow . . .** Stewart, 2003, p. 301.

94 **Even the usually shy . . .** *CSPD*, 15 May 1619, item 34; Stewart, 2003, pp. 303, 298.

94 **James's only consolation** . . . *DNB*, Diego Sarmiento de Acuña, Count of Gondomar in the Spanish nobility (1567–1626).

95 **Their private talks began** . . . Gardiner, 1907, vol. 3, p. 338.

95 **Others did not find** . . . *CSPV*, 19 Mar 1620 [NS], item 295.

96 **Elizabeth now began to write** . . . Lockyer, 2014, p. 83.

96 **The reaction in London** . . . *CSPV*, 11 Dec 1620 [NS], item 652; Stewart, 2003, p. 308.

98 **Parliament was recalled in late November** . . . http://www.historyofparliamentonline.org/volume/1604–1629/survey/parliament-1621 [accessed 1 Dec 2016].

99 **James acted promptly.** Nicholas, 1766, vol. 2, p. 252.

99 **Goring had been** . . . http://www.historyofparliamentonline.org/volume/1604-1629/member/goring-sir-george-1585-1663 [accessed 2 Dec 2016].

99 **After lodging the motion** . . . Russell, 1977, p. 309.

99 **Whatever qualms** . . . Halliwell, 1848, p. 157.

100 **This outcome has been taken** . . . Nicholas, 1766, vol. 2, p. 220; Lockyer, 2014, p. 109. See also Robert Bireley, 2012, pp. 6–7 for details on the relationship between the Spanish and German empires at this time.

101 **Just before he was due to depart** . . . Pursell, 2000, p. 445.

101 **As he was about to leave** . . . Redworth, 2003, p. 154, n. 2.

101 **The prince had been sending letters** . . . Lockyer, 2014, p. 134; Carlton, 1995, p. 36.

102 **[note] According to Glyn Redworth** . . . Redworth, 1994, p. 409; Redworth, 2003, pp. 58–9.

Periwigs

103 **After Charles had first broached** . . . D'Ewes, 1974, p. 118; Redworth, 2003, p. 59.

104 **Breaking diplomatic protocol** . . . Redworth, 2003, p. 172.

104 **Encouraged by these diplomatic signals** . . . Stewart, 2003, p. 111.

105 **In the event, it was James** . . . Porter, 1897, p. 41.

105 **Cottington's intervention** . . . Bergeron, 1999, pp .150–1.

109 **The sight of Anne** . . . Lockyer, 2014, p. 139.

110 **As she pirouetted** . . . Moote, 1989, p. 147.

111 **Their coats once more attracted** . . . Wotton, 1672, pp. 214–17.

111 **Having 'saucily' opened** . . . Bergeron, 1999, p. 185.

The House of the Seven Chimneys

112 **At 5 p.m., on 7 March 1623** . . . Howell, 1726, p. 132; Redworth, 2003, p. 82.

112 **Nevertheless, here they were** . . . Chamberlain and McClure, 1939, vol. 2, p. 488; Bergeron, p. 186.

113 **Gondomar went off immediately** . . . Redworth, 2003, p. 82.

114 **Though there might be something intriguing** . . . Redworth, 2003, p. 65.

114 **Nevertheless, the sheer audacity** . . . Redworth, 2003, pp. 82–3.

115 **Crowds gathered** . . . Porter, 1897, pp. 48–9; Bergeron, 1999, p. 187.

118 **On Sunday, barely a week** . . . Anon., 1623b, p. 18 ff.

119 **A few days later** . . . Bergeron, 1999, pp.155–6, 188–9.

120 **George also enclosed 'consolatory' letters** . . . Lockyer, 2014, pp. 152–3; Porter, 1897, p. 52.

120 **In the midst of all this** . . . Howell, 1726, p. 135.

121 **The infanta played her part** . . . Redworth, 2003, pp. 90, 97–8.

122 **The awkwardness and lack of encouragement** . . . Redworth, 2003, p. 92.

123 **On Saturday 17 May** . . . Howell, 1726, p. 136.

124 **[note] The reasons for the break-down of negotiations** . . . Cross, 2007.

124 **There was also the position of Charles's sister** . . . Howell, 1726, p. 136.

124 **A despondent mood** . . . Bergeron, 1999, p. 190.

124 **The patent formally conferring** . . . Hacket, 1693, p. 125; Bergeron, 1999, p. 193.

125 **The promotion made** . . . Porter, 1897, p. 61.

125 **A previous English envoy** . . . Porter, 1897, p. 38; Bergeron, 1999, p. 190; Bellany and Cogswell, 2015, loc. 3600.

126 **Back home, Charles owned** . . . Burke and Cherry, 1997, pp. 148–9; Redworth, 2003, p. 112 ff; Brotton, 2006, pp. 23, 17.

127 **They arranged for five camels** . . . Redworth, 2003, pp. 112–15.

Secret Intelligencers

127 **Wallingford House stood next** . . . 'The Admiralty', in *Survey of London: Volume 16, St Martin-in-The-Fields I: Charing Cross*, ed. G. H.

Gater and E. P. Wheeler (London, 1935), pp. 45–70; British History Online http://www.british-history.ac.uk/survey-london/vol16/pt1/pp45–70 [accessed 13 Nov 2016].

128 **Before leaving for Madrid** . . . Hacket, 1693, pp. 125–6.

128 **Speculation erupted, and was picked up** . . . D'Ewes, 1974, pp. 134–5.

129 **James Hay – the Earl of Carlisle** . . . Chamberlain and McClure, 1939, vol. 2, p. 499.

129 **However, with the rumours** . . . D'Ewes, 1974, pp. 135–6, 144; Cogswell, 2005, pp. 36–8.

130 **Fears swept through the country** . . . Chamberlain and McClure, 1939, vol. 2, p. 494.

131 **Around the same time, two senior members** . . . D'Ewes, 1974, p. 147; Whiteway and Murphy, 1939, p. 55; D'Ewes, 1974, p. 139; Chamberlain and McClure, 1939, vol. 2, p. 499; *CSPD*, 21 Jun 1623, item 35.

131 **William Whiteway, a Dorchester merchant** . . . Whiteway and Murphy, 1939, p. 53.

131 **The Wallingford House circle became** . . . Hacket, 1693, pp. 137–8; Lockyer, 2014, p. 160.

132 **Then, on 14 June** . . . Bergeron, 1999, p. 167.

A Farewell Pillar

132 **George and Charles had been in Madrid** . . . Lockyer, 2014, p. 148.

133 **A departure date of late August** . . . Bergeron, 1999, pp. 197–9.

Fool's Coats

135 **When George's father-in-law** . . . D'Ewes, 1974, p. 156.

135 **Reaching London Bridge** . . . *DNB*, George Abbot (1562–1633).

136 **Elsewhere in the kingdom** . . . D'Ewes, 1974, pp. 163–4; Chamberlain and McClure, 1939, vol. 2, p. 515.

137 **James, meanwhile, raced south** . . . Chamberlain and McClure, 1939, vol. 2, p. 516. Chamberlain writes that they met at Royston, but D'Ewes noted that James had gone to Theobalds: D'Ewes, 1974, p. 164; *CSPD*, 9 Oct 1623, item 31.

137 **The three retired** . . . Hacket, 1693, p. 165.

137 **The day after the reunion** . . . *CSPD*, 10 Oct 1623, item 32; James, VI of Scotland and I of England, 1984, pp. 427–8.

138 **Meanwhile, the news-mongers** . . . Whiteway and Murphy, 1939, p. 57.

138 **Hinojosa and Coloma** . . . Nichols, 1828, vol. 4, p. 932.

138 **'Matters are still kept** . . . Chamberlain and McClure, 1939, vol. 2, p. 516; *CSPD*, [16] Oct 1623, item 59.

138 **George seemed to be** . . . Hacket, 1693, p. 133.

138 **Bedraggled members** . . . Chamberlain and McClure, 1939, vol. 2, p. 516.

139 **A deadly incident** . . . Paisey, 2005; Walsham, 1994; Anon., 1623a, pp. 12–13.

140 **The king took little interest** . . . *CSPD*, 20 Oct 1623, item 81.

140 **As the weeks passed** . . . Ruigh, 1971, p. 21.

140 **The king made a show** . . . Chamberlain and McClure, 1939, vol. 2, p. 524.

140 **These overtures were followed up** . . . Paisey, 2005.

141 **All was not as it seemed, however.** Chamberlain and McClure, 1939, vol. 2, p. 519.

141 **In November, James's loyal servant** . . . Ruigh, 1971, p. 23.

ACT III: THE GREATEST VILLAIN IN THE WORLD

The Honey and the Sting

145 **The mission to Madrid** . . . Bergeron, 1999, p. 195.

145 **Yet his reception** . . . Chamberlain and McClure, 1939, vol. 2, p. 516; Ruigh, 1971, p. 23.

145 **Since plummeting from power in 1621** . . . Bacon and Spedding, 1861, p. 432.

146 **George was responsive.** For observations about the poverty witnessed in Madrid, see Redworth, 2003, p. 80; Villiers writes of how the nuncio 'works as maliciously, and as actively as he can against us' (Bergeron, 1999, p. 187); for references to the witch and the devil, see Bergeron, 1999, p. 195.

146 **George sent off** . . . Bacon and Spedding, 1861, pp. 423, 442–3.

The English Junta

149 **George reacted** . . . *CSPV*, 15 Dec 1623 [NS], item 219.

149 **The prince joined in** . . . Stewart, 2003, p. 330.

149 **Meanwhile, George set about** . . . Bacon and Spedding, 1861, p. 443.

149 **George adopted a similar approach** . . . Lockyer, 2014, p. 175.

150 **George responded by staging** . . . Laud, 1695, pp. 8, 10; Chamberlain and McClure, 1939, vol. 2, p. 532.

151 **'They are very closely united'** . . . *CSPV*, 2 Feb 1624 [NS], item 260.

151 **A select group of privy councillors** . . . Chamberlain and McClure, 1939, vol. 2, pp. 535, 542, 543, 539.

152 **In an extraordinary declaration** . . . Bergeron, 1999, p. 175.

A Secret Matter

153 **Thursday, 12 February 1624** . . . *CSPV*, 23 Feb 1624 [NS], item 275.

153 **On 19 February, the ceremonies** . . . Ransome, 1996, p. 11.

154 **Looking tired and ill** . . . Baker, 2015: '19th February 1624'; D'Ewes, 1974, p. 181; Chamberlain and McClure, 1939, vol. 2, p. 546.

155 **But James had not been** . . . Baker, 2015: '19th February 1624'.

The Banqueting House

156 **Francis Bacon had compared ambition to choler** . . . Bacon and Kiernan, 1985, p. 115.

156 **The duke struck** . . . Wilson, 1653, p. 264.

157 **The MPs were entranced.** Bellany and Cogswell, 2015, loc. 3372, 795; Hacket, 1693, p. 190; Lockyer, 2014, p. 193; Wilson, 1653, p. 264.

159 **Even the libellers** . . . ESL, Oi2.

159 **The appreciative and patriotic mood** . . . Baker, 2015: '1st March 1624'.

Countless Difficulties

160 **The vigilant Venetian ambassador** . . . *CSPV*, 23 Feb 1624 [NS], item 275.

160 **As the diplomatic machinations** . . . *CSPD*, 2 Mar 1624, item 13.

160 **James, meanwhile, lingered** . . . Bergeron, 1999, p. 200.

161 **Though his 'rheum'** . . . *CSPV*, 22 Dec 1623 [NS], item 225.

161 **The French ambassador** . . . Stewart, 2003, pp. 332–3; Lockyer, 2014, p. 185.

The Forger of Every Mischief

162 **As the king moped** . . . *CSPV*, 29 Mar 1624 [NS], item 317; *CSPD*, 1–2 Mar 1624, items 8–17.

163 **Delegates were swiftly chosen** . . . *HoL*, 8 Mar 1624, 'Advice of both Houses to the King, concerning Treaties with Spain'.

165 **Nevertheless, despite this litany** . . . *HoL*, 8 Mar 1624, 'King's Answer'.

165 **The despondent and confused** . . . *CSPD*, 5 Mar 1624, item 81; *HoL*, 14 Mar 1624; Holles records five subsidies and ten fifteenths; elsewhere the demand is six subsidies and ten fifteenths.

165 **The queasy archbishop** . . . Baker, 2015: '8th March 1624'.

165 **The following week** . . . Baker, 2015: '11th March 1624'; the pithy summary of his letter to Carleton is in *CSPD*, 20 Mar 1624, item 4; *CSPD*, 15 Mar 1624, item 77; *CPSD*, 17 Mar 1624, item 90; Bergeron, 1999, letter B20.

167 **The endless negotiations** . . . *CPSD*, 17 Mar 1624, item 90; Baker, 2015: '19th March 1624'.

167 **On Sunday 21 March** . . . Baker, 2015: '21st March 1624'.

A Game at Chess

168 **In the opening 'Induction'** . . . Middleton, 1625, sig. B^r.

170 **'This vulgar pasquin'** . . . Holles, 1983, vol. 2, pp. 288–9.

170 **Tumbling out of the Globe** . . . Whiteway and Murphy, 1939, p. 18.

171 **Some speculated that the 'gamesters'** . . . Howard-Hill, 1991, pp. 283, 278.

171 **Humiliatingly, James's 'first notice'** . . . *Acts of the Privy Council of England*, vol. 39, 1623–1625, ed. J. V. Lyle (London, 1933), pp. 303, 305; British History Online http://www.british-history.ac.uk/acts-privy-council/vol39 [accessed 2 Dec 2016].

Hobgoblins

172 **For what the British had not realized** . . . Elliott, 2002, p. 321 ff.

172 **Their first attempt had come soon** . . . *CSPD*, 20 Mar 1624, item 4.

174 **According to Francesco's own report** . . . Ruigh, 1971, pp. 271–3.

174 **The most specific and scandalous charge** . . . Bodleian Tanner MSS 82:90 ff206–208; Hacket, 1693, p. 132.

174 **At around the same time** . . . Ruigh, 1971, pp. 271–2.

175 **Brett's brother-in-law and patron** . . . Hacket, 1693, pp. 196–8. For a discussion of the veracity of Hacket's account of Williams's involvement, see Nichols, 1828, vol. 4, pp. 961–2, n. 1; Ruigh, 1971, pp. 274–5, nn. 21, 22.

178 **Meanwhile, there were signs** . . . Ruigh, 1971, pp. 283, 286–7, 291.

179 **Other accounts capture** . . . Wilson, 1653, p. 271; *CSPD*, 25 Apr 1624, item 50.

180 **The duke also provided a stout defence** . . . Ruigh, 1971, p. 291.

180 **And yet without Steenie** . . . *CSPV*, 17 May 1624 [NS], item 388.

To Ride Away an Ague

181 **On this occasion George was treated** . . . Lockyer, 2014, p. 195.

181 **The onset of the illness** . . . Bellany and Cogswell, 2015, loc. 1971; *CSPV*, 17 May 1624 [NS], item 388.

181 **By mid-May** . . . *CSPD*, 15 May 1624, item 86.

181 **On 25 May, James came to London** . . . Lockyer, 2014, p. 196.

182 **He had earlier promised** . . . Bergeron, 1999, letter B23.

183 **No more was needed** . . . Bergeron, 1999, letter J30.

183 **Of course George was too ill to go** . . . Bergeron, 1999, letters J31 and J32.

183 **George responds teasingly** . . . Bergeron, 1999, letter B24.

184 **As George regained his strength** . . . Bergeron, 1999, letter B2.

The Price of a Princess

185 **George made his formal return** . . . Lockyer, 2014, p. 198; *CSPD*, 29 May 1624, item 61.

185 **The Spanish envoys, meanwhile** . . . Ruigh, 1971, p. 301.

186 **The efforts of Cranfield's brother-in-law** . . . Nichols, 1828, vol. 4, p. 984.

187 **With all immediate threats** . . . Lockyer, 2014, p. 201.

187 **Early signs were encouraging.** Chamberlain and McClure, 1939, vol. 2, p. 568.

187 **At Windsor, George took Effiat to one side** . . . For contrasting

interpretations of Buckingham's first meeting with Effiat, see Lockyer, 2014, p. 200, and Schreiber, 1984, p. 68.

188 **They proved to be tough.** *CSPV*, 20 Jun 1624 [NS], item 448; 5 Jul 1624 [NS], item 476.

188 **Despite these setbacks, George . . .** Lockyer, 2014, p. 200.

189 **Throughout the negotiations . . .** Bergeron, 1999, letters J33, B5, B33 and B36.

189 **But George's letters . . .** *CSPD*, 7 Jul 1624, item 26; Bergeron, 1999, letter B38.

190 **Only one letter during this period . . .** Chamberlain and McClure, 1939, vol. 2, pp. 439, 573; Bergeron, 1999, letter B39.

190 **Despite these family distractions . . .** Whiteway and Murphy, 1939, pp. 74–5, 79; Chamberlain and McClure, 1939, vol. 2, p. 588.

191 **An English agent crossed the North Sea . . .** *CSPV*, 2 Dec 1624 [NS], item 685.

191 **Not everyone was convinced.** *CSPV*, 6 Dec 1624 [NS], item 687.

192 **A formal event was organized . . .** *CSPV*, 3 Jan 1625 [NS], item 730.

192 **Finally, on 31 January 1625 . . .** Lockyer, 2014, p. 227.

193 **As James's secretary put it . . .** Bellany and Cogswell, 2015, loc. 2028; Chamberlain and McClure, 1939, vol. 2, p. 584.

193 **The fortified city of Breda . . .** *CSPV*, 7 Mar 1625 [NS], item 842; Lockyer, 2014, pp. 227–8; Bellany and Cogswell, 2015, loc. 2039.

194 **When he heard the news . . .** Bellany and Cogswell, 2015, loc. 2028.

195 **Meanwhile, agents arriving in London . . .** Schreiber, 1984, pp. 85–6; *CSPV*, 26 Feb 1625 [NS], item 818.

195 **Confirming suspicions . . .** Lockyer, 2014, p. 224.

195 **Rumours swirled . . .** *CSPV*, 14 Mar 1625 [NS], item 853; Cecil, 1663, pp. 237–8.

196 **William Whiteway, the Dorchester merchant . . .** Whiteway and Murphy, 1939, p. 84.

What an Age We Do Live In

196 **'Dear Dad' . . .** Bergeron, 1999, letter B40.

197 **The king's mood was further lowered . . .** Chamberlain and McClure, 1939, vol. 2, p. 604; *CSPD*, 12 Mar 1625, item 48; Birch, 1848, vol. 2, p. 504.

197 **A range of treatments were prescribed** . . . Culpeper, 1653, pp. 182, 166.

199 **'A tertian in the spring** . . . Chamberlain and McClure, 1939, vol. 2, p. 606; *CSPV*, 28 Mar 1625 [NS], item 869.

199 **Around this time, the 'cunts' turned up** . . . Bergeron, 1999, p. 211.

199 **Remington was not a member** . . . Bellany and Cogswell, 2015, loc. 2263.

200 **Mayerne, the king's chief physician** . . . Trevor-Roper, 2006, pp. 273–5.

200 **The number at Theobalds** . . . Holles, 1983, vol. 2, p. 302.

201 **For all their eminence** . . . Margaret Pelling and Frances White, 'PADDY, Sir William' and 'MOORE, Dr John', in 'Physicians and Irregular Medical Practitioners in London 1550–1640 Database', London, 2004; British History Online http://www.british-history. ac.uk/no-series/london-physicians/1550-1640 [accessed 2 Dec 2016]; Munk's Roll, http://munksroll.rcplondon.ac.uk/Biography/ Details/3174 [accessed 2 Dec 2016].

201 **George was at Theobalds on 11 March** . . . Bellany and Cogswell, 2015, loc. 2128; *CSPV*, 28 Mar 1625 [NS], item 869.

203 **The king started to suffer a violent fit.** Hacket, 1693, p. 222; Bidwell and Jansson, 1992, vol. 3, pp. 57–8, 68–9.

204 **In the midst of this melee** . . . Bellany and Cogswell, 2015, loc. 1923.

205 **On Friday 25 March** . . . Nichols, 1828, vol. 4, p. 1032; Stewart, 2003, p. 346.

206 **'I ascended the pulpit** . . . Laud, 1695, p. 15.

206 **Recovering himself, George** . . . Wotton, 1672, p. 219.

207 **Charles's succession was proclaimed** . . . Howell, 1726, p. 174.

207 **Not everyone was pessimistic.** Chamberlain and McClure, 1939, vol. 2, p. 618.

ACT IV: WE THE COMMONS

Poisonous Applications

211 **His charcoal moving across the paper** . . . Held, 1976, p. 547; Brotton, 2006, p. 10; Bellany and Cogswell, 2015, loc. 3393; Martin, 1966.

213 **It was May 1625** . . . Memegalos, 2013, p. 18; *DNB*, Henrietta Maria [Princess Henrietta Maria of France] (1609–69); Plowden, 2001, p. 20.

214 **One, a complex work by the celebrated poet Hugh Holland** . . . Holland, 1625; Bellany and Cogswell, 2015, ch. 2.

215 **The procession was enormous** . . . Salvetti and Skrine, 1887, p. 16; Nichols, 1828, vol. 4, p. 1036 ff.

215 **George, barely recovered from his sickness** . . . Chamberlain and McClure, 1939, vol. 2, p. 615; *CSPD*, 16 May, item 50 (postscript); http://www.historyofparliamentonline.org/volume/1604-1629/member/howard-sir-thomas-1587–1669#footnote25_w2ubkci.

216 **Later that day, he was visited** . . . Memegalos, 2013, p. 18.

216 **During James's final weeks** . . . Bellany and Cogswell, 2015, loc. 4532.

216 **George and his company galloped** . . . *CSPD*, 25 May 1625, item 88.

217 **George's formal introduction** . . . Petitot, 1824, p. 403.

217 **Vain or not, *tout le monde*** . . . Lockyer, 2014, p. 236.

217 **The one person who did not** . . . Wotton, 1672, pp. 220–1; Charles, 2011, pp. 114–17.

218 **George would not allow** . . . *DNB*, John Tradescant the elder (d.1638).

Anne of Austria

220 **George's love life** . . . Lockyer, 2014, pp. 152, 160.

221 **However, what George did not realize** . . . The report is contained in Peuchet, 1838, p. 27 ff. A translation of the section of the work relating to Buckingham appeared in the *Morning Chronicle* (Anon., 1839). Some question the report's credibility, describing it as a 'pastiche'. It certainly has picaresque, even absurd, qualities which draw into question its authenticity, and perhaps explains its influence over fiction at the time it was published, inspiring novelists such as Alexandre Dumas, author of *The Three Musketeers*. Jacques Peuchet (1758–1830), who included the report in his collection of police archives, has been described as a 'journalist and publicist', but did produce a number of archival collections, e.g. *Collection des lois, ordonnances et règlements de police depuis le 13e siècle jusqu'à l'année* (Paris, 1818). See Hoefer, 1862, vol. 39, pp. 770–1. A Guillame Bautru (also spelled Beautru or Botro), the agent mentioned in Peuchet's account, turns up in a number of contemporary sources

and was associated with Anglo-French negotiations at the time
of George's visit to France. See for example *CSPV*, 17 Dec 1625
[NS], items 371 and 373, where 'Botro' is described as 'a servant of
the [French] queen mother and consequently a dependant of the
cardinal [Richelieu], a friend of Buckingham and who knows
the secrets of the Cabinet and the intentions of the Duke of
Chevreuse and of the queen herself'. See also Leveneur, 1863,
pp. 84–5.

223 **George and the duchess . . .** Mademoiselle de Flotte is probably
Marie de Hautefort, who may have got the name 'Maiden of the
Fleet' through her grandmother, Catherine Le Voyer de Lignerolles,
known as 'la Dame de la Flotte'. Hautefort was known to be close to
Louis XIII. See, for example, La Porte, 1755, p. 202.

225 **Anne now flouted the king's orders . . .** Michaud and Poujoulat,
1838, p. 15 ff.

225 **In London, a lack of news . . .** Plowden, 2001, p. 22–3.

226 **The party set off on its long journey . . .** *CSPD*, 9 Jun 1625,
item 48.

226 **That evening she was introduced . . .** Cecil, 1663, pp. 253–4.

227 **Later that day, the weather deteriorated . . .** Michaud and
Poujoulat, 1838, pp. 19–20; Petitot, 1824, pp. 404–6.

And So the Devil Go with Them

228 **Since King James's death . . .** Bellany and Cogswell, 2015, loc.
2314, 2326.

228 **George was made first gentleman . . .** Salvetti and Skrine, 1887,
pp. 3, 6; *CSPV*, 25 Apr 1625 [NS], item 25.

229 **There was a slackening . . .** Birch, 1848, vol. 1, pp. 12, 10.

229 **The orderliness left . . .** *CSPV*, 2 May 1625 [NS], item 38.

229 **The king's nuptials . . .** Birch and Gamache, 1848, pp. 24–5.

229 **Henrietta's twelve-hour Channel crossing . . .** Leveneur, 1863,
pp. 89–90; Birch, 1848, pp. 29–31; Plowden, 2001, pp. 25–7.

231 **Lord Keeper Williams, responsible for helping . . .** *CSPD*, 13
Jun 1625, item 62; Bidwell and Jansson, 1987, pp. 641–2; *CSPV*,
24 May 1625 [NS], item 73.

232 **As always, the parliamentary session . . .** Bidwell and Jansson,
1987, p. 28.

232 **The following week, the 'ceremony . . .** Salvetti and Skrine,
1887, p. 23.

232 **Meanwhile, the mood in the House . . .** Sharpe, 1996, p. 3.

233 **In this hostile environment** . . . Bidwell and Jansson, 1987, pp. 28, 361.

234 **Instead George appointed Sir Edward Cecil** . . . http://www. historyofparliamentonline.org/volume/1604-1629/member/cecil-sir-edward-1572–1638 [accessed 2 Dec 2016].

234 **The Spanish were making moves** . . . Salvetti and Skrine, 1887, p. 22.

235 **While she was staying at Hampton Court** . . . Leveneur, 1863, pp. 93–4.

235 **The king gave a short opening address** . . . Bidwell and Jansson, 1987, p. 402.

236 **On 9 August, George** . . . Bidwell and Jansson, 1987, p. 435 ff.

237 **Soon after, George went to the Hague** . . . Wotton, 1672, p. 223.

239 **George suggested she would get** . . . Leveneur, 1863, pp. 118–20.

239 **Henrietta relented** . . . Cornwallis, 1842, p. 143.

240 **As the wet, miserable spring** . . . *CSPV*, 21 Aug 1626 [NS], item 705. According to Garnett's entry in the *DNB*, he was executed in St Paul's Churchyard, not at Tyburn.

240 **Such antics had left Charles** . . . Halliwell, 1848, pp. 262, 270.

241 **As this was going on, Charles revealed** . . . Ellis, 1825, vol. 3, p. 244; Plowden, 2001, p. 49.

All Goes Backward

241 **Two weeks later, Eliot wrote** . . . *CSPD*, 9 Dec 1625, item 44; 22 Dec 1625, item 38.

242 **A sense of gloom descended** . . . Chamberlain and McClure, 1939, vol. 2, p. 626.

242 **The vice admiral had long been** . . . Hulme, 1957, p. 81.

243 **Where George admired audaciousness** . . . Forster, 1872, vol. 1, p. 69.

243 **When he was released** . . . http://www.historyofparliamentonline. org/volume/1604-1629/member/eliot-john-1592-1632 [accessed 2 Dec 2016].

The Knot Draws Near

244 **Henrietta Maria's dowry** . . . *CSPD*, 18 Dec 1625, item 10; *CSPV*, 3 Jul 1626 [NS], item 640.

244 **Opposition was poorly organized** . . . Bellany and Cogswell, 2015, loc. 4657.

244 **On 15 January 1626** . . . Forster, 1872, vol. 1, pp. 277–9.

245 **Meanwhile, and presumably with the help** . . . Bodleian Rawlinson, C674 ff22–24; Bellany and Cogswell, 2015, loc. 4685.

246 **Hogg's interrogator** . . . *CSPD*, 26 Dec 1625, item 54; Bellany and Cogswell, 2015, loc. 1867.

246 **Charles opened Parliament** . . . *HoL*, 6 February 1626; British History Online http://www.british-history.ac.uk/lords-jrnl/vol3/pp492–494 [accessed 2 Dec 2016].

246 **The initial response was muted** . . . Forster, 1872, vol. 1, pp. 285–9.

248 **Commenting on the debacle** . . . Salvetti and Skrine, 1887, p. 48.

Common Fame

248 **He attended the House of Lords sporadically** . . . Lockyer, 2014, p. 97.

248 **The proposal may have reflected** . . . Chamberlain and McClure, 1939, vol. 2, p. 630.

249 **Nevertheless, in a summary** . . . Lockyer, 2014, p. 296.

249 **One of the bones of contention** . . . http://www.historyofparliamentonline.org/volume/1604-1629/member/eliot-john-1592–1632 [accessed 26 Jan 2017]; Bidwell and Jansson, 1992, vol. 2, pp. 165, 170.

250 **On 11 March, members of the king's Council** . . . Bidwell and Jansson, 1992, vol. 2, pp. 256–7.

250 **Then Dr Samuel Turner got to his feet.** Bidwell and Jansson, 1992, vol. 2, pp. 268–9.

251 **The following day, the royal secretary** . . . Bidwell and Jansson, 1992, vol. 4, p. 333.

The Bottomless Bagg

251 **In early March 1626** . . . http://www.historyofparliamentonline.org/volume/1604-1629/member/bagg-james-ii-1592-1638 [accessed 26 Jan 2017].

251 **As part of these efforts, Bagg** . . . Gardiner, 1872.

252 **Meanwhile, Turner was to receive** . . . Bidwell and Jansson, 1992, vol. 2, pp. 284–5, 288, 299, 316–17.

253 **Turner's talk of public** . . . Coast, 2016, pp. 23–6; Anon., 1691, pp. 255–7.

254 **The following day, at a joint meeting** . . . Bidwell and Jansson, 1992, vol. 2, pp. 392, 404 ff.

254 **And so the wrangling continued** . . . Coast, 2016, p. 32.

254 **Concerned that the case** . . . Bidwell and Jansson, 1992, vol. 3, p. 39.

The Forerunner of Revenge

255 **On 18 April 1626, Rubens** . . . Bellany and Cogswell, 2015, loc. 3386; Eglisham, 1626a.

256 **Eglisham was a colourful figure** . . . Bidwell and Jansson, 1992, vol. 4, p. 335.

257 **In the early 1600s, Eglisham** . . . Chadwick, 1941, p. 571.

257 **Reflecting the fringe existence** . . . *CSPD*, 18 Jan 1630, item 60; Bellany and Cogswell, 2015, loc. 3058.

259 **On Sunday, 16 June 1622, Hamilton** . . . Chamberlain and McClure, 1939, vol. 2, p. 441.

260 **Eglisham affirmed** . . . Eglisham, 1626b.

Great Matters of Weight

261 **On Monday, 24 April 1626** . . . Bellany and Cogswell, 2015, loc. 4787.

261 **In fact, what was afoot** . . . Bidwell and Jansson, 1992, vol. 3, pp. 53, 56.

262 **However, copies of Eglisham's tract** . . . Bellany and Cogswell, 2015, loc. 4829.

262 **Besides the vivid details** . . . Eglisham, 1626b.

263 **The committee at least was up** . . . Bidwell and Jansson, 1992, vol. 3, pp. 53–87; *HoL*, 17 May 1644.

267 **What about the testimony** . . . Keynes, 1966, p. 147.

A Silly Piece of Malice

269 **Little is known about Butler.** *CSPD*, 27 May 1625, item 57; Bergeron, 1999, p. 211; *CSPD*, 28 Apr 1626, item 86; Bellany and Cogswell, 2015, loc. 5156.

269 **Whatever his relationship to George** . . . Eglisham, 1626b.

270 **Charles instructed Henry Wotton** . . . Smith, 1907, vol. 2, pp. 291–3.

Dissolution

271 **'The arraignment of the Duke . . .** Salvetti and Skrine, 1887, p. 61.

271 **Still under house arrest . . .** Bidwell and Jansson, 1992, vol. 4, pp. 150–1; vol. 2, p. 108.

271 **In the hush that followed . . .** *CSPV*, 29 May 1626 [NS], item 596.

273 **In a characteristically abrupt . . .** Bidwell and Jansson, 1992, vol. 1, pp. 328–39.

273 **The following day, the finalized list . . .** The full text is contained in *HoL*, 15 May 1626.

273 **On the same day, a letter . . .** Proceedings of the House of Lords, 2 May 1626 (Bidwell and Jansson, 1992, vol. 2, p. 202).

276 **As the official record of the event . . .** John Rushworth, 'Historical Collections: The impeachment of Buckingham (1626)', in *Historical Collections of Private Passages of State*: Volume 1, 1618–29 (London, 1721), pp. 302–58; British History Online http://www.british-history.ac.uk/rushworth-papers/vol1/pp302–58 [accessed 23 Oct 2016].

276 **In the Commons there was uproar.** Bidwell and Jansson, 1992, vol. 2, p. 239.

276 **Carleton's speech . . .** Bidwell and Jansson, 1992, vol. 2, p. 241.

277 **Yet even as Carleton tried to intimidate . . .** Bellany and Cogswell, 2015, loc. 5645.

277 **The night of the MPs' arrests . . .** Birch, 1848, vol. 1, p. 104.

278 **At three that afternoon . . .** John Rushworth, 'Historical Collections: 1626, June–1627 (March)', in *Historical Collections of Private Passages of State*: Volume 1, 1618–29 (London, 1721), pp. 374–422; British History Online http://www.british-history.ac.uk/rushworth-papers/vol1/pp374–422 [accessed 21 Oct 2016].

279 **An MP who had kept . . .** Bidwell and Jansson, 1992, vol. 2, p. 449.

The Devil and the Duke

279 **Like all of London's theatres . . .** Bellany, 2008, p. 44.

279 **On Friday, 13 July 1628, Dr John Lambe . . .** Goldstein, 1979.

280 **This is when Lambe's name . . .** Chamberlain and McClure, 1939, vol. 2, p. 601; Birch, 1848, vol. 1, p. 296.

280 **Though the association . . .** Birch, 1848, vol. 1, p. 252.

280 **By the time John Lambe** . . . ESL, Oiii5; Birch, 1848, vol. 1, p. 169; Bellany, 2008, pp. 58–61.

281 **Whatever play was put on that day** . . . Bellany, 2008, pp. 37–9; Anon., 1628; Goldstein, 1979.

The Scrivener's Tale

282 **A few hundred yards** . . . *DNB*, John Felton (d.1628).

283 **News of its damning indictment** . . . Lockyer, 2014, p. 442.

283 **Felton, it emerged** . . . Bellany and Cogswell, 2015, loc. 7685; Wotton, 1642, p. 23; Holstun, 1992, p. 527.

I Am the Man

285 **News of the emergency** . . . Long, 1888, pp. 44–5.

286 **On 22 August, George wrote** . . . Lockyer, 2014, p. 453.

Sad Affliction's Darksome Night

287 **In London, the Tuscan agent** . . . Salvetti and Skrine, 1887, p. 162.

287 **With zeal and justice** . . . *DNB*, John Felton (d.1628).

288 **In one of the many editions** . . . Anon., 1649, sig. [A3r].

289 **Of honour, power, and pleasure** . . . ESL, Pi21, Pi22; Bellany and Cogswell, 2015, loc. 7695.

289 **Here lies the best and worst** . . . 'Epitaph on the Duke of Buckingham', cited in Shirley, 1833, vol. 6, p. 449.

Index

Natasha Walter is the author of two non-fiction books, *The New Feminism* and *Living Dolls: The Return of Sexism*. She has worked as a journalist, columnist and reviewer for the *Guardian*, the *Observer* and the *Independent*, and is the founder of the charity Women for Refugee Women. She lives in London with her partner and their two children. *A Quiet Life* is her first novel.

Praise for *A Quiet Life*:

'A troubling, understated novel, almost hypnotic in the completeness with which it inhabits the mind of its impressionable central character'
SARAH WATERS, 'Best books for summer', *Guardian*

'Impressive . . . easily competing with the claims of such experienced novelists as Sebastian Faulks and William Boyd to the territory' *Guardian*

'A writer of game-changing skill and sensitivity. Few novelists can combine serious feminism with romance and adventure and make it work . . . a literary page-turner' *Times*

'Brilliant' JULIE MYERSON, 'Best holiday reads', *Observer*

'Evokes the period with brilliant precision and detail'
Sunday Times

'Elegant, slow-burning . . . leaving you with no choice but to read on' *Metro*

'Walter is a natural when it comes to fiction' *Litro*

'A superb, sophisticated and radical book that refreshes the parts other spy novels cannot reach . . . Meticulously researched and disarmingly told, *A Quiet Life* is historical fiction at its best, finding vast uncharted territories within a period we might have thought we knew'

CHRIS CLEAVE, author of *Everyone Brave is Forgiven*

'A tour de force. Walter has taken us inside a life in hiding, in a novel about love, about political ideals and about the entrapment both create'   LINDA GRANT

'As well as having a gift for cool, elegant phrasing, and a fine sensitivity to psychology . . . Walter proves to be a hard-working and accomplished storyteller'   *Guardian*

'A brilliant observer of period, place and upper-class mores'
Daily Mail

'Riveting'   *Good Housekeeping*

'This ambitious debut fuses espionage, wartime romance, and enquiry into female identity and power'   *Mail on Sunday*

'Exquisitely detailed'   *Red Magazine*

'It is in the characterisation of the multifaceted Laura that the novel really sings'   *Independent*

Also by Natasha Walter

NON-FICTION
Living Dolls: The Return of Sexism
The New Feminism